First Steps in Practitioner Research

A guide to understanding and doing research in counselling and health and social care

Pete Sanders
and
Paul Wilkins

PCCS BOOKS
Ross-on-Wye

First published 2010

PCCS Books Ltd
2 Cropper Row
Alton Road
Ross-on-Wye
Herefordshire
HR9 5LA
UK
Tel +44 (0)1989 763900
www.pccs-books.co.uk

The authors wish to acknowledge the work of Damian Liptrot on the series:
'Incomplete Guides to Research Methods for Counsellors' published by PCCS Books in 1993.
Several sections of the current book owe much to Damian's work.

First Steps in Practitioner Research:
A guide to understanding and doing research in counselling and health and social care

ISBN 978 1 898059 73 8

Cover designed in the UK by Old Dog Graphics
Printed by Ashford Colour Press, Gosport, Hampshire, UK

Contents

3   Doing practice-based research

Acknowledgements

The 'Steps' series of books has a complex structure that involves a huge amount of work. The possibilities for errors are manifold and it is mostly due to the skilful and diligent work of our copy-editor and proofreader Sandy Green that this book has been published. This simple acknowledgement hardly seems sufficient to honour her part in the work.

We are grateful to Damian Liptrot for his generous permission to use his work as the framework for some of the chapters and to Isabel Gibbard and Kirshen Rundle whose contributions helped bring the day-to-day realities of research alive. We also thank Laura Aitken, Heather Allan, Peter Cardew, Mick Cooper, Robert Elliott, Sheila Haugh, Hilary Keenan, Katie McArthur, Caroline Muir, Peter Pearce, Gillian Proctor, Maggie Robson, Rosemary Smith, Helen Spandler, Sheila Spong and Leonie Sugarman for invaluable feedback on early drafts of the book.

introductions

The 'Steps' series

This book is part of a 'family' of related books designed to lead you through what you need to know to begin your training and practice in counselling and psychotherapy or the application of counselling as a complement to other activities in a wider context.

Some of you will be encountering the *Steps* series for the first time. The series is characterised by the way in which the usual conventions of academic writing are modified and adapted. They are written in such a way as to directly address you, the readers. This isn't about being different for the sake of it. Each author who contributes to the series, as well as being a practitioner and writer across the broader field of the helping professions, is or has been a counselling trainer. So in these books we are using our training skills and (amongst other things) for the most part relating to you as we would to a new group of students.

You will also already have noticed another peculiarity of books in the *Steps* series. Each page has an unusually wide margin. On most pages (as this one) you will find something written. Here, we have given references to the other books in the series and you will find other references (and all sorts of things) in the margin as you work with this book. What we have done is to write the main text so that it can be read without interruption or diversion. However, there are many points at which there is more that at least some of you may like to know. In the margin is where you will find 'extra' information. This includes references, explanations of terms used in the main text and activities that will aid your learning. We will say more about how we have used the margins in this book later.

Another important feature of this book is that it is not about any particular approach to research. It is designed to be of use to you and to facilitate your learning irrespective of the theories that underpin your training programme and your own specialism in helping practice.

This book

We have written this book in a single voice. This isn't because we agree on everything – it would be very difficult to find any two helping professionals who do. Research is not a monolith; it is

Sanders, P (2002) *First Steps in Counselling: A students' companion for basic introductory courses* (3rd edn). Ross-on-Wye: PCCS Books.

Sanders, P (1995) *Step in to Study Counselling: A students' guide to tackling counselling training and course assignments* (3rd edn). Ross-on-Wye: PCCS Books.

Sanders, P, Frankland, A & Wilkins, P (2009) *Next Steps in Counselling Practice: A students' companion for degrees, HE diplomas and vocational courses* (2nd edn). Ross-on-Wye: PCCS Books.

Although this series is conceived as comprising interrelated books, each also stands alone. However, as well as offering a progression into which it is possible to dip in or out at any point, they share a style and approach.

represented by many voices, each of which speaks of research with a different tone, accent or dialect, each of which comes from a different perspective. Helping professions embrace a range of quite different views. We think that this difference is important and valuable in the context of training (and continuing professional development for that matter). It is by hearing, reflecting on and evaluating what these many voices have to say that you can defend yourself against blind, creaking orthodoxy and stimulate your own questioning and learn and develop as a practitioner. As well as in the main body of the text, throughout this book you will find the diversity of approaches to research represented in the margins.

How we have used the margins

In our introduction to the *Steps* series, we have already said a bit about how, in general, the extra-wide margin is used to convey 'extra' bits of information and to suggest activities that will help you understand the points being made in the main text. This is true of this book too but we have also put other things in the margin. In the margins of this book, you will find:

IN THE MARGINS

In addition to the notes references in the margins, you will find various types of box and text.

Activities – to make this book more personal and to facilitate your learning, from time to time we use the margin to invite you to undertake a brief activity. This will inevitably slow down your reading, but just as in your training, a new dimension is added by active engagement, getting directly involved with the ideas, perhaps remembering or noticing aspects of your own life and experience, or taking sides in arguments and debates, or registering your responses to ideas or scenarios we put in front of you. Since some of you will be working with this book alone, the activities are designed to be done by a single person but for those of you who are using the book while undertaking training it may often be useful to work with a friend or colleague from the programme because discussion and the attempt to put an idea or feeling to someone else is an excellent way of increasing your grasp of it.

RUNNING GLOSSARY will define words as we go along that we think might be specialist or technical.

Notes – we include 'notes' in the margin when, to the interest of some of you, there is more to say about a particular point we have raised in the text. This may involve the expansion of some point of theory, a point of detail about a professional organisation, the definition of a term we have used, something interesting about someone we cite or quote or, indeed, anything else we think may be valuable or interesting to know.

Note

As you probably know, in academic writing a list of works cited or quoted, 'references', is usually compiled at the end of the piece.

References – we have put references in the margins for two main reasons. Firstly, we didn't want to interrupt the text by doing this in the conventional way but also, perhaps more importantly, because we wanted you to be able to see what we are referring to at the point at which we make the reference.

Notes from research/life – these are occasional illustrative 'stories' in the margin. These are accounts based on something that happened to one of us or a student, supervisee or colleague of ours. These tales are sufficiently removed from the 'actuality' of any particular event as to contain not even a hint of a breach of confidentiality. The purpose of these stories is to make something we have written about in the main text clearer by offering an example and, of course, so that you can think about what you might have said or done in similar circumstances.

If you want to know more about – this category is a slightly different way of introducing further reading. Sometimes we will introduce texts, sometimes web-based material. Where possible and appropriate we also try to give an indication of the level of difficulty of the text, or the level of experience at which we think it is aimed.

HELP! – we hope these short margin notes do exactly what they say on the label.

Getting started with using the material in the margin yourself

You have already encountered the way we use the margin to give you references we think may be helpful or interesting to you and you already have an example of one of our 'notes'. We have also told you a bit about the interactive element of this book – the 'activities' we suggest in the margin. We would like to take this a little further and invite you to take part in an activity at this point.

Take a look at the activity suggested in the margin. Think about it for a moment or two and then, if it seems as if it might be at all useful, give it a go.

Language

Related to the nature of the questions we ask in research, indeed to everything we write here, there are seriously important issues about the language of the text, about stereotyping and oppressive imagery. There are a lot of snide jokes and unhelpful misconceptions about political correctness. We have no wish to be po-faced or pious, but attempts to diminish the abuse of power in creating images which risk stereotyping or in using language which may demean others seem important to us, even if they are sometimes easy targets for parody.

We have tried to avoid stereotyped and oppressive imagery, and ensure that 'participant' and 'researcher' roles are fairly distributed, so that any power residing in positions is not unreasonably attributed to age, gender, race, sexuality and sexual preference, religious affiliations, appearance or abilities.

Note from research
Notes to illustrate points we are making and to encourage you to think about your own research. They are loosely based on things that happened to one of us or one of our colleagues, supervisees or students.

Note from life
Life experiences which help elaborate a particular point in the text.

HELP!
Times when we think you may feel like hitting the panic button and putting the book down. Hopefully we offer some ...

Note: Learning styles
This book has been deliberately written to encourage exploration, learning from all of your experience and adapting material to your own needs. However, it is still possible to limit yourself to the way the book appears to structure learning. Remember that everyone has their own way of learning: their learning *style*. Just because the margins in this book suggest certain reading or certain activities, don't think that this is the right or only way.

Activity: Your learning style(s)
Consider the following questions:
1. *Do you prefer to do learning activities:*
   - *on your own?*
   - *with a partner?*
   - *in a group?*
2. *Do you prefer learning by:*
   - *thinking through abstract ideas?*
   - *experience (doing something, then reflecting on it)?*
   - *sometimes by thinking, sometimes by doing – it depends upon what you're learning?*
3. *When 'getting your head around' something new do you prefer to:*
   - *draw a diagram of it to make sense of it?*
   - *draw a picture of it to make sense of it?*
   - *talk about/discuss it to make sense of it?*
   - *another way of symbolising the material?*

As authors, we have most of the public characteristics of representatives of the dominant group in the 'mainstream' of our culture, but we very much want readers from across the whole range and diversity of our society to recognise themselves as researchers and participants in practitioner research.

Like everyone else who is trying to be aware of these issues while writing in English, we have struggled with the fact that it is impossible to write using ungendered singular pronouns. The so-called neutral pronouns (he and his) are not gender neutral at all and there is no acceptable neologism that is genuinely inclusive. We have used a variety of devices to try to get round this, sometimes using 'he' and sometimes 'she' to refer to people of both or either gender group, and sometimes using the third person plural (they/ their) because it is not gendered, although it may not always be grammatically entirely correct.

Recording your experiences of research

Another way of getting a hold on ideas and understandings (both intellectual and personal/emotional) is to *write* about your learning on a regular basis. Many people keep a personal journal and whilst they would not think of giving it up they may not think of extending it to become a developmental tool or act of personal data collection.

There are so many forms that such a journal could take, from literally day-to-day comments and observations of self/ others, developing thinking and reactions, etc., to weekly or occasional reflections, perhaps particularly when hitting a brick wall or solving a problem in your research, or after supervision. Some people like to ensure that responses and reactions to every book or article they read are recorded as potential source material, whereas others see the journal as more nearly a therapeutic tool, in which they explore only their developing understanding and feelings about themselves, as individuals and researchers.

As an alternative or an adjunct to a journal you might also wish to consider a READING LOG, where at very least you record the full title and reference of everything you read that relates to your research and related literature review.

It may also be helpful to discover sooner rather than later what kind of RESEARCH LOG you need to be keeping. This kind of record keeping will be useful if you intend to do any sort of research. The kind of research log you keep will be influenced by many factors: in some cases by course requirements, for others it would be necessary to keep a research log from the moment you start thinking about doing some research, because at some point you are likely to want to write the research up, and you may well regret not having a record of your early thoughts.

READING LOG is a record of the theory and practice-related books you have bought, borrowed, read, along with brief notes about the book: what you found useful, memorable quotes, etc with page numbers.

RESEARCH LOG A 'research log' is a record of the process by which your research was undertaken, along with documentation of both positive and negative results. Essentially, it is the diary of your research process – what you did, when you did it, what happened, what was productive, what was less so.

Data

We decided to follow common popular use of the plural 'data' to mean both singluar and plural. When we tried using 'a datum' for the singluar case, some readers found it stopped them in their tracks.

How the book works

We have decided not to create a primarily *academic* sourcebook of research because we take the view that there are a number of such texts about already – what we find lacking, in our face-to-face teaching and when we survey the market, is a companion text for students and anyone wanting to learn about research from the ground up and maybe start looking at their own practice with a more critical, research-informed eye. Practitioners are increasingly being expected to audit their work and we wanted to provide a user-friendly starting point. We hope the text explores this territory in a rigorous and demanding way, without losing sight of the fact that very large numbers of helping practitioners and those in training do not have a formal academic background or interests. In every chapter we hope you will find material and activities that will stimulate not just your intellect but an interest in research.

It is also the case that a book is unlikely to be the most significant medium for stimulating many aspects of research understanding that require a richer interactive approach than the written word. We imagine you will have opportunities to avail yourself of a variety of experiences, with individuals (tutors, peers, colleagues and supervisors) and with groups, using a wide range of activities. It won't always be grim stuff; research often brings laughter, joy, a sense of strength and purpose, although we do not deny that it can be daunting and awaken fears about competence in mathematics and logic along the way. We intend you to have fun with our book. Yes, take it seriously (because that is how we mean it) but play with it too. We wish you well as you continue to learn about how rich and rewarding practitioner research in the helping professions can be.

Note
By this, we mean that there are not pages of highly referenced research theory in this book. It is a book about, and for, absolute beginners. There *are* plenty of references in this book, but in the main they are not included to justify points of discussion or theory. They are there to encourage exploration and further reading. Academic books, replete with references include:

Denzin, NK & Lincoln, YS (2000) (eds) *Handbook of Qualitative Research* (2nd edn). Thousand Oaks, CA: Sage.

McLeod, J (2003) *Doing Counselling Research* (2nd edn). London: Sage.

Robson, C (2002) *Real World Research: A resource for social scientists and practitioner researchers* (2nd edn). Oxford: Blackwell.

First Steps in Practitioner Research Internet Resource

First Steps in Practitioner Research readers will find much of the margin information, including references and live web links on the PCCS Books website <www.pccs-books.co.uk>. Click on 'VIP section' on the left of the home page, then 'click here to access the protected area'. Type in the password 'FSIPR01'.

Note
You can copy and paste references and link directly to the websites we feature in the book without typing in the URLs.

what is research and why bother?

Introduction

One of our reasons for writing this book is that the very idea of 'research' immediately puts people off. However, we believe that helping practitioners are natural researchers, each of us well able to contribute to the pool of knowledge on which our professions depend. We also think that it is helpful if all health and social care practitioners get to know at least a little about research and how it can be done. It really isn't all that scary and whatever your form of practice and how you think about people and the work you do, there is likely to be a way of doing research you will not only easily understand but actually enjoy. Research is rewarding, research is involving, research can be fun (or, at times, be difficult, exasperating, frustrating) but most importantly it is a normal, natural human activity for which we are all innately skilled. Undertaking our own research can be personally satisfying and possibly (through, for example, doing a higher degree) bring about professional advancement. Knowing enough about research to read the reports of others with understanding may help make us more effective as practitioners as it helps us sort the wheat from the chaff of 'evidence'.

There seems to be a widespread belief that research is about measuring things and that it is done by men (sic) in white coats in mysterious places called laboratories. And of course this is true – for some research, some of the time. However, in many ways research is an everyday activity; something we all do all the time. It is a natural human characteristic to be curious about the world around us, the people we meet and the experiences we have. We are constantly seeking to explore and explain whatsoever we encounter and to make sense of it all. This is the bedrock of research.

As practitioners, we are continuously noticing things about our clients and patients, their circumstances, how effective we are as we work with them and so on. In this way we refine our knowledge, sharpen our abilities and find new ways of implementing our new, growing understanding. In this way we are continually researching our working environment. As helpful as it is to us as individuals, it is much more helpful if we can find a way of telling others about what we have found out. This too is part of the research process. Of course, there is a bit more to it than this. A whole set of beliefs, conventions

Note

By this we mean all care workers – qualified and unqualified. Indeed anyone who works in one-to-one or group settings as a helper: counsellors, psychotherapists, nurses and other healthcare practitioners, social workers, support workers …

Note

We are not crazy! We think that in everyday life, human beings are natural testers of theories. We say more about this in Chapter 2.1 starting on p 21.

Note

We firmly believe that research is not only an activity for highly qualified scholars with years of experience or postgraduate students, and that 'beginners' can and do make valuable contributions to knowledge through doing research. If you are just setting out on a research project as part of your undergraduate or diploma studies or are a practitioner wanting to know how to conduct research then this book is as much for you as anyone else.

Note

The conventions, language and culture of social sciences research can appear – and be – very excluding. You need to know the jargon in order to be part of the club. But don't give up, 99% of the language is simply short cuts – terminology to name something quite complicated in a couple of words. The point of much of this book is to explain this jargon in simple everyday terms so you will not be excluded. The RUNNING GLOSSARY will also help.

Note

John McLeod (2003: 4) gives 'a useful working definition of research' as 'a systematic process of critical inquiry leading to valid propositions and conclusions that are communicated to interest others'. He distinguishes research from learning in part because the former 'requires the symbolization and transmission of [newly acquired] understandings in the public domain'.

McLeod, J (2003) *Doing Counselling Research* (2nd edn). London: Sage.

META-STORY The story that tells everybody's story, the 'big story', or the story of stories.

SAMPLE A small part or quantity intended to show what the whole is like. So, for example, rather than interview all patients of an NHS trust in order to find out what they think about the service, a researcher might decide to select a proportion of them that in some way are likely to represent the views of them all. More formally, a sample is a section from a POPULATION serving as a basis for the whole population.

POPULATION All the cases conforming to, or affected by, the set of circumstances pertaining to the research. For example, all the patients of an NHS Trust, all adults abused as children and so on.

We expand on samples and populations in Chapter 2.4.

and practices have grown up around the world of research and it is helpful to understand these. That is what this book is about.

But don't be fooled, at its heart research is an ordinary activity and whatever it is you want to discover, explore or explain, there is a way appropriate to the issue and that will suit you as an individual. Perhaps it helps you to know how likely something is to happen or what chance there is that something you do (or don't do) will have an effect on your client. There are a number of approaches to research that may help you do this. Alternatively, perhaps you are interested in the stories people have to tell about their experiences and the meaning they give to these. Again, there are a number of research strategies, any one or more of which may be helpful. It is an introduction to these and many other ways of doing research that we present this book.

What is research?

Conventionally, conservatively and in the simplest terms, research is systematic study conducted with the intention of answering a question. The hope is that this will lead to the establishment of 'fact' and, in turn, increased understanding and knowledge. For example, a way of understanding how adults who experienced childhood trauma cope with its effects in later life would be to collect the stories that some people who were traumatised as children have to tell about this (perhaps by recording interviews) and then to find a way of producing a 'META-STORY'. Usually, a final step in the research process is to communicate what has been found in such a way as to interest and inform others. This can be in writing, through a presentation or in some other form.

In the example about adults traumatised as children, what is systematic is the recruitment of a SAMPLE of people who have the experience (and therefore the knowledge), the collection of that knowledge in more or less the same way from each individual and then the 'processing' of the collected information, firstly in order to be able to understand the general experience, and then to be able to present it in a communicable form. Arguably, unless the new understanding or discovery that happens through posing and answering a question is somehow told to others, it is 'personal learning' rather than research.

In a way, the view of research we give above is conservative and traditional but it is certainly one that has dominated the exploration and examination of practice – and, for the very good reason that it provides useful information, it will continue to be important. Research of this kind has been described as *informative;* that is, to do with the collection and dissemination of information. However, there are other ideas about research and broader definitions.

Approach to research	Definition
Informative*	To do with describing some set of circumstances or domain of experience and offering some explanation of what is found. It is also about the dissemination of findings to interested parties.
Transformative* *Informative and transformative research are often interdependent.	Concerned with exploring practice within a particular setting with a view to changing the behaviour of the researchers (perhaps by developing new skills) or their attitudes. It may also result in changing systems or organisations. Transformative research is often the kind known as action research or action inquiry and may have 'political' aims or the aim of changing social situations.
Developmental	This occurs when the researcher(s) is/are 'altered' in what may be described as in the direction of constructive personality change by the research activity *per se*. It is a by-product of the research process when that involves the development of high levels of self-understanding, self-reflection and productive engagement with others (most frequently transformative or expressive research). Developmental research occurs when the researchers are investigating aspects of their own experience.
Explanatory	This is about classifying, conceptualising and building theories. Observation, hypothesis formation, experimentation and analysis are the main strategies for the implementation of explanatory research. It is descriptive and informative. The questions behind such research are usually 'what?', 'how?' and 'why?' so explanatory research is close to the conventional view of research.
Expressive	This is to do with understanding the meaning of experience, allowing its meaning to become apparent. It requires the researcher(s) to partake deeply of the experience under investigation and to reflect deeply on what happens to them and around them. It may involve intuition and creativity as well as cognition. There is no attempt at detached analysis. It is essentially an exploratory approach in which synthesis is a principal strategy.

John Heron (1996: 48-9, 91-2) defines and discusses informative and transformative research and Wilkins (2000: 17-20) concisely explains action research. Wilkins (2000: 20) and Mitchell-Williams et al. (2004: 332) consider research as a developmental process. Reason and Hawkins (1988: 79-80) cover the differences between explanatory and exploratory research.

Heron, J (1996) *Co-operative Inquiry: Research into the human condition.* London: Sage.
Mitchell-Williams, Z, Wilkins, P, McClean, M, Nevin, W, Wastell, K & Wheat, R (2004) The importance of the personal element in collaborative research. *Educational Action Research 12*(4), 329-46.
Reason, P & Hawkins, P (1988) Storytelling as inquiry. In P Reason (ed) *Human Inquiry in Action: Developments in new paradigm research* (pp 79-101). London: Sage.
Wilkins, P (2000) Collaborative approaches to research. In B Humphries (ed) *Research in Social Care and Social Welfare: Issues and debates for practice* (pp 16-30). London: Jessica Kingsley.

POSITIVISTIC/POSITIVISM A doctrine asserting that sense perceptions are the only admissible basis of human knowledge and precise thought. In research, that the validity of knowledge can only be assured by experimental science.

These and other alternative approaches to research were developed because old-style, POSITIVISTIC, informative research did not provide adequate tools to answer the questions that seemed important to people wanting to explore and understand human experience and how human beings make sense of the world. These newer approaches are based on the premise that if you want to know about human experience, the best thing to do is to ask a human being – and, in some approaches, that the human being each of us knows best is ourselves. It is also true that for some inquirers there are philosophical (and perhaps ethical) dilemmas in doing research *on* people. This has led to the development of a number of methods of inquiry that involve others as co-researchers, that is, that are about research *with* people. Often practice with people implies a set of attitudes and values rarely employed in traditional research. Many newer approaches are more directly concerned with these values.

Although these different approaches have come to prominence in recent times, there is nothing new in this (apparent) division in ways of knowing. In classical Greece, there were notions of *logos* and *mythos* as different, complementary and mutually dependent ways of knowing and arriving at 'truth'. *Logos* equates with the rational, pragmatic and 'scientific' way of thinking which came to dominate Western approaches to inquiry. As the word suggests, it is to do with logic. *Mythos,* on the other hand, is about meaning rather than practicalities. It is the way cultures, societies and individuals express insight, intuition and deep (but possibly 'irrational') understanding. Myths are the stories which give form to this understanding. Arguably, shaping, telling and listening to stories can be research in its own right. Western science may be understood to have lost the necessary connection with *mythos,* but newer methods of exploring human experience can be seen as attempts to redress this. In this book, as well as explaining the core concepts of traditional research, we take a broad view of what constitutes research and show that to draw *logos* and *mythos* together once more is likely to enrich our understanding of human experience, the ways in which we construct meaning, and the diversity and universality of our existence.

Note

For more about storytelling as research see:

Reason, P & Hawkins, P (1988) Storytelling as inquiry. In P Reason (ed) *Human Inquiry in Action: Developments in new paradigm research* (pp 79-101). London: Sage.

Wilkins, P (2000) Storytelling as research. In B Humphries (ed) *Research in Social Care and Social Welfare: Issues and debates for practice* (pp 144-53). London: Jessica Kingsley.

Ways of 'knowing'

Increasingly as research in the helping professions expands from a purely 'scientific' approach to the acquisition of knowledge, understanding the frame of reference from which the researcher operates has become essential – firstly to the researcher so that predispositions can be understood and allowed for as the research proceeds and findings are interpreted, secondly to the reader/receiver so that the lens through which the researcher's conclusions were viewed and presented can be taken into account.

Because there are many ways of thinking about how we know things it is very likely that in your reading about research you will come across a few technical terms that are to do with the systems of knowledge that underpin particular approaches, that is, the EPISTEMOLOGY of the approach. Every approach to research is characterised by a particular EPISTEMOLOGY, ONTOLOGY and AXIOLOGY, whether these are made explicit or not.

To some extent, when you do research yourself, how you do it will be guided by how you think we construct or discover knowledge, what you believe to be the nature of human beings, and the ethical and personal values you bring to your study. It is like this for all researchers. For example, a belief that people are rational beings and that there is an objective truth out there waiting to be discovered may lead a researcher in the direction of POSITIVISM and experimentation. Those who believe that we acquire our knowledge of things from experience and observation will be attracted to EMPIRICISM. Alternatively, the researcher may think in more humanistic terms and see all knowledge as subjective (i.e. depending on the interpretations of the knower) in which case a PHENOMENOLOGICAL approach which is concerned with conscious experience from the point of view of the experiencing person may be most appropriate. There again, a belief that we construct our knowledge and understanding of the world by reflecting on experience and that each of us comes up with a personal framework to make sense of our experience points towards a CONSTRUCTIVIST approach. There are many more possibilities and each blend of EPISTEMOLOGY and ONTOLOGY leads to one or more research methods.

This isn't the end of it: really most of what we have been talking about so far is the knowledge of ideas, what we think and why we think it. There are other forms of knowledge. For example, there is the knowledge of how to do something, practical knowledge. Additionally, some people think in terms of experiential knowledge, which is learning from direct encounters with people, places or things. And then there are more mystical approaches to knowledge which emphasise a TRANSPERSONAL dimension. Again, each of these can influence or even dictate an approach to inquiry.

What can research do?

There are many reasons for conducting a piece of research but perhaps the primary drive is the burning desire to 'know' on the part of the researcher. But what is there to know? Taking person-centred therapy as an example, researchers may have questions about the necessary and sufficient conditions for therapeutic

EPISTEMOLOGY Philosophy concerned with the nature of knowledge (what is it?), the source of knowledge (how do we know what we know?) and the scope of knowledge (what, if any, are the limits of knowledge?).

ONTOLOGY The branch of METAPHYSICS concerned with the nature of being and, of special relevance to research, with particular theories about the nature of being and kinds of existence.

AXIOLOGY The study of the nature of values and value judgements (aesthetic or moral). In the context of research, axiology is most likely to be important in terms of moral or ethical values.

METAPHYSICS Philosophy concerned with abstract concepts such as the nature of existence or of truth and knowledge.

POSITIVISM See page opposite.

EMPIRICISM A philosophy where sensory experience (instead of reason) is the source of understanding, i.e. that knowledge of the world comes from outside the person.

PHENOMENOLOGICAL approaches to understanding and psychology are based on the study of immediate experience, where 'truth' or 'knowledge' comes from the perceptual field of the individual, rather than an external authority. Based on the work of the philosopher Edmund Husserl.

CONSTRUCTIVIST Constructivism is a philosophy of learning founded on the premise that, by reflecting on our experiences, we construct our own understanding of the world we live in. Each of us generates our own 'rules' and 'mental models' which we use to make sense of our experiences. (From <www.funderstanding.com/content/constructivism> retrieved 11/11/2009)

TRANSPERSONAL Literally beyond (trans) the person, transcending the rational, physical and sensory to the mystical.

Activity

When you think about your own understanding of human beings and human experience, where would you place yourself in terms of the above major philosophical attitudes to research? What is it you like to know? And how do you prefer to know it?

OUTCOME STUDIES/OUTCOME RESEARCH refers to research (usually in the field of medicine or health and social care) in which the outcome of care practices and/or treatment is investigated. The focus is often on the impact of care procedures on the quality of life of the subjects (efficacy) but it could also include an evaluation of, eg, cost-effectiveness (efficiency).

Moustakas, C (1990) *Heuristic Research: Design, methodology and applications.* Newbury Park, CA: Sage.

Ellis, C & Bochner, AP (2000) Autoethnography, personal narrative, reflexivity. In NK Denzin & YS Lincoln (eds) *Handbook of Qualitative Research* (2nd edn) (pp 733-68). Thousand Oaks, CA: Sage.

Note

Collaborative research methods (see p 150 and throughout this book) are very appropriate with helping practitioners. For example, Helen Traylen (1994) found co-operative inquiry to be the most significant of three research methods she used when she researched the experience of health visitors. She says the co-operative inquiry 'helped the health visitors not only to express what they felt about their real problems but also to move towards a more open and constructive relationship with their clients, with each other, with other agencies, and with their managers' (p 81).

Traylen, H (1994) Confronting hidden agendas: Co-operative inquiry with health visitors. In P Reason (ed) *Participation in Human Inquiry* (pp 59–81). London: Sage.

personality change (certainly a lot of effort has gone into attempting to establish the truth of psychotherapy theory hypotheses), or the comparative merits of person-centred therapy and other approaches to therapy, or its cost-effectiveness with respect to drug treatments, or its efficacy with particular client groups and so on. Such research can be seen as attempts to establish the 'evidence-based' credentials of person-centred therapy and are often called OUTCOME STUDIES. For these investigations an informative, explanatory form of research is likely to be appropriate and the findings amenable to being published in a mainstream academic or professional journal (see Chapter 3.4).

As an alternative to investigating outcome, researchers might be interested in the experiences of clients and practitioners. This may involve the deep reflection by a practitioner/researcher on a particular aspect of skill or technique in an attempt to achieve an intimate understanding of it 'from the inside'. This could lead to consideration of heuristic inquiry (see pp. 217–21) or autoethnography (see p. 149) as research processes (see Moustakas, 1990; Ellis & Bochner, 2000). Other questions might centre on the client experience and involve researchers in in-depth conversations with clients trying to reach an understanding of, for example, their therapeutic process. A number of strategies are then available to make some sort of consensus account of that experience. Or perhaps the researcher will decide that the power to determine the subject, nature and course of the research should be with the people it is about rather than a person in the defined and controlling role of 'researcher'. An initial question might be 'What is it like to be an occupational therapist?' but quite how this is understood and answered would be decided by the co-researchers as a group. Broadly speaking, if the appropriate method is chosen, research can contribute to the knowledge of and/or insight into almost any question that can be framed. Of course, the answer might be 'you can't get there from here' but this too contributes to the sum total of knowledge. Any of this research may contribute to the formulation or advancement of theory and/or improvements in practice.

Why should helping practitioners do research?

A really good question about research is 'Why should I bother doing it? What's in it for me?' Those of an academic bent might answer that it is about scratching the itch of curiosity, finding out the answer to something you really want to know. Behind this lies the notion that researchers are driven purely and simply by the need to know – and some of us are, some of the time. Maybe you are or will be. A more pragmatic answer might be that doing research might help you advance in your profession. This may be through studying for a higher degree (both Masters and Doctoral programmes will require students to undertake some relevant independent research) or perhaps getting research published will be viewed positively by employers and potential employers. Another reason may be to obtain funding to ensure the survival, advancement or establishment of a service. One way to establish that a service is appreciated, required, cost-effective and so on is to do some research to demonstrate this.

However, perhaps the best reason for doing research is that it will in some way improve the lot of clients. This may be because it enhances your knowledge and skills and, when it is published, others have the opportunity to be similarly advanced, or because it shows service improvements are worthwhile, or that it establishes a fulfillable need, and so on. Also, research raises the profile of a profession. This recognition is important when it comes to funding, employment status, etc. Moreover, separately and together via their practice, helping professionals have access to phenomenal amounts of data. Perhaps there is a professional and ethical obligation to use this data for the greater good.

As practitioner-researchers, a wealth of information lies at our fingertips and we and others might benefit greatly if we find ways of looking at our own practice with the critical eye of a researcher. It may be that the institution or service you work for collects information on all service users. This may be ready-made data. A good example is the use of CORE (Clinical Outcomes in Routine Evaluation) data demonstrated by Isabel Gibbard in Chapter 3.5.

Perhaps you notice a trend of some kind in your service or amongst your clients and you have a hunch about it. Research will help you establish the truth and usefulness of that hunch. Perhaps you wonder about some aspect of yourself in relation to practice. There are ways of reflecting on this so as to contribute to the sum total of knowledge. In these, and many other ways, helping professionals can use their working situations to feed their research endeavours. However, if one practitioner has access to information on which to base research, think how much more several practitioners have. Research need not be a lonely activity.

We want to encourage you to think creatively about your work, your ideas and the questions you have and how you might contribute to knowledge of your profession and how it operates. We owe it to ourselves and our clients to offer the best service we can. Research improves and enhances what we can do and how we can do it. So, with this book as your primer, find a way of doing research that suits you and suits your purpose and get out there and have some fun.

Last but not least, we want to emphasise the importance of practitioner research. Although we have been saying otherwise in the first part of this section, please do not assume that research is

Activity

Looking back at the table about approaches to research, do you think Helen Traylen (see previous margin note) was conducting informative, transformative, developmental, explanatory or expressive research? Why do you think as you do? How easy or difficult is it to decide? Does her study fall neatly into one category?

Note
This argument – somehow tapping into the (potentially) huge amounts of data held by individual practitioners – provides the thrust for the notion of the harnessing of 'practice-based evidence'. All those who receive systematic helping and care would benefit if the collective wisdom of everyday practice could be somehow captured and put to use. We will return to this several times in this book.

Note
The CORE system is for managers and practitioners working in counselling and psychological therapy services. It provides a framework for responding to the increasing demand in health and other sectors to provide evidence of service quality and effectiveness. Using its various tools enables researchers to obtain quality information about client groups and service performance. The CORE website <www.coreims.co.uk> provides guidance on how to use the system, publishes accounts of its use and much more. It is explained in more detail in Chapter 3.5, pp 299-304.

only done by researchers or students with a research-based assignment to do as part of a training course. There are several reasons why research done by practitioners on their own and their colleagues practice is crucial to the future of health and social care work.

We are deliberately not going to list these reasons, since we hope you will discover your own – research is nothing without the enthusiasm of the researcher, and this can only come from within. However, we do think that the move towards evidence-based practice gives practitioner research some energy and 'edge'.

You may have started this book with the idea that your work situation required some data collection and report-writing skills, but that research was not appropriate. If you're reading this chapter you may have changed your mind or become fascinated by the research side of things. We argue that health and social care professionals should be numerate and 'research method literate' in order to claim back some lost social science territory and fight their corner, rather than be pushed to the margins of research whilst the behavioural *scientists* get on with the *real* business of *proving* which approaches are *effective*.

The italics in the previous sentence are there to remind us of the key words that grant-makers and fundholders look out for when planning what services can be afforded in the financial year. Our message is simply that research methods are here and accessible. Health and social care practitioners can go to the ball too and, if armed with a little understanding and some common sense, you will not turn into a pumpkin when midnight comes. Projects, studies, investigations, research, scientific investigations, call them what you will, all have to meet certain quality criteria before they are deemed acceptable. In order to plan and carry out an acceptable piece of work, or judge the work of others, you will need an understanding of research methods.

quantity versus quality

One of the first things the beginning researcher encounters is an apparent ideological divide in approaches to research. Newcomers to the world of social sciences research would be forgiven for thinking they had stumbled into an ideological war zone when people start debating the pros and cons of quantitative versus qualitative research methods. So, how do you, new to research, bright-eyed and bushy-tailed, wanting to investigate something, reach a preliminary decision about which of these warring parties to ally yourself with?

In this chapter we explain the battle lines, although in fairness it has to be said that in recent years there has been a good deal of bridge building to find some ground on which both parties can stand safely without coming to blows. For many of us, our first belief about social science research is that it comprises 'scientific' methods, numbers and statistics. If your first reaction to this is terror, then on introduction to qualitative methods you may feel lost in vagueness and confusion. So what is the debate all about? What is quantitative research? What is qualitative research? What can each of them do?

At the heart of the issue lies a fundamental difference in philosophy. This difference is not a new one and should be familiar to health and social care practitioners since a variation of it appears in the philosophies underpinning different approaches to helping. This difference is fundamental because it is in many ways irreconcilable and exclusive. In other words it is difficult, if not impossible, to hold both views at once, rather like religious views. You either believe in God or you don't. It is difficult to build a world-view on a 'maybe' or a 'yes and no' answer. Such views are also often held with some passion and many people are not open to changing these views. It's not that people are rigid when it comes to thinking about social science research, it's just that rather like finding a helping approach that is congruent with their personality, people discover that certain approaches to research resonate with or are more in accord with their views on life, the universe and everything. By reading this chapter and perhaps some of the ones that follow you will be able to place yourself in relation to approaches to research. You may decide that the certainty of a quantifiable approach is for you, or perhaps you will decide that you value the stories people have to tell over measurement. However, although there is a fundamental philosophical

Note

Although it is often presented as if there is a fundamental separation between quantitative and qualitative approaches to research it is not uncommon to use both together in an effort to answer a particular research question. One such approach is called 'mixed methods design'. Two main types of mixed methods design are: mixed methods and mixed model research.

In a mixed research method you use quantitative data for one stage of a research study and qualitative data for a second stage of a study. In a mixed model design you use both quantitative and qualitative data in one or two stages of the research process.

The mixing of quantitative and qualitative approaches happens in every stage of a research. For example, in his examination of the working alliance in online therapy with young people, Terry Hanley (2009) used both a questionnaire on which he performed a quantitative analysis, and conducted interviews which were analysed for key themes using a qualitative technique.

Hanley, T (2009) The working alliance in online therapy with young people: Preliminary findings. *British Journal of Guidance and Counselling* 37(3), 257-69.

IF YOU WANT TO KNOW MORE ABOUT
mixed methods design

you could look at:

Cresswell, J & Plano-Clark, V (2006) *Designing and Conducting Mixed Methods Research.* London: Sage.

Johnson, R & Onwuegbuzie, A (2004) Mixed methods research: A research paradigm whose time has come. *Educational Researcher* 33(7), 14-26.

divide here and many people opt for one side or the other, it is important to remember that approaches to research have been developed to do different things. They are essentially tools. So, although you can wire a plug with a bread knife and hack off a chunk from a loaf with a screwdriver, it is more efficient to do it the other way round, and a hammer is useless for either task but just what you need to knock in a nail, to some extent whether you do quantitative or qualitative research will depend on what your question is and in what form you want your answer. This chapter and the ones that follow will not only explain the ideological divide but help you towards deciding which is the best tool in the box for the task you have in mind. Whatever you decide for yourself, remember that it isn't that quantitative approaches are 'better' or 'worse' than qualitative approaches (we certainly don't believe that) merely that they are different. This difference means that they have different uses for different people in different circumstances.

Some philosophical differences between quantitative and qualitative approaches can be expressed in many different ways

• structure	structurelessness or 'chaos' •
• outcome	process •
• objective	subjective •
• external frame of reference	internal frame of reference •
• neutral and detached	involved •
• 'science'-centred	person-centred •
• analysis	synthesis •
• taking apart	putting together •
• variables are identified and measured	complex variables that interact and are difficult to measure •
• numbers	thoughts, feelings, words, patterns •
• reduction to simple units	complexity and pluralism •
• people as objects	people as persons •
• measurable and observable	experiential •
• abstraction of facts	description of experiences •
• deduced from fact	elaborated from intuition •
• technology	nature •
• **quantity**	**quality** •

The overwhelming conventional wisdom of our technological culture is that we all process the world in rational and 'scientific' ways. We form little hypotheses about the world, test them and then act upon our findings. It must surely follow then, that the way to find the 'truth' is to pursue the same 'method' in research. We put these words in quotes because each one carries with it assumptions and behind each assumption lies a debate. The main assumption was that there was no other way of looking at the problem. This way of looking at the discovery of 'truth' is called POSITIVISM and was the dominant research method, so much so that it remained more or less unchallenged for decades. In the world of research, numbers have been (and to a large extent still are) where the power is – just think about the drive for 'evidenced-based' treatment. However, from the point of view of helping professionals, there are lots of things we want to know that quantitative approaches just can't tell us. Not only that, there is an argument that numbers are a distraction from what is really worth knowing. In the story of *The Little Prince*, de Saint-Exupéry (1991: 15-16) puts this rather well:

> Grown-ups love figures. When you tell them you have made a new friend, they never ask you any questions about essential matters. They never say to you, 'What does his voice sound like? What games does he love best? Does he collect butterflies?' Instead, they demand: 'How old is he? How many brothers has he? How much does he weigh? How much money does his father make?' Only from these figures do they think they have learned anything about him.

That we can even have this debate is a tribute to the pioneers of qualitative research methods. The language used in research is at the heart of the debate for the same reasons that it lies at the heart of issues of oppression because of colour, gender, etc. Language is important because it interacts with our thoughts and feelings – helping define and give shape to them at the same time as being defined by them.

If we look in a little more detail at the meanings behind some of the words and phrases used in research, we will get a better picture of the positive features of a qualitative position. For some, there is also an ethical dimension behind the choice of an approach to research. This too, involves language and the thought and attitude behind it. Quantitative research into aspects of human behaviour is performed on *subjects* ideally with their informed consent but still as something done to one human being by another. In qualitative research, it is more usual to talk of *participants,* which implies greater agency on the part of the people involved – other than the

---

IF YOU WANT TO KNOW MORE ABOUT
POSITIVISIM

you could look at
Encyclopædia Britannica Online <www.britannica.com/EBchecked/topic/471865/Positivism> retrieved 02/02/2010, or

Friedman, M (1999) *Reconsidering Logical Positivism*. Cambridge: Cambridge University Press.

Or, if you are really keen, go back to the original description and definition set forth by Auguste Comte in 1848: Google Books, <books.google.co.uk/books?id=SgaHpaeZAewC&dq=positivism&printsec=frontcover&source=in&hl=)> retrieved 08/03/2010.

De Saint-Exupéry, A (1991) *The Little Prince*. Glasgow: Egmont Books.

POSITIVISM A doctrine asserting that sense perceptions are the only admissible basis of human knowledge and precise thought. In research, that the validity of knowledge can only be assured by experimental science.

Note
We have defined a number of terms on p 5, Chapter 1.1, and there is a RUNNING GLOSSARY throughout the book.

principal researcher or even *co-researchers* – which is an even greater step towards a democratic and involving way of doing research *with* people rather than *on* people.

The role of the researcher

Both approaches recognise the powerful effect that the researcher has on the research, from choice of area to be studied, the hypothesis or question asked, through to the collection and treatment of data. Human beings have profound effects on other human beings, so our research method must acknowledge this and deal with this in some way. If the researcher gets too close to the subjects under study, they may influence the subjects' behaviour.

In quantitative studies, this recognition is expressed as an attempt to remove all trace of the researcher and the effects of their person from the research; to remove the contamination of the human touch. Elaborate controls are enacted to prevent the researcher from having any noticeable effect (see Chapter 2.5). Also, the researcher, being human, is likely to have *their* judgement adversely affected by too close proximity to the subjects under study.

In qualitative studies, this human interaction is deliberately exploited. The researcher tries to understand the complexities of the effect they might have by getting involved in the study, possibly as a participant. Qualitative methods seek understanding of the process of the effect of the researcher by empathic understanding rather than neutral objectivity.

Variables and measurement

Measurement of something isn't quite as simple as it sounds. Even the most hard-line quantitative researchers will agree that accurate measurement of anything is impossible, it's just a question of what degree of inaccuracy you're prepared to put up with. Another problem is that very few things stay constant for long enough to make a measurement useful; as soon as you've measured it it's changed, so you have to measure it again, then it changes again, and so it goes on. Add to that the fact that when you measure something you nearly always change it; that is to say that the very act of measuring something causes it to change and thus to invalidate the first measure.

All quantitative approaches are dependent upon measurement and can be seen as the constant (if, in some people's view, vain) attempt to measure things as accurately as possible, given all of the drawbacks. Variables are seen as elements of the world which the researcher controls and manipulates.

A qualitative approach, on the other hand, takes either the view, 'If measurement is so problematic, why bother?' or the view,

QUESTIONS TO CONSIDER
• *Which is the best position from which to understand the effect of the researcher: outside or to one side of the 'action' – or right in the middle of it?*
• *In order to collect the best data, should the researcher be involved in the middle of the process or neutral and detached from it?*

'Measurement is an insult or violation of the human processes we are seeking to sensitively understand' and so proceeds to try to find better ways to capture the meaning in the world that has relevance to the study in hand. This search for better ways involves assuming that there is no such thing as 'objective' reality, but that reality is socially constructed. The best way of understanding reality then, is from the point of view of the main protagonists in the study.

Variables, therefore, are understood as elements of the world which emerge through a non-invasive process of inquiry and are then described or portrayed in the process of data collection. They are not seen as simple unitary items but as complex interwoven strands of experience the essence of which will be destroyed by inappropriate unravelling. Description rather than measurement is seen as the prime method of data capture.

> *QUESTION TO CONSIDER*
> • *Will measurement of the variables capture the meaning without distorting it or is measurement so intrusive and 'insulting' that it changes or even destroys the meaning?*

Treatment of data

Once you have captured the meaning of the world in some form of data, the question is, how are you going to make sense of it? It could be that the form in which the data comes – numbers, words, pictures, audio or video recordings, etc. – begins to suggest certain ways of treating it. On the other hand, it could be that we are so conditioned to count numbers that we just can't think of anything else to do with them! All kinds of research are to some extent the story of how much we are prepared to wrestle with ourselves and our preconceived ideas as we try to make sense of the data.

Untreated data as it arrives from collection is called raw data. It is usually a jumble of notes, numbers, lists, tapes, in an apparently undisciplined pile. We have likened this raw data in quantitative studies to a raw diamond (see Chapter 2.3): an apparently charmless stone within which lies beauty waiting to be revealed by the skill of the diamond cutter. Statistical description and analysis are the diamond cutter's tools.

Qualitative researchers look at data differently:
- the first difference is that in qualitative research we may be interested in the patterns on the surface of the rough stone. We may consider these natural patterns to be of more intrinsic value than any enhancement, amplification or exploitation of the qualities of the stone through *artificial* treatments
- the next difference is that in qualitative research we will wish to use treatments which involve humans as the instruments of treatment, rather than mechanistic tests or numerical models. We want the data treatments to be of human beings and by human beings, since it is these qualities in the data which we value and wish to preserve through congruent treatment

SYNTHESIS Putting things together in familiar or novel ways to see what patterns are made and to understand how they might fit and work together. This is called holism (see p 22).

ANALYSIS Taking things or ideas apart, or separating things into their constituent parts to see how the parts fit and work together. In scientific terms this is called reductionism (see p 22).

QUESTIONS TO CONSIDER
- *What forms can data take?*
- *Should data treatment be natural, human and congruent with the data, or does it need treatment with special statistical instruments to reveal the order inherent in it?*
- *How can we best express this congruence in the way we treat our data?*

Note – data are* …
Wikipedia has the following entry for the term 'data' which we think assumes a quantitative definition. (We look at the nature of qualitative data in Chapter 2.8, p 187.)

> … groups of information that represent the qualitative or quantitative attributes of a variable or set of variables. Data (plural of 'datum', which is seldom used*) are typically the results of measurements and can be the basis of graphs, images, or observations of a set of variables. Data are often viewed as the lowest level of abstraction from which information and knowledge are derived.

Retrieved 03/04/2010 <http://en.wikipedia.org/wiki/Data>

*We explain our general use of 'data' as both singular and plural on p v, in 'Introductions'.

- the third difference is that in qualitative research we do not say that the process of the treatment is just as important as the outcome. *We understand that the process is the outcome.* The process of treating data is the process of discovering meaning in the data and since it is human researchers that have chosen and implemented the treatment, we are simultaneously making, discovering and describing the meaning in the data
- the final difference is that in qualitative research we are looking for patterns and qualities, not numbers and quantities. In order to achieve this we may have to consider putting data together to SYNTHESISE meaning rather than take the data apart into ever smaller units to ANALYSE meaning. This is a little like those pictures made up of dots that make no sense when you stand close to them. In order to see the meaning in the pattern, you have to first of all turn your back on the picture, walk a long way from it, screw up your eyes and look at it with half-closed eyelids. Then you see the pattern. In qualitative data analysis, we try what might seem to be rather disconnected or bizarre ways of treating data. The common sense which they all bring is that they each try to use a uniquely human attribute or aptitude in order to bring out or discover the meaning inherent in the data

These differences are variations on the technology–nature dimension (listed in the box on p. 10). On this dimension the difference between quantitative and qualitative methods is the difference between believing that we can (only) advance through technology, or, on the other hand, that we cannot enhance nature through artificial processes, all we do is destroy it.

Purpose of research

You would be forgiven for thinking that there is only one purpose of research – to discover the truth. Not an unreasonable assumption, but nevertheless one that on checking turns out to be a little short of the mark (see Chapter 1.1). The point about the debate between qualitative and quantitative philosophies is that one side acts as though truth exists in some absolute form, that there is obviously only one way of discovering truth and that any suggestion otherwise is heresy. This is the quantitative version that we have all grown up with.

The philosophical position underpinning qualitative approaches suggests that *meaning* is socially constructed and that 'truth' is subjective and therefore variable depending upon your point of view. (Even some research physicists now take this line.) So what is the purpose of research if there is no absolute truth? It is to seek an understanding of the contexts of truths, to discover meaning, to explore experience and even to construct new meaning, new understanding and to effect social and/or political change. Where the quantitative researcher seeks the small truth from a limited sample in order to generalise it to the big truth of the population, the qualitative researcher seeks to contextualise the truths. Only by understanding the context can we understand the viewpoint of the actors in the context which generated the view of truth and so come to some tentative explanation.

Quality, quantity and health and social care

The challenge presented by qualitative research is to let go of our notions that facts are important and that the only things worth knowing are discovered by controlling variables, counting things and applying logic to the numbers. Imagine if you can a subjective, process-oriented research in which feelings are felt and then subjected to a process of chaotic synthesis.

The words used in qualitative research are words we use to indicate human processes because the human researcher, with all of their wonderfully complicated influences, is put at the heart of the research process. In quantitative approaches the human factors are excluded as far as possible because they are thought to contaminate the outcome. Qualitative research is of people, about people and done by people.

In this book, we will use our understanding of helping approaches to aid our understanding of a qualitative approach to research methods wherever possible. Helping approaches can be thought of in terms of several 'dimensions' similar to the ones listed on p. 10. Some are more subjective, intuitive, unstructured and 'person-centred', whilst others are more objective, structured, fact and natural science-centred. For example, most counsellors will be familiar with the philosophical, theoretical and practical bases of behavioural counselling and person-centred counselling, and the consequent differences between them. There are similar philosophical differences in other health and social care professions. We will use these two approaches to counselling to illustrate the different approaches to research. Some researchers and readers might think that the analogy has limited use and we welcome the debate. If readers start thinking about and debating the issues in this way, the analogy will have achieved its first objective.

A behavioural approach to counselling and person-centred counselling can occupy the two poles of a continuum, with many degrees of difference and combination of ideas and practice between them, yet their basic philosophies remain inherently and exclusively different. Some are of the *fundamental* kind, some are more flexible and might indicate areas of compromise.

QUESTIONS TO CONSIDER
- *What is the purpose of research?*
- *Is it to generalise from small SAMPLES to POPULATIONS, make predictions and find causal explanations or to create and understand contexts, understanding the perspectives of others and understanding the part our collection and treatment of that data has played in the final explanations?*

SAMPLE A small part or quantity intended to show what the whole is like. So, for example, rather than interview all patients of an NHS trust in order to find out what they think about the service, a researcher might decide to select a proportion of them that in some way are likely to represent the views of them all. More formally, a sample is a section from a POPULATION serving as a basis for the whole population.

POPULATION All the cases conforming to, or affected by, the set of circumstances pertaining to the research. For example, all the patients of an NHS Trust, all adults abused as children and so on.

We expand on samples and populations in Chapter 2.4.

Where do you stand on these issues as they are presented? What concepts do you see as fundamental to your belief system? What ideas of your own are missing from this list (it is not intended to be comprehensive)?

Behavioural counselling	Person-centred counselling
Learning processes are responsible for change	The human tendency towards purposeful, positive self-fulfilment is responsible for change
Feelings can be manipulated by thoughts	
Observable behaviour is of prime importance	Experiences are of prime importance
Logical rational processes are thought to guide behaviour and mental life	Logic and rationality are not important in the understanding of people Persons each have a unique logic
External frame of reference is used	The internal frame of reference is used
Measurable elements of behaviour are sought and quantified in order to evaluate change	Only that which the person sees as important is used, whether it be behaviour or experience, measurable or not. Measurement is not seen as important
Empirical/pragmatic approach to effectiveness of therapy – if it works, use it	The person determines what is important
The 'person' is thought of as a 'behaviour machine' or sometimes even a black box, the contents and workings of which are less important than the outcome, i.e. the behaviour	The person is seen as central to the process, enigmatic and autonomous, wise and powerful
Trust in the scientific principles of learning gives this method its power and integrity	Trust in human processes of change gives this method its power and integrity
Behaviourism	**Person-centred humanism**

Practitioners occupying the extreme poles of these methods approach the whole process of counselling and personal change in fundamentally different ways. Researchers occupying the extreme poles of research METHODOLOGY approach the whole process of data collection and analysis in fundamentally different ways. So much so that at the extreme edge of subjective 'human-centred' research the very words 'data' and 'analysis' have little or no meaning, whereas they are at the very heart of traditional POSITIVISTIC, quantitative research.

- a behavioural counsellor looks at the client objectively in the same way as the quantitative researcher tries to distance themselves from the process of research in order to become an objective, neutral data collector
- a behavioural counsellor deals in measurable, quantifiable behaviour in the same way that a quantitative researcher does
- a behavioural counsellor applies the laws of learning in the same way that a quantitative researcher applies the laws of empirical science

On the other hand,

- a person-centred counsellor will put the client at the centre of the process, just as the qualitative researcher does
- the person-centred counsellor sees the change process as a relationship event, just as the qualitative researcher sees research as a relationship between the researcher and the things being researched (much more of this from Chapter 2.6 – 2.8)
- the person-centred counsellor will trust and follow the client's process in the same way that the qualitative researcher trusts and follows the research process – wherever it may lead
- the person-centred counsellor understands that the self of the therapist is an integral part of the process and must enter the relationship congruently or authentically, just as the qualitative researcher needs to understand their own self and their role in the process of research

This analogy can be developed further. Perhaps you don't agree with some of the statements above, or you might like to see how far it goes before it starts to break down. Either way we have found it a useful tool for understanding some of the issues at the heart of the qualitative/quantitative debate. Behavioural and person-centred counsellors follow these paths because they believe in different models of humankind and human change processes. These differences follow us into the world of research too. Those who follow a humanist, person-centred philosophy would generally seek to carry it into research. They believe that people-research should put people and people-processes at its centre.

METHODOLOGY A coherent collection of theories and practices relating to a field of inquiry; the underlying principles and rules of organisation of a process of inquiry.

POSITIVISTIC/POSITIVISM A doctrine asserting that sense perceptions are the only admissible basis of human knowledge and precise thought. In research, that the validity of knowledge can only be assured by experimental science.

Note
To make our argument clear, we have over-simplified a bit here. Traditionally, not all qualitative research was quite as involving and 'relational' as you may infer from what we say. For example, classical ETHNOGRAPHY involved detached observation by a 'neutral' observer and detailed description of what was seen and so (at least arguably) had more in common with EMPIRICISM than PHENOMENOLOGY.

ETHNOGRAPHY A branch of anthropology dealing with the methodical, scientific description of human societies and cultures. No particular method is specified – what is important is that whatever the method of investigation it leads to describing people, their interactions and beliefs through writing.

EMPIRICISM A philosophy where sensory experience (instead of reason) is the source of understanding, i.e. that knowledge of the world comes from outside the person.

PHENOMENOLOGY An approach to understanding and psychology based on the study of immediate experience, where 'truth' or 'knowledge' comes from the perceptual field of the individual, rather than an external authority. Based on the work of the philosopher Edmund Husserl.

Attempts to control, quantify, measure or objectify the person distort the elements under study to such a degree as to make the research invalid.

Of course, it is not only person-centred counsellors who seek a method of research that is congruent with their world-view. The principles of qualitative research are not exclusively person-centred. The analogy we have used may give that impression, but as you read on it will become clear that some of the debates in research methodology are about developing methods of study which are congruent with the philosophical bases of helping approaches, rather than hostile or damaging to them or that, of necessity, make them invalid as a consequence of the data collection process.

- the first question a beginning researcher interested in studying an aspect of health and social care should ask themselves is,
  'What event, activity or approach do I want to ask questions about?'

- and then,
  'What theoretical and philosophical assumptions regarding the nature of humankind and the change process underpin it?'

- finally,
  'What way of studying it would be at least congruent with it and perhaps even enhance it?'

You don't have to be an expert on research methods to come to some sort of useful answers to these questions. Many of us have already found our natural leaning in terms of helping approaches. We feel a resonance or harmony with certain ways of doing things. Sometimes we go along with this leaning and sometimes we deliberately go in another direction to challenge the cosy, comfortable feelings of merely confirming our prejudices.

Wherever you stand on this you will have a sense of how you prefer to do things, how *you* prefer to study and discover important 'truths'. From this starting point you have taken your first step in research, regardless of your leaning towards qualitative or quantitative ways of knowing; you have considered yourself and your place in the process – your 'method' if you like. Successful research must be appropriate to the topic being researched. And equally important, it can only be done by a researcher who feels comfortable in their skin as a practitioner and researcher – knowing that they are being true to themselves as well as their topic. In the following chapters we will look at some popular research methods and some guidelines and principles to follow to make sure you get your chosen research method as valid as you want it to be.

Qualitative and quantitative ways of thinking and working

Consider the following three examples of study, in which people come to grips with finding something out. Each starts with a problem or question which an individual or group wish to have answered.

1. Janet, a college counsellor, was interested to notice that each year, during enrolment, there was a stream of anxious, disoriented new students arriving at the counselling service. Whilst this was 'good for business' and made her yearly figures look good, she was sure that the college should be able to help these students more but she wasn't sure how. She thought it was important to see what the students felt about it themselves. At the beginning of every academic year she visited classes to talk about the counselling service, so when she visited the English department she asked the staff to help in her project. They agreed and got the students to write a story about arriving at college, based on what it was like for them. The staff then asked the students to write another story based on a perfect first week at an ideal college. Finally, the staff got the student group to make written recommendations to the college principal on how to improve the college 'welcome' to new students.

2. On arriving at her new job as lecturer, Aysha was appalled to find that the college had no counselling service and no plans to start one. She wanted to marshal evidence to persuade the college management that a counselling service was indeed needed. She wrote to all the other colleges in the region to find out how many had counselling services and of what type. She devised questionnaires for staff, students, parents and employers to find out whether a counselling service would be seen as an asset and whether students thought they would benefit from having someone to talk over their personal problems with. Finally, Aysha tabulated all her results and presented them in a written paper for the academic board.

3. Bill, another lecturer at a neighbouring college, also without a counselling service, found that in his role as personal tutor, students were coming to him with their problems. Sometimes he felt completely out of his depth and would worry at night about whether he was handling the situation well. Whilst realising that a college counselling service could be the answer, he wasn't sure how to find out about counselling or how best to convince the senior management. Bill put a notice up in the staff common room asking if any other staff encountering the same problem would like to meet to discuss what they should do. Eight other tutors turned up to a meeting and decided to meet as a support group one lunchtime every week. Through talking about the problems that they suffered themselves as a consequence of listening to the problems of others, they got a clearer picture of what was needed in college to support students and the mostly untrained staff who listen. The group decided to invite some senior managers to one of their meetings to find out for themselves exactly what the problem was and how it affected students and staff.

What do you think of these three pieces of 'research'? Did any of them seem more 'real', giving 'hard' data which would be more credible? Did any methods seem more congruent with counselling approaches? Did any methods 'speak' to you as being more in harmony with your own preferred way of doing things? Numbers 1 and 3 are examples of more qualitative methods, whilst 2 is an example of a comparatively quantitative method.

Whatever side of the ideological divide you come down on, research is about formulating and answering questions. The first skill of the researcher is learning how to frame questions in such a way as they can be answered. That is what the next part of this book is about.

Quantity, quality or a mixture?

From what you hear and read (and perhaps even from the way we have organised this book) you might think that there is a polarisation between quantitative methods and qualitative methods and that never the twain shall meet – perhaps even that one of these meta-methods is better than the other. We don't think that this is true. Each approach to research has its merits and uses. In fact we believe there is a case for the integration of qualitative and quantitative methods to be adopted as the routine starting point in social sciences research. For example, CORE (Clinical Outcomes in Routine Evaluation) is seen as a pluralistic research paradigm by its advocates, see p 302.

An aim we have in this book is to tell you about the basic building blocks of research. It is from these that you will be able to determine what sort of researcher you are and how to implement research strategies which have meaning for you. In this chapter, one of our objectives has been to make it clear that one of the first tasks of a researcher is to choose an appropriate approach to the question to be answered, that is, to choose the best tools for the job. In other words, it is for you to decide what specific research method(s) you wish to employ and you can do this in any combination that makes sense to you and which you can justify to others.

According to your particular sympathies and the nature of the job to be done, this may lead you in the direction of quantitative research and hypothesis testing using, for example, specific scales, tests or instruments. The data generated from this is then susceptible either to:
- certain statistical processes (see Chapters 2.2, 2.3, 2.4 & 2.5)
- listening to and recording the stories people have to tell you about their experiences, and ways of distilling these (see Chapters 2.6, 2.7 & 2.8)
- a mindful mixture of these two basic categories of approaches to research (quantitative and qualitative)

There are established ways of doing the latter, for example
- mixed methods designs (see pp 9 & 25)
- some innovative ways of incoporating pluralistic data into case studies such as Hermeneutic Single Case Efficacy Design (HSCED) developed by Robert Elliott, (see p 103 for a brief pointer).

Then there are ways of working with data in approaches normally thought of as qualitative but which include elements of counting or measuring, for example, some forms of content analysis (see pp 203-7) and Q-sort (see pp 226-8). Not only that but some methods of data collection are in hybrid form. For example, it is possible to construct a questionnaire in which both quantitative and qualitative information is collected (of course, these must then be processed differently).

So, you need not choose to work *only* with quantitative methods or only with qualitative methods. These can be combined in any number of ways and to varying degrees. If you think that a combined approach makes more sense or would be more useful then you can take one 'off the shelf' or invent your own. It is harder to do the latter, but all research methods were invented because the developer couldn't find a research method which would answer the question in hand in the way that made sense to the researcher.

asking questions

Throughout this book we are trying to relate the business of research to everyday examples that crop up in most peoples' lives, putting the subject in everyday language, and eliminating or explaining technical terms and jargon. The same is true for the chapter headings, as we hope will become obvious. We could have called Chapter 2.3 'Descriptive Statistics', but that may have put readers off. By the same token, we could have started the book with a chapter called 'Generating HYPOTHESES', but, again, that doesn't relate very closely to peoples' lives and besides, what is a hypothesis anyway? Perhaps it is better to think about research as a way of asking and answering questions (although it can also be about exploring something or changing something). This chapter is about how a 'research question' (the starting point for most researchers) can be framed in such a way as to create a reasonable chance that it may be answered.

As each of us goes around the world we try to understand the workings of our world and so we ask questions. 'Who are you?' 'How much is that?' 'Where did that come from?' 'What is the meaning of this?' 'How does this work?' 'Why did that happen?' and even 'How did I get here?' Clearly these questions vary in difficulty, and research describes a process by which we try to answer some of these questions.

When considering the best way of getting to an answer, or even how to frame a question, we find that in research, as in life itself, there is considerable disagreement over which way is best. Of course, this is because there is no 'best' way of doing research. How you pose and answer a research question depends entirely on what it is you want to find out, who or what may be able to give you something approaching an answer, the means and resources at your disposal, who you want to be able to understand what you find out and so on.

It may seem that in some areas of life, both the question and the method of seeking an answer are strikingly obvious. However, we would do well to challenge our ideas of the obvious because so much of what seems 'obvious' to us is based on cultural views which, to say the least, are local (not everyone in the world shares our culture) and temporary (how many 'civilisations' throughout history have come to grief through the complacent view that they

HYPOTHESIS A supposition made on the basis of limited evidence (from, for example, observation or experimentation) as a starting point for further investigation. Or, if you prefer, a proposal intended to explain certain facts or observations.

Note

A HYPOTHESIS that holds up after testing accrues a degree of certainty (or, more accurately, an increased probability that it is true) and becomes a THEORY.

THEORY A tentative insight into the natural world (including human behaviour); a concept that is not yet verified but if true would explain certain facts or phenomena.

Note

As you will see from our definitions, neither a hypothesis or a theory is proven to be 'true' but whereas (to put it crudely) the first is a guess ('I wonder if …'), the second is supported by evidence ('Given x and y it seems to me that …'). One of the best known theories is Darwin's ideas about the evolution of life. Lots of evidence but, as yet, nothing that proves it beyond doubt.

had the 'right' answer?). It has been obvious to the greatest thinkers of their age that the world is flat, that it is the centre of the universe around which the stars rotate, that black people are sub-human, that children need smacking, that standards in education are falling, that counselling works, etc. Good research avoids taking the 'obvious' as read and involves researchers in an honest assessment and declaration of the stance they take in their investigations. Especially in qualitative approaches to research which involve at least a degree of interpretation, it is important the researchers 'locate' themselves. That is, offer the reader relevant information about their outlook, experience and so on.

There have been many attempts to categorise the *ways of finding things out* in the world. Although philosophers have been thinking about them for thousands of years, we'll attempt the arrogant illusion of briefly summarising the situation as it is today. There are two broad methods by which human beings come to understand the world about them, *analysis* and *synthesis*. These share something with the notions of *Logos* and *Mythos* respectively.

Logos and *Mythos* are described on p 16, Chapter 1.1.

Analysis	Synthesis
Taking things or ideas apart, or separating things into their constituent parts to see how the parts fit and work together. In scientific terms this is called reductionism.	Putting things together in familiar or novel ways to see what patterns are made and to understand how they might fit and work together. This is called holism.
For example, trying to understand the workings of the human body by dissecting it into its constituent organs and systems and understanding their individual functions. This is the main method adopted by Western science.	*For example, trying to understand the workinmgs of the human body by looking at it as a coherent, indivisible unit connected to the universe and natural forces in the world through invisible energy channels. More of an Eastern tradition, it has gained in popularity in the West in recent years.*

Note from life
As a child, Pete learned how his bicycle worked by taking it apart and reassembling it, seeing how the parts fitted and moved together.

Since both of these words have common uses in our culture you would be forgiven for believing that analysis alone describes the one true process by which we come to understand the world around us. It certainly is *one* valid method to gain knowledge and we have many examples from our own experience of gaining understanding through analysis.

Some people argue that our technological culture perpetuates the myth that analysis is the only way to reach an understanding of anything. However, computer technology and theoretical physics (surely the heartland of analytical science) have recently come together through a new explanation of the universe, life and everything. This new explanation (an aspect of 'new physics' which is to do with, amongst other things, quantum theory) is called *chaos theory*. This is the very essence of synthesis. In this theory, order in the universe is achieved through chaos – the random combinations and interactions of very small events. When computers are instructed to mimic such chaos, the result is complex irregular patterns called *fractals* that can look like and, so it is argued, explain the origin of coastlines, snowflakes, coral reefs, leaves on trees, the pattern of small blood vessels in our lungs and so on.

We have known for some time, however, that reductionism falls down under some circumstances. When Pete studied psychology at university it was assumed by most psychologists that reductionism was the one true way to understand the workings of the human mind. The argument went something like this:

In order to understand, say 'psychotic mental illness', we should:

- first look at the individual mentally ill people
- then look at their individual psychotic behaviours
- then look at the components of that behaviour
- then look at the biological bases of that behaviour (hormones, nervous system and genetics)
- then look at the chemical bases of the biological systems, and finally
- when we can reduce the problem no further, we can eliminate psychosis by:
  - correcting chemical imbalances (drugs)
  - repairing a faulty nervous system (brain surgery) and, when we develop the right technology
  - adjusting genetic imperfections (gene therapy screening for, and terminating, deviant foetuses, or changing human characteristics through genetic engineering)

The prevailing dominant model in psychiatry is the medical model, and the first two 'solutions' have been tried over many years with contentious results which, depending upon who you read, vary from the cautiously promising to the failing disastrously. Gene therapy is still at an experimental stage. We can already test the unborn child for many conditions from Down's syndrome to cystic fibrosis. How long will it be before we can choose between not only boy or girl, but intelligent or super-intelligent, neurotic or extrovert, 'psychotic' or … ?

A 'cure' for 'psychosis' still eludes us and we are turning to

IF YOU WANT TO KNOW MORE ABOUT
new physics and chaos theory

the following books might be a good starting point:

Al-Khalili, J (2004) *Quantum: A guide for the perplexed.* London: Weidenfeld & Nicolson.

Gleick, J (1989) *Chaos: Making a new science.* London: Vintage.

Rogers, CR (1951) *Client-Centred Therapy*. London: Constable.

ANALYSIS Taking things or ideas apart, or separating things into their constituent parts to see how the parts fit and work together. In scientific terms this is called reductionism (see p 22).

SYNTHESIS Putting things together in familiar or novel ways to see what patterns are made and to understand how they might fit and work together. This is called holism (see p 22).

QUANTITATIVE relating to quantities. In research it involves measuring things and 'describing' them with numbers. For example, 'on a scale of 1–10, indicate how helpful this definition is where 1 = Very unhelpful , and 10 = Very helpful'.

synthesis in the form of holism to help our understanding of 'psychotic' behaviour. Not so long ago, psychologists and psychiatrists were keen on the idea of 'dualism': that mind and body were split, i.e. two separate entities. Much of the current medical model of mental illness has this assumption at its heart. Now the same doctors are busy trying to put the body and mind back together again, into one integrated whole, as evidence emerges to show us that people, as Carl Rogers wrote in 1951, '... react as an organised whole ...' (p. 487).

A psychologist trying to argue against using the results of brain surgery as a method of understanding brain function, wrote that we would not try to understand the workings of a television and its constituent parts by taking a working television, arbitrarily removing a component and observing the results. If we removed a component, then switched the television on only to see multicoloured wavy lines on the screen and hear a loud buzzing noise, we might simplistically and erroneously conclude that the purpose of the component we had removed was to prevent coloured wavy lines and buzzing sounds. For years, the main method of understanding brain function was this very technique of removing a small part of a brain and observing the results. To this day, our understanding of most of the anatomy of the human brain is based on these conclusions. (It must be said, though, that on a very crude level, the majority of the early observations are holding up quite well to modern day scrutiny using less invasive methods.)

If we are to avoid making grand mistakes in our thinking, we need to have a broad view of the 'possible' in research. Both ANALYSIS and SYNTHESIS can be valid methods of research. Although we *can* seek answers to our questions through reductionism and holism, the first part of this book is going to concentrate on one set of methods based on the gathering of QUANTITATIVE data. This in itself is a somewhat contentious issue because measuring things is associated with a particular philosophical view of the world namely:

Positivism   based on the idea that there is a fixed observable world which we all experience in a similar way. Knowledge is limited to observed facts and that which can be deduced from those observed facts. Research based in the positivist paradigm is usually *quantitative* – that is, to do with measurement and, in the social sciences, often involves statistical manipulation of data. Crucial to positivistic research are the concepts of *validity* and *reliability* (see Chapter 2.2). In simple terms, validity refers to the ability of the research procedure to perform the task claimed for it – for example, that a test actually measures what it purports to measure – while reliability refers to the capacity of the procedure to produce similar results when implemented by different people, at different times or in different situations. In health and social care, the purpose of such research is often to allow the prediction of outcome – that is, to establish chains of cause and effect: 'if this patient is treated in this way then this will happen'. Positivistic research can also be 'experimental' – that is, to do with the manipulation of variables, an underlying question being 'what happens if …?' However, in the context of health and social care, experimental research raises ethical problems because it may involve doing something to individuals that may be to their detriment, or withholding something of potential benefit.

This view is not held by everyone. In particular it is challenged by the ideas of:

Phenomenology that our knowledge is based on our experience, on attending to phenomena as they are directly and subjectively experienced. This viewpoint is most often associated with qualitative methods (see Chapters 2.6, 2.7 & 2.8).

However, we must point out that the use of measurement and numbers does not preclude the use of individual experience. There are research methods that combine elements of measurement with the interpretation of stories people have to tell about their experience. The emphasis of these new approaches is to keep the process of human experience at the centre of the inquiry whilst at the same time understanding the effects of any measuring methods on that central experience.

Approaches to answering questions that use measurement but also value and make use of accounts of human experience are attempts to pull together two major traditions. In the 1980s, a number of social science researchers began to search for a 'human' science. While they appreciated what positivistic, quantitative research could tell them, they were of the view that there were questions it could neither frame nor answer. Mostly, these questions were to do with the nature of human experience. For example, positivistic research isn't very good for investigating dreams, fantasy, creative thinking and any number of emotional experiences.

Often, these researchers also had ethical concerns about the nature of research, in particular they sought to develop methodologies in which the people the research was about would be involved as decision-makers rather than as passive subjects. In other words, one

IF YOU WANT TO KNOW MORE ABOUT
phenomenology

Carol Becker has written an introductory text, Ernesto Spinelli introduces phenomenological psychology and Clark Moustakas describes phenomenological research methods. Online resources include the Stanford Encyclopedia of Philosophy <www.plato.stanford.edu/entries/phenomenology/> and the Center for Advanced Research in Phenomenology <www.phenomenologycenter.org/phenom.htm> both retrieved 07/01/2010.

Becker, CS (1992) *Living & Relating: An introduction to phenomenology.* Newbury Park, CA: Sage.

Spinelli, E (1989) *The Interpreted World: An introduction to phenomenological psychology.* London: Sage.

Moustakas, C (1994) *Phenomenological Research Methods.* Thousand Oaks, CA: Sage.

Note
There is an approach called 'mixed methods design' which incorporates the advantages of both approaches into one study (see also Chapter 1.2, p 9). These advantages are:

Triangulation if they confirm each other, the results from the use of different approaches increase the validity of findings.

Complementarity clarifies and illustrates results from one method with the use of another method.

Development as the research progresses, the findings from one method help determine the use of other methods or steps in the research.

Initiation stimulates new research questions or challenges results obtained through one method.

Expansion provides richness and detail to the study exploring specific features of each method.

After **Green, JC, Caracelli, VJ & Graham, WF (1989)** Towards a conceptual framework for mixed methods design. *Educational Evaluation and Policy Analysis 11*(3), 5-18.

Also see **Cooper, M & McLeod, J (2007)** A pluralistic framework for counselling and psychotherapy: Implications for research. *Counselling and Psychotherapy Research 7*(3), 135-43.

Note

Carl Rogers, in the 1960s, began to experience a tension between two points of view: the desire to understand how people experience themselves and the world subjectively and an interest in the behaviour of people from the standpoint of a 'neutral' observer (see Kirschenbaum, 2007: 315-17). It was another 20 years before Rogers (1985) wrote of methods he did think suitable to explore human experience.

Kirschenbaum, H (2007) *The Life and Works of Carl Rogers.* Ross-on-Wye: PCCS Books.

Rogers, CR (1985) Toward a more human science of the person. *Journal of Humanistic Psychology 25*(4), 7-24.

Note from life

A potential problem with measurement is that, unless it is clearly specified, the scale used may not be the one assumed to be used! For example, in 1999 NASA lost a $125 million Mars orbiter because a Lockheed Martin engineering team used English units of measurement while the agency's team used the more conventional metric system for a key spacecraft operation.

Note

The ground-breaking book about new paradigm research appears to be currently out of print and unfortunately difficult to obtain:

Reason, P & Rowan, J (1981) *Human Inquiry: A sourcebook of new paradigm research.* Chichester: Wiley.

thrust was to develop research *with* people rather than *on* people. These approaches were collectively known as 'New Paradigm' methods. These new methodologies offer the following criticisms of traditional approaches:

- social science research that follows a traditional method tends to be rationalistic, i.e. it *assumes* that human experiences, thoughts and feelings follow, and are the result of rational, logical, decision-making processes. This turns out to be a dangerous assumption to make and the results of applying a rational methodology to irrational experience or behaviour are either:
  - that the results do not offer useful or actionable explanations of human behaviour, or
  - that the method imposes rationality upon the irrational human processes and thus *masks* their true nature. (This has serious implications for any view of human experience or behaviour based on rational decision making)
- whenever you measure something, the scale itself imposes a meaning upon the measurement. A researcher, then, will only ever find what she or he is seeking because the measurements used limit and define the frame of reference of the people being studied
- since the researcher has selected and defined the variables to be measured (as well as the measurement methods), the results will do nothing more than reproduce the researcher's frame of reference

The conclusions of these criticisms, then, are that traditional methods:
- fundamentally mask the true nature of human experience
- find what the researcher expects to find
- yield explanations that will not work as predictors of human behaviour in the real world

Does this sound familiar? Theories about how people change have, in general, failed over the years to offer practical explanations for human behaviour in everyday situations. Recently, social scientists working in the area of health education have been disappointed to discover that traditional theories of attitude formation and change fail to predict or explain people's attitudes and behaviour surrounding safe sex, condom use and the risk of contracting HIV.

The new paradigm research now under way suggests that traditional methods asked the wrong questions in the wrong way and came up with an over-simplistic, rational view of why people *know* one thing, *believe* another thing and *do* yet another. The good news for us all is that we (i.e. human beings) are much more complicated than some theorists would have us believe. So, an alternative way of thinking about research becomes important and relevant.

Such a new way may:

- tend to do away with the fear of subjective speculation
- place a stress on disciplined personal commitment rather than methodology
- do away with many of the 'oughts' in selecting HYPOTHESES in that there would be a greater openness to subjective experience
- allow PHENOMENOLOGICALLY based hypotheses as well as chemically based, genetically based or behaviourally based hypotheses
- do away with the tendency to research only what is measurable
- avoid placing method at its core
- discover meaning rather than statistical significance
- emphasise the dedication and humanity of the researcher
- most importantly, it would stress the importance and centrality of the subjects of investigations as subjective, experiencing human beings

In new paradigm research:
- there is no illusion that there is one objective truth to be discovered, no certain knowledge
- there is an acceptance that no one method or methodology is supreme. Rather than a 'best' tool for research, there are many tools and the choice of which to employ depends on the nature of the question and the form in which the answer is desired
- there is a valuing of 'indwelling', intuition and imagination
- the notion of 'subjects' of research is replaced by the concept of 'co-researchers' or participants

Whilst the emergence of these new methods is vitally important, the quantitative approaches are still the most frequently used in contemporary research and the skills associated with data collection and presentation are very useful in a wide range of activities from planning and evaluating systems to writing annual reports. What we write about quantitative methods is based on the notion that whatever method is chosen, it will be worthless without accurate, valid data. We will cover this in the chapters that follow. Because it is the most common POSITIVISTIC, quantitative approach, in particular we are going to concentrate on a way of doing research that involves suggesting an explanation for something observed or guessed at and then finding ways to see if the explanation is 'true'. This is usually thought of as a 'hypothesis-testing' approach and it is formally called the HYPOTHETICO-DEDUCTIVE METHOD.

We have used the general example of *asking questions* about the world up to now. However, in quantitative research, a problem is never 'asked' as a question, but stated as a hypothesis. A hypothesis is simply a statement of belief about some aspect of the world that is, as yet, unknown. It involves making a prediction that something will happen, if tested.

HYPOTHESIS A supposition made on the basis of limited evidence (from, for example, observation or experimentation) as a starting point for further investigation. Or, if you prefer, a proposal intended to explain certain facts or observations.

PHENOMENOLOGY Definition on p 25.

Note
We will look at statistical significance in Chapter 2.5, pp 92-3 & 98.

Note
These ideas draw on Carl Rogers' notion of 'authentic science' as well as the 'new paradigm' of humanistic research. See Rogers (1985) and Hutterer (1990).

Rogers, CR (1985) Toward a more human science of the person. *Journal of Humanistic Psychology* 25(4), 7-24.

Hutterer, R (1990) Authentic science: some implications of Carl Rogers's reflections on science. *Person-Centered Review* 5(1), 57-76.

POSITIVISTIC/POSITIVISM A doctrine asserting that sense perceptions are the only admissible basis of human knowledge and precise thought. In research, that the validity of knowledge can only be assured by experimental science.

HYPOTHETICO-DEDUCTIVE METHOD A scientific method whereby we formulate a hypothesis that predicts what is going to happen in a given situation. We then set about testing the hypothesis to see if its prediction is true.

…/ continued overleaf

continued ...

Actually, as a safeguard against the tendency for researchers to 'prove' what they set out to find, good hypothesis-testing research involves trying to prove the hypothesis false. This is because it takes only one instance of a hypothesis failing to disprove it but to establish a hypothesis as universally true requires the examination of every possible case in which it applies.

The classic example is that, from the perspective of Europeans, the hypothesis that all swans are white seemed true until the voyages of Tasman and Cook. The hypothesis survived as North America was explored but once the description of Australian swans was conveyed to Europe it fell because although all five species of swan in the northern hemisphere are white, those of Australia are black.

Questions and hypotheses

In life we ask questions, e.g. 'What is the moon made of?' In research we state hypotheses, e.g. 'The moon is made of green cheese.'

This hypothesis is a statement about something and involves the implicit prediction that if we visit the moon, we will find that it is made of green cheese. There are several reasons why we state hypotheses in research and, although there are advantages and disadvantages, the big advantage is that they simplify the issue to a manageable size.

1 on a simple level, a hypothesis narrows down the possibilities which we have to investigate – when we try to answer the question there are literally millions of possibilities, whereas all we can do with a hypothesis is prove it or disprove it

2 it is possible to verify the likelihood of our prediction being responsible for our results using statistical procedures (because these involve an estimate of probability). We can only do this if we state the problem in the form of a hypothesis. It won't work if we ask a question. (More of this in Chapter 2.5.)

3 the problem with hypotheses is that unless we hit upon the right one, we have to generate hypothesis after hypothesis, i.e. when we send a cheese taster to the moon to test our first hypothesis, she returns to say that the moon is definitely not cheese, it tastes a bit like caviar but she's not sure. Our second hypothesis might then be that the moon is made of caviar. So up goes the fish roe expert who returns to tell us that it's not like any fish roe he's ever tasted and we generate yet another hypothesis

Finding out what the moon really is made of could take a long time if we follow this method, and we find that in the realm of practitioner research, direct observation of events is almost impossible. In the social sciences in general we have evolved methods to overcome the indirect nature of the observations we can make.

To continue with the example of the moon hypothesis, it's rather like not having the technology to send a human to the moon, but being able to send a mouse and watching it through a telescope.

So to find out if the moon is made of green cheese we find a mouse that we know likes green cheese and send it to the moon. We watch it through our telescope to see if it is tempted to take a nibble. To our delight we see the mouse clearly eating the moon's surface. We take photographs and publish our results to the astonishment of the scientific community and give much-acclaimed lectures on the subject until some maverick scientist suggests that we hadn't checked that our mouse would only eat green cheese and nothing else. Our rival has a hypothesis that the moon is made not of green cheese at all but marzipan. And so the research continues.

In this brief example lie all the problems and challenges of quantitative research in the social sciences. These will unfold as you read the book and we deal with examples closer to your everyday work than whether the moon is made out of green cheese.

The first chapters of this book will take you through understanding measurement, presenting numbers for clarity and ease of understanding, choosing the right method to test your hypothesis and, finally, writing up or reporting your results in an appropriate format. We hope you find the contents and style stimulating, informative and fun.

'Good' questions and 'bad' questions

All research and data collection have a social and political context. The dominant culture and government in power determine what gets funded and what doesn't. This means that at any one time there are 'Good' questions and 'Bad' questions. As practitioners we have a duty to collect data in ways that:

- do not contravene our professional codes of ethics
- are within the limits of principled ethical research as determined by fellow researchers (more of this in Chapter 3.2 'Researching Ethically')
- add to human understanding in a developing, empowering way rather than a limiting, disenfranchising way

Over the years, much of social science research has failed to meet up to similar criteria. Instead of asking the general question …
   How can we construct the world so that each of us can reach our full potential?

… social scientists have succumbed to cultural or political pressure and asked questions like:
   Why are we different?
   Who is the best?
   How can we separate the best from the worst?

If you are white, middle class, educated, able-bodied, heterosexual and male, you will have been well served by social science research questions of the latter type. The hidden part of this type of question is usually 'In order to protect the interests of the best'. For *best* read white, middle class, etc. Before collecting data, think hard why you're doing it and what the question *really* is that you're trying to answer. In any event, be sure to read Chapter 3.2 'Researching Ethically' before proceeding with your investigation.

The great car driving and cooking cover-up – Pete's story

The first time I tried to learn about statistics and research methods, I failed miserably. I just couldn't understand what it was all about. It seemed incredibly complicated and anyway, I had convinced myself that I was no good at maths. Does this sound familiar?

I understand statistics and research methods now, but I have never forgotten that panicky, hollow feeling of complete blankness when staring at pages of incomprehensible jargon especially when the author was explaining it in what s/he thought were 'simple terms'. I felt even worse when I realised that the explanation could not get any more simple!

My real problem was that I had to pass the statistics part of my psychology degree and I needed to be able to apply statistical tests to the practical work I had been doing. What was I to do? I took comfort from what I call 'the great car driving and cooking cover-up'. I discovered that not only could I apply the statistical tests more-or-less correctly without having the foggiest idea what they were all about, but also that no one could tell that I didn't really understand. This way of working was known and used by thousands upon thousands of social science graduates who, like me, understood little yet appeared to understand it all. So what is this great cover-up?

The vast majority of car drivers do not know how cars work. Yet they are excellent drivers and get the vehicle safely from A to B without any problem whatsoever. Ask the average driver why the car goes faster when they press their foot on the accelerator and they will simply not know. They may say something about more petrol getting to the engine, but that's about it. This was roughly my state of knowledge about research methods and statistics.

I learned how to select appropriate methods by getting hold of the equivalent of a good cookbook and simply following the recipes. I didn't know why I needed baking powder in my sponge cakes, but I knew that if I followed the recipe no one would know and they would say 'What a brilliant cook!' (This level of non-understanding is fine as long as nothing goes wrong. If the car breaks down I phone the service station, if my soufflé falls flat, I phone my mum.)

It is quite possible to adopt the same approach to research methods and data collection if it all seems double Dutch. Although statistical tests are beyond the scope of this book, if you extend your research horizons you may find that you need to use one, so you will be relieved to learn that there are several 'cookbook' style texts and computer applications listing statistical procedures, when to use them and providing simple methods for data entry*. If this book itself proves too difficult, try to adopt a 'cookbook' approach and a 'recipe-following' mentality. You may wish to come back to the book after a while and find that it makes more sense second time round. Although we have written this book rather like a story – there's a logic to the order (a plot if you like) – remember that you don't have to read the chapters in order. Whichever way you choose, we would really like you to have fun!

* Two texts that have helped thousands of social scientists for years are:

Clegg, F (1983) *Simple Statistics: A course book for the social sciences.* Cambridge: Cambridge University Press.

Rowntree, D (2000) *Statistics without Tears: An introduction for non-mathematicians.* London: Penguin.

On p. 55 we briefly explain how computers are used for processing data and how we demonstrate the rudiments of this using Microsoft Excel in this book.

In order to get to know a bit more about quantitative research you are going to have to know a bit more about numbers and how they can be used. A lot of this isn't difficult really. Most commonplace day-to-day activities depend upon quantification – the assignment of numbers to objects or events to describe their properties. Lots of everyday questions ask for precise or approximate measures. How old are you? How many of those to do you get to the kilo? How much does that cost? How far is it from here to there? Attempting to express your requirements without numbers would be a slow, cumbersome and rather vague process. We'll show you what we mean.

Suppose you are driving to work when you notice that you need to fill your car with petrol. You put ten gallons in the tank and pay the cashier. As you put the change in your pocket, you glance at your watch and realise that if you wish to speak to your colleagues before you see your first client, you'd better hurry up. How many times have you used numbers in this example? Imagine, if you can, doing all of those things without reference to numbers. Difficult if not impossible!

In fact, not only would you have used numbers, you also would have performed many of the functions and used many of the skills referred to in this book:

- measuring things
- describing things using numbers
- making predictions using numbers

We are so used to describing the natural world in terms of numbers that it may come as a bit of a shock to some readers to discover that the natural world sometimes doesn't fit into a number system quite as easily as we would like. The degree to which the natural world and numbers *actually do* fit together determines the types of calculation we can do with those numbers.

For example, most of us would like to think that adding 100 to 100 gives us 200. However in certain domains of the natural world this is not true – one such domain is temperature. If we take a pan of boiling water ($100°C$) and add it to another pan of boiling water ($100°C$) the result is not a pan of water at $200°C$, but a pan of water still at $100°C$. Temperature doesn't add up like money, for example.

There are special rules to govern the way numbers relate to temperature. Of course, we all know this. All of us that have ever boiled an egg or made a cup of tea, that is. We have learned the common-sense rules of numbering things in the natural world.

Scales of measurement

SCALE A graduated range of values forming a standard system for measuring or grading something.

So, as we mentioned above, the degree to which things don't add up helps define the type of calculations we can do – clearly adding temperatures together doesn't work in the same way as, for example, adding up the money in your pocket. In the late 1940s a statistician called Stevens came up with four ways in which we can match numbers to events in the world. He called these four ways *scales of measurement* and we need to understand them before we can start measuring things in the world.

However, some of these scales may not seem to have much to do with measurement if you think that measuring something is always going to be like measuring the weight of a parcel with scales or the length of a desk with a tape measure. Remember that you are automatically making assumptions about what measuring is and how it works because you have learned the common-sense rules about measuring things. One of the really interesting things about research and data collection in the social sciences is that our assumptions about what is common sense get challenged almost every day. So suspend your assumptions and enter into the world of numbers with fresh eyes.

Most of the things practitioners are interested in measuring are to do with people – what people do, think and feel. This is the most difficult, frustrating, interesting and fun area of numbers that we've ever come across. However there is some information that can help us avoid making some very simple mistakes.

1. Nominal scale of measurement
Definition
This is when we use numbers to name objects and events in the world. Instead of using a word to identify an object or event we use a number. The number itself has no meaning, it just tells you that the item is different from other items. Some examples are:

Everyday examples
1 Catalogue shopping – the Acme Safety Fryer has the number 421/2894 in the current Acme Electrics Catalogue. The item before it in the catalogue (the AutoFry Master Fryer) has the number 421/1541 and the item after it (the Supertricity Safety Elite Fryer) has the number 421/2375. The numbers aren't even consecutive. They tell you nothing except that the items are different and, most

important of all, they allow the Acme computer to identify the product you are ordering.

2 National Insurance numbers – more everyday, nominal measurements. We like to think of ourselves as named, free individuals but, at least to the state, we are also a number. Our National Insurance numbers are the 'name' by which we are known to the Department of Work and Pensions computer. The National Health Service knows each of us by yet another number. Neither of these means anything other than to indicate who we are.

3 Motor Vehicle Licence numbers – the registration number of your car is a 'name' that contains several pieces of information, including the year and region in which it was first registered.

Research examples

1 In a recent piece of research the numbers of clients choosing each of four helping professionals were compared. The four practitioners were simply identified by a single number: 1, 2, 3 and 4.

2 Dividing clients up according to their gender (male and female) is nominal scaling.

3 Let's say we want to categorise the types of problem that clients present during their first interview. We might name the categories 'psychosexual', 'abuse', 'bereavement', etc. and number the categories 1, 2, 3, and so on:
Category 1: Psychosexual problems
Category 2: Abuse
Category 3: Bereavement

What does it enable us to do?

The nominal scale describes categorising or classifying things as the most basic form of measurement. There is no arithmetical basis for putting such categorised items into any sensible order, so all that we can do is count how many there are. The Acme Electrics computer can count how many 421/2894s were sold today, yesterday, last week, etc. We can count how many clients came to us with housing problems, debt problems, etc. What we can't do is to add them up in any sensible way (421/2894 + 421/1541 or category 1 + category 3) or multiply them together to get a meaningful answer, because we're using the numbers as names.

In recent years the advent of computers has meant that we have become more familiar with nominal scaling since computers don't understand names for categories half as well as they understand numbers. It's also easier to obtain long lists of numbers than it is to compile long lists of names.

2. Ordinal scale of measurement
Definition
This is when we not only use numbers to identify objects or events, we also put them in an order. (*Ord*inal – *Ord*er). The number now has some meaning – the second number comes after the first and before the third. It is sometimes known as putting things in rank order, or ranking, and is a true measurement method. Some examples are:

Everyday examples
1 Places in a competition – first-, second- and third-placed songs in the Eurovision Song Contest can be placed in order, or *ranked*.

2 Hotels and restaurants – are graded in certain guides by the number of stars or crowns they are allocated: five stars for the best down to one or no stars for the worst.

3 Arranging a class of school children in order of height is ordinal scaling (ranking the children by height). We can go from the tallest to the shortest or the shortest to the tallest, it doesn't matter, it's still ordinal scaling.

Research examples
1 We might want to know how highly our clients value our service and ask them to rank 'counsellor', 'doctor', 'solicitor', 'social worker', 'estate agent', in order of importance to them.

2 An occupational therapy service might rank their OTs in order of popularity. (How would you do this?)

What does it enable us to do?
Ranking is the most basic way of comparing things. Before we can put things in order we have to compare them in some way – height, price, effectiveness, value, etc. Some of these qualities are subjective (the two research examples above, for instance) and you will find that ordinal scaling is quite a handy and very popular way of trying to measure people's thoughts and feelings. Like nominal scaling it's difficult to do arithmetic on ranks since there's no way of knowing what the gap is between the ranks. For example, how much better is the song that came first in the Eurovision Song Contest than the song that came second? Similarly, if you see a list of children's names in order of height, you can't tell from that list whether the tallest was one foot or one inch taller that the second

tallest and so on down the list.

It's interesting to note that most people try to collect the most information they can in any given situation – particularly where ranks are concerned. If someone learns that Lewis Hamilton won the British Grand Prix, or that Aston Villa beat Manchester United, they often want to know the margin of victory. Who won is only half the story; we also want to know by how much. It's as though we *know* the shortcomings of ranking alone.

3. Interval scale of measurement
Definition
In interval scaling we not only rank the items, we give them numbers that indicate the gaps or *intervals* between the ranks. On an interval scale the units of measurement are equal. Interval scaling is getting to look more like our common-sense methods of numbering, but it still has a trick or two up its sleeve.

Everyday examples
1 Testing in schools, e.g. GCSE Mathematics – a score on a test of ability is an example of interval scaling. We know the gap between each unit is equal – the difference between 50 and 55 is the same as the difference between 90 and 95.

2 Temperature in degrees Fahrenheit or Celsius – our old friend temperature is back, still not adding up but definitely on an interval scale when measured in Fahrenheit or Celsius.

Research examples
1 There are many PSYCHOMETRIC TESTS around which purport to measure various human attributes. Some readers may be familiar with some which measure anxiety for example. When you obtain a score on such a test, say from 0 to 100, the intervals between each score are supposed to be equal.

2 Rating scales – these are sometimes used in practitioner research to rate the performance of the practitioner from bad (ineffective) to good (effective). They use various ranges: for example, some are five-point scales, some are nine-point scales (other ranges are possible) with the mid-point being 'minimally effective', e.g.:

PSYCHOMETRIC TEST Any standardised procedure for measuring aspects, qualities or attributes of mental functioning including, eg, sensitivity, memory, 'intelligence', aptitude or personality.

Activity
Type the term 'psychometric test' into an online search engine. You will find links to tests that purport to 'measure' your personality, your career prospects and much more. You could try one or two of the free ones.
• *What do you think of these tests?*
• *How can you tell if they do what they say they do?*

Note
Scales of this type are called LIKERT SCALES.

LIKERT SCALE A psychometric scale commonly used in questionnaires. The most widely used scale in survey research. When responding to a Likert question respondents specify their level of agreement to a statement. The scale is named after its inventor, Rensis Likert. We look at Likert scales on p 136 in Chapter 2.7.

1	2	3	4	5
poor ———————————		minimally effective	———————————	excellent

It is generally *assumed* (how can we be sure that the intervals are *equal*?) that such scales are examples of *interval scaling*.

What does it enable us to do?
We can do some simple arithmetic on this level of scaling – addition, subtraction, multiplication, division, arithmetic mean (taking an average), square roots, etc. Interval scales can be rather seductive, though, and it's not what we can do with them but what we can't do with them that we need to understand. There are two problems:

- some scaling that looks like interval scaling isn't really. A good example of this is IQ (Intelligence Quotient). Many people think that IQ is an interval scale, but it is really difficult to prove that the gaps between the units are equal. (We could also have a good debate about whether the rating scale above is really interval scaling – what do you think?) Can we say that the difference between IQs of 120 and 125 is the same as the difference between 50 and 55? Are five IQ points always the same wherever they are? In contrast, an increase of five degrees Celsius *is* the same wherever it is on the Celsius scale

- it's OK to do the basic arithmetic on an interval scale as long as you don't want to get a ratio between two measures on it. A ratio just doesn't work on an interval scale because the scale doesn't have a *meaningful zero point*. If you score 0 in a geography test it doesn't mean that you have no geographical knowledge. Also, if you record a temperature of 0 degrees Celsius, it doesn't mean that there is no temperature. This is evidenced by the fact that when you've reached 0 on the Celsius scale you're only at 32 on the Fahrenheit scale. So what about ratios? You can't say that I know twice as much about geography as you if I got 60 in a test and you got only 30. Nor is it true to say that it's twice as hot at 30 degrees centigrade as at 15 degrees centigrade – your body should tell you that

4. Ratio scale of measurement
Definition
Now we not only have a rank with equal intervals, but also a meaningful or absolute zero – one where zero means zero quantity of the thing being measured. So a ratio scale is interval scaling with an absolute zero point.

Everyday examples
1 There are so many: length, weight, time, etc. All have equal intervals and a meaningful zero. We can 'measure' no length, no weight and no time – and these measurements indicate zero quantities of these things.

2 Temperature, again! Yes, it's here too, as a ratio scale when measured in degrees Kelvin. The Kelvin scale has an absolute zero at which there is no temperature and *everything* freezes. It's a theoretical temperature that has never been achieved in practice (-273° Celsius if you're interested). This example illustrates another important point. That is that the absolute zero on a ratio scale doesn't have to be practically achievable – just theoretically possible.

Research examples

1 Let's say we want to work out the average number of sessions each client has had. We could compare self-referred clients and clients referred by another agency:

> Self-referred clients average   8.4 sessions
> Other agency-referred clients average   4.2 sessions

We can now say that the self-referred clients have, on average, twice as many counselling sessions as the other agency-referred clients. Only with ratio scaling can we do this.

Note
Later in the book, we will be looking in some detail at the term 'average' and explaining the three types of average: 'mean', 'median' and 'mode'. See Chapter 2.3, pp 52-64.

2 We could compare two types of helping activity with ratio scaling by looking at the average length of sessions conducted by psychiatrists and the average length of sessions conducted by counsellors:

	Psychiatrists	Counsellors
Average session length (minutes)	18.1	54.3

This time we can say that, on average, counsellors' sessions last three times as long as sessions with psychiatrists.

What does it enable us to do?

That question has already been answered in the two examples above. All arithmetical calculations can be performed on a ratio scale and that allows us to apply the most powerful statistical analyses to our measurements (more of this later). We can do all the basic arithmetic that we could do on an interval scale and now make meaningful ratio comparisons between measurements and averages. Most people want to be able to make these powerful statements about their measurements, but you must make sure you have ratio data first. Many people will want to know what will happen if they don't get it right.

What if I want to compare measurements in a ratio but my measurements aren't on a ratio scale?

The short answer is you shouldn't do it. In the real world of research, journal articles are read by folk just waiting for the authors to make mistakes in their assumptions about the measurements. The result of getting this wrong is that your conclusions will be erroneous and useless. In extreme cases, the maths you try will just look silly – you can't take the average of male and female. However, mistakes aren't always that obvious and there are several genuinely grey areas where people argue about the nature of measurements.

What if I don't know if my measurements are ordinal or interval?

This happens more often than you might think, and not only to beginners! A good example of this is the argument over whether IQ, or the rating scales mentioned above, are interval or ordinal scaling. In the end, researchers may well say that they are *assuming* that the rating scale they are using is interval, even though they can't prove it, just so they can use a more powerful piece of arithmetic on it. This won't stop other researchers arguing with them and, ultimately, even though all sorts of evidence and argument is brought to bear, there will probably still be disagreement. Then you, the reader, will have to decide for yourself. Do the researchers' assumptions make their arithmetic, and thus their conclusions, silly or not? This is where it gets to be fun!

IQ also suffers from not having a meaningful zero point, thus not being ratio scaling. If someone scores zero in an IQ test it doesn't mean that they have zero intelligence. Also, ratios don't work with IQ either: we wouldn't say that a person with an IQ of 150 is twice as intelligent as a person with an IQ of 75, or the same as three people with an IQ of 50 each! (Will a woman with an IQ of 150 solve the problem quicker than three women with IQs of 50?)

On the subject of IQ, it will not surprise you to learn that the publishers of Intelligence Tests claim that they are interval data, and the opponents of IQ testing claim that they aren't, and thus the conclusions frequently drawn by users of such tests are INVALID. What do you think?

VALIDITY is a quality of data which roughly says that the data is what is claims to be. We will be looking in detail at the types of VALIDITY on pp 40-2 later in this chapter.

Continuous and discrete measurements

In addition to working out how well our measurements match a number system, we need to work out how to collect them. This is where the notion of continuous and discrete measurements comes in. It's quite simple really: either we are forced to measure in whole units (discrete) or we can use fractions or partial units (continuous).

Definitions

Continuous can be broken down into partial or fractional units. Continuous measurements can be seen as points on a line. The accuracy of the measurement doesn't depend on the size of the units.

Discrete can only be expressed in whole units or categories. The accuracy of the measure is dependent upon the size of the unit since we have to stick within the categories available or round up or down to the nearest whole unit. The activity here is counting.

Everyday examples

Continuous: feet and inches, pounds and ounces, minutes and seconds. These things can be *measured*.

Discrete: categories, e.g. male and female, or putting people into age bands, 0–9 years, 1–19 years, 20–29 years, etc. Here, we are *counting* the number of people in each category.

Research examples

Continuous: measuring the time each telephone counselling session takes.

Discrete: counting the number of service users in each of four age bands:

What does this enable us to do?

	under 20	21–40	41–60	60+
Number of patients in 2006	10	29	14	6

This is just another way of understanding the properties of the numbers we are collecting. Try to get used to figuring out what you can and can't do with the numbers you collect and what limits your measurements impose upon the calculations and conclusions you can draw. Most people treat all measurements as continuous. Take the famous 'average' family size of 2.4 children. It's clearly impossible to have 0.4 of a child, so we must be careful and clear when expressing ideas in numbers, otherwise we may find that our readers get the wrong idea.

When using discrete measurements, the kind of data we end up with is called *frequency data*, or the number of times a certain thing happens. So, in the example above, we are counting the number of times or the frequency with which people aged 60+ were clients of our service in 2006.

Our measurements need another two qualities before they are worth the paper they're written on: *reliability* and *validity*. We'll look at these qualities one at a time.

Validity

Definition
A measure is said to be valid when it measures what it claims or intends to measure.

Examples
It's a bit like the law requiring goods to be 'fit for their purpose'. A TV has to receive broadcast signals, a kettle has to hold and heat up water, an intelligence test has to measure intelligence and a 'helping professions' aptitude scale has to measure a person's aptitude for working in health and social care. If they don't do what they claim to do, they are not valid measures. A kettle is not a kettle if you can't boil water in it and a test isn't a helping professions aptitude scale if it doesn't measure aptitude for being a helping professional. Validity is measured on a scale from 0 to 1.

Note
Both validity and reliability are calculated using correlation. Correlation (co-relation) is the degree to which two things vary together in some sort of synchrony. It is a measure of the level of association between two variables. We look at this later in this chapter (p 44) and again in Chapter 2.5, pp 105-10. Correlation coefficients have values between 0 and 1.

0	LOW VALIDITY		HIGH VALIDITY	1
No validity	Doesn't measure what it claims Isn't fit for its purpose		Does measure what it claims Is fit for its purpose	**Complete validity**

There are four main *types* of validity.

1. Surface or face validity
Definition
Where the validity of the measure is judged simply on whether it seems to be or looks appropriate. This is a very rough-and-ready test of validity.

Examples
As consumers, we all know that you can't judge the fitness for purpose of a household appliance just by looking at it. The same applies to measurements in social science research. Face validity is useful, however, for eliminating things that are real no-hopers from the start. A kettle with no spout, for example, or a helping professions aptitude scale that asks what the person had for breakfast, the colour of her eyes or his inside leg measurement, may be judged by some as having low face validity.

2. Concurrent validity
Definition
Where we compare our measure with another measure of the same thing taken at the same time.

Examples
We might check to see if the potatoes are cooked by measuring the time they have been boiling, but we could get a concurrent measure of validity by sticking a fork into them as well. Let's say we want to measure staff attitudes to the counselling service in a Further Education College, so we give a questionnaire to all staff and, to estimate the validity of the measure (is it really tapping into staff attitudes?), we might compare the results with the number of referrals from staff. Staff may say that they support the counselling service, but their behaviour as referrers may not support this. Our questionnaire would then have low validity.

3. Predictive validity
Definition
Here, we are assessing validity by trying to relate our measure to some future event, to see if it can predict a certain outcome that we would normally associate with high validity. Sometimes, we may be using a measure specifically to act as a predictor – like forecasting the weather by looking at seaweed and pine cones.

Examples
Staying with the weather example, you may know that there are some 'old-fashioned' methods of forecasting the weather using natural objects. Some people reckon that when the pine cones open we're in for a dry spell. Let's suppose that we wanted to estimate the validity of using pine cones as predictors of the weather. We could measure the degree of openness of the pine cones by using a ruler (our measure), then note the weather changes over the next few days (the future event) and estimate how high the validity of pine cone forecasting is.

If we have long waiting lists at a social care agency, we might want to devise a test to give to prospective clients to screen them so that we only accept those who will definitely benefit from its service. We would give the test to all prospective clients and then compare the clients' results with follow-up measures which tell us how much benefit the clients got from the service. (We would first have to establish the validity of the measures we used to test the benefit gained from the service!)

<table>
<tr><td>

Replication

The terms *reliability* and *validity* are expressions of the desire to establish the trustworthiness of not only individual measurements but also hypotheses and theories. When applied to this 'meta-level' we would normally try to achieve this trustworthiness by the process of replication. This is, in effect, a form of test–retest reliability done at the level of whole studies or even genres of research. For example, if we wanted to establish the validity and reliability of the notion that youth workers embedded in the community help lower the rate of Anti-Social Behaviour Orders, we would not be content to conduct a single study in one part of the country. We would have more trust in our conclusions if the study was repeated in a number of locations and that the results had been *replicated*.

A definition of *replication* from About.com is: 'A term referring to the repetition of a research study, generally with different situations and different subjects, to determine if the basic findings of the original study can be generalised to other participants and circumstances.' Retrieved 03/04/10 <http://psychology.about.com/od/rindex/g/def_replication.htm>

</td></tr>
</table>

4. Construct validity
Definition
This is a form of validity which is usually of interest only to those engaged in high-level research. It is an attempt see how far the theoretical notion (construct) on which we've based our measure is what it says it is.

Suppose a deodorant manufacturer claims that their product will increase your personal magnetism. Is this claim valid, we might ask? In the first instance, validity here hinges upon the existence (validity) of the notion (construct) of 'personal magnetism'. What do you think? Does personal magnetism exist, or not? Social science is littered with such notions that have no basis other than that established by construct validity. Intelligence is probably the best-known example. Think of an idea or notion in social science theory and you could try to establish the validity of it. How about empathy, transference or mindfulness, as examples?

The actual process of establishing the validity of a construct is rather complicated and involves advanced statistical procedures, so we won't go into detail here. Basically, the process involves measuring lots of characteristics which you think are evidence of the main construct and comparing the measures of these subsidiary characteristics. The assumption is that the construct you are trying to validate is the one thing which links all the other measures. At this level of calculation some people find it difficult to distinguish between the lies, the damned lies, and the statistics!

Reliability

Definition
Sometimes called *consistency*, it refers to the likelihood of getting the same results over and over again if we repeated the measure in the same circumstances. There are two main areas in social science research where reliability is important: one where the reliability of an observation or observer is at issue; the second is where the reliability of the measuring device itself is at issue.

Reliability is represented on a scale from 0 to 1 in a similar manner to validity (take a look at the diagram and margin note on p. 40).

Inter-observer reliability
Definition
When two or more observers agree on what they've observed (high inter-observer reliability).

Everyday example
So that teachers can be fair in their allocation of marks, they often

'cross-mark' assignments. This is where two or more teachers mark the same piece of work and compare marks to make sure that they are working to the same standard.

Research example

Let's say two counselling colleagues wish to rate the performance of another counsellor in a particular session. They video-record the session and sit down to watch it, rating scales in hand. When it's over, they compare notes – if their ratings agree or are very close, then there is high inter-observer reliability. If they disagree and their ratings are very different, there is low inter-observer reliability. In a research setting, it's important to obtain high inter-observer reliability and this is usually achieved by training the observers in the proper and consistent use of the rating scale. It is not uncommon for *many* observers to be used in a piece of serious research since this should increase the inter-observer reliability. Can you work out why? (The answer is in Chapter 2.4, 'Distributions, Populations and Samples'.)

Reliability of a measure

There are a few ways of estimating this depending upon the type of measure you're using. Most of these ways are only really important if you're devising a PSYCHOMETRIC TEST and since we don't think we'll be getting on to that in this book, we'll just describe one type that has possible applications in practitioner research.

Test–retest reliability
Definition

This is simply the taking of repeated measurements. Results that are similar indicate a reliable measure, whereas wildly different results indicate an unreliable measure.

Everyday example

Measuring the same thing twice is the most commonly used everyday method of checking reliability. In physics at school it was usual to learn to measure everything three times and take the average of the three measures. Whilst this isn't necessary for most everyday measures, many people still find that measuring something twice prevents us from making simple mistakes such as misreading the tape measure, so most of us do a second measurement without even thinking about it.

Research example

It is common practice to make sure that any test or questionnaire you devise, however simple, is reliable. The simplest method is to give it to a small group of people twice with a week or so gap in-

PSYCHOMETRIC TEST Any standardised procedure for measuring aspects, qualities or attributes of mental functioning including, eg, sensitivity, memory, 'intelligence', aptitude or personality.

Note
Some of these other ways of measuring reliability include 'split-half reliability' and 'parallel-forms reliability', if you want to look some up.

Note
Whilst validity and reliability are most often thought to tell us something about the *measure*, we have come to appreciate that, in all areas of science, they can also be telling us something about the *measurer*, and we are not simply referring to inter-observer reliability. The most accurate and sensitive measuring device can be rendered useless in the hands of someone who doesn't know how to use it properly. There will be more on this in Chapter 2.5, 'Quantitative Research Methods'.

between. Agreement between the test and the re-test results means high reliability. Big differences between the test and re-test results mean low reliability.

Correlation

Both reliability and validity depend upon a statistical procedure called correlation. It is based on the idea that two things may be associated or co-related, for example:

- my weight *increases* as I eat *more* food, or
- the amount of petrol in my car's fuel tank *goes down* as I drive *more* miles

We cover this procedure in more detail in Chapter 2.5 'Quantitative Research Methods', but for now it is just necessary to know that:

- in the case of validity, for example, correlation means that the more open the pine cones are, the less it rains (predictive validity) and
- in the case of reliability, for example, correlation means that the same people getting a high score on our helping professions aptitude scale on Monday also get a high score when we give them the test on the following Friday (test–retest reliability)

Great care must be taken when using correlation, since it can't tell us anything about cause-and-effect relationships. It just tells us that as one thing varies, so another thing varies in a consistent way. For example, in the 1960s and 70s the suicide rate in the UK fell. At roughly the same time, more and more telephone helplines were founded and became widely known. This looks as if one thing might have caused the other. However, in this same time period there was a change in the domestic gas supply. Toxic coal gas was replaced by non-toxic natural gas. Previously, gassing was a common way for a person to commit suicide. So, there is another possible cause for the drop in the suicide rate. Did one, both, or neither of these contribute to the fall in suicide? What do you think? How could you find out for certain? Chapter 2.5 covers this and other issues regarding correlation in more detail.

Note
Samaritans, the most well-known telephone helpline in the UK dedicated to listening to people contemplating suicide, was informally founded in the mid 1950s by Chad Varah. If you are interested in how the Samaritans came into being look at: <http://www.samaritans.org/about_sam aritans/governance_and_history/why_ samaritans_started.aspx> retrieved 11/12/ 2009.

using numbers to describe things

It is not enough to measure and count accurately, reliably and validly. We have to make sure that other people can understand our measurements. This means presenting them in a clear and concise form, often having to summarise them so that they can be taken in at a glance.

When we have finished measuring and counting, we are left with what's known as *raw data*. It's called raw data for a fairly obvious reason: like a raw diamond, its value can't be appreciated until we've treated it in some way. There's just too much to be taken in and it's more than likely all jumbled up. So, in order to appreciate a raw diamond, it is cleaned to reveal its true form and cut into a pleasing shape, in sympathy with its natural structure, to enhance its inherent beauty. We do the same with raw data. We have to 'clean it up' using treatments that work with, rather than against, the trends in the data. We have to try to reveal the true form of the data and, if possible, enhance the subtle messages buried under the apparently chaotic surface.

This chapter is all about that first stage of the 'clean up' where we are trying to see the true shape of the data. The techniques are all very basic and you may well be familiar with some if not all of them. However, what we will try to do is explain why we use certain ways of describing and summarising data under different circumstances. In order to understand this you will have to read and understand Chapter 2.2, 'Measuring Things', since all the explanations hinge upon the type of measurements we've made, i.e. nominal, ordinal, interval or ratio. What we are beginning to do here is to introduce you to statistics. There is no need to be discouraged. In a way, we are also using statistics when we talk about averages, percentages, decide whether the odds of winning the lottery justify the purchase price of a ticket and so on. Statistics is just a branch of mathematics that allows the displaying, summarising and comparison of numerical data. Its usefulness in research is that it gives ways of presenting complex findings in a simplified way, sometimes graphically and that it provides means of establishing the probability that hypotheses are true or untrue. Also, statistics can form a basis from which to make statements about *probability* and *significance* (see below). In lay terms, in the case of, for example, 'evidence-based' research, it is by the use of

Note

In recent years, the world of work in health and social care has been heavily influenced by *evidence*. Like it or not, this evidence comes in the form of numbers. Increasingly, our abilities and even integrity as a practitioner or helper lies in our ability to understand evidence, provide evidence and debate evidence. We all have to have a facility with numbers. In your experience, are health and social care practitioners, therapists and helpers able to express themselves accurately, concisely and authoritatively using numbers?

The emphasis of this book is on practice-based evidence which raises the further question: when might *you* need to display your information in numerical form?

statistical procedures that researchers can make authoritative statements about the efficacy of an action or treatment or to compare different approaches.

Summarising and describing results in pictures

One of the first things we can do in order to see the 'shape' of data is to arrange it in some sort of 'picture'. The simplest sort of picture is a table.

Tables

Tabulating numbers is a very old and very simple procedure. It means taking the dozens of scraps of paper on which you've written your measurements and summarising them in one place. Suppose we want to look at the use of a counselling agency in 1992. We collect the figures from each counsellor and summarise them in Table 2.3.1.

With a quick glance at this table, we can learn several pieces of information and with a longer look come to understand some of the possible workings of the service. We may ask questions about the data – why does Counsellor 2 have fewer clients? Why does Counsellor 1 have so many female clients and so few male clients?

Of course, it would occur to most of us to do it like this and now we can see that there are some further pieces of information we could have included to aid understanding. We could have added to the same table some information about the time the counsellor spent working for the agency (full or part-time) and the counsellor's gender (male or female) – Table 2.3.2.

Clearly, even this doesn't answer all the questions that we might have. Indeed, we may have to tabulate more data about the counselling agency in order to answer more questions, or we may never be able to answer all questions with simple tables. At this stage the message is simple – don't overlook the humble table as a method of expressing your results.

Charts, graphs and histograms

These even more pictorial methods of displaying summarised data are increasingly employed to make the information more accessible. Data are not all alike. There is more than one type of data which we can collect and this affects how the data can be summarised and described. We'll briefly introduce each of three types and then explain each in more detail.

HELP!
If the thought of drawing tables and graphs sends shivers up your spine, this can be done practically at the touch of a button if you enter your data into presentation software like Microsoft PowerPoint (and know which button to press). We will show how this is done in the Appendix on p 309. In the present chapter we show you the *principles* of drawing your data on charts and graphs so you can understand what they mean.

	NUMBER OF CLIENTS IN 1992		
COUNSELLOR	FEMALE	MALE	TOTAL
1	54	12	66
2	12	14	26
3	32	42	74
4	38	19	57
5	50	21	71
TOTALS	**186**	**108**	**294**

Table 2.3.1 Number of clients using the counselling agency in 1992

COUNSELLOR	M/F	FT/PT
1	F	FT
2	M	PT
3	M	FT
4	M	FT
5	F	FT

Table 2.3.2 Counsellor gender and status at counselling agency

Note
See Chapter 2.2, 'Measuring Things'.

Frequency data This is where we have *counted* things in categories, e.g. '60 clients out of 100 improved after 10 weeks of person-centred therapy' is a statement of frequency. This statement is of little use because, without some further manipulation, it does not allow comparison with any other group treated in the same way. If the same information is expressed as a *frequency distribution* then comparison becomes possible. For example '60% of clients improved' is a statement of frequency distribution. If a similar study was conducted with a different number of clients and the findings from this too were expressed as a frequency distribution ('45% of clients improved') then, because the findings are in the same form, it is easier to compare the two studies. Of course, without knowing something about the clients in each study, what constituted 'improvement' and how it was measured and how, where, when and who provided the 'person-centred therapy', comparison remains problematic.

To display frequency data we use pie charts, bar charts (histograms) and frequency distributions or polygons.

Other data Here we have *measured* something, e.g. time. For this we use data curves or graphs.

Correlation data Measuring two variables and seeing how they are related. For this we use *scattergrams* which will be covered in the section on correlation beginning on page 105 of Chapter 2.5.

1. Frequency Data
Counting can only be represented by illustrating how the frequencies of occurrence of events in the various categories are distributed amongst those categories. Frequency distributions are very important graphical representations in statistics, as we shall see in later chapters.

Example
Let's say that an agency wants to look at its record of working with people with drug abuse problems. They decide to follow up a month's worth of their clients for a year and look at the number of drug-free months since the end of service use (when each client ended the treatment programme) for the cohort of clients in question. They collect the results and summarise them in a table.

One hundred and sixteen clients finished the programme at the agency in September 2006, all of whom were followed up each month until August 2007 to see if they were still drug-free (a pre-condition of joining the agency programme). So in September there were 116 drug-free clients and, as each month went by, the number of ex-clients returning to drug-taking increased. They were recorded by making a down-stroke for each client per month in groups of five, with the fifth client being represented by a diagonal stroke

MONTH	TALLIES	NUMBER OF EX-CLIENTS RETURNING TO DRUGS	NUMBER OF EX-CLIENTS REMAINING DRUG FREE
1		0	116
2		0	116
3	II	2	114
4	I	1	113
5	III	3	110
6	ЖН II	7	103
7	ЖН ЖН II	12	91
8	ЖН ЖН ЖН	15	76
9	ЖН ЖН IIII	14	62
10	ЖН ЖН	10	52
11	ЖН II	7	45
12	III	3	42

Table 2.3.3 Number of clients returning to drugs and remaining drug free by month from September 1991 to August 1992

(column 2). These tallies were totalled for each month in column 3 and subtracted from 116 as each month went by, as shown in Table 2.3.3.

We must now decide which measure (the number of ex-clients returning to drugs, or the number of ex-clients remaining drug-free) to use. There is no set procedure here; you must decide for yourself which best fits the purpose of the research, and this is a matter of opinion. It's more common in statistics to use the former, because it helps us see the shape of the distribution of the frequencies more easily.

So first, we'll show what the number returning to drugs per month distribution looks like and we will be explaining this shape in much more detail in Chapter 2.4. Next, we'll use the numbers remaining drug-free. This will give you a chance to see both ways of representing the results. This second method of counting (numbers remaining drug-free) is called *cumulative* because the additions (or in this case subtractions) *accumulate* and we work with the running totals.

We now turn the above table on its side to make frequency the horizontal axis and 'categories' the vertical axis. For each column of frequencies (1 and 2) we plot the frequencies against the month on a separate chart. If we draw a line linking each point we have for column 1 (number returning to drugs per month), Chart 2.3.4. Then, drawing a line linking each point for column 2 (number remaining drug-free per month) we get Chart 2.3.5 below.

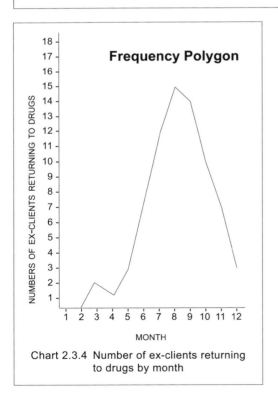

Chart 2.3.4 Number of ex-clients returning to drugs by month

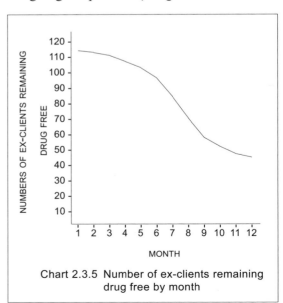

Chart 2.3.5 Number of ex-clients remaining drug free by month

If we draw vertical bars to represent the numbers in each category, instead of drawing lines to join them together, we have a bar chart or histogram:

Chart 2.3.6 Bar chart or histogram

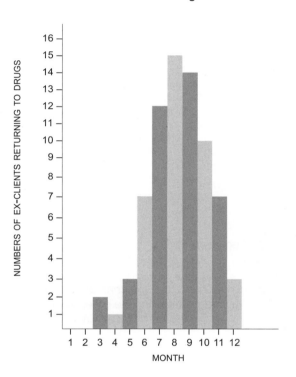

Chart 2.3.7 Cumulative bar chart or histogram

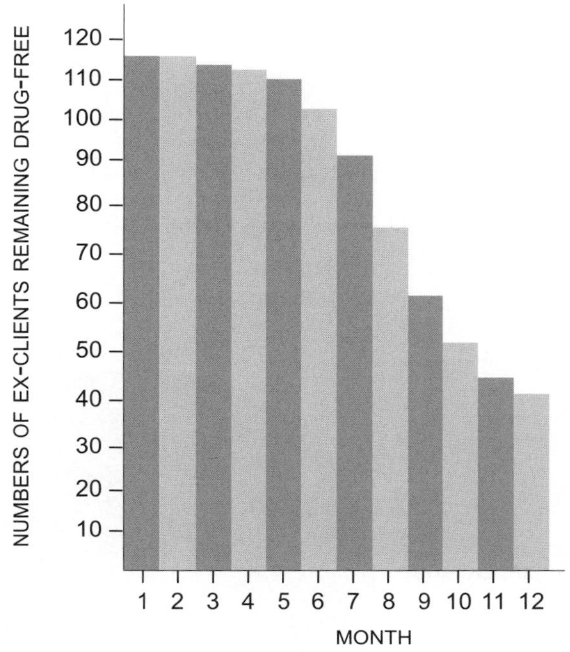

Note
We'll learn why a pie chart isn't such an informative way of representing this kind of data in Chapter 2.4, 'Distributions, Populations and Samples'.

Although we could use the above data to draw a *pie chart* (see following page), it would be less useful than these histograms or frequency polygons.

Instead, we'll use some different, nominal, data to illustrate the best use of a pie chart. Suppose our college counselling service wants to report its activities to the Academic Board. We want to show how much students from each of the five faculties used the counselling service in 2006. Our tabulated data on the next page can be translated into a pie chart by using the calculation above the table if you don't have access to a computer spreadsheet program which will do it for you. The calculation is simply a way of changing the number of something (students in a particular faculty) in a finite total group into the proportion represented by the pie segment in degrees (you need a protractor to draw the segments in degrees).

Note
We include how to *calculate* the segments of a pie chart so that if you don't have access to a computer, you can still create a visual representation of your data with impact. For those with a computer, you will find pie-chart and several frequency graphs (bar charts and polygons) available at the click of a button on Microsoft PowerPoint and equivalent presentation programs. If you don't have one of these, free pie-chart calculators are available on the Internet. The latter are easy to use and use vibrant colours. We explain how to use PowerPoint for graphing and charting on p 309 in the Appendix.

Pie Chart

Note

In the pie chart below we have put the segment names next to the segments, but it is also common to have a key showing the colour/pattern next to the name:

Pure Science

Arts and Humanities

Though this can be difficult when dealing with shades of grey.

FACULTY	NO. OF CLIENTS (X)		DEGREES
ENGINEERING	14		27
PURE SCIENCE	19		36
ARTS AND HUMANITIES	75	$\frac{X \times 360}{\Sigma\ X} =$	142
SOCIAL SCIENCE	60		113
BUSINESS STUDIES	22		42
Σ X TOTAL	190		360

Table 2.3.8 Number of clients attending the college counselling service by faculty in 1992

On p. 54 we explain what these mathematical symbols Σ and X (and others) mean.

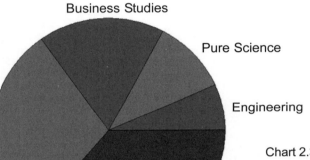

Business Studies

Pure Science

Engineering

Social Science

Arts and Humanities

Chart 2.3.9 Pie chart of number of students attending the college counselling service by faculty in 1992

2. Other data

Measurements (as opposed to frequency counts) are represented graphically on data curves. A counsellor trainer was interested in looking at the improvement in skills ratings of her trainees on a nine-point scale over the period of a year-long course. Three trainees agreed to take part and submitted tape-recordings of their work with clients every month for ten months. The tapes were rated by the trainer and recorded in Table 2.3.10.

	SKILLS — TAPE RATING									
TRAINEE	SEP	OCT	NOV	DEC	JAN	FEB	MAR	APR	MAY	JUN
1	6	5	7	7	6	6	5	4	3	3
2	5	5	5	5	4	4	3	3	2	2
3	7	7	6	6	5	5	5	4	4	3

Table 2.3.10 Skills rating of trainees by month. Skills rating scale from 9 (low) to 1 (high)

The results were represented graphically by using ratings on the vertical axis and time in months on the horizontal axis. Note that the vertical axis scale has been 'turned upside-down'. This is because an improvement in the trainees' performance is indicated by a *lower score*, we can then see on the graph an improvement is indicated by *upward* movement. All three trainees' ratings are drawn on the same graph.

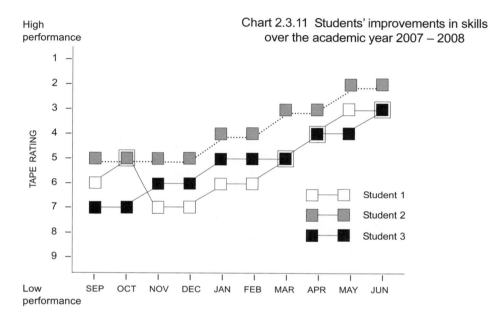

Chart 2.3.11 Students' improvements in skills over the academic year 2007 – 2008

It is sometimes very helpful to draw several sets of data on the same set of axes since it allows the reader to quickly appreciate any trends in the data or values around which many performances cluster. The tendency for results to group around certain values that represent the middle portion of a distribution is called *central tendency* and is covered more fully in the next section in this chapter.

Summarising and describing results with numbers: Descriptive statistics

If, as is often the case, we have a large number of measurements, it is sometimes not possible to present a visual picture until we have first done some preliminary numerical summarising and describing. This is not difficult at all; in fact most people do it instinctively when they say 'on average'. The 'average' is only one of the features of sets of scores that it is useful to know and we will look at the different terms used to describe these important (and useful) features.

Note
Before we move on to the next section, remember that if you're not familiar with drawing graphs, we cover how to do it on a computer in the Appendix.

Note
We're putting inverted commas around the word 'average' because its common meaning has become sufficiently different from its technical meaning to invite misunderstanding.

Everyday example

In schools, there are often class tests in each subject. When the results are read out, there are four things most pupils want to know. The first is their own score. Probably each person fantasises about getting 80 or 90 out of 100. Maybe they also have a nightmare where they get 90 out of 100 only to discover that everyone else had scored higher than 90! So the second piece of information everybody requires is the (roughly) average score. Then they can place themselves somewhere in relation to the average. Mostly, this is still not enough because everybody wants to know by how much they missed the top mark and by how much they escaped the indignity of bottom of the class (and that is the last piece of essential information).

So in order to really understand how well they have done, each pupil needs to know:
- their own score
- the average score
- the top score
- the bottom score

These four features of a set of data are also essential for statistical analysis. Knowledge of these four features, plus the number of scores (i.e. the number in the class), allows us to do some very powerful calculations and make some powerful assumptions about the data. Statisticians would use the following terms, and we should get used to thinking in terms of them and using them routinely:
- Average *Measure of central tendency* of the scores
- Top score and bottom score *Measure of Spread* or *Dispersion* of the scores

1. Measures of central tendency

An 'average' is a measure of central tendency – the extent to which a set of scores group around a mid-point. Statisticians have devised measures of central tendency that can be used with each of the scales of measurement.

Mode

The mode is the most frequently occurring value in a set of scores, the most 'popular' so to speak. It can be found (hardly 'calculated') by simply looking at the data. If there are only a few scores, the mode is not a very useful measure of central tendency. It is, however, often quoted for large samples. If a histogram or frequency polygon is plotted, the mode is the peak of the histogram or polygon.

Example

A group of seven speech therapists decides to see to what degree they agree on standards of speech therapy. They watch a videotaped speech therapy session and rate it individually on a nine-point scale, where 1 is an excellent performance, 9 is a poor, non-therapeutic performance and 5 (the mid-point) is minimally acceptable practice.

The mode (modal rating) is 4 (the most frequent rating), and you can see this by glancing at Table 2.3.12.

SPEECH THERAPIST	RATING
1	3
2	4
3	2
4	4
5	3
6	5
7	4

Table 2.3.12

Advantages:
- the only measure of central tendency that can be used with nominal data
- very simple to calculate, especially with large sets of scores
- very useful with sets of scores that do not have a symmetrical distribution (more about this later in the chapter)

Disadvantages:
- not a very powerful measure – it can't be used in further calculations and, if you use it with any data that is more than nominal, you are leaving a lot of the information contained in the data untapped
- there may be more than one mode in any set of scores. Such sets or distributions of scores are called bimodal (two modes) or multimodal (many modes)

Median

The median is defined as the value that has as many scores above it as below it: the 'middle' score, so to speak. So using the data set above, seven speech therapists rate the same videotape of a speech therapy session on a nine-point scale. To find (again, we can hardly call this a 'calculation') the median, we arrange the scores in ascending (or descending) order and locate the middle most score, as follows:

> **HELP!**
> If you're worried about the arithmetic involved in these calculations we show you how to use spreadsheets like Microsoft Excel to work out the mode, median and mean in the box on pp 56-7. We explain why we are doing this in the box on p 55.

2, 3, 3, 4, 4, 4, 5 median = middle score (2, 3, 3, *4*, 4, 4, 5) = 4

If we have an even number of scores, then the median is the point halfway between the two middle scores (the average of the two middle scores) after putting all the scores in rank order. An eighth speech therapist turns up to rate the tape so the median is now:

2, 3, 3, 3, 4, 4, 4, 5 median = (3+4)/2 = 3.5
(Also note that the set of scores now has two modes: 3 and 4: it has become bimodal.)

Advantages:
- a measure of central tendency, purpose-built for use with ordinal data (you can use the mode, but the median is almost as easy to

calculate and uses more information inherent in the data than the mode)
- easy to calculate even with large sets of scores
- very useful with asymmetrically distributed sets of scores (again, more about this later in the chapter)

Disadvantages:
- not the most powerful measure of central tendency since it has only limited use in further calculations and, if you try to use it with interval or ratio data, you will be under-using the information contained within the data

Arithmetic Mean

This is a commonly used measure of central tendency which is usually called the 'average' in everyday language. It is calculated by adding together every score and dividing by the number of scores:

$$\text{Mean} = \frac{\text{total of all scores}}{\text{number of scores}}$$

This can be expressed as a mathematical formula using symbols that represent the words used above. It's a good idea to learn the symbols used in statistics since it saves a lot of time by cutting down on the large number of words required to explain simple numerical ideas. So here are some symbols used pretty universally in statistics. We'll use them throughout the rest of this book and you'll find them in other books too.

Glossary of common symbols used in statistics

X = scores in general or any score in the set

$\overline{X}$ = the mean score

You can, if you choose, use other letters to denote the scores (particularly if you have a number of sets of score which you want to compare). Then, putting a bar over the letter indicates that this is the mean value. The first score in the set would be indicated by adding a subscript 1, the second subscript 2, and so on. So if the scores are $A_1, A_2 \ldots A_n$, (where 'n' is the final number in the set), then $\overline{A}$ is the mean.

Σ = the sum of (whatever follows)

ΣA = the sum of all the As

N = the number of scores in the set

The mean has a formula using these symbols as follows:

$$\overline{X} = \frac{\sum X}{N} = \frac{\text{The sum of all the Xs}}{\text{The number of Xs}}$$

The mean for the scores given in the above example for the median, is:

$$\overline{X} = \frac{2+3+3+3+4+4+5+5}{8} = \frac{29}{8} = 3.625$$

HELP!

If you're worried about the arithmetic involved in these calculations, we show you how to use spreadsheets like Microsoft Excel to work out the mode, median and mean in the box on the next pages. We explain why we are doing this in the box below.

Advantages
- the mean is the most powerful measure of central tendency: it can be used in the most advanced calculations
- can be used with interval and ratio data
- uses all the information in the data

Disadvantages
- takes a little while to calculate (and you can make mistakes)
- very sensitive to extreme scores and is 'pulled' away from the centre of the scores in asymmetrical distributions (more about this next)

Calculating statistics in the 21st century

Although we have included the equations and show a worked example, we do not expect you will be doing the calculations by hand. Calculating and arithmetic in the 21st century are activities almost always performed on a personal computer. We are using the equations here so that you can see how these descriptive statistics work from first principles upwards, and also so you can get used to the symbols (S, X, etc.) used in statistics and data processing.

There are several computer programs which make calculating the mean, median, mode, variance and standard deviation, and processing data in other ways, very easy. We'll use *Microsoft Excel* in this part of the book as an example, since it's the one you're most likely to use. If you use something else, don't worry, most spreadsheets (they're 'number processors' – like word processors but for manipulating numbers) work in very similar ways. They are often supplied with your computer and will come with instructions. If a spreadsheet is supplied as part of your computer software bundle, it will almost certainly be part of an 'office' suite of software.

We need to mention SPSS (its full title – which no one uses – is *Statistical Package for the Social Sciences*) which is often available as part of the online student support services provided to students doing research-based degrees (Masters and PhD). It is a large, sophisticated program with huge capacity for data processing and many ready-configured statistical procedures. If you are an independent researcher (as part of an agency or a private practitioner) you might find SPSS rather expensive, but SPSS can be purchased by individual students if you're registered with an educational institution. It's always worth asking your tutor or librarian if any statistical packages are available to students on your course.

It is beyond the scope of this book to run even part tutorials in SPSS (though we give a few screen illustrations, here and there). We recommend the following book to support its use for beginners:

Pallant J (2007) *SPSS Survival Manual: A step-by-step guide to data analysis using SPSS for Windows (Version 15).* Buckingham: Open University Press.

You will also find free tutorials online if you enter 'SPSS Tutorials' into a web search engine.

Calculating the mode, median and mean using Excel

Enter your data

We will use the scores from the speech therapists' ratings used in the calculations on the previous pages.

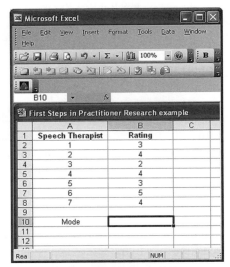

• Enter the titles of your columns 'Speech Therapist' and 'Rating'. You can use any consecutive columns you wish, but for convenience we used columns A and B

• Enter the speech therapist numbers in the cells in column A

• Enter the ratings in column B opposite the appropriate therapist number

• Click on a cell below them and enter some text to indicate the statistic you are calculating (mod, median or mean). In this case we have entered 'mode', since we are calculating that first

• Click on the adjacent cell: the one that you want the mode to be shown in. Your screen should now look like the one illustrated top right

You are now ready to make any number of calculations on the data you have entered

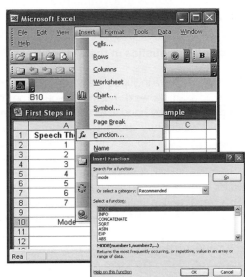

Calculating the mode

• Click on 'insert' on the toolbar

• Choose 'function' from the dropdown menu

• A pop-up box titled 'Insert Function' will appear

• Type 'Mode' into the search box at the top, (you can ignore the 'select category' box)

• Click the 'Go' button. Your screen should now look like the middle one illustrated on the right

• Select 'mode' from the 'select a function' box and click 'OK'

• Click OK on the next screen ('Function Arguments') and the mode will be inserted into the cell you chose, as illustrated in the bottom diagram on the right

	Speech Therapist	Rating	
1	Speech Therapist	Rating	
2	1	3	
3	2	4	
4	3	2	
5	4	4	
6	5	3	
7	6	5	
8	7	4	
9			
10	Mode	4	
11			

Calculating the median

• After you have entered your data as shown previously, except at step 4, type the word 'median' into the box:

• Click on 'insert' on the toolbar

• Choose 'function' from the dropdown menu

• A pop-up box titled 'Insert Function' will appear

• Type 'median' into the search box at the top, (you can ignore the 'select category' box)

• Click the 'Go' button. Your screen should now look like the one illustrated on the right

• Select 'median' from the 'select a function' box and click 'OK'

• Click OK on the next screen ('Function Arguments') and the median will be inserted into the cell you chose, as illustrated in the second diagram on the right

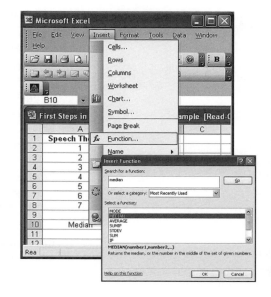

Calculating the mean

• After you have entered your data as shown previously, except at step 4, type the word 'mean' into the box:

• Repeat steps 2-4 above

• Type 'mean' into the search box at the top, (you can ignore the 'select category' box)

• Click the 'Go' button. Your screen should now look like the second one illustrated on the right

• Excel will select and highlight 'Average' in the 'Select a function' box. This is correct: it uses the word 'average' to denote the arithmetic mean.

• Click OK on the next screen ('Function Arguments') and the mean will be inserted into the cell you chose, as illustrated in the diagram below

1	Speech Therapist	Rating	
2	1	3	
3	2	4	
4	3	2	
5	4	4	
6	5	3	
7	6	5	
8	7	4	
9			
10	Median	4	

1	Speech Therapist	Rating	
2	1	3	
3	2	4	
4	3	2	
5	4	4	
6	5	3	
7	6	5	
8	7	4	
9			
10	Mean	3.571428571	

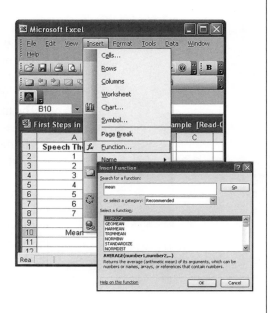

Examples of using measures of central tendency
The mean. The ages of 5 social work clients are 45, 43, 49, 42 and 47.

The mean age is $\dfrac{45+43+49+42+47}{5} = \dfrac{226}{5} = 45$

This seems like a meaningful summary since everybody in the sample is within 4 years of that age. However, if the ages were 25, 62, 23, 29 and 67, the mean age is also 45. But this time, the mean tells little about the population and is potentially misleading. Means are useful and meaningful only when there are not extreme values.

The median is the central value when all the scores are arranged in order of size, and for the two data sets above, the lists are thus 42, 43, 45, 47, 49 and 23, 25, 29, 62, 67. The median for the first is 45 while that for the second it is 29. The median is, therefore, probably more meaningful than the mean when there are extreme scores but all it tells the reader is that there are as many individual items with a lower score as there are with a higher score.

Note
We cannot emphasise enough how important it is to keep your raw data. It's best to keep it in its original form so that you (or anyone else who wishes to check) can return to it for confirmation or to retrieve lost data.

The mode. In order to tailor counselling services appropriately, university students were asked several questions regarding their lives, including the age at which they became sexually active. One hundred (50 male, 50 female) student's responses were tabulated:

Age of sexual activity	10	11	12	13	14	15	16	17	18	19	20	21	Total
Number of students	1	0	3	11	16	12	12	13	16	11	3	2	100

If we calculate the measures of central tendency we find as follows:
• The mean = 16.05
  What do we conclude from this? That on average students 'lose their virginity' aged 16?
• The median = 16
  The median seems to confirm this.
• The mode: there are two, 14 and 18, so the distribution is bimodal.
  What does this tell us? How can we explain the two modes?

The presence of two or more modes (Chart 2.3.13) usually tells us that the distribution is showing us that we have collected data from two populations with regard to the variable in question. So somehow the researchers have collected data from two 'groups', one of which tends to lose their virginity around the age of 14 the other around

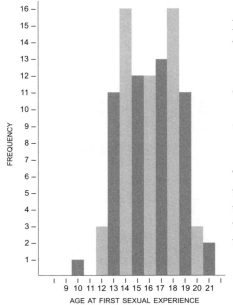

Chart 2.3.13 Frequency of age of first sexual experience in university students

the age of 18. A quick look back at the raw data explains what is going on: the female students' responses tend to group around age 14 and the male students' responses tend to group around age 18.

If we draw the distribution we can clearly see the two modes. In order to illustrate the distributions of the two groups we could draw two frequency polygons on the same set of axes (Chart 2.3.14).

2. The shape of the distribution of scores

Next, we need to look at the meaning of the shape of the distribution of scores and how this interacts with the measures of central tendency. It's all very well and good talking about central tendency – where the bulk of the scores lie – as if such a quality could be measured reliably. However, the truth, as we have just seen, is that central tendency is, as its name suggests, a *tendency*, and as such may be slightly different depending upon the method of measurement.

This is particularly relevant when we have a set of scores that is not distributed evenly about its mid-point. These distributions are asymmetrical – the first half of the distribution is not the same shape as the second half. We have seen that there are some symmetrical distributions that have interesting causes too (bimodal or multimodal ones) but these are rare, frequently explain themselves and require further investigation if an explanation isn't immediately apparent.

Suppose we gave a 'nursing aptitude test' to two successive intakes of trainees on a nurse training programme in 2007 and 2008. Look at the histograms drawn from the two sets of scores in charts 2.3.15 and 2.3.16 below.

The first set is distributed symmetrically about its mid-point, the second set is distributed asymmetrically. This lack of symmetry in a distribution of scores is called *skew* and can be either positive or negative. A positively skewed distribution is bunched up towards the left with a longer tail to the right. A negatively skewed distribution is the other way round – with a longer tail to the left.

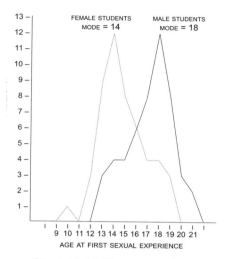

Chart 2.3.14 Frequency of age of first sexual experience of female and male university students

Note
These results are still intriguing. Why should the female sample have a lower modal age than the male sample? The counselling service generated a number of hypotheses, including that the university had more male overseas students and that these were likely to be more sexually conservative than UK students. How could they test this and what hypotheses can you come up with to explain the graph above?

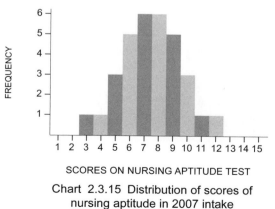

Chart 2.3.15 Distribution of scores of nursing aptitude in 2007 intake

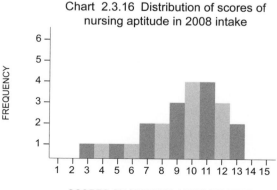

Chart 2.3.16 Distribution of scores of nursing aptitude in 2008 intake

Whilst skew in a distribution is caused by many things, one thing can be relied upon – it exerts varying degrees of 'pull' on the different measures of central tendency. The mode is affected least by skew, the mean is affected most as follows:

Chart 2.3.17 A positively skewed distribution

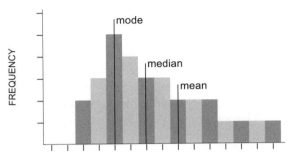

Chart 2.3.18 A symmetrical distribution

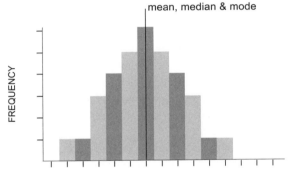

Chart 2.3.19 A negatively skewed distribution

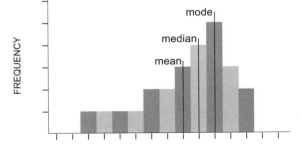

This feature helps us in two ways:
- if you know your distribution is skewed, don't use the mean – it's the least accurate measure of where the bulk of the scores lies in these circumstances
- if you want to quickly find out whether you've got a skewed or symmetrical distribution, you don't have to draw it out – just work out the mean, median and mode. If they lie fairly close together, in no particular order, you've most likely got a symmetrical distribution. If they are spread out in the order, mode, median, mean (or the reverse) then you've most likely got a skewed distribution

You may well be saying to yourself 'So what if I *do* have a symmetrical or skewed distribution, what difference does it make?' The answer is that skew in itself doesn't mean much. But you should remember that the numbers we collect are *always* telling us something – they may, of course, be simply telling us that we've collected a rather ordinary, unremarkable set of numbers. This is generally good news since, generally speaking, the more ordinary the distribution, the more powerful statistical procedures we can use (more of this in the next chapter). Skew is a feature of distributions of scores which has ramifications for the statistics we can use, but we don't have to trouble ourselves with that in this book, and probably not in the kind of practitioner research most readers will be interested in.

3. Measures of spread, dispersion, variance or deviation

The degree to which a group of scores is bunched up or spread out around a mid-point is an important piece of information about measurements. It tells us by how much the scores vary from each other or from the mean (or what the variability is in the scores). This is sometimes talked of in terms of the degree to which scores deviate from the mid-point.

Example

Again, staying with the example used earlier on p. 53 of the eight speech therapists who rated the same videotaped speech therapy session. Let's suppose that, in addition, a group of eight speech therapy *students* also rated the tape. Below are the results of both 'teams' of raters; the qualified speech therapists and the students and on the next page the histograms of the two sets of scores.

Speech Therapists' Ratings: 3 4 2 4 3 5 4 3
Students' Ratings: 4 3 1 5 7 4 2 8

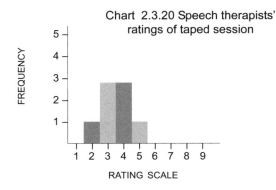

Chart 2.3.20 Speech therapists' ratings of taped session

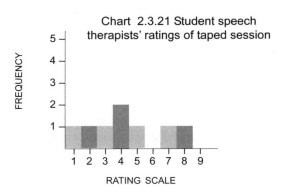

Chart 2.3.21 Student speech therapists' ratings of taped session

Note

What are the scores are telling us? In this case, more dispersed rating scores tell us that there is less agreement amongst the raters. We could hypothesise that the tutors' ratings, bunched up together, showed they agreed with each other, whereas the students did not agree with each other. This lack of agreement might mean that either the students didn't know how to use the scales or were not clear about what the skills of speech therapy are. Since they are students, either or both explanations are reasonable.

Now, as you can see, the 'spreadoutness', or *dispersion,* of the two groups is markedly different. The speech therapists' scores are bunched up around the mean, whereas the students' scores are more spread out or *dispersed.* Another way of saying this is to say that there is more *variation* in the students' scores, or more *variability.* Yet another way of saying the same thing is to say that the students' scores *deviate* more from the mid-point.

So if the measure of central tendency is where the bulk of the scores lie, then scores can be closer or further away from the measure of central tendency used. The different ways of saying this can be summarised as follows:

When scores are **closer** to the mid-point of the distribution:	When scores are **further away** from the mid-point of the distribution:
They look **bunched up**	They look **spread out**
They are **less dispersed**	They are **more dispersed**
They have **less variation**	They have **more variation**
They **deviate little** from the mid-point	They **deviate a lot** from the mid-point

There are a number of ways to express or describe the degree to which the scores in a distribution are dispersed. Some of these methods involve calculations which are more complicated than the mean and pie chart formulae earlier in the chapter. If the thought of more complicated calculations makes you break out into a cold sweat, don't worry, we will look at how to do this on a computer later in this chapter and show you how make a computer draw graphs and charts in the Appendix.

The simplest way of describing the dispersion of a set of scores is the *range.*

Range

The range is the difference between the highest score and the lowest score. The following marks in a social work exam were achieved by students on a certain course in subsequent years and placed in rank order from the lowest to the highest:

2005/6   39, 39, 45, 50, 52, 56, 56, 65, 67, 71, 75, 81
   mean = 58
2006/7   46, 48, 48, 51, 54, 56, 56, 62, 67, 68, 68, 72
   mean = 58

By a coincidence the marks in the exam show that the mean exam mark was the same in both years. Is this the end of the story that the numbers can tell us? Let's calculate the range to find out what the dispersion is. This is easily done since the marks are in rank order (although this isn't necessary when working out the range, it does help avoid silly mistakes):

Range = Difference between the highest score and the lowest score.

2005/6 range = 81 – 39 = 42
2006/7 range = 72 – 46 = 26

As you can see, there is a big difference between the ranges. This tells us that the marks in 2005/6 were more dispersed or spread out than the marks in 2006/7. If there is a pass mark of 45% and a distinction gained at 75%, then the range has quite an important effect on how these marks would be viewed. In 2005/6 two people failed, yet there were two distinctions awarded. In 2006/7 there were no fails and no distinctions, everyone was more 'average'.

   The tutors on the course might want to try to explain this by looking at the way they selected the students at the beginning of the course, or whether the teaching differed from year to year, or whether the examinations were equally hard. What do *you* make of these results?

   Easy and useful though it is, the range has a severe drawback. Since it only takes into account the two most extreme scores, it cannot give a good description of a skewed distribution or one that has a single extreme score sticking out at one end:

2, 2, 3, 4, 4, 4, 5, 7, 8, 72   range = 70 – 2 = 70

The range of 70 for the above set of scores is, to say the least, misleading!

Advantages
- the range is quick and easy to work out
- for rough-and-ready appreciation of results, it's fine

Disadvantages
- not very powerful, i.e. it doesn't use all the information in the data
- can't be used in more complex calculations
- loses its usefulness when a distribution is skewed or has one extreme score

The road to the standard deviation

The standard deviation is the most useful and probably the most frequently used measure of dispersion. It is powerful and, with a calculator, quite easy to work out. It's also not too difficult to understand the idea behind it as long as we follow the logic. Along the way to understanding the rationale, we can learn the reasoning behind two other, less useful and less often used, measures of dispersion, the *mean deviation* and the *variance*. We're not going to show you how to calculate the mean deviation here because quite frankly, hardly anyone ever uses it, but it's useful to know what it *means* so that you can understand the standard deviation.

Mean deviation

The mean deviation is short for 'mean deviation from the mean' which sounds complicated but is a very simple idea. The idea is this: since we are trying to measure dispersion, we take a fixed point in the middle of the scores (the mean) and measure the deviation of each score from it, then we calculate the mean of all of these deviations.

Now it won't have escaped those budding mathematicians amongst you that some scores lie above the mean and some lie below it. The mean of a set of scores is like a fulcrum, it is the point at which the distribution balances so that there is just as much of the distribution above the mean as below it. So, maybe you've guessed it: if we calculate the mean deviation as described above, it will be zero because the deviations below the mean (midpoint) will be negative and will perfectly cancel out the positive deviations above it.

In order to solve this problem, the mathematicians used the fact that, since, if you multiply two like signs together you always get a positive, why not use the squared deviations (they'll always be positive) before calculating the mean of them?

Variance

That's exactly what the variance is: the mean of the squared deviations from the mean. The formula is:.

Important note

Distributions and samples

As you read this section, you must bear in mind that the type of data you have will affect the equations used in calculating the variance and standard deviation.

The crucial factor is whether your data is from a population or a sample of measurements. The meanings of the terms 'population' and 'sample' are explained in some detail in the next chapter 'Distributions, Populations and Samples', and you'll have to either wait for the full explanations or jump forward to the next chapter to get an idea of the differences. Either way, the actual differences this makes to the equations is a matter for advanced statistics, and we will not be covering things to that level of detail (you'll be relieved to discover).

As we go along we show the different equations (in fact the differences simply mean using either 'N' or 'N-1'* as the denominator). The data we are using in the simple worked example involves the number of sessions worked in a given week by the counsellors in a drop-in agency. Because we are using data from *all* of the counsellors and *all* of their sessions, this is population data. This means that we use 'N' as the denominator.

*On p 54 we explain the symbols 'N' etc.

$$\text{Variance} = s^2 = \frac{\Sigma(X-\overline{X})^2}{N}$$

If we wanted to calculate the variance longhand using this formula, we would find it very laborious. There is an alternative formula that allows us to square each value of X as we find it, then add them together and subtract the square of the mean just once at the end.

$$\text{Variance} = s^2 = \frac{\Sigma X^2}{N} - \overline{X}^2$$

If what we're after is a single number that expresses the dispersion of a collection of scores, the variance looks as though it might just do. Indeed, it is used in many more complex calculations and summaries of data, but when we have a symmetrical distribution or, better still, a normal distribution (*see* Chapter 2.4, 'Distributions, Populations and Samples'), the standard deviation has that extra ingredient: *standardness*.

Standard deviation

In mathematical terms, the standard deviation (SD) is simply the square root of the variance. That's why the symbol for the variance is s^2. In maths taking the square root of a number has a stabilising effect on the number. It also, in this case, gives us a number with which we can measure the distribution in the same units of measurement as the data we have collected. We'll give you a definition of what the SD does in everyday language below. Here's the formula for the SD and a worked example using the number of sessions worked in a week by seven counsellors in the Midshires drop-in centre (so we use the population variance calculation):

> **HELP!**
> Don't worry if the variance equation looks complicated. As we have explained in previous margin notes, we are showing you the equations and worked examples so that you can (if you wish) get down to the most basic building blocks of understanding. Whilst we don't expect you to plough through the calculations (unless you want to), *we do recommend you try and stick with the bits of text between the equations*, since we think it really is important that you understand the logic of variance and standard deviation (especially in the next chapter). These concepts are key to understanding how things like effect sizes are worked out – and effect sizes are currently all the rage in outcome research and meta-analysis. Hang on in there!

Important note
Remember, *don't try to calculate this*. There's no need to do this longhand any more – we'll show you how to do this in Excel (like we did with the measures of central tendency) overleaf.

COUNSELLOR	NUMBER OF SESSIONS	SESSIONS SQUARED
1	12	144
2	14	196
3	16	256
4	14	196
5	13	169
6	15	225
7	18	324
	$\Sigma X = 102$	$\Sigma X^2 = 1510$

Table 2.3.22

MEAN

$$\overline{X} = \frac{\Sigma X}{N} = \frac{102}{7} = 14.571$$

VARIANCE

$$s^2 = \frac{\Sigma X^2}{N} - \overline{X}^2$$

$$= \frac{1510}{7} - 14.571^2$$

$$= 215.714 - 212.314$$

$$= 3.40$$

STANDARD DEVIATION

$$s = \sqrt{3.40} = 1.84$$

Standard Deviation is a measure of how tightly all the scores in a sample range are clustered around the mean. Tight bunching results in a relatively small SD while a sample with a greater variation produces a larger SD. For example, the standard deviation of the ages 45, 43, 49, 42, 47 is 5.74 while that for 25, 62, 23, 29, 67 the standard deviation is 43.74 yet for both the mean is 45.

A useful application of standard deviation statistics in social science research has been through the concept of *effect size*. Effect size is a way of quantifying the effectiveness of a particular treatment relative to another. It has become the statistic of choice when trying to compare results from two or more studies which have used different samples of participants, different methodologies and different measures. In outcome studies (its main use) effect size offers a way of standardising the effect of the treatment groups against any comparison or control groups practically regardless of the measures, samples and methodologies used in the original studies.

In the next chapter we will cover the methodological framework within which outcome studies are organised. We'll also look at the so-called 'gold standard' or randomised controlled trials (RCT) favoured by the National Institute for Health and Clinical Excellence (NICE). However, we think that outcome studies and RCTs are beyond the scope of the book and the resources of the vast majority of readers. We will be introducing these methodologies in order that readers will be able to understand how they are organised, how to interpret the results and to enable critical reading of research, since few studies, 'gold-standard' or not, are beyond critique.

OUTCOME STUDIES/OUTCOME RESEARCH refers to research (usually in the field of medicine or health and social care) in which the outcome of care practices and/ or treatment is investigated. The focus is often on the impact of care procedures on the quality of life of the subjects (efficacy) but it could also include an evaluation of, eg, cost-effectiveness (efficiency).

Calculating the variance and standard deviation using Excel: Are you using population data or sample data?

As we mentioned in the sidenote on p. 64, whether your data comes from a population or sample of measurements will affect the equations used in the calculations.

In real terms this means that if you are using data from a sample of measures, you will use N–1 as the denominator when at the stage of calculating the variance, whereas if you are using data from a population of measures, you will use N as the denominator.

This logic is carried through to using any kind of computerised calculation, whether it is Excel or SPSS. The only slight difficulty is locating the correct calculation for your data. In Excel this is done at the 'select a function' stage as follows:

- Population variance = VARP
- Sample variance = VAR
- Population SD = STDEVP
- Sample SD = STDEV

If you want to check the actual equations being used by the program, click 'Help on this function' at the bottom of the 'Insert function' pop-up box.

Calculating the variance and standard deviation using Excel

Calculating the variance – using the data from the worked example on p. 65

After you have entered your data as shown in the box 'Calculating the mode, median and mean using Excel' on p. 56, except at step 4, type the word 'variance' into the box:

- Click on 'insert' on the toolbar
- Choose 'function' from the dropdown menu
- A pop-up box titled 'Insert Function' will appear
- Type 'variance' into the search box at the top
- Select 'Statistical' in the 'Select a category' box
- Click the 'Go' button. Your screen should now look like the one illustrated on the right
- Select 'VARP' (we have explained why in the note on p. 64 and the box on the facing page) from the 'select a function' box and click 'OK'
- Click OK on the next screen ('Function Arguments') and the variance will be inserted into the cell you chose, as illustrated in the second diagram on the right. Remember to round the values up or down

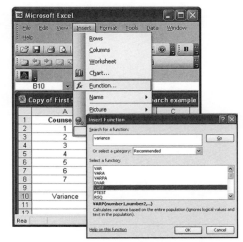

	A	B	C	D
1	Counsellor	Session		
2	1	12		
3	2	14		
4	3	16		
5	4	14		
6	5	13		
7	6	15		
8	7	18		
9				
10	Variance	3.387755102		
11				

Calculating the standard deviation

After you have entered your data (see above) except at step 4, type the words 'standard deviation' into the box:

- Follow steps 2-4 above
- Type 'standard deviation' into the search box at the top
- Select 'Statistical' in the 'Select a category' box
- Click the 'Go' button. Your screen should now look like the one illustrated on the right
- Select 'STDEVP' (we have explained why in the note on p. 64 and the box on the facing page) from the 'select a function' box and click 'OK'
- Click OK on the next screen ('Function Arguments') and the SD will be inserted into the cell you chose, as illustrated in the bottom diagram on the right. Remember to round the values up or down

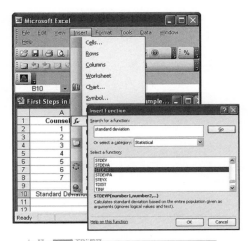

	A	B	C
1	Counsellor	Session	
2	1	12	
3	2	14	
4	3	16	
5	4	14	
6	5	13	
7	6	15	
8	7	18	
9			
10	Standard Deviation	1.840585532	
11			

Distributions

The term 'distribution' has already cropped up in the previous chapter. We need to have a much deeper understanding of what a distribution of scores *is* because an understanding of certain types of distributions is at the root of understanding all statistics.

We would like to start off with an example that all readers could relate to, but no one draws graphs in 'everyday life' so it's difficult to think of an 'everyday example'. We'll use height (as in 'Jim is 5ft 10ins') as our example for this section, since we all have some height and we all understand the simple issues involved. This example will also serve the purpose of introducing some of the issues behind research methods and, although we'll not be making too much of that now, we'll be returning to these issues soon.

Let's say we want to find out the mean (average) height of people in Britain. 'All the people in Britain' is then the *population* we wish to measure. (We're using the term *population* here statistically, not demographically – see later in this chapter on p. 72.) There is only one way to do this and that is to measure the height of all the people in Britain then calculate the mean. Now that would clearly be impossible, or at least not worth the effort. So what should we do? A statistician would say that the best that we could do would be to *estimate* the mean height of people in Britain. In other words, in the absence of being able to measure the height of everyone in Britain and take the mean, we're going to have to do something that will give us a close enough guess. How do we do this?

Most readers will know that the way to do it is to measure the height of a few British people in the hope that they are *representative* of British people in general. Then we can calculate the mean of this small, hopefully representative, group with the expectation that the mean will be near enough to the national mean to suit our purpose. In this way, we will have *estimated* the national mean.

We decide to follow this procedure and so we measure the height of twenty people and calculate the mean. We also decide to represent these heights that we've collected graphically. If you've read Chapter 2.3, you'll know that this sort of data is best drawn as a *histogram*. We start by counting the number of people at each height interval (in feet and inches) as follows:

> **HELP!**
> If you find it difficult to grasp what follows, don't panic. Take some comfort from the fact that we include these chapters on quantitative research for good reason. They are here because it is important to understand the basic building blocks of quantitative research when working with people. If you don't get at least a rudimentary grasp of these methods, you stand a chance of wasting your time and that of your participants.
>
> Also, we want to acknowledge that research involving human participants is complex and requires sensitive, respectful application of techniques. We think this can only be done if the researcher has a grounding in these techniques so that they can apply them with respect. You may like to read on regardless, in the expectation that all will fall into place as you go along, or leave it for a day or two before re-reading it.
>
> We appreciate that some people have real difficulties with numbers and if this way of thinking still doesn't suit you, yet you want, or have to work with quantitative data, in extremis, you can revert to 'cookbook mode' and follow the steps like a recipe.

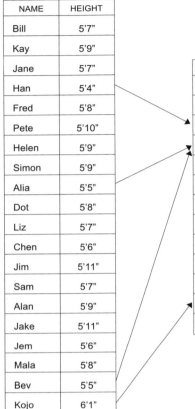

NAME	HEIGHT
Bill	5'7"
Kay	5'9"
Jane	5'7"
Han	5'4"
Fred	5'8"
Pete	5'10"
Helen	5'9"
Simon	5'9"
Alia	5'5"
Dot	5'8"
Liz	5'7"
Chen	5'6"
Jim	5'11"
Sam	5'7"
Alan	5'9"
Jake	5'11"
Jem	5'6"
Mala	5'8"
Bev	5'5"
Kojo	6'1"

Table 2.4.1 Measuring, counting and tabulating height in a sample of 20 people

HEIGHT	FREQUENCY
5'2"	
5'3"	
5'4"	I
5'5"	II
5'6"	II
5'7"	IIII
5'8"	III
5'9"	IIII
5'10"	I
5'11"	II
6'0"	
6'1"	I
6'2"	

You can see how each person's height becomes a tally in the second table, from Hannah, the shortest, through Alia and Bev, up to Kojo, the tallest. This second table shows the *frequency* with which each height occurs within our group of twenty people. This is the way we generated Table 2.3.3 on p. 48.

The histogram we have drawn (Chart 2.4.2) is a 'frequency distribution'. It is called a *distribution* because it is a graphical representation of how the twenty heights in our table are spread or *distributed* across the scale of heights from 5ft 2ins to 6ft 2ins (these are just the limits we have chosen on our graph). The term *frequency* is used because it charts the number of times (the frequency with which) each height interval occurs in our sample. The histogram is, in logical terms, made up of building blocks, each one representing one person and their height measurement. So we can see where each of the twenty people measured actually is in the distribution if we draw it as a series of blocks. We do this next to illustrate the way a frequency distribution works – you would never want to do this when presenting real data.

You should be able to fill in the missing names in

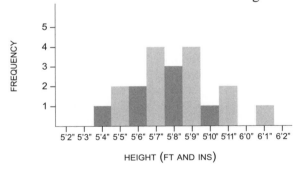

HEIGHT (FT AND INS)

Chart 2.4.2 Histogram of the distribution of the height of 20 people

Note

If we calculate the mean following the formula on p 54, we find that the mean height of our small group is 67.95 ins, or 5ft 8ins rounded up to the nearest inch. You could also work out the median and mode to test your knowledge.

the histogram on the right. Whenever we take a measurement and represent it in a histogram we can always 'find it' there, so to speak, in the same way as we can 'find' Sam's height measurement in this histogram. This is because all of the measurements can be found in what's known as the *area under the curve*. We can see this in the histogram in the margin (Chart 2.4.3) if we imagine that the mid points on the top of the bars of the histogram have been joined together to make a curve. We have done this by hand in the illustration – the shaded portion is the area under the curve. The corner bits left out tend to be cancelled out by the extra corner bits included.

For small numbers, as you can see, the curve looks jagged and uneven, which makes it difficult to use as an indication of the overall shape of the distribution. The term 'area under the curve' makes much more sense for large frequency distributions of hundreds of measurements. Such distributions lose their jagged edges and begin to look much more like curves. This is illustrated in Chart 2.4.4 and if we continue the process for the whole population we get to Chart 2.4.5.

This area under the curve *can* be used in calculations, but it's not really necessary to understand why or how at this stage. We're only showing it here so that you can understand how this demonstrates a further and much more useful feature of a frequency distribution, namely that since all of the measurements in a frequency distribution can be 'found' in the area under the curve, we can quickly answer questions such as 'How many people are taller than 6 ft?' (going back to Charts 2.4.2 and 2.4.3: answer = 1), or 'How many people are shorter than Fred?' (answer = 9). This feature has only limited use in a small group, but if the small group really *is* representative of the whole population, then the proportions, or percentages, of people taller or shorter than a particular height will hold true for the population also.

So if five out of twenty people are shorter than 5ft 7ins in our representative group (see Chart 2.4.3), we can expect the same proportion of the population of Britain in general to be

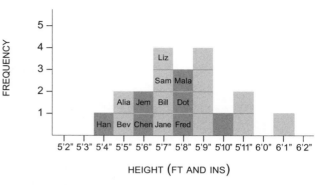

Chart 2.4.3 Illustrating the location of individual measurements in a frequency distribution

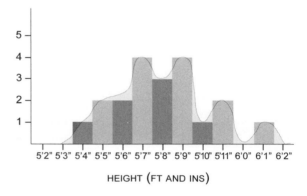

Chart 2.4.4 Illustrating the area under the curve

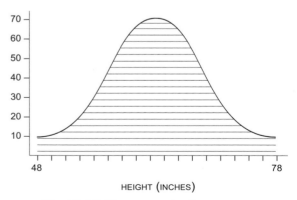

Chart 2.4.5 The area under the curve

shorter that 5ft 7ins, i.e. one quarter of the population of Britain is shorter than 5ft 7ins. By the same token a reader at 5ft 10ins would know that they are taller than three-quarters of Britons.

A social work related example might be to find out how many clients are seen, on average, by a social worker in a typical week. We could start by a taking a small group of British Association of Social Workers (BASW) members and counting how many clients they saw in a typical week. We could then draw the frequency distribution and work out the mean. If our small group was representative, we could assume that our data was a close enough estimate of BASW members in general. We could then make statements about the average number of clients seen by BASW members: for example, 50% of BASW members see 'n' number of clients per week.

The next tasks are, firstly, to find out what samples and populations really are and, secondly, to find out just how to take a *representative* sample.

Populations and samples

So far we've looked at the general techniques of collecting our measurements and presenting them in meaningful and attractive ways. The contexts in which the measurements are made are vitally important for three reasons:

1 as we have already learned, the context helps us understand the power of the measure (i.e. whether our measure is nominal, ordinal, interval or ratio)

2 the context helps us ensure that our measure is valid and tells us how reliable it needs to be

3 it's the context that directs us to a particular part of the world to collect our measurements

So now it's time to ask ourselves the question 'What are we collecting this information for?' There are many reasons for collecting data, but, with respect to quantitative data this book will concentrate on just two rather broad purposes for its collection:

1 taking measurements to describe one circumstance, or identifiable whole group of circumstances for a report or case study. A good example of this would be recording client numbers and demographic details (age, gender, ethnic origin, etc.) for the annual report of a social work service or agency

2 taking measurements so that we can make general statements about a larger group of people or circumstances than the one we have used. So, although in a study to evaluate the effects of counselling we might have taken measures from twenty students at one particular college, we want to be able to *generalise* our findings to all students at that college or all students in the country

What separates the above two examples is that the first deals with a *population*, the second, a *sample*. Here are the definitions and some further examples:

Population: The total number of people, objects, events or measurements sharing one or more features.

Examples

People: all the patients of a health centre, all the people aged under sixteen in Britain, all the approved social workers in the British Association of Social Workers (BASW)

Objects: all the baked-beans produced by Heinz in the week beginning 11/1/08, all the cars in Europe, all the copies of this book

Events: all the reported road accidents in Wales in 2007, all the occupational therapy sessions in any NHS hospital, all the responses a particular therapist could ever possibly make in any counselling session

Measurements: the heights of all the people in Britain, the ages of all of the members of BASW, all the lengths of all the pieces of string in the world

Sample: Simply a part of a population. Specifically, any part of any population specified by the person taking the sample.

Examples

People: the first twenty patients that walked through the door at a health centre last Tuesday morning

Objects: the baked bean tins selected at random by the AcmeFood Quality Control Department during the week 11/1/08

Events: two road accidents seen on holiday in Wales in 2007

Measurements: the heights of the twenty people used in the example on p. 70

Some things now become obvious from the above examples:
- that populations and samples are largely what you make them. They are defined and manipulated by the researcher
- that whilst some populations are real and finite (i.e. all of the patients of a particular health centre), some are conceptual, virtual, imaginary or infinite, e.g. all the responses a given therapist could ever make in any counselling session
- that some real populations, though finite, are difficult or impossible to measure, e.g. the lengths of all of the pieces of string in the world
- that there are many different ways in which we can arrive at a sample from any given population. We will look at this in some detail later in this chapter
- most importantly for the budding researchers amongst you, when

we start seeing *possible measurements* as populations, we open up a whole new area of potential in the way we treat measurements as numbers

When to use a population: If the population is small and discrete (well defined) then it's best to use the population, rather than a sample. So, if you are writing an annual report for a speech therapy service, it will be appropriate to use the population of measurements, e.g. all the clients who used the service in the year of the report.

When to use a sample: If the population is large and difficult to access, you will have to take a representative sample and then *generalise* your findings to the population as a whole. So if a large professional organisation were to ask you to find out what their members in private practice charge, you would have to take a small sample of members to ask, then generalise your findings to the whole population of members.

The point of much quantitative research is the *generalisation* of findings from the *sample* to the *population* from which it is drawn.

If we define our population as all the heights of all the people in Britain, that means that our range of measurement goes from 0ft 0ins to very tall (it's one of those populations that it's impossible to measure). That's the population of measurements. Now any sample of heights we choose to take (like the heights of the people in our small group, or the *sample* of twenty on p. 70) is then just a very small part of the distribution of the frequency of occurrence of the *possible heights* that people in Britain can be.

Note
You can select an appropriate method of sampling when you read through the various methods later in this chapter.

HELP!
You may want to go into 'cookbook mode' at this point if what follows confuses you even after a couple of reads-through. Join us again for the 'Representative samples – what they are and how to get them' section on the next page.

Chart 2.4.6 Illustration of the location of our sample in the population

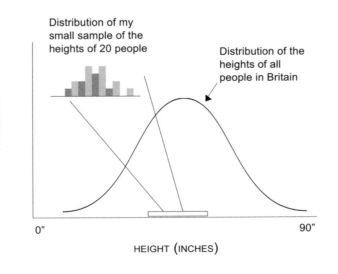

Distribution of my small sample of the heights of 20 people

Distribution of the heights of all people in Britain

FREQUENCY

0"   90"

HEIGHT (INCHES)

Chart 2.4.6 above illustrates this, although it would not be possible to draw it to scale – the curve for the population would go off the page! It's important to understand that the large curve is a hypothetical distribution since we have not, cannot, and never will be able to, measure the heights of all the people in Britain. If you're at the 'So what?' stage by now, here's the punch line.

Statistics enable us to let our *real* sample average 'stand in' for an *imaginary* average from a population that's impossible to measure – but only if we've taken every possible step to ensure that our sample is *representative*.

The crucial thing to understand here is that all measurements themselves belong to a population of possible measurements. The heights of the twenty people in our small sample are just twenty examples of all of the heights that people in Britain can possibly be. We can liken it to taking photographs while on holiday. Holiday snaps 'represent' the places you saw, the people you met, the fun you had. They are, literally, 'snapshots', frozen moments from all of the possible moments in that holiday. The photographs are the 'measurements' – the whole holiday is the population of 'possible measurements'. So when possible measurements are themselves seen as populations of measurements, all the *real* measurements we can make in a research study become part of the huge range of possible measurements that we've defined as the population. We can have then:

- *a sample of participants in our study* (nurses, therapists, students, clients, passers-by, members of the general public or whoever), and
- *a sample of their responses or measurements* (height, professional ability, rating on an anxiety scale, opinions about what works in helping, or whatever)

So when we say that a sample must be *representative*, not only do the people we measure have to be a representative sample of people, but the measurements that they yield must be a representative sample of possible measurements. We would not, for example, measure the heights of the people in our sample whilst they were standing on tiptoes, wearing shoes or stooping. If we didn't take such precautions, we would have taken either an unrepresentative sample of heights or a representative sample of the heights of say, stooping people, which would be no use at all in our quest to estimate the mean height of people in Britain.

Representative samples – what they are and how to get them

A representative sample is one that contains within it all the essential characteristics of the population from which it is drawn and in the correct proportions.

Note
A good online free resource to help you with sampling is Alison Galloway's workbook at <www.tardis.ed.ac.uk/~kate/qmcweb/scont.htm> retrieved on 02/03/2010

An example of this is when pre-election pollsters search for the parliamentary ward that most closely mirrors the features of the nation as a whole. They hope that because the chosen ward contains all the essential characteristics (those that affect voting behaviour) of the nation, in the correct proportions, the result declared in the chosen ward will predict the national result.

Similarly, in our attempt to estimate the average height of Britons we are hoping that the sample of twenty people in our study contains all the essential characteristics (those that affect height) of the population of Britain.

How do we obtain a representative sample? Whilst it is true to say that it is not easy to get a 'cast-iron guarantee' that a sample is representative, we do know that statistical procedures are quite forgiving if we fall short of perfection. The aim is to be as correct as possible in our sampling procedure so that, although we know we are not perfect, we can put ourselves beyond criticism. In other words, we should be able to demonstrate that we did the best we could given the circumstances. How do we do this?

There are several sampling techniques that can be used in different circumstances to get the best possible sample. Our decision will be based on what we are trying to achieve in terms of:

- *validity and reliability*: if we are doing a small project for professional training at our place of work, we would not go to the same lengths as we would if we were doing government-funded research into the effectiveness of music therapy.
- *expense and convenience*: good sampling takes time and costs money. Even our government sponsors may not want to fund our attempts to get that *perfect* a sample.
- *the research method we are employing*: for example, surveys require different sampling methods from experimental studies.

All the following methods can yield a representative sample given the right situation. Some are more difficult (or impossible) to do properly under some circumstances, e.g. we *couldn't* have taken a random sample of the population of Britain. A sample is unrepresentative if some error has crept in and the sample is said to be *biased*. Statisticians can calculate some kinds of error (random errors) quite easily and include allowances in statistical procedures for a certain amount of random error (they know that data collection is a fallible process). Researchers then try to include as many random methods in their sampling as possible so as to take advantage of this feature of statistical tests.

Random sampling
Description: The sample is selected by chance with each member of the population having an equal chance of being selected.

Method: Assign a unique number to each member of the population then select numbers at random. If the population is small, write the names or numbers on paper and then draw like a raffle until the desired sample size is achieved. If you have a large group you can generate random numbers online.

Example: All clients who attended the Drug Rehabilitation programme in 2007 were given a number and then twenty were drawn from a hat to take part in a post-treatment study.

Systematic sampling

Description: Each member of the population has an equal chance of selection, as in the random sample, but the sample is chosen systematically according to a fixed method (or *system*) rather than by chance.

Method: The members of the population fall in a natural order or are put in an order before a proportional sample is taken, e.g. one in every 100 (this is called the sampling ratio), then a random starting point is chosen. The starting point is chosen at random between one and, in this case, 100.

Disadvantage: If there is some unsuspected regularity or rhythm in the order, an error or *bias* will be introduced.

Example: All 2,650 first-year students enrolling at the university were arranged in order of age. A sample of 100 was required, so a number between 1 and 26 was chosen (19) by using a random number generator (see margin note). Then every twenty-sixth name was chosen from the list until 100 had been chosen, starting at number 19.

Stratified sampling

Description: In many situations the researcher will have some knowledge of the characteristics of the population. In stratified sampling, this knowledge is put to use. Each known characteristic of the population (age, sex, ethnic origin) is a stratum from which cases are sampled.

Method: Use your knowledge of the population to look at the proportions for each stratum, e.g. 54% males, 46% females, 20% aged under twenty, 34% aged between twenty-one and forty, 46% aged over forty. Then sample randomly from each stratum in accordance with these proportions. (This is known as a *stratified random sample*.)

Advantage: If information about the strata is accurate and the sampling is properly done, this method delivers the most representative sample with fewer possibilities of bias or error.

Example: In a survey designed to improve careers service publicity, the college looked at its student population and found the following proportions in the following strata: 59% female, 41% male, 11%

Note

There are several ways to generate random numbers 'automatically' online. Basic generators of lists of integers include <http://www.random.org/integers> (retrieved 02/03/2010) or more sophisticated configurable ones with tutorials, eg, <http://www.randomizer.org/form.htm> (retrieved 02/03/2010). Put 'random number generators' into an Internet search engine and choose one that meets your needs.

It is possible to generate random numbers in Microsoft Excel, but there are bugs in certain versions of the software and we recommend the use of online generators for simple sets.

declared disabled, and various proportions in different ethnic minorities. The researcher then took a random sample of 200 from the 5,000 students so that 118 were women (59% of 200), eighty-one men, twenty-two self-declared disabled, and so on throughout the ethnic groups.

Cluster sampling

Description: This relies on the existence of natural groups such as houses, blocks of flats, streets, people in a family, children in a classroom. A cluster sample is one in which a set number of cases is sampled from each cluster or naturally occurring group.

Method: Take a naturally occurring cluster that is relevant to your situation, then select from it at random the number of cases you require.

Example: In order to discover attitudes towards the hospital occupational health service, a sample of ten staff is taken at random from each department in the hospital. Note: if we were doing this on attitudes towards a college careers service and were choosing ten students at random from each course in the college, care must be taken to ensure that the same people are not chosen twice, i.e. that the course groups do not overlap.

Convenience or opportunity sampling

Description: Not really a bona fide sampling method, just what most people do most of the time. It has been said that the social scientist's choice of sample is largely dictated by *convenience*. That's why so many psychology experiments are done on psychology students ... they're convenient. Much small-scale research is conducted on passers-by (because the *opportunity* is there) rather than going to the trouble of using a proper sampling technique.

Method: Choose whoever is convenient whenever you have the opportunity.

Advantages: It's cheap and should not be ignored. Nearly all sampling has an element of convenience and opportunity about it. Absolutely proper sampling is really expensive in time and money.

Disadvantages: Truly horrendous risks of bias. If you have a biased, unrepresentative sample, then you cannot generalise your results. This would render useless most research since the aim is to be able to generalise from the sample to the population.

Example: A psychologist wanted to study conformity but, to avoid the time and expense of a random sampling method, she used her undergraduate psychology students. Her findings could later be criticised for telling us little about conformity in the general population because psychology undergraduates may not be representative of 'ordinary' people.

Note

All of these methods can be combined in order to get the right balance between precision and convenience. As mentioned above, all sampling in the real world contains an element of convenience, but most stratified, cluster and systematic samples contain an element of randomness or chance too.

Example of choosing a sampling method

Imagine we are commissioned by a fictitious professional body – National Association of Helping Professionals (NAHP) – to find out how much their members charge. What sort of sampling would you use? You would have to take the following steps:

1 you would need access to the NAHP membership file. Even though NAHP have asked you to do this study, you should consider the ethical and possibly legal issues in using the membership list (see Chapter 3.2, 'Researching Ethically')

2 there are several things you could do to protect the confidentiality of members, e.g. deal with membership numbers rather than names

3 a random sample would be possible by using a random number generator to select from the list of membership numbers. This would not be the best method though, because there is still a chance that your sample may be biased. For example, members in the south east may charge more than members in the north of England. Your random sample may not get the proportions of members in these geographical clusters right

4 cluster sampling would be better, using, e.g. postcodes to group members into areas. You could then take the right proportions of members from each geographical cluster at random. This would make sure that the proportions of the membership as a whole, in each region, were accurately reflected in your sample

5 you might consider getting even more sophisticated if you wanted to ensure that each professional section (nursing, social work and counselling) within NAHP (these would be strata) gained proportional representation in your sample. There is a problem here, though, because an individual member can be in more than one division

6 you might then decide, for convenience, that your geographical clusters according to postcodes are as far as you can go, given the time and effort involved in disentangling any strata in the population from the membership list

Note
Talk over issues of confidentiality and security of data with your research supervisor and issues of privacy and data protection with NAHP.

The normal distribution

You may have noticed that some of the distributions illustrated in this book have the appearance of a symmetrical 'bell-shaped' curve. If you happened to be in the habit of going around getting samples of measurements of natural events in the world and plotting them as curves you would find that this bell-shaped curve kept cropping up over and over again. It seems as though this shape is a natural property of some distributions of measurements.

It is also possible to obtain this shape *theoretically* if we assume that the measure is derived from *many small factors acting at random*. This shape is called the 'normal distribution' curve. It is

Note

In short, the normal distribution demonstrates that many everyday measures contain a fair amount of random variation since it was originally a description of the distribution of random variation. This unsurprising 'fact' allows us to make assumptions about the distribution of anything which contains a lot of random variation.

Note

We realise that the way height is determined is actually much more complicated than this, even at the level of genetics, but hope that the example will work in an everyday sense to explain the effect of many randomly acting variables. The normal distribution is a *theoretical* distribution of probabilities of effects of randomly acting variables. We can't actually measure them or their effects.

Note

In statistics, variables that contribute to a measure that pushes the mean higher are likely to be called 'positive' factors and variables which contribute to a measure which pushes the mean lower are likely to called 'negative' factors. In cases where we look at human characteristics it might be important to avoid such value-laden terms, ie, associating being taller with a 'positive' value, and being smaller as being 'negative'.

generally assumed that the normal distribution theoretically matches the process by which things actually come about in the real world.

The normal distribution curve is important not only because it seems to describe events in the natural world but also because it describes the distribution of probabilities that certain things might happen. It is used in this way, as a *probability distribution* by statisticians, as the basis for some powerful statistical procedures. Although these procedures are beyond the scope of this book, it's important to know *how* we get a normal distribution so that we can appreciate *why* we keep on seeing this shape over and over again in the data we collect and plot. Also, we will explain shortly how the standard deviation can be used to split up the normal distribution into handy standard chunks.

An example of a normal distribution

A normal distribution is what we get when a large number of random variables are influencing a measure. In order to demonstrate how this works, we'll go back to our 'height of people in Britain' example. You may have noticed that the shape of the distributions on pp. 71 and 74 follows the bell-shaped normal distribution curve. This is because the distribution of heights of humans is approximately normal. That is to say many of us have a height not that far from 'average', a few are noticeably shorter or taller and even fewer are very short or very tall.

How does this come about?

- height is determined by a whole host of factors (or *variables*) – some inherited, some as a result of upbringing, e.g.
  - inherited factors – height of your mother, height of your father, height of your maternal grandmother, height of your paternal grandmother, etc.
  - 'upbringing' factors – your mother's diet whilst she was pregnant, her health whilst she was pregnant, whether you were breast-fed, your diet as an infant, childhood diseases, etc.
- each one of these factors may affect your height in a such a way as to make you taller, or in a way that makes you shorter
- each one of these factors is independent of each other – the height of your paternal grandmother does not affect your diet during infancy
- whether any factor (for example, how tall your paternal grandfather was) contributes to making you taller (maybe he was 6ft 6ins) or shorter (maybe he was only 4ft 6ins) is determined by chance, i.e. at random
- we now have all of the ingredients for a normal distribution: a large number of factors exerting a varying effect on the outcome; each acting independently, and each acting at random

It is easy to show how this actually makes a normal distribution –

you can do this demonstration yourself with four coins.

Let's suppose that an individual's height is determined by many factors acting at random. Each factor can be represented by a coin with an equal chance of exerting its effect in such a way as to make you taller (heads) or in a way to make you shorter (tails). If we limit our example to considering four factors (four coins) A, B, C, and D, then an individual's height will be the result of how many 'taller' factors (heads) and how many 'shorter' factors (tails) they end up with out of four.

The tallest individual, then, is one with four 'taller' factors (heads), the shortest with four 'shorter' factors (tails) and an individual of average height has two heads and two tails.

Now we need to look at how likely it is that a given individual is going to be tall, average height or short. This is done by working out how many ways there are of arranging our four factors into tall, average, short and so on. You can follow the logic with four coins of your own if you wish:

- the tallest individual is one having all four coins heads up. There is only one way of obtaining four heads. Similarly there is only one way of obtaining the shortest individual – four tails
- there are, however, four different ways of getting a taller than average individual with three heads and one tail, as shown in the margin. Similarly there are four different ways of getting a shorter than average individual with three tails and one head
- there are, then, following this logic, six different ways of getting two heads and two tails – the average height individual

Now, if we plot these numbers of different ways against the number of heads we will have the beginnings of a normal distribution.

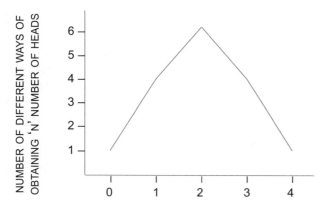

'N' NUMBER OF HEADS FROM 4 COINS

Chart 2.4.7 Distribution of the number of different ways four coins can land heads or tails

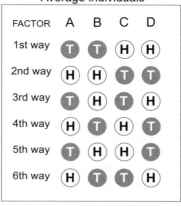

The larger the number of variables, the smoother and more bell-shaped the curve will be – and remember a normal distribution is the result of a large number of variables acting in this way. We can see this bell shape emerge when we use just ten variables:

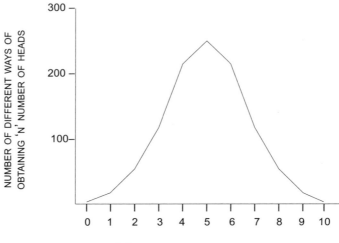

Chart 2.4.8 Distribution of the number of different ways ten coins can land heads or tails

This is what is known as a *probability distribution*. We've just described the likelihood of coins landing heads or tails – the probability of four heads, three heads or two heads landing each time four coins are tossed.

What use is the normal distribution?

The normal distribution is a model distribution and can be treated as a template, if you like, for many of the measurements that you may make even though you have not collected enough to plot a smooth curve. The rough rule of thumb is to ask yourself, 'Is the variable I am measuring likely to be the result of many independent factors acting at random?' If the answer is 'Yes' then the normal distribution and its features may be of use to you. Its main useful features are (i) its symmetry and (ii) the fact that the area under the normal curve (see p. 71) can be divided up in a standard way by using the standard deviation (see p. 65), which we will look at shortly.

Symmetry: We know that the normal distribution is symmetrical about the mean – the mean divides the area under the curve into two equal halves.

The standard deviation (SD): The SD measures off from the mean constant proportions of the area under the curve of the normal distribution. The following example explains its use:

Note
This distribution of probabilities is also reflected in real life. You can test it if you like by taking your four coins, tossing them a few hundred times and plotting the results. There is a strong chance that your real distribution will approximate the one illustrated above.

Note
It's important to understand and remember that the SD measures off the same proportions of the distribution in a symmetrical distribution. We illustrate how useful this is in the example.

Example

The Midshires Drop-in Helping Agency (MDHA) has decided to evaluate its work as a part of the annual audit required by some funding bodies. This year they have decided to use a simple measure called the General Contentment Quotient (GCQ). This measure – simple to administer and complete – has 10 items (questions). MDHA chose it for the following reasons:

- it is simple to administer – only a 20-minute training is needed
- it is non-invasive and easy to complete
- it is a general scale. This is important since the MDHA provides a wide range of services from benefits advice through debt counselling to psychological therapies. The directors wanted a single measure to evaluate the service as a whole
- it has been widely used, tested and standardised:
  - it is normally distributed
  - scores of -2SDs (two standard deviations below the mean) and lower are strongly associated with factors such as high suicidality, high risk of problems with alcohol and drug use, and high incidence of petty crime
  - Scores of - or +3SDs (three standard deviations, either below or above the mean) are strongly associated with incidence of severe mental health problems. The +3SD scores are associated with manic episodes and unrealistic expectations verging on delusional states (life can't be *that* good)
- the main funding bodies approve its use

The questionnaire asks participants to put a cross on a ten-point scale for each of ten items, e.g.

> **How much do you enjoy life at the moment?**
> Not at all | | | | | | | | | | Complete enjoyment

The properties of the GCQ distribution are as follows:

    mean   = 55
    median = 55
    mode   = 55
    standard deviation = 11

The fact that the mean, median and mode are all the same value indicates that the distribution is symmetrical. This goes some way to confirming that it is indeed a normal distribution. When plotted, it looks like the graph on the right.

Note
There is no 'General Contentment Quotient'. In order to generate a short example to illustrate our points, we have brutally simplified the type of measure that might be used. There are a few non-specific measures which can be used in general outcome studies of this low-key type. In Chapter 3.5 you can read about this kind of research in action in a real-life setting.

Note
'Standardised' means that the test in question has been administered to large numbers of people in the general population and the results compared with other similar or equivalent PSYCHOMETRIC instruments. After a considerable amount of data has been collected, it is possible to make valid and reliable predictions (within certain confidence limits, see Chapter 2.5, pp 92-3) regarding what different scores on the test are likely predict.

PSYCHOMETRIC Defined in margin overleaf.

Note
A test with simple items like this can be easily translated, or read to the client or completed by anyone with limited literacy by having the scale explained to them (and the only response required is an 'x').

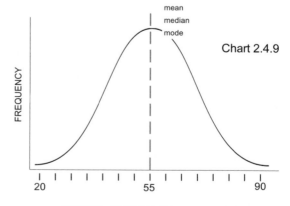

Chart 2.4.9

The first level of usefulness of the standard deviation lies in the fact that it measures off constant proportions of the area under the normal curve. This means that whatever the values are on the axes of our distribution, whatever the measures are that we've been collecting, the proportions remain the same. If we want to use the case example of the GCQ we must transpose this information onto the curve illustrated in the graph at the bottom of the previous page, as follows – as we measure 11 (the SD of the CGQ) from the mean in each direction, the proportions of the area under the curve stay the same.

Chart 2.4.10

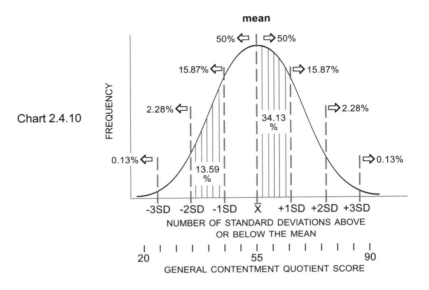

Note

In this idealised example we have created a fictitious PSYCHOMETRIC TEST, a fictitious helping agency and, naturally, fictitious results. In particular you might ask what proportion of the general population are 'at risk' from suicide, alcohol and drug problems, petty crime and severe mental health problems?

How would you find out, and how would you know the figures were trustworthy?

PSYCHOMETRIC TEST Any standardised procedure for measuring aspects, qualities or attributes of mental functioning including, eg, sensitivity, memory, 'intelligence', aptitude, personality, or symptoms.

In popular press parlance we can see that out of 1000 people tested, the GCQ predicts that,

- twenty or so are almost certain to be experiencing severe problems leading to greatly increased risk of suicide, alcohol or drug problems and/or be involved with petty crime
- one or two people will be suffering from severe mental illness
- between 1 SD above and below the mean we can assume that most people measured (around 7 out of ten) will be reasonably content with their lives

The usefulness of this feature is that we don't have to plot any scores to work this out, since we know the rules:
- 50% of the curve above (or below) the mean
- 15.87% of the curve above (or below) one standard deviation
- 2.28% of the curve above (or below) two standard deviations and
- 0.13% of the curve above (or below) three standard deviations

In terms of GCQ scores, we know the mean (55) and the SD (11), which means that when we count in 11s above or below the mean we find, as illustrated on the graph above:

$$55 + 1DS = 66 \qquad 55 - 1SD(11) = 44$$
$$55 + 2DS = 77 \qquad 55 - SD(2 \times 11) = 33$$
$$55 + 3SD = 88 \qquad 55 - 3SD(3 \times 11) = 22$$

Policy issues

This helps us understand the meaning of an individual's score. Someone coming in to the centre with a score of 25 would be in the bottom 1% of the population in terms of contentment with their lives and much more at risk in terms of general mental health issues. Another person drops in for legal advice with a score of 43, which suggests that whilst they need help, they are only just outside the mainstream in terms of life contentment.

Using the scores of people as they come to the agency asking for help raises policy issues:

- if the agency has a waiting list, should people with a lower score be seen earlier?
- should people with a very low score, e.g. 25 or lower, be referred to specialist mental health services?

Is the service necessary?

The SD also helps us understand the type of people in general who come in to the MDHA for help if we know their scores on the GCQ. The agency will get an idea of where in the population they are drawing their clients from. How discontent with life are their clients compared with the average person? This might raise issues for the funding bodies, since they might not think it a good use of grants if clients of the agency have a contentment quotient within the top 50% of the population (above average contentment) before they receive a service. How far removed from 'average contentment' should the typical client of a service be before funding is considered?

Is the service effective?

The original purpose of the research was to present evidence for the effectiveness of the service the agency provides to include in the annual audit and report. MDHA decided to ask all people who dropped in to access help to fill in a GCQ questionnaire (the pre-service measure). They then asked all clients to fill in the same questionnaire at the end of their last session or service meeting (the post-service measure). Of the 347 new clients in 2008, 198 completed both pre- and post-service questionnaires. The results were collated and a simple calculation revealed the following:

- pre-service mean score on the GCQ = 31.6
- post-service mean score on the GCQ = 40.3

Note
This method of data collection has advantages – it is reasonably convenient – and disadvantages – the data will be drawn from a sample that is unrepresentative in at least two ways: first, it comes only from those willing to take part (which might bias the scores), and second, some people may drop out of the service before they fill in the second questionnaire.

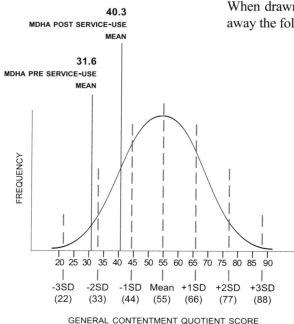

40.3
MDHA POST SERVICE-USE
MEAN

31.6
MDHA PRE SERVICE-USE
MEAN

FREQUENCY

20 25 30 35 40 45 50 55 60 65 70 75 80 85 90

-3SD   -2SD   -1SD   Mean   +1SD   +2SD   +3SD
(22)   (33)   (44)   (55)   (66)   (77)   (88)

GENERAL CONTENTMENT QUOTIENT SCORE

Chart 2.4.11

When drawn on the GCQ distribution curve we can see straight away the following features of the data:

- the people dropping in for help were, on average, in the part of the population with the lowest contentment scores, at risk of higher suicidality, drug use problems and mental health problems, and therefore in greater need of help
- after they had used the service their quality of life had improved to bring them closer to the average person

The data will help the directors and funders decide whether the service is needed. It looks as though the people using the service come from the groups in society with the lowest quality of life. And it also is clear that the service improves people's perception of their contentment with life.

It would help if we could have an idea of how much improvement in the test scores would indicate an effective service.

Standard deviation and effect size

We have explained that the power of the SD is that it is standard – it provides a measure that is independent of the scales or tools used. So when we want a standardised unit to compare results across different methodologies, measuring tools and sample parameters (the number and type of subjects, the number and type of treatment sessions), the SD fits the bill.

It forms the basis of one of the ways we can calculate 'effect size' (see Chapter 3.1), which itself is another statistic that helps us compare results across different studies as above.

$$\text{Effect size} = \frac{\text{post-service mean} - \text{pre-service mean}}{\text{standard deviation}}$$

$$\text{Effect size} = \frac{40.3 - 31.6}{11} = 0.79$$

As we explain in Chapter 3.1, p. 250, an effect size (based on 'difference') of 0.8 or more can be thought of as a 'strong' effect. In other words, the service provided by MDHA would be deemed effective. This is the kind of 'evidence' the funding bodies require.

It should go without saying that real life is not as simple as the idealised example we have created for the purposes of simple illustration.

Note

We explain the principles of effect size and look at it in connection with meta-analysis in Chapter 3.1. Here we simply use one of the effect size calculations to illustrate the usefulness of the standard deviation in understanding the effect of a helping service in terms of outcome.

QUESTIONS TO CONSIDER
- *Given that data collection is always a balance between convenience and economy on the one hand and accuracy and validity on the other, do you think that there are corners that should never be cut in research?*
- *If so what are they?*

In Chapter 1.1, pp. 7-8, we said that this book

[does] not assume that research is *only* done by researchers or students with a research-based assignment to do as part of a training course. ...You may have started this book with the idea that your work situation required some data collection and report-writing skills, but that research was not appropriate. If you're reading this chapter you may have changed your mind or become fascinated by the research side of things. We argue that health and social care professionals should be numerate and 'research method literate' in order to claim back some lost social science territory and fight their corner, rather than be pushed to the margins of research whilst the behavioural *scientists* get on with the *real* business of *proving* which approaches are *effective*.

The italics in the previous sentence are there to remind us of the key words that grant-makers and fundholders look out for when planning what services can be afforded in the financial year. Our message is simply that research methods are here and accessible. Health and social care practitioners can go to the ball too and, if armed with a little understanding and some common sense, you will not turn into a pumpkin when midnight comes. Projects, studies, investigations, research, scientific investigations, call them what you will, all have to meet certain quality criteria before they are deemed acceptable. In order to plan and carry out an acceptable piece of work, or judge the work of others, you will need an understanding of research methods.

Throughout the current chapter we will refer to all studies, projects, etc. however small or grand as 'investigations' or 'studies', whichever fits best in the sentence. Please don't be either overwhelmed or insulted by the terms. In this chapter we shall be looking at the basic methods that you might employ for your investigation. You may want to know:

- how one thing affects another thing, e.g. does the distance between the helper and client affect the degree to which the client likes the helper?
- whether two things go together, e.g. does the self-esteem of

Note

In this book we cover the rudiments of what are known as 'descriptive statistics', up to and including standard deviation. We are assuming that if you want to do research which involves more complex *inferential statistics*, you will need to move on to a specialised statistics book and possibly a book covering more complicated research methodologies.

The first two of the following books have served many thousands of social science researchers very well over the years, and the last one is a very recent well-reviewed text. More advanced students will get recommendations from their tutors and research supervisors.

Clegg, F (1983) *Simple Statistics: A course book for the social sciences.* Cambridge: Cambridge University Press.

Rowntree, D (2000) *Statistics without Tears: An introduction for non-mathematicians.* London: Penguin.

Yang, K (2010) *Making Sense of Statistical Methods in Social Research.* London: Sage.

For an introduction to inferential statistics on the computer software Statistical Package for the Social Sciences:

Pallant J (2007) *SPSS Survival Manual: A step-by-step guide to data analysis using SPSS for Windows (Version 15).* Buckingham: Open University Press.

You will also find free tutorials online if you enter 'SPSS Tutorials' into a web search engine.

clients increase as the number of counselling sessions increases?
- patterns of things or events, e.g. does the non-verbal behaviour of the client change from the start of a session to the end?

Each of these investigations could require a different method of research. You may get some ideas from reading other research papers, or have done some low-key research already. There are qualitative research methods that would be appropriate to investigating the questions above and we will come to these later in the book. Just now, we are going to concentrate on methods using measurements and statistics. This chapter will deal with the basic ways of organising an investigation:
- experimental methods
- case studies
- longitudinal and cross-sectional studies
- correlation techniques
- observational methods (including surveys)

Each has its advantages and disadvantages, but it is necessary to understand each before deciding which is the most appropriate. We hope you're confident enough by now to not be put off by the jargon words. Whilst it's not absolutely essential that you learn them, it does make life easier when 'talking research'.

'Things' and 'people'

Note
Whilst the word 'subjects' is still the dominant vocabulary at the scientific end of the quantitative social science research continuum, it is considered a little hard-line in the more humanistic zone of health and social care, counselling and psycho-therapy research. It is more acceptable to call the people that we are collecting data from, 'participants'.

Before we go any further, it could be an idea to stop talking about 'things' and introduce the term 'variables'. Simply put, a *variable* is anything that can vary, change and be measured. All the things mentioned so far in this chapter are capable of varying and being measured, so they could be classed as variables.

At the same time we'll stop talking about 'people' that we might use in our investigation to collect results from and start talking about 'subjects'. Human volunteers in quantitative social science investigations are mainly called *subjects*. How these subjects are obtained and organised will depend upon the type of investigation you are conducting, as will what you measure and how you measure it.

Hypotheses: Stating your ideas

Before you start your investigation you must have had an idea of what you wanted to investigate and possibly of what you might expect to find. In research, the idea you have or the prediction you might make is called a hypothesis. We have looked at this notion from a slightly different angle in Chapter 2.1, 'Asking Questions'. For example, you might have the idea that ingestion of alcohol affects driving ability, or you may think that clients undergoing person-centred therapy are more articulate than clients undergoing play therapy.

A hypothesis is simply a formal statement of your idea or theory, made in a way that allows it to be tested. In the examples above, the ideas cannot be really tested in their current form; they need to be turned into testable hypotheses. In order to do this we have to make a statement or prediction about something that is measurable. Researchers call this *operationalising*. It simply means stating something in terms of the operations or measurable events which make the 'something' in question happen. So, for example, 'Ingestion of alcohol affects driving ability' is imprecise (it doesn't say how much alcohol) and unmeasurable (how do you measure 'driving skill'?). It could, however, become 'There will be a difference in the number of cones knocked down on a set driving test between subjects who have drunk four units of alcohol and subjects who have drunk no alcohol.'

Similarly, 'Clients undergoing person-centred therapy are more articulate than clients undergoing play therapy' is also unmeasurable (how do you measure how articulate someone is?). It could be written as 'Clients undergoing person-centred therapy will use longer words than clients undergoing play therapy.'

As you can see, the ideas have now been stated in a form in which they can be tested, and a conclusion can be drawn as to their accuracy. In effect they are now hypotheses. But you might have guessed that there would be more than one type of hypothesis. In fact there are two hypotheses which we need to propose at the outset of our investigation.

Imagine that you have read your horoscope for today which suggests that 'things are going to become clearer'. Now that you have read the beginning of this chapter and fully understand the concept of operationalising statements, you may decide that your horoscope has come true. The astrologer has made a prediction (a hypothesis) and you have observed that it is correct, possibly because you believe in astrology and wanted it to be accurate. The same may be true if you were to only formulate one hypothesis for your investigation. Either consciously or unconsciously you could work to make it come true, to influence the results so that they support your hypothesis. The way to avoid this is to formulate two hypotheses that basically say the opposite of each other. The purpose of your investigation is then to obtain results that will indicate which of the two hypotheses is correct or proven.

The null hypothesis (H_0)

The null hypothesis is the hypothesis that says that the most likely outcome of your investigation is that nothing will happen, no effect will be detected and any detectable effect will be the result of pure

HELP!
You may get a 'these people are barking mad' feeling as you read about hypotheses. Part of the problem is that the 'real' explanations of the null hypothesis are statistical and beyond the scope of this book. Such explanations can sound a bit silly when simplified and taken out of a statistical context. We are trying to tread the difficult line between giving enough of an explanation without going too far into statistics versus making it so simple that it's incorrect. You can skip this section if the explanations seem superfluous to your needs (but we recommend you stick with it).

chance rather than anything systematic that you've done. If the null hypothesis is proved, statisticians say that the results of the investigation are 'not significant' (this will be explained later in this chapter on pp. 92-3 & 98). Examples of null hypotheses are:

- there will be *no difference* in the number of cones knocked down on a set driving test between people who have drunk four units of alcohol and people who have drunk no alcohol
- there will be *no difference* in the length of words used in a session by clients undergoing person-centred therapy and clients undergoing play therapy

At the beginning of your investigation, you will be expected to state the null hypothesis. This is just *one* of the *two* hypotheses you will have to state in order to ensure that one of them is proven. The null hypothesis is important in itself because it's the one calculable point in probability statistics, i.e. the point at which chance exerts its effect. As we move away from this 'chance' point, the likelihood that the results are due to something you've done increases until you can say with some confidence that the null hypothesis is not proven.

If the null hypothesis basically says that *nothing will happen* other than by chance, then the other hypothesis says that *something will happen* and not by chance but as a result of some systematic intervention by you, the investigator.

The alternate hypothesis (H_1)
This is the other hypothesis, which states that something will happen as a result of the investigation. It's the hypothesis we've looked at a page or two ago and just to refresh your memory, our two examples were:

- there will be a difference in the number of cones knocked down on a set driving test between people who have drunk four units of alcohol and people who have drunk no alcohol
- clients undergoing person-centred therapy will use longer words in the therapy session than clients undergoing play therapy

This alternate hypothesis is the one that is most familiar and logical to people new to research. As researchers, we are looking for sufficient evidence to be able to accept or prove the alternate hypothesis. If the evidence is strong enough, statisticians would say that the results are *significant* (see pp. 92-3 & 98). The story doesn't end there, since to complicate matters just a little bit more, there are two types of alternate hypothesis.

1 One-tailed alternate hypothesis
As we have already said, any alternate hypothesis states that there will be a significant effect. However, sometimes we can say more

than just that *there will be an effect*. We may have an idea about the *direction* of that effect. By direction we mean that not only would you expect there to be a difference between the length of words used by clients undergoing person-centred therapy and play therapy but that you expect the person-centred therapy clients to be the ones who use longer words. So you are predicting *not just any difference* either way but a *specific difference*. You can say what *direction* the effect will take.

The hypothesis we used in our second example above, 'clients undergoing person-centred therapy will use longer words than clients undergoing play therapy' is an example of a *one-tailed alternate hypothesis,* since it not only says that there will be a difference in the length of words used, but also that it is the person-centred therapy clients who will use longer words.

2 Two-tailed alternate hypothesis

This type of hypothesis simply states that there will be an effect *and no more*. You state this sort of hypothesis when your idea or theory cannot make a prediction about the direction of any effect, i.e., whether the effect will make something specifically *more* or *less* than (or faster or slower than, etc.) something else. So we would state that there will be a difference between two things without saying which of the two things would end up the greater.

The other hypothesis that we used as our first example above, 'there will be a difference in the number of cones knocked down on a set driving test between people who have drunk four units of alcohol and people who have drunk no alcohol', is an example of a *two-tailed hypothesis* since it predicts a difference only. It doesn't say whether the people that have drunk the alcohol will knock down more or fewer cones than those who have not drunk any.

At this point two or three questions occur to most people.

Question Why are they called one- and two- *tailed* hypotheses?
Answer Because the two extremes of a normal distribution are called the 'tails' of the distribution. The calculable statistical point at which things are caused by chance alone occurs at the centre of a particular, normal distribution used by statisticians. To the left of this point lie all the probable results indicating one direction of the effect in question and, to the right, results indicating the other direction of the effect. In our example using alcohol and driving skill, the point in the middle of the distribution is the point of no difference (the null hypothesis) and the two tails of the distribution indicate fewer cones knocked down by the drinkers to the left and more cones knocked down by drinkers to the right.

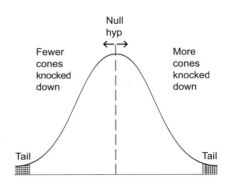

Chart 2.5.1

If your prediction states the direction of the effect, it is predicting that the results will be found in only one of the tails and, if you can't predict the direction, your results may be found in either of the two tails. Hence 'one' and 'two-tailed' hypotheses.

Question Which is better, one- or two-tailed hypotheses?
Answer Neither is really better than the other, it just depends upon which is best suited to your investigation. If you think that your idea or theory leads you to 'know' which way your results are likely to turn out, choose a one-tailed hypothesis. If you are not so sure, stick to a two-tailed hypothesis. There is a statistical reason for assuming that you can be more confident in your results if you have chosen a one-tailed hypothesis. This is simply because any statistical procedure you employ only has to look in one half of the distribution illustrated above if your hypothesis is one-tailed. Any more explanation than this is beyond the scope of the present book.

Question Can you have a one- or two-tailed *null* hypothesis?
Answer No. We hope this answer is obvious from the answer to the first question above. There is only one null hypothesis.

'Significant' effects

The results of any investigation can, in statistical terms, have a quality known as 'significance'. Rather than merely looking for an effect, it is customary to look for a significant effect. If, for example, we had carried out our alcohol and driving skill investigation and found that the drivers who drank alcohol knocked over an average of fifteen cones whereas those not drinking alcohol knocked down only an average of fourteen: there is obviously a difference in performance, but the difference is quite small. We cannot be *confident* that the difference is actually due to what we did in the investigation. The difference is so small it could just as easily be due to chance. If we did the experiment again, we might not find the same pattern of results. We would describe a result like this as being *non-significant*.

If the difference was larger, we might be more confident that this was due to what we had done in the investigation rather than to chance factors. If we repeated the procedure, we would probably obtain similar results. In this case we would describe the effect found in the results as *significant*. When we think the effect in the results is large enough to be regarded as significant we can reject the null hypothesis (which states that there will be no effect and any small effect is due to chance) and accept the alternate hypothesis. If the difference is very small, the opposite happens and we accept the null hypothesis.

Note
Here we are using the term 'significance' to explain the concept. It has a particular use when talking about the levels of probability required to actually define what is significant and what is non-significant. In our example in the text, we hope it is clear that a study showing such a small difference would not be taken as proof of the alternate hypothesis at a *common-sense level*.

Establishing the level of significance statistically helps us make the leap from anecdotal evidence (or proof) to a more scientific level of evidence (or proof). One swallow doesn't make a summer, nor does one cone mean that four units of alcohol critically degrade driving skill.

Of course, we are making this study and these results up. Please don't drive after drinking any, let alone four units of alcohol!

Note
We talk about being *confident* that an effect is due to our manipulation of variables, and you will see that statistical significance is sometimes referred to as a *confidence limit* or *confidence interval*.

Question: How do I know when an effect is large enough to be significant?

Answer: A very good question, and one that we wish we didn't have to answer right here. This is the key to all research and, frustratingly enough, the way we have planned this book, the answer lies outside our brief. Whether an effect is large enough is a statistical decision, in fact the quality we're after is called '*statistical significance*'. It is based on the likelihood or probability that the results are due to chance.

This chance factor is worked out by a statistical test (there are several to choose from covering different types of research methods) which will tell you whether the effect is large enough or not. The test will base its decision on things like the number of measurements you have taken, what scale of measurement (nominal, ordinal, etc.) you have used and what research method you have chosen. The process is a little like consulting an oracle – you ask a question ('Is my effect large enough?') and the test pronounces its decision after looking at the evidence.

Question: What do you mean by 'the likelihood or probability that the results are due to chance'?

Answer: Probability statistics are really beyond the scope of this book (see margin for suggestions), but to answer the question simply, it's up to you, the researcher, to select a level of chance that you have faith in. Would you be satisfied that there was a 50/50 chance your results might be due to chance? Probably not, since that's only as good as tossing a coin. There are conventions to guide you – most social science researchers are satisfied with a chance of less than one in twenty that their results might be due to chance factors. In probability terms, this is referred to as the *0.05 level of significance*.

If you want or need to take your research to the point of deciding upon the statistical significance of your results, you will have to get another book (see margin) which lists and details the statistical tests that can give you the decision, i.e. the effect either is or is not large enough.

You may, of course, not need or want to take the analysis of your data so far. You may be happy to use a rule of thumb or just look at the face validity of any effect you may have obtained. Whilst this may be perfectly acceptable for some applications, it is very easy to be deceived by numbers. It may be worthwhile taking your results to someone with some research experience who may be able to give you a ballpark estimate. In the meantime, part of the answer is covered in the explanation of one- and two-tailed hypotheses on pp. 91-2. We also briefly look at statistical significance as it applies to the different research methods later in this chapter.

A little more on significance, confidence limits and probability

The statistical significance of a result, the confidence with which we view it, are two *ways of talking* about the same thing: how scientists try to answer the question 'What are the chances of that happening?' In particular, since we arrange our hypotheses in terms of chance (read what we have written about the null hypothesis on pp 89-90) we are trying to figure out and explain how likely it is that the results are due to chance or whether it is likely that they are due to the manipulation of the independent variable. These concepts of significance and confidence are a way of creating a scale of *how* likely that is.

In everyday life, people tend to use rules of thumb (heuristics) to make judgements on the likelihood of something happening. We do it all the time but human beings' rules of thumb are prone to influence from personality traits, learning and contexts. So how do you *feel* about the chances of the following?

- the weather forecast predicts a 20% chance of rain in Manchester today
- a person is told they have an 80% chance of recovery from cancer after chemotherapy

Expressed as chances, the above figures tell us that there is a 1 in 5 chance of rain in Manchester. Would you take an umbrella? And if there is a 4 in 5 chance of recovery, how optimistic might the person in question feel? Immediately we can appreciate how vulnerable our responses to probability are to our personality, previous experiences and context.

On the next page we continue in the margin with an example. In the meantime, ask yourself how *confident* you are (expressed as a percentage, eg, 75% confident) that your helping practice brings tangible benefits to your clients/patients.

.../ continued opposite

Experimental method

An experiment is, in principle, a very simple thing to organise. This is true whether the subject matter is physics, chemistry, medicine or, for that matter, social work. All you have to do is arrange things so that all variables are kept the same or eliminated, except one. This one variable is allowed to change or, rather, is *manipulated* by the researcher and the effects are observed. Then any effects can be said to be due to, or caused by, the changes in the manipulated variable. Note we said *in principle*. In practice, it's a different thing altogether.

Variables and the experimental method

The variable that we manipulate is called the *independent variable*. The variable that we measure any changes in as a result of manipulation of the independent variable is called the *dependent variable*. The variables we wish to eliminate or keep constant are called *extraneous variables*. The attempt to eliminate or keep extraneous variables constant is called *controlling* the extraneous variables.

Example To continue our 'Does alcohol affect driving skill?' example, the *independent variable* (IV) is the amount of alcohol ingested by our subjects. We manipulate this quantity. The *dependent variable* (DV) is the number of cones knocked down (our measure of driving skill). We control *extraneous variables* by keeping the car and the driving skill course constant.

Confound it!

If we fail to control variables, they run the risk of becoming *confounded*. A confounded variable is an extraneous variable that is left free to vary in a *systematic* way, i.e. a way that makes it impossible for us to separate its effects from the effects of the independent variable. Let's suppose we had used two cars in our alcohol and driving skill study and one of the cars had faulty steering. If the faulty car was used for one condition only (it doesn't matter which one) then it would be a confounded variable. We wouldn't know whether it was the car or our manipulation of the independent variable which was responsible for any difference in performance. The use of standard control procedures (below) will eliminate or reduce this possibility.

An experiment is the only research method that can reveal a cause and effect relationship between the independent and dependent variables. There is no mystery to this, it's simply because if only one thing has changed (the IV) then it must be responsible for changes in the DV. The key to this is control. We must be sure that nothing else has changed. This turns out to be more difficult than it seems, and the real skill of constructing an experiment is controlling all the *relevant* extraneous variables (there's no point in controlling variables which have no bearing on your subjects) without affecting the independent variable or the integrity of your measurements.

Control! Control!

The main difference between social science research and physical science research is that people's behaviour is not as consistent and well ordered as the behaviour of atoms and molecules (notwithstanding the predictions of quantum physics). Many of the methods of control used in the social sciences have evolved to take this feature of humankind into account. The 'human factor' causes certain well-defined effects which need specific attention as follows.

1. Order effects

Practice effect: This is where your subjects need a little time to get used to whatever procedure you are asking them to perform. So if you are asking your subjects to complete a rating scale for service provision, a simple solution would be to give them a couple of 'dry runs' or *practice trials* before you start recording the results. This has the further benefit of making sure they understand the experimental procedure properly.

Fatigue effect: Fairly obviously the opposite effect to practice effect where subjects' performance tails off towards the end of a series of trials.

Order effect: This is an effect which is literally caused by the order in which the conditions in your experiment occur. For example, if we wished to investigate the effect of the students' gender on ratings given to their practice videotapes by counselling course tutors, there might be an order effect, since we would have to show either a male tape first or a female tape first, which in itself might colour their perceptions of subsequent tapes.

Controlling order effects

Order effects are controlled by either *randomising* the order of presentation of items or conditions, or *counterbalancing* – a technique where you would give half your subjects the conditions A and B in the order AB, while the other half of your subjects would have the conditions in the order BA. These techniques distribute the order effects evenly across both (or *all* if there are more than two) conditions.

2. Primacy and recency effects

Psychologists have discovered that people can remember the first and last things in a list (names, events or whatever) much better than things in the middle. These effects are called primacy and recency. They affect our everyday lives and have an effect in

continued ...

Would you stop gambling at 4 tosses, 6 tosses? The decision is a personal one, reflecting something of our personality, financial resources and views on the trust-worthiness of bar staff. *So how can research in the social sciences ever get past this personal (and therefore highly variable) decision?*

Choosing a significance level

Two types of mistake can be made: a *type 1 error* is when we claim that an effect is due to the independent variable when it is really due to chance. This sometimes happens when we choose a significance level that is too close to chance. A *type 2 error* is when we set a significance level that is too rigorous, ie, we think that the effect is due to chance when it is really due to the independent variable.

To solve the dilemma, interested parties agree to a loose convention. In social science research it is convention to adopt a significance level of 0.05. This is expressed as $p \leq 0.05$ which means that the probability that the results are due to chance is *less than or equal to* 0.05. If you look back at the table of probabilities of a fair coin landing heads a number of times in succession opposite, you will see that the 0.05 level is around a run of four tosses. Take a coin from your pocket or purse and toss it a few times to get a sense of how possible this is (you'll be surprised).

Significance levels other than the 0.05 level can be chosen, eg, if you want to challenge a well-established theory with your research, it is convention to choose a significance level of $p \leq 0.01$ or *1% probability* or *one chance in one hundred*. You wouldn't want to challenge a well-established theory unless you were *very confident* your results were not due to chance.

Note

Although technically primacy and recency are the quintessential order effect, they are typically dealt with separately in their own category.

experiments too. They are well-defined types of order effect. Watch out for them in observations (you may forget what happened in the middle of the observation) and questionnaires (subjects tending to opt for the first and last choices offered) as well as experiments.

Controlling primacy and recency
Since primacy and recency are a special type of order effect we would control for them in the same way as for other order effects, by employing randomisation or counterbalancing.

3. Experimenter effects
This is an example of the 'human factor', where the experimenter themselves can affect the results in certain ways. Firstly, by having expectations about the outcome of the study and unintentionally passing these on to the subjects; secondly, the experimenter's personality, demeanour and appearance can affect the results, e.g. subjects will behave differently for an officious white-coated experimenter than for a laid-back, scruffily dressed experimenter.

Controlling experimenter effects
This is achieved by keeping the experimenters' personality as neutral and as constant as possible. Use only one experimenter, who should present a neutral persona and always use standardised instructions. Standardised instructions are written down, checked to make sure they make sense and are comprehensive, then read out to each subject. *Example* 'Thank you for agreeing to take part in this study. Its aim is to ... I will be pleased to answer any questions you may have about the study afterwards. Can you see the equipment on the desk? When you see the red light go on, please talk into the microphone until ... Do you understand the instructions? Are you ready?'

4. Demand characteristics
When people are put in novel or unfamiliar situations they try to work out what's going on, the 'rules' of the situation if you like. These are called the demand characteristics of the situation. Subjects in experiments (or any kind of investigation for that matter) try to guess and respond to these demand characteristics of the experiment. Human beings are not passive participants, far from it, they are trying to figure out what the experimenter wants them to do, and to behave accordingly. The subjects pick up subtle clues from the experimenter and the environment.

Controlling demand characteristics
This effect wreaks havoc in medical treatment trials, e.g. where a new treatment method is being compared with a placebo. The only way to get rid of it is to do what's known as double-blind trials (see

Note
A particular form of experimenter effect where the experimenter's expectations about the outcome can be subtly communicated to the participants has historically been known as *experimenter bias*. More recently, experimenter bias has been receiving considerable attention in health and social care research as 'researcher allegiance'. Mick Cooper (2008: p 48) defines this as 'The tendency for researchers to "find" results that support their own beliefs, expectations or preferences.' He goes on to explain that outcome studies have to be adjusted for this factor in order to make meaningful comparisons in meta-analyses.

Cooper, M (2008) *Essential Research Findings in Counselling and Psychotherapy: The facts are friendly.* London: Sage.

Note
Demand characteristics were first high-lighted by Orne (1962). All researchers would do well to consider his words (p 777):
'... the subject agrees to tolerate a considerable degree of discomfort, boredom, or actual pain, if required to do so by the experimenter. Just about any request which could conceivably be asked of the subject by a reputable investigator is legitimized by the quasi-magical phrase, "This is an experiment," and the shared assumption that a legitimate purpose will be served by the subject's behavior.'

Orne, MT (1962) On the social psychology of the psychological experiment: With particular reference to demand characteristics and their implications. *American Psychologist 17*, 776-83.

p. 116) where not only do the subjects not know what condition they're in, the experimenters don't know either. That way the experimenters can't pass on, even unwittingly, any subtle clues about the preferred outcome of the study.

5. Random error

If you think that you've kept one step ahead of the effects listed above, you've still got to control for random errors. These are much less predictable than the systematic effects above and less amenable to control. Random errors cannot be eliminated but they can be reduced and their effects spread evenly around all of the conditions so that they affect each subject equally. Temperature fluctuations, lighting variations, decor, what happened on the way to the laboratory, will all exert their random effect on the results.

Controlling random error

We must make sure that they don't (a) get too large (there might then be too much random error to see any real effect) or (b) turn into systematic errors. These are errors which systematically vary and might distort the result, for example, by running all the subjects in condition A on a bright, crisp, sunny winter morning and all subjects in condition B on a dark, cold winter afternoon. We would then have a confounded variable, i.e. one muddled up with our independent variable. We must also make our procedure 'tight' to reduce the overall level of random error by appropriately high degrees of control throughout.

Hypotheses and the experimental method

Experiments are mainly looking for differences between conditions, but if you are using more than two conditions you will, in the most simple of cases, be looking for a *trend*. Your alternate and null hypotheses should reflect this.

Null hypothesis: 'There will be *no difference* in the length of words used by clients undergoing person-centred therapy and clients undergoing play therapy.'

Alternate hypothesis: 'Clients undergoing person-centred therapy will use *longer* words than clients undergoing play therapy' (one-tailed). Or: 'There will be a *difference* in the length of words used by clients undergoing person-centred therapy and clients undergoing play therapy' (two-tailed).

If you have more than two conditions, your hypotheses should mention the fact, explicitly or implicitly, by talking about increases, decreases or referring to a *trend* in the results:

Null hypothesis: 'There will be no change in speech therapist performance as the ambient noise level in the consulting room increases.'

Experimenter effects, demand characteristics and power

In Chapter 3.2, p 259 we look at power issues and dual roles, concentrating mainly on qualitative research methods. Here we are describing, in a fairly matter-of-fact way, how interpersonal and structural power play out in quantitative research. Using 'scientific' language like 'experimenter effect' and 'demand characteristics' tends to conceal the fact that we are really looking at, and trying to limit, the influence one person with a lot of relative power (the experimenter) has over a person with relatively little power (the subject).

The famous obedience studies performed by Milgram (1963) – where the 'experimenter' dressed in a white coat persuaded the subjects to administer electric shocks – and Haney, Banks and Zimbardo (1973) – where students acted out increasingly submissive and violent roles as prisoners and guards respectively – were as much about the power vested in the role of experimenter as they were about human obedience.

The role of researcher in social science research is a powerful one and we must work hard to limit the influence implicit in the role. Do not underestimate it, nor think that you need not take steps to deal with it. The different methodologies use different techniques to deal with this considerable challenge. Quantitative methodology uses instrumental techniques to deal with it as we have seen, but it is difficult to control for something you have no awareness of. The best starting point for dealing with power issues in research is to engage with them on a personal level.

Milgram, S (1963) Behavioral study of obedience. *Journal of Abnormal and Social Psychology 67*, 371-8.

Haney, C, Banks, WC & Zimbardo, PG (1973) A study of prisoners and guards in a simulated prison. *Naval Research Review 30*, 4-17.

Alternate hypothesis: 'There will be a decrease in speech therapist performance as ambient noise level in the consulting room increases.' (If you think about it, the prediction of a trend is most likely to be a one-tailed hypothesis.)

Significance and experiments

Since experiments are looking for differences between conditions, we will talk about *significant* differences. A significant difference is one that is large enough for us to be confident that it is not due to chance but to a real, replicable difference. In other words, if we were to take another similar sample of subjects, we would get a similar difference.

One of the main considerations in an experiment is the size of your sample (or samples) of subjects. Because the experimental method employs rigorous control of variables, you will not need as large a sample size as you would in, for example, a correlation study (p. 105). There is a law of diminishing returns when it comes to sample size and experimentation. In most cases your effort will not be greatly rewarded if you strive for a sample size of more than twenty subjects, if you have tightly controlled extraneous variables. A large sample size is no substitute for a well-sampled group of subjects, an appropriate design, and very tight control on the extraneous variables.

Organising your experiment

There are three basic ways of conducting experiments, the main difference being the manner in which subjects are used in or allocated to the different conditions of the experiment.

Question: Is there a limit to the number of conditions I can have in an experiment?

Answer: In theory no, but there are practical limits. The point of having conditions in experiments is to see if there is any *difference* between them. When there are just two conditions this is relatively easy to see and test with statistical procedures. When three or more conditions are used, we would be looking for a trend in the results rather than a difference. It is possible, in advanced research, to have conditions in a grid – like a table, say 3 x 3 or 4 x 4. These grids have exotic names like 'split-plots' and 'latin squares' and they are beyond the scope of this book. For now we will restrict ourselves to (i) two by one (difference) designs, (ii) three or more by one (trend) designs and (iii) two by two (chi-squared or association) designs. These will become clearer as we proceed through the different ways of organising an experiment.

In some cases, one of the conditions will act as a control condition whereby the results obtained become a 'baseline' against which any changes in the dependent variable during the experimental condition(s) can be compared. In the alcohol and driving skill example, the no alcohol condition acts as a control. Now you have to decide which type of experimental method to use. These are called *experimental designs* and you have three basic types to choose from.

1 Repeated measures design

In this design, all subjects take part in all conditions of the experiment. It's called repeated measures because we repeat the measurement of the DV on the same people in both conditions. Statisticians refer to this design as *related measures* because the measurements in the different conditions are related by virtue of being taken from the same group of people. The alcohol and driving skill experiment is repeated measures.

Repeated measures advantages
The most obvious advantage is that this type of design gives the greatest degree of control over subject variables. As the same subjects perform in both (or more) of the conditions of the experiment, the results give a greater indication of the effect of the independent variable on their performance. For example, if a subject had poor eyesight during the no alcohol condition of the experiment, they would still have poor eyesight in the alcohol condition. Similarly, if they were a nervous driver in the first condition, they would still be a nervous driver in the second – and difference in their driving ability can be more readily attributed to the effect of the alcohol. This may not be the case if different subjects were used for the two conditions of the experiment – subject variables such as eyesight, tolerance of alcohol, etc. could affect the results.

The other significant advantage of the repeated measures design is that it requires fewer subjects. If you decide to have twenty subjects in each condition, using a repeated measures design, the same twenty subjects would perform in both conditions. If a design were used which required different subjects in the different conditions of the experiment, you would need forty subjects (twenty for each condition).

Repeated measures disadvantages
To refer back, once again, to the alcohol and driving ability example: if a repeated measures design were used, subjects would perform in both conditions of the experiment. This in itself could cause order effects, i.e. if the same driving test were to be used in both conditions (having done the test once in the first condition) the subject's performance in the second test would be affected by the fact that they have now practised the course. It could be that they perform better because of their knowledge of the course, or they may have

Note
Repeated measure and related measures are two terms for the same thing. Related measures is more often used in statistics, but it means the data has been generated by a repeated measures design.

become tired and irritated and therefore perform worse. If they are not using their own car, they may have become used to the vehicle, again, improving their performance for the second condition. These disadvantages are particularly associated with the repeated measures design, and they must be controlled.

One way to avoid order effects is a technique known as counterbalancing (also known as the ABBA procedure), in which half the subjects perform one condition of the experiment first (condition A), and the other condition later (condition B); the other half of the subjects perform the experiment in the opposite manner (condition B then condition A). Although the subjects will all still suffer from order effects, the overall effect has been balanced out and should not affect the results of the overall group.

The other possible means of avoiding order effects is to randomise the presentation of the conditions. For the current example, the experimenter (the person conducting the experiment) would toss a coin, if it came down heads the subject would perform in the alcohol condition first, if it came down tails then they would perform in the no alcohol condition first. This may not seem like the most scientific of methods, but when you only have two alternatives, tossing a coin is a reasonable rough and ready way of achieving randomisation. Another method is pulling pieces of paper out of a hat. For serious research you might want to use a random number generator.

In some cases it will be impossible to avoid order effects. For example – if you are comparing one therapeutic approach to another – you couldn't submit subjects to one therapy, see if they got better and then submit them to another approach and see if they showed an even greater improvement. In instances such as this, you would require different subjects for the different conditions of the experiment.

2 Matched pairs design

The design is basically an attempt to create a repeated measures design, but using different subjects in each of the conditions. This involves matching the subjects into pairs on the basis of variables that you consider are relevant to the experiment. Each member of the pair performs in one condition of the experiment, and the result from one member of the pair is directly compared to that of the other member. Usually, in order to conduct an experiment using a matched pairs design, potential subjects must be given a pre-test to find someone to match them up with. For example, you may wish to test potential subjects on a driving test and count the number of errors they make. You would then pair two people who had made four mistakes each, another two people who had made five mistakes, and so on.

Note (repeat of note on p 77)
There are also several ways to generate random numbers 'automatically' online. Basic generators of lists of integers include <http://www.random.org/integers> (retrieved 02/03/2010) or more sophisticated configurable ones with tutorials, eg, <http://www.randomizer.org/form.htm> (retrieved 02/03/2010). Put 'random number generators' into an Internet search engine and choose one that meets your needs.

It is possible to generate random numbers in Microsoft Excel, but there are bugs in certain versions of the software and we recommend the use of online generators for simple sets.

Matched pairs advantages
This design gives a reasonable degree of control over subject variables (assuming you have matched them on the appropriate variables) and, as subjects only perform in one condition of the experiment, there are no order effects to control.

Matched pairs disadvantages
The first disadvantage is the need to decide what variables to match the subjects on. Earlier, it was suggested that you could match subjects on the basis of driving ability. However, there are other significant variables that have been ignored, such as body size, metabolic rate, age, etc. that could all affect their tolerance of alcohol, and therefore affect the results.

Even if you do decide what variables to match your subjects on (and are convinced that no one reading your report will immediately decide that you have missed at least three important variables), there is the logistical problem of finding sufficient numbers of adequately matched subjects. This will take a great deal of time and effort and may prove fruitless.

Many books suggest that identical twins are perfect subjects for use in a matched pairs design. Do not spend several years of your life searching for a sufficient number of identical twins. This idea is, to use a technical term, 'Rubbish'. For the most part you will be using adult subjects. It is highly likely that adult identical twins will have different partners, different jobs, different incomes, different experiences and different most-things, and may be no more matched than any other two people of similar age and gender.

Whilst, in theory, a matched pairs design is the preferred choice if a repeated measure is not possible, in practice it is a difficult design to use unless you are striving for the utmost rigour.

3 Independent groups
Quite simply, the name says it all. Different subjects perform in the different conditions of the experiment, with each subject performing in only one condition of the experiment. The two groups are independent of each other.

Independent groups advantages
There are no order effects and there is no need to match subjects.

Independent groups disadvantages
Because completely different people take part in the different conditions of the experiment, there is a lack of control over subject variables. If care is not taken, any difference in the results between the conditions of the experiment may be due to the type of subjects in each condition. For example, in deciding which subjects perform

Note
Matching might sound relatively easy in the example we use in the text, but in health and social care research it is very difficult to know what variables to match subjects on beyond the strikingly obvious. Since matching takes a lot of time and effort and 'wastes' a lot of subjects (if no matches can be found), it is not a hugely popular design and will be almost certainly out of the range of possible designs for beginning and/or practitioner-researchers.

Whilst matching subjects in practitioner research is likely to be more trouble than it's worth, in funded OUTCOME STUDIES it is a respectable way of doing your best to overcome the inherently low power of the independent groups design (see below).

OUTCOME STUDIES/OUTCOME RESEARCH refers to research (usually in the field of medicine or health and social care) in which the outcome of care practices and/ or treatment is investigated. The focus is often on the impact of care procedures on the quality of life of the subjects (efficacy) but it could also include an evaluation of, eg, cost-effectiveness (efficiency).

in which condition of the experiment, if it is simply left to the choice of the experimenter, they may (either consciously or unconsciously) allocate subjects to the conditions in such a way as to influence the results. It may be that the conservatively dressed, neat and tidy, calm and respectable-looking subjects may be allocated to the no alcohol condition, whilst the wild-eyed, boy/girl-racer types, who look as if they drive an XR4 Turbo Egoboost are all allocated to the alcohol condition. It may be that there is a difference in driving ability between the two groups, but this may be due to the choice of subjects rather than the intake of alcohol.

The way to avoid subject variables having an effect on the results is simple. Subjects should be randomly allocated to the conditions (in any previously mentioned experimental method). In theory, this should give a representative mix of subjects in each of the two conditions and eliminate the effect of subject variables. The other disadvantage of the independent groups design is that more subjects are required, but there is no easy way to solve this problem.

4 Chi-squared (χ^2)

This is a particular statistical test that is applied to a particular form of independent groups design where the experimenter is looking for the degree of association between two variables.

Example A college career service asked all its visitors whether they would prefer a male or a female advisor. The results could be tabulated (on the left) in a 2 x 2 table by separating the male visitors' responses from the female visitors' responses.

In a 2 x 2 association table like this we are looking for a diagonal pattern in the results to indicate an association between the two variables like this:

	Male advisor preferred	Female advisor preferred	Total
Male clients	32	21	53
Female clients	14	49	63
Totals	46	70	116

high	low	or	low	high
low	high		high	low

Although chi-squared specifically refers to the statistical test used to tell us if we have a significant association, you do not have to perform the test. There is value in collecting and displaying data in this way since there is a striking visual impression of association when one exists.

Case studies: Bringing a systematic framework

Whilst most research methods require a reasonably large number of subjects, case studies provide an opportunity for far more detailed consideration of a question by restricting the number of subjects used and increasing the degree to which the individuals are studied. For example, we may choose to study a therapeutic method by concentrating on two individual clients from the beginning to the end of their therapy. The report would be largely narrative, i.e. a detailed description of the progress of the therapeutic process. Although most case study research makes use of one or more qualitative methods (see Chapter 2.7) they do have a place in quantitative research too since it is possible to bring systematic elements to the design as we shall see below.

Case study advantages   Case studies provide us with a great amount of detailed information. They are capable of revealing, and concentrating on, any developmental process or the effects of a sequence of events. In a helping setting, the subjectivity of a case study, cited as a disadvantage below, is seen as a distinct advantage.

Case study disadvantages   As the sample size is small, generalisation to a larger population is difficult, if not impossible. You may have deliberately chosen subjects who were not 'typical' anyway. A second difficulty is the analysis of the results. There is not much scope for numerical analysis (see below), but content analysis (see also p. 203) is a popular method of data analysis which acknowledges the various subjective viewpoints.

Systematic case studies

Many people think that when we begin to control some of the complex factors which give case studies their richness, they lose much of their power to inform our work through the elaboration of the experience of one or two individuals. Others, such as Robert Elliott (2002a, b), has argued for some time that systematising some of the elements of case study design brings sufficient scientific sensibility whilst retaining many of the essential human qualities.

Elliott's work concerns the development of a novel mixed quantitative/qualitative design he calls 'Hermeneutic Single Case Efficacy Design' (HSCED) in which he creates a network of triangulating evidence from a number of sources. Whilst this is too sophisticated to drop into at this entry level of practitioner research, it is worth making a mental note, since if you progress to a more advanced course requiring research, it is a design which deserves attention and certainly qualifies for both Stiles' theory-building and enriching (see margin) forms of research.

Note

Case study design is a popular methodology in Masters and first degrees because it is a relatively manageable research project for an individual practitioner. If you intending to progress to higher degree research and are interested in case-studies, we recommend the work of Bill Stiles. He has developed the idea of case studies as theory-building devices, arguing that well-designed qualitative case studies can be considered scientific research. He proposes two purposes of case study research:

- enriching: where data, knowledge and theory can all be enriched by the narrative element of case study research
- theory-building: where complex data from certain case studies can challenge, modify and develop existing theory. See:

Stiles, WB (2007) Theory-building case studies of counselling and psychotherapy. *Counselling and Psychotherapy Research 7*(2), 122-7.

Stiles, WB (2009) Logical operations in theory-building case studies. *Pragmatic Case Studies in Psychotherapy 5*(3), 9-23.

If you are embarking on case study research, we also recommend you register (free) for the *Pragmatic Case Studies in Psychotherapy* journal, where there is a huge range of research available: <http://pcsp.libraries.rutgers.edu/index.php/pcsp/index>

Elliott, R (2002a) Hermeneutic single case efficacy design. *Psychotherapy Research 12*, 1-20.

Elliott, R (2002b) Render unto Caesar: Quantitative and qualitative knowing in person-centered/experiential therapy research. *Person-Centered and Experiential Psychotherapies 1*, 102-17.

Note

Robert Elliott's blog is an excellent source of news views, articles on psychotherapy research and he gives details of schemes for systematic case study design: <http://pe-eft.blogspot.com>.

Longitudinal and cross-sectional studies

These are two different methods primarily concerned with looking at development over time. They approach the problem in different ways by using subjects in a different manner. To illustrate the advantages and disadvantages of both methods we will take the question 'How soon after treatment do most drug users relapse?'

Longitudinal studies

The obvious way to study this question is to find a group of drug users who have undergone treatment and study the same group of subjects over a particular period of time: this would be a longitudinal study. We could interview each subject every month, note whether they have resumed drug use or not, and count how many have resumed each month. Using the same subjects throughout keeps subject variables constant. However, it may be that a realistic period for such a study would be three years, whereas you may wish to have the study completed within three months, in which case a longitudinal study would not be appropriate. Well-conducted longitudinal studies do yield powerful, persuasive data.

Cross-sectional studies

COHORT A group of people sharing one or more common, defining characteristics, eg, an age cohort would be one of people all born in the same year.

A cross-sectional study would also interview former drug users at monthly intervals after receiving treatment but, rather than using the same subjects throughout, different COHORTS of subjects would be interviewed at the same time (one group who had finished their treatment one month ago, another group who had finished their treatment two months ago, etc.). Whilst this would take considerably less time, we have no way of knowing whether one group is comparable with another. Also, circumstances may have changed as the different COHORTS are studied. We can see how social attitudes may change over time, will have various effects on COHORTS of different ages, and may interfere with any conclusions we could draw in a cross-sectional study. We could be looking at attitudes formed fifty to sixty years ago possibly being acted out today.

Design issues

In terms of experimental design, a longitudinal study can be looked at as a repeated measures design, whereas a cross-sectional study would be independent groups. We would need to use this information when writing up our investigation or considering statistical analysis of our data. One feature of the example used is that we might expect our results to show a *trend*, i.e. in this case a consistent difference over time. (For an example of how to display your data from these kinds of studies, turn to the example on p. 51.)

Correlation

So far, we have looked at the experimental method where the independent variable is manipulated and the dependent variable is measured whilst all other variables are controlled. Any change in the *measured* variable is attributed to the *manipulated* variable – a cause and effect relationship. However, sometimes it is not possible, practicable or desirable to conduct an investigation in this way. It may be difficult or impossible to deliberately manipulate a particular variable, or it may be impossible to control other variables that may affect the result. In a correlational investigation, the two variables under study are simply measured and we look to see if there is a relationship between them. A correlation indicates the degree to which two *naturally occurring* variables are related.

Note
By 'naturally occurring' we mean not actively manipulated by the researcher.

There are three basic types of relationship between two variables; one is not better or worse than the others, they are just different:

Positive correlation

One variable increases as the other variable increases.

Example: If we were to get a number of subjects and measure the height and weight of each subject, we would probably find that the taller the subjects, the heavier they are. As height increases, weight increases.

Negative correlation

One variable increases as the other decreases.

Example: We could look at the relationship between the volume of your sound system and the happiness of your neighbours. As the volume of your sound system increases, the happiness of your neighbours decreases.

No correlation

No real pattern to the results.

Example: If we measured the shoe size and intelligence (using an intelligence test) of a group of adult subjects, we would probably find that there was no noticeable pattern in the results. Knowing their intelligence would not give us the confidence to buy the right size slippers for their birthday.

More examples Let's look at the relationship between ice cream sales and deaths by drowning at seaside resorts. If you collect the data and calculate a correlation coefficient (see pp. 107-9), you will find that there is a very strong positive correlation. As ice cream sales at the seaside increase, more people drown (or, as more people drown, so ice cream sales increase).

We cannot, however, say that one has caused the other – simply that they go together. Although we can never prove this, we can make a guess at a likely explanation. In common with many correlations, a third, hidden, variable may be identified that is related to both. One guess may be temperature: so as temperature increases, more people buy ice creams *and* more people go swimming (so more are likely to drown).

Should we find, for example, a positive correlation between income and self-esteem, it would be an error to think that high income *causes* high self-esteem and low income *causes* low self-esteem. It could be that there is a third factor involved and related to both – education, perhaps (i.e. the more education, the greater the income, and the more education, the greater the self-esteem). At this point, you may be thinking of someone that you know who has little money and feels great about themselves. Remember that, as with other techniques in research, correlation depends upon sampling and we are interested in general trends rather than individual cases, so moving data from the anecdotal to the more scientific.

Scattergrams: Showing a correlation as a graph

Having measured some subjects' scores on two variables (usually referred to as variable '*x*' and variable '*y*'), we can get a visual impression of the correlation, the degree to which they are related by drawing a simple kind of graph called a *scattergram*.

Worked example We were interested in the relationship between counselling ability and creativity. Each subject has taken a 'counselling ability test' and a 'creativity test' so we have a score for counselling ability and creativity for each subject. We call the counselling ability score, variable *x* and the creativity score, variable *y*.

Then we draw two axes on graph paper covering the range of scores for each variable, with variable *x* along the horizontal axis and variable *y* on the vertical axis as illustrated in the chart below.

Subject	Score on variable x	Score on variable y
1	100	46
2	122	37
3	113	48
4	145	29
5	98	72
6	122	38
7	133	32
8	140	19
9	122	36
10	106	60

Note

For those of you with a moderate amount of data, you might prefer to use a presentation software like Microsoft Excel to draw your scattergram. We've included a brief guide to using the graphing tools in the Appendix on p 309.

Note

The two forward slashes on the axis tell us that the axis in question does not start in scale at a zero point. Zero would be much further to the left if you look at the values on the axis.

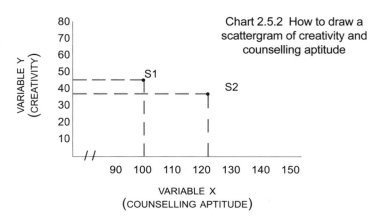

Chart 2.5.2 How to draw a scattergram of creativity and counselling aptitude

Then enter the scores by taking Subject Number 1's variable *x* score (100) and variable *y* score (46) and plotting them as illustrated above using dots or little crosses to mark the spot. Repeat this procedure for all ten subjects and you should end up with a scattergram that looks like Chart 2.5.3.

Now we can see a pattern to these results. Subjects who scored low on variable *y* scored high on variable *x* and vice versa (high on *y* and low on *x*). This pattern is typical of a negative correlation. It's much easier to see a pattern in the results when drawn as a scattergram than it is if you gaze at columns of numbers. The following scattergrams illustrate typical correlations as indicated:

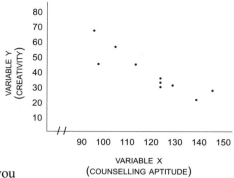

Chart 2.5.3 Scattergram of creativity and counselling aptitude

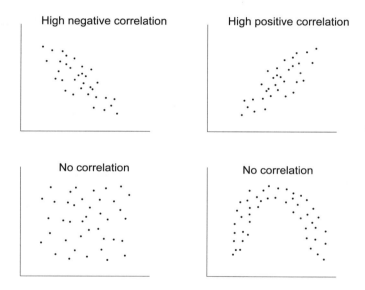

Chart 2.5.4 Illustrations of four scattergrams

If you look again at the last scattergram in the figure above you will notice something unusual. It demonstrates one of the limitations of correlations since there is clearly a relationship between variable *x* and variable *y*, described by the upside-down U-shaped scattergram. However because the slope to the left cancels out the slope to the right, the correlation for such a set of scores would be zero. This neatly illustrates why drawing scattergrams is always a good thing to do in addition to calculating a correlation coefficient.

Correlation coefficients: Defining the strength of the relationship in numbers

If a scattergram gives a visual impression of the relationship between two variables, then a correlation coefficient gives us an indication of both the strength and direction of a relationship as a numerical value.

Correlation coefficients range between -1, through 0, to +1. All the sign does is indicate the direction of the relationship (we explained this above in the scattergrams section). A correlation of 0 would indicate that there is no relationship between the two variables (as in the shoe size and intelligence example). The closer to 1 (or -1) the coefficient gets, the stronger the relationship between the variables until (and this is *very* rare in social science data) at 1 (or -1) we have a perfect relationship.

- a correlation coefficient of .85 indicates a very strong positive correlation
- a correlation coefficient of -.74 indicates a very strong negative correlation
- a correlation coefficient of -.22 indicates a weak negative correlation
- a correlation coefficient of .16 indicates a weak positive correlation

> The number of calculations available depend upon the edition of Microsoft Excel you are using, so don't be put off if only three correlation coefficients are offered where we say you should be offered four. And of course, this number might change in future upgrades.

You may come across correlation coefficients when reading research papers or you may want to calculate one for your data. If you have collected data and wish to calculate a correlation coefficient, we show a step-by-step procedure for calculating one of the most simple using Microsoft Excel below.

Calculating a correlation coefficient using Excel

Using the data from the worked example on p. 106, enter your data

After you have entered your data and put descriptors into the columns (see Chapter 2.3, p. 56) your screen should look like the one illustrated on the right.

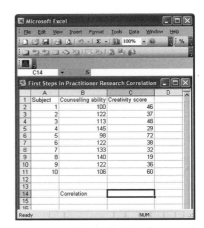

- Click on 'insert' on the toolbar

- Choose 'function' from the dropdown menu. Your screen should now look like the bottom illustration on the right

- A pop-up box titled 'Insert Function' will appear

- Type 'correlation' into the search box at the top

- Select 'Statistical' in the 'Select a category' box

- Click the 'Go' button. Your screen should now look like the one illustrated at the top of the facing page

- You now have to decide which type of correlation calculation you want. Several are available (on Excel you can choose from four, but there are still more available in statistical manuals and on SPSS). Your choice will depend upon many factors which we are not able to cover in this book. For the sake of this illustration we suggest you choose 'CORREL' and click OK

- Another panel will pop up, called 'Function Arguments'
- Enter the cells where your two data sets for one variable (use 'Counselling ability' since it's first) in Array 1, by typing in 'B2:B11' This tells Excel to use the values in the cells B2 through to B11. Then enter the second variable locations (Creativity) into array 2 by typing in 'C2:C11'
- The 'Function Arguments' box will now look like the bottom illustration *on the right*. You will notice that this panel actually gives the correlation coefficient result as -0.883113414
- Click 'OK' and the value will be entered into the cell on your page and it will look like the final illustration below
- Note that the correlation coefficient calculation has returned a negative value

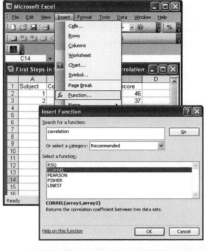

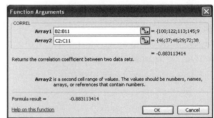

1	Subject	Counselling ability	Creativity score	
2	1	100	46	
3	2	122	37	
4	3	113	48	
5	4	145	29	
6	5	98	72	
7	6	122	38	
8	7	133	32	
9	8	140	19	
10	9	122	36	
11	10	106	60	
12				
13				
14		Correlation	-0.883113414	
15				

Drawing a scattergram is covered in the Appendix on p. 309 where we give a short tutorial on using the graphing capabilities of Microsoft PowerPoint.

Hypotheses and correlation

In a correlation we are looking for a *relationship* between two naturally occurring variables and your hypotheses should reflect this. Other than this, the 'rules' for stating hypotheses are the same as for experiments.

Null hypothesis 'There will be no relationship between counselling ability and creativity.'

Alternate hypothesis 'There will be a relationship between counselling ability and creativity' (two-tailed), or 'There will be a positive (or, if you choose, negative) correlation between counselling ability and creativity' (one-tailed).

In the case of correlation, a two-tailed hypothesis states that there will simply be a relationship, without predicting the direction, whereas a one-tailed hypothesis states that not only will there be a relationship but also whether it is expected to be positive or negative. In the example we have used, a positive correlation would show that as creativity increases, so does counselling ability.

> QUESTION TO CONSIDER
> *The correlation coefficient calculation above returned a value of -0.88.*
> - *What does this tell us about the relationship between counselling ability and creativity?*

Note

We refer to a rough rule of thumb regarding the significance of correlation coefficients as follows:

To be significant at $p \leq 0.05$

• a small sample size of 10 requires a coefficient of around ±.6

• a large sample size of 50 requires a coefficient of around ±.25

However, you can get a good estimate of the probability of your correlation coefficient occurring by chance by putting in your parameters (coefficient and sample size) into an online calculator such as <http://faculty.vassar.edu/lowry/rsig.html>.

Note

We look at the meaning of the levels of statistical significance, eg, $p \leq 0.05$, on pp 93–5.

Note

Observational methods as qualitative techniques are looked at in Chapter 2.7.

Significance and correlation

A significant correlation is one that is large enough that we are confident it is not due to chance but to a real, replicable relationship. In other words, if we were to take another similar sample of subjects, we would get a similar correlation.

In the case of correlation, sample size and significance are related in the sense that if you have a small sample (e.g. 10), you will need a very high correlation coefficient to achieve significance (around ±.60). Conversely, if you have a large sample size (above 50 for example) you will need a relatively small correlation coefficient (around ±.25). A complicating factor is that the larger the sample size, the more difficult it is to get a sufficiently large correlation coefficient.

A correlation coefficient is worth working out even if you have no intention of carrying your work through to the 'statistical significance' stage, since it, like measures of central tendency and dispersion, is telling you something about your data. You can always use a rough rule of thumb to tell you whether your correlation may be due to chance by using the numbers in the paragraph above.

Observational methods

Observations are intended for accurate *description* and then hopefully meaningful *explanations* of behaviour. This method is primarily intended for the study of behaviour in natural settings where an experiment would not be possible or desirable because of the effect it may have on natural behaviour. Whilst the behaviour being observed should be natural and unmanipulated, the simple fact of being observed may itself have an effect on the behaviour of the subjects. As counsellors we know the disturbing effects of having our work observed! There are a number of ways of minimising this and other undesirable effects:

• the subjects are simply allowed to become *accustomed to the presence* of the observers (or their apparatus). This does take time and if you wish to observe behaviour in a specific situation, such as a first counselling interview, then this may not be appropriate

• the observers (or their apparatus) could be *concealed* from the subjects. This would minimise the effects of being observed but would create other problems. Visibility and lines of sight would become a problem, thus restricting the range of behaviour that could be observed, and there is also the ethical consideration of whether the subjects know that they are being observed

• this option is where the observer becomes part of the group that is being observed – *participant observation*. In some ways the study will become more realistic, but the behaviour of the observer may affect that of the other members of the group.

They may also become involved in the process that is occurring, and become less accurate or objective in their description of what is happening, and it is difficult for other observers to verify the observations made by the participant. It would be an extremely difficult study to replicate

Observations are very good for showing sequences of events, and could therefore be thought to be good for showing how one behaviour causes another. But, it should be remembered that there will be a large number of uncontrolled variables in a natural situation, and this will make it difficult to infer 'cause and effect' relationships. It is also worth remembering that observations of this sort require constant description of behaviour. Even if some sort of shorthand code is developed for noting behaviours, an observation will generate a great deal of information, which will have to be presented in some way – if sequences of behaviour are to be shown, it is very difficult (if not impossible) to put this information in mathematical form.

So far we have assumed that the observation taking place is both natural and continuous. It may be that, in order to limit the amount of information generated or to restrict the range of behaviours studied, we have to impose a degree of control over the environment, restricting the range of behaviour studied to pre-determined categories, or sampling behaviour at certain time intervals, rather than monitoring it continuously. Of course there will be advantages and disadvantages to each method.

Controlled or structured observation
If you wished to observe behaviour during counselling interviews, it may be the case that continuous, natural observation would be an appropriate method. However, if you wanted to observe a group session, the difficulties involved may cause you to consider imposing a degree of structure.

Note
Examples of a qualitative approach to this would be non-participant observation (p 165) and ethnography (p 202).

You may wish to control the environment to a degree by holding the session in a particular room because it offers good visibility. This imposition of a particular environment may have some effect on the behaviour of the subjects. It may also be the case that continuous monitoring and a full description of all behaviours is not possible. This requires incredibly fast recording or, if the recording is mechanical, a huge amount of transcription. In any event, you may have to structure your observation using one of the following methods:

1. Event sampling
In this method the researcher has to produce a set of categories of behaviour so, to continue the group session example from above, a list of observable behaviours could be:

Agrees, disagrees; gives information, seeks information; shows aggression, shows support; shows humour, mediates.

Each time one of the behaviours occurs, a tick is placed against that category for either the whole group or individual group members. There are however, a number of problems with such a simple method:

Problem 1: It will, for example, show you the number of occurrences but not the sequence of behaviours. It could be that many people said 'I agree' after contributions at the beginning of a group, but that the whole second half of the group was taken up with a bitter disagreement. Just counting occurrences would miss this.

Problem 2: The categories themselves can be a problem. How well defined are they? The categories should be mutually exclusive, i.e. behaviour should only fit into one category, with no overlap. In the above example, would you know how to distinguish between 'agrees' and 'shows support'?

Problem 3: If there is only one observer, then objectivity becomes an issue of validity (e.g. the humour category could be, to say the least, a matter of personal taste). If there is more than one observer, then inter-observer reliability (see pp. 42-3) becomes an issue.

Observation should not be seen as an easy option compared to experimentation. Observations require just as much planning, preparation and rigour as any other research method.

2. Time sampling

Rather than continuously monitoring the behaviour of subjects, this method samples the behaviour of subjects at predetermined time intervals, e.g. the behaviour of a particular subject may be noted every minute, every ten minutes or whatever. Observations would continue at the given intervals until the observation period had ended. You could simply write down the behaviour to record it or use a category (see above). Whilst the main advantage of this method is to reduce the amount of information that has to be recorded, it suffers from the same problems as event sampling and has one of its own:

Problem: You may fall prey to cycles of behaviour in a session which will distort your results. One way round this is to sample behaviour at random time intervals (use a random number generator to generate the time intervals, say in minutes or seconds); although this is much more effort, it could be worth it.

Note
We explained how to generate random numbers in the margins on pp 77 & 100.

Content analysis

It is possible to view many areas of human endeavour (e.g. media output) as human behaviour and, when this is sampled using the above methods, the content can be recorded and analysed. So we might conduct a content analysis of a news bulletin on the radio by taking a transcript and analysing its content. Or we may sample a whole day's television programmes every hour on the half hour. Content analysis is also a *narrative* technique when used in people's descriptions of their experiences. The same problems and cautions regarding sampling of behaviour and observer validity and reliability, apply.

Surveys and questionnaires

Most surveys use some form of questionnaire: a fixed set of questions followed in a set pattern for all subjects. Three issues arise when we consider conducting a survey: firstly, sampling; secondly, the design of the questionnaire; and thirdly, administering the questionnaire.

Sampling for surveys and questionnaires

Advanced researchers would talk about sampling stimuli (questions), sampling responses (answers) and sampling respondents (subjects), but at this level we need only attend to the problem of sampling subjects (obtaining the people who are going to answer our questions). We will be looking in a slightly less sophisticated way at questionnaire design in the next section.

We have covered most of the sampling issues in Chapter 2.4, 'Distributions, Populations and Samples'. The main difference between a survey and other methods is the size of the sample. Because there is no control of extraneous variables, and the measurements themselves (people's opinions) are subject to un-predictable variation, the larger the survey sample the better. We can say this now in the certain knowledge that expense, time and effort will impose their own limits on your surveying endeavours. You will, no doubt, wish to use your survey or questionnaire results to generalise from your sample to the population in general, and this will be the driving force behind your intentions. If your sample is not representative, you will not be able to generalise your findings with confidence and your efforts will have been in vain. A sample of around 10% of such a population would be very respectable.

The remaining question is what sort of sample should you go for? To answer this question we refer you to Chapter 2.4. There are advantages and disadvantages to each sampling method. For a simple study with a discrete population, such as all the students at a particular college, some form of stratified sampling (see p. 77) is best.

Questionnaire design

It may seem the easiest thing in the world to produce a set of questions and give them to subjects, but questionnaire design is an

Note
Narrative research is introduced on p 200 and content analysis as a qualitative method is described on pp 203-7.

IF YOU WANT TO KNOW MORE ABOUT
questionnaire design

you could try (beginners' text first):

Robson, C (2002) *Real World Research: A resource for social scientists and practitioner researchers* (2nd edn). Oxford: Blackwell.

Bradburn, N, Sudman, S & Wansink, B (2004) *Asking Questions: The definitive guide to questionnaire design – For market research, political polls, and social and health questionnaires.* San Francisco, CA: Wiley.

art in itself and there are several pitfalls awaiting the inexperienced.

- try to limit the number of items (questions). Besides overloading or boring your subjects (this will affect their responses), the sheer length of your questionnaire may well be the deciding factor as to whether the subject completes it. Use only questions that are essential to your investigation
- pilot your questionnaire at various stages of completion – try it out on a few subjects to see if it works; if there are too many items, missing items, offensive items, confusing items, ambiguous items, inappropriate instructions, etc. piloting will bring these to light
- you should also ask a small group of subjects to make suggestions regarding what questions you should ask. This way you will be asking relevant questions rather than ones that *you* think are important and help to avoid the possibility of just finding what you wanted to find
- think very carefully about the type of questions you ask. Try to avoid open-ended questions, since you will only have the difficult job of categorising them later. Ask questions with 'yes'/'no' answers, or on a scale from 1 (very satisfied) to 6 (very unsatisfied). This will also help you express your results numerically. There is a phenomenon called *regression to the mean* that not only afflicts statistics but also people. It means that people are likely to go for a middle of the road answer or a 'don't know' option if at all possible. So don't give them the opportunity of opting for a mid-point, by using a scale without one (i.e. with an even number of options), 1–6, for example
- you should consider how you ask the questions. For example, you should not ask leading questions in a way that indicates the questioner's preference, e.g. 'Would you agree that abortion is the senseless murder of innocent humans by selfish, self-centred women who will burn in hell for the rest of eternity? Yes or No?' You could reword this so as to give no hint about your own opinion, e.g. 'Are you in favour of abortion on demand? Yes or No?'

Questionnaire administration
Firstly, you will need to give some thought to maximising the response rate to your questionnaire. In other words, even though you select, say, 100 subjects, only 60 of them may complete the questionnaire.

The best response rate is achieved by administering your questionnaire in person. In this case there will be little problem other than getting your selected subjects to agree to answer your questions. Even then, be prepared to have a number of refusals. It only gets worse from now on, since every other method gives you a much worse response rate. Here are some simple procedures to help maximise your response rate:

- if you send the questionnaire out by post always include a covering letter explaining the purpose of the study
- you may offer anonymity to your respondents. Make sure you keep your promise and show that you have done if anyone checks
- provide stamped addressed envelopes for subjects to send back completed questionnaires
- aim for a 70–80% response rate. Below 50% and your sample runs the risk of becoming unrepresentative
- always thank your respondents for taking part – in advance if at all possible

Interviews

Administering your questionnaire in person is one of two types of interview you may wish to conduct as part of your data collection. You can choose an informal, unstructured interview or a formal, structured one. If you have prepared a set of questions in the form of a questionnaire, you will be conducting a formal, structured interview in which all subjects are submitted to the same procedure. The results are then more readily generalised. However, subjects are more likely to recognise the procedure as routine and clinical and be less spontaneous in their responses.

Since your intention will usually be to generalise your results, an informal interview is probably not the best method to use as the lack of standard procedures makes it difficult to control any stray variables and thus compare results from different subjects. The information gained is difficult to submit to any type of formal analysis, but it may be useful in formulating further questions for study. Also, there is a growing trend to use narrative evidence and submit it to content analysis. An unstructured interview is a suitable method to collect such data. The one remaining problem with this method is the tedium of the transcription of the interview. A half-hour interview can take several hours to transcribe and, if you have a limited number of specifics things to discover, may also contain a lot of irrelevant information.

> *QUESTIONS TO CONSIDER*
> *Only experimental methods can reveal cause and effect relationships, but the level of control is sometimes so intrusive that some people argue that the point of the experiment is lost. This could be particularly true when it comes to counselling studies, when the subjects might be at their most vulnerable.*
> - *Do you think experiments are worth the bother?*
> - *Do you think there is a better way of investigating counselling?*

Randomised controlled trials: The 'gold standard' in quantitative research?

We are finishing off this chapter with a section on randomised controlled trials (RCTs) although we could just as sensibly included it at the end of Chapter 3.1. Indeed there is probably more logic in the latter since conducting an RCT is almost certainly beyond the resources (time, energy, professional connections and research capability) of an independent practitioner or student up to doctoral level. Our purpose in including this methodology here is so readers can appreciate the lineage of RCTs in terms of quantitative research

Note

Notes on the numbered points in the text:

1. Use independent diagnosticians to apply the diagnostic tools to prevent experimenter bias in the selection of participants.

2. Randomisation can be problematic since simple coin tossing whilst effective, will almost certainly lead to unequal groups (and less statistical power). But any method used to create equal groups will dilute the random nature of the allocation.

3. Allocation concealment controls the demand characteristics (see p 96), even at an unconscious level, affecting how the participants perceive how they are treated.

4. Difficulties in ensuring the trustworthiness of the measurements of symptoms are overcome by triangulation – several tests are done in parallel. The tests themselves can then sometimes have an effect, either therapeutically positive or negative.

5. This is an essential component in order to eliminate experimenter effects, including experimenter allegiance (p 96).

6. Most therapeutic interventions requiring an interpersonal dimension are difficult if not impossible to 'mask' in this way, since most treatment conditions are self-evident. Some studies have tried to use a dynamic but benign activity as a control, assuming it to have no therapeutic effect. Sometimes, however, such effort has been frustrated by finding that the control activity is indeed therapeutic and not benign.

Norcross, JC, Beutler, LE & Levant, RF (eds)(2005) *Evidence-Based Practices in Mental Health: Debate and dialogue on the fundamental questions.* Washington, DC: American Psychological Association.

Wall, S (2008) A critique of evidence-based practice in nursing: Challenging the assumptions. *Social Theory and Health* 6(1), 37-53.

Webb, SA (2001) Some considerations on the validity of evidence-based practice in social work. *British Journal of Social Work* 31, 57-79.

methodology and how RCTs use the notion of control of variables to establish (in the view of its advocates) an unequivocal causal link between the independent and dependent variables.

The methodological features which give an RCT its power to reveal causal relationships are:

1 a representative sample of people from the population under study

2 the random allocation of the participants to the treatment and control groups

3 concealment of the allocation from the participants, i.e. so that they do not know whether they have received a treatment or not. In medical trials this is done by giving a placebo dosage. In the care professions this is usually done by having an active but demonstrably benign process as the control activity

4 selection of appropriate measures of functioning pre- and post-treatment
   • this can be problematic, since in many health and social care settings, there is a plethora of psychometric instruments and disputes can arise over whether demonstrable, enduring improvements in symptoms have been achieved

5 use independent assessors to determine the pre- and post-treatment scores

6 if possible, apply 'blinding' or 'masking' to the study
   • this is where the design of the study prevents the participants, treatment providers and outcome assessors knowing which participants received treatment and which received control. This is a more wide-ranging design feature than 'allocation concealment' above, since in blinding, only the executive researcher knows the allocation

The rationale for RCTs is that since all sources of bias are controlled, only one element (the treatment versus no treatment experience of the participants) is left to vary. Therefore any change in symptoms must be due to the treatment condition.

Disadvantages

RCTs are not without their critics, and the criticism is substantial and well-argued. At the heart of one stream is the idea that such an instrumental method is terminally flawed when used 'on' human psychology. Another is concerned with the philosophy of comparison with the (methodologically unsound?) way they are used in drug trials. Readers wishing to follow the vigorous debate regarding the applicability of RCTs (essentially a methodology originating to test physical medicine interventions, such as drugs) to health and social care can enter any aspect of the topic into a search engine and pursue their interest. We offer three references which open up debate.

Introduction

When it comes down to it, in social science at least, qualitative research is based on the idea that the way people make sense of their experience and communicate it to others is by telling stories. Most of our everyday communication is in the form of stories and rich in metaphor. 'I was on my way home yesterday – it was coming down cats and dogs – like stair rods it was – and I was thinking about my clients when I stepped off the kerb and this blue streak came hurtling round the corner and nearly knocked me into the middle of next week.' That's an ordinary story which somehow conveys something of the quality of an experience as well as the bare fact that someone was nearly hit by a car on a rainy night.

Qualitative research is about drawing out the salient features of an experience rather than attempting to measure it. To put it another way, storytelling is how we make sense of our lives and qualitative research is about discovering (or creating or co-creating) meaning through listening to and collecting stories.

We could try to list all the possible categories of story which would be admissible to a research project, but since qualitative methods have broadened our expectations beyond measuring things with mere numbers, it is only our imagination that limits our research. Literally anything can be considered as a collectable story for qualitative study: from words in diaries and journals, through pictures and drawings, to intuitions and feelings and so much more. We are no longer constrained by the idea that we have to be able to get a reliable measure of a particular variable.

That does not mean, however, that we do not carefully and diligently collect our stories and rigorously subject them to some form of treatment in order to discover and understand what information the stories may yield. It is important to remember that, in parallel with quantitative data collection and analysis, the collection and processing of stories for qualitative research is rigorous: both are mindful and disciplined activities. We must also keep in mind the methods of processing we intend to use as we begin to plan how we will collect our stories in the first place. A laissez-faire approach to research will nearly always end in an inconclusive jumble of information from which little can be learned.

Note

To be fair, not everybody agrees with this view and some would undoubtedly consider it simplistic, seeing qualitative research as much too complex a field to easily define. For example, in their compendium of qualitative approaches to research, Norman Denzin and Yvonna Lincoln (2000: xv) state that, because of its open-ended nature, there is 'perpetual resistance against attempts to impose a single, umbrella-like paradigm over the entire project' of qualitative research.

Denzin, NK & Lincoln, YS (2000) (eds) *Handbook of Qualitative Research* (2nd edn). Thousand Oaks, CA: Sage.

Note

This is in contrast to an inconclusive jumble of information which can be marshalled into some shape from which we can learn.

Stories, storytelling, human communication and human inquiry

There is a lot in the literature about the importance of stories as communication. For example, Cragan and Shields (1995: 91-2) take the view that 'regardless of context, all human communication exhibits the characteristics of narration or stories' and Rennie (1994: 234) points out that in much of social science, storytelling is considered to be a fundamental way in which people make sense of their lives.

Then there are those such as Bettleheim (1976) and von Franz (1982) who write of how metaphor speaks widely and generally and the importance of symbols and archetypes in understanding life and life events. For these authors, fairy stories are not simply entertainment but ways of transmitting knowledge and life experience from one generation to another. Jones (1996: 10) writes of the dramatherapy paradox that 'what is fictional is also real' and Goddard (1996: 4) has pointed out the 'metaphorical nature of everyday talk'. The work of Kwansah-Aidoo (2001) on the importance and relevance of stories in Ghanaian culture indicates that the significance of stories is not confined to Western societies.

So, there are many reasons to believe that storytelling and metaphor are the ordinary language of ordinary people, a universal mode of communication understood in some way (however deeply or shallowly) by both teller and listener. Because they are a natural form of expression, it makes sense to use them in any investigation of human experience: as a means of inquiry, as a way of processing data and as a way to present findings.

References

Bettleheim, B (1976) *The Uses of Enchantment.* London: Thames & Hudson.

Cragan, JF & Shields, DC (1995) *Symbolic Theories in Applied Communication Research: Bormann, Burke & Fisher.* Cresskill, NJ: Hampton Press.

Goddard, A (1996) Tall stories: The metaphorical nature of everyday talk. *English in Education 30* (2), 4-12.

Jones, P (1996) *Drama as Therapy: Theatre as living.* London: Routledge.

Kwansah-Aidoo, K (2001) Telling stories: The epistemological value of anecdotes in Ghanaian communication research. *Media, Culture and Society 23*(3), 359-80.

Rennie, DL (1994) Storytelling in psychotherapy: The client's subjective experience. *Psychotherapy 31,* 234-43.

Von Franz, ML (1982) *An Introduction to the Interpretation of Fairy Tales.* Irving, TX: Spring Publications.

In this book, we are telling you the story of how we have made sense of research – well, more strictly, we are telling you *a* story of research. It is the one we have agreed on at this time, for this purpose. There are other stories we could tell and there are certainly other stories that others could tell. For example, a research book written by a particle physicist probably wouldn't start where we started, cover the same ground in the same way or end up at the same place. But it would be equally valued as an account (story) of research. So, you could actually find out a lot more about research by reading this book, a book on particle physics research and several other books written from different perspectives. The art of putting all these stories together in a systematic way and then telling other people *your* story of research is what qualitative research is about. It means somehow collecting stories (listening, reading, watching), doing something to them to decide what they mean (interpreting, processing) and telling a new story (reporting your findings). Behind a qualitative research strategy is:

- a desire to understand other people's experience and interpretations of phenomena. 'Data' are the stories people have to tell
- an acceptance that 'reality' shifts with time and experience – that we live in a subjective universe and reality is whatsoever people perceive it to be
- a recognition that values (of both the researcher and the researched) are important and must be taken into account in the process of research and in conveying findings to others

Qualitative research is about exploration and discovery – theories and hypotheses are evolved from the stories told – if at all. The primary 'instrument' is the human person of the researcher who gathers information (stories) under natural conditions rather than by experiment. What the qualitative researcher is after is real, rich, deep and meaningful stories of a particular experience or set of experiences.

You will notice that we are only a few paragraphs into qualitative research and we are already using different language from when we were writing about quantitative research. For example, qualitative researchers rely on collecting stories and *interpreting* their data rather than *manipulating* variables and 'analysing' the data. We also indicated something else important about qualitative research when we said this book was *our* story of research and that it was somehow shaped by the time at which we told it and the purpose for which we told it. In other words, it is not a definitive story of research; there are many, many others. We happen to think that it is a useful story but it is a limited story. However, it is purposeful and 'fit for purpose' and that is important. Also different is the emphasis on *values*. There are other ways in which the language and concepts of qualitative research differ from those of quantitative research and we will introduce and explain some of these as we go along.

For the most part, qualitative researchers have neither the intention nor the possibility to come up with definitive answers. Rather, qualitative research tells you something about a particular thing as 'told' by one or more people who record it, process the record in some way and then tell a third person what they think they have found out from the original storytellers. Although, to keep things simple, we are using the notion that stories are 'told' and this implies that they are spoken and a lot are, they can also be observed (you might learn the stories of client experience by watching video tapes of actual sessions) or portrayed expressively (as, for example, paintings, drama, dance). So a process of qualitative research might be something like this:

- the researcher asks a question of a participant 'tell me about

Note

There are many examples of researchers collecting and making sense of the stories people have to tell in order to understand some aspect of their experience. For example, Riches and Dawson (1996) collected the stories of bereaved parents in an attempt to understand the part grief played in marital tension and Usher and Monkley (2001) used the stories told by four intensive care nurses as a way of understanding what constituted effective communication in their professional setting. You could try your own search using Google Scholar or a similar search engine (see pp 238-9 for how to do this) – you may be surprised just how many studies you find.

Riches, G & Dawson, P (1996) Making and taking stories: Methodological reflections on researching grief and marital tension following the death of a child. *British Journal of Guidance and Counselling 24* (3), 357-65.

Usher, K & Monkley, D (2001) Effective communication in an intensive care setting: Nurses stories. *Contemporary Nurse 10*(1-2), 91-101.

Note

This list is an adaptation and expansion of something Paul wrote (see Wilkins, 2000: 147).

Wilkins, P (2000) Storytelling as research. In B Humphries (ed) *Research in Social Care and Social Welfare: Issues and debates for practice* (pp 144-53). London: Jessica Kingsley.

MEDIATION In common use it means trying to achieve reconciliation, but here we mean that something has interrupted, interceded and changed some thing or process.

what happened to you when …'

• the participant reflects on the question and 'tells' a highly personal story as a largely internal, impressionistic process. This story may or may not be an exact answer to the question asked

• as the participant communicates that story through speech, writing a journal, painting a picture etc. it is MEDIATED and modified. A process of interpretation and, possibly, censorship or creative enrichment occurs

• the researcher records the story as it is told – but recording too involves MEDIATION and it is likely that the process of MEDIATION involves moderation and/or modification

• the researcher processes the collected story in some way, deciding what bits are significant and what the story means (we'll tell you more about some ways to do this later). There is a process of sifting, sorting, exclusion and interpretation

• the researcher then compares the findings to what is already known and takes this previous knowledge and opinion into account

• lastly, the researcher presents what has been found and what it means in such a way as to make it understandable to others. This too is a process of MEDIATION

In this process, there are five stages between the participant's inner experience and what gets presented by the researcher as the answer to the question originally asked – and, in the first place, that might have been understood by the participant differently from the way the researcher meant it – perhaps without either person knowing. A further complication is that another researcher, even if posing the same question in the same way, will have made different interpretations along the way and reached different conclusions.

In Chapter 2.2 we told you about the importance and meaning of validity and reliability and that these are fundamental to good (quantitative) research. To recap, quantitative social science researchers are concerned to establish the reliability and validity of their measurements in the same way that physical scientists do – by taking repeated measures and comparing them to other scientists' measures. If the measures look respectably alike (in a numerical sense) they are deemed to be reliable and valid. Validity is about knowing that measurements can be trusted and reliability is about knowing that, if the same procedure is conducted by a different person, a similar conclusion will be reached. Well, the procedure we have outlined above doesn't involve measurement so validity isn't an appropriate concern and we have indicated that different researchers are likely to experience and process qualitative data in different ways to reach different conclusions. So, is qualitative research unreliable? Strictly speaking, in the technical way we have been using the word, we suppose we have to say yes.

This seems like a problem doesn't it? If the concepts of validity and reliability don't apply to qualitative research, how can we know it means what the researcher says it means? There seems little point in going to all the trouble of planning a study, collecting and interpreting the data for it to be dismissed as not to be trusted. It is a prime concern that research findings are trustworthy and it is a point of difference between qualitative and quantitative methods as to how best to go about establishing this feature. Since qualitative work is about processes, stories and understanding the humanness of being human, it would not be appropriate to seek validity in numbers. Other more naturalistic methods of ensuring that qualitative results are trustworthy must be found. This has proved to be difficult because we are so used to numbers and their historical association with facts (numbers just *are* reliable and trustworthy – after all, two plus two is four).

Trustworthiness

By now, you are very possibly saying to yourself 'Why should I bother, it all seems complicated and if I do qualitative research is it going to mean anything anyway?' You could be right, qualitative research might just amount to a distorted opinion *unless* it is very clear:

- who is doing the research (From what frame of reference? With what interest and experience? With what beliefs and ideals?)
- who or what they are researching (Who were the participants? What is it about them that led the researcher to think they know the answer to the question?)
- how they are conducting the study and processing the stories they collect
- that the methods used in conducting the research are credible and suited to the task

Only if you know these things can you understand how the researcher has interpreted the stories, why they did it that way and what has coloured the interpretation along the way. Given this information, you can make a judgement about the final story the researcher is telling (which, traditionally, would probably be labelled 'discussion') and make your own interpretation. In other words, while qualitative research may not be valid or reliable in the technical sense, it can and must be trustworthy. Trustworthy qualitative research produces a deeper, more complex understanding of human experience than is usually achieved using quantitative methods.

There have been various attempts to describe how qualitative research can be trustworthy. One way is to try to find equivalents

Note

There is a discussion of the criteria for evaluating the validity of qualitative research (ie, its trustworthiness) in John McLeod's book on counselling research (pp 93-6).

McLeod, J (2003) *Doing Counselling Research* (2nd ed). London: Sage.

Note

The term 'trustworthiness' as a criterion for adequacy and plausibility of qualitative research seems to have first been used by Guba (1981). Lincoln and Guba (1985) devote a whole chapter to how trustworthiness may be established in their seminal work on naturalistic inquiry.

Guba EG (1981) Criteria for assessing the trustworthiness of naturalistic inquiries. *Educational Technology Research and Development 29*(2), 75-91.

Lincoln, YS & Guba EG (1985) *Naturalistic Inquiry.* Newbury Park, CA: Sage.

Table 2.6.1
Comparative standards for
qualitative and quantitative research

Standard	Qualitative Research	Quantitative Research
Truthfulness	Credibility	Internal validity
Applicability	Transferability	External validity
Consistency	Dependability	Reliability
Neutrality	Confirmability	Objectivity

POSITIVISTIC/POSITIVISM A doctrine asserting that sense perceptions are the only admissible basis of human knowledge and precise thought. In research, that the validity of knowledge can only be assured by experimental science.

to the criteria used in quantitative research. In this way, a very simple model for trustworthiness is shown in Table 2.6.1.

Many of the older ways of doing qualitative research do hark back to POSITIVISTIC, physical science methods. From this perspective, some of the ways trustworthy qualitative research is achieved are by:

- *having a well-calibrated measuring instrument* (in qualitative research the principal instrument is the researcher). Ways in which this may be achieved include by establishing the background, authority and experience of the researcher (see 'locating yourself' below)

- *triangulation* – basically, having more than one source. To some extent, when conducting your research, you should look at the possibility of verifying the truth of your claims using two (or more) sets of results, having two or more researchers acting independently or by making use of more than one method of inquiry. For example, the results of observations may be backed up with information derived from a questionnaire administered to some or all of the subjects or the results obtained from your study may be compared with those previously obtained in similar studies

- *repetition of the measurement* – we hope, self-explanatory

- *analysis of negative cases* – although this isn't used all that much it is really a qualitative version of the null hypothesis we talked about when we were telling you about quantitative research. It involves making a real attempt to find from fieldwork and the literature instances that disprove or qualify your findings. This simply means looking at your data and attempting to explain why certain cases or findings don't seem to fit into the strong trends and patterns evident in the majority of cases. Doing this openly, discovering and acknowledging the reasons for the negative cases, gives your readers the opportunity to accept (or otherwise) your interpretation of the findings. Do not cover up or attempt to disguise and results that don't fit. They will always prove to have an interesting story to tell. Analysis of negative cases establishes trustworthiness by opening the data and its interpretation to a wider scrutiny. Any personal biases will be limited by the research equivalent of 'washing your dirty linen in public' and 'trial by publication'

- *participant consultation* – this is a way of checking that the perceptions and views of those contributing stories to the research are accurately reflected in what has been recorded and the subsequent findings. Perhaps the simplest way to do that is in the first place to agree the record ('Is this what you said?') and in the second place to show your informants your findings, the question being something like 'Does what I say here reflect your experience?'

However, another view is that the standards applicable to quantitative research are not directly transferable to qualitative research and that the criteria in Table 2.6.1 are actually an attempt to squeeze the quart of qualitative research into the pint pot of POSITIVISM. This is especially true of some of the more subjective or collaborative 'new paradigm' approaches which we explore in various places throughout the book. However, regardless of the approach to qualitative research, the question of its trustworthiness remains paramount. If you aren't going to go through the business of using a quasi-quantitative strategy to establish trustworthiness, how else can you do it? Well, most of the time it comes down to 'having a well-calibrated instrument' (see above). Qualitative research rests on the idea that it is about human encounter. After deciding on a research question and how to answer it, the first step is for one (or more) human beings to collect information (data, stories) from one or more other human beings. It is by knowing something about the researcher and the motivation behind the research and how it was done that others can get a flavour of this encounter and make some judgement about the trustworthiness of the research process and the findings. If someone reading your research report knows enough about you to understand the lens through which you view the world then they can more readily understand what you are saying and why you say it the way you do. The first part of a good report of qualitative research should contain enough information about the researcher for the readers to understand the researcher's frame of reference. This is sometimes known as 'locating yourself'. Of course, to do this effectively requires that you first take a critical look at yourself in the context of your research.

Note
We agree with John McLeod (2001: 188-9) who takes the view that the question of validity in qualitative research comes down to whether the researcher is plausible and trustworthy. He says '[i]t seems to me that here, the *personal* qualities of the researcher, his or her integrity, courage, honesty and commitment to the task of inquiry, actually make a difference.'

McLeod, J (2001) *Qualitative Research in Counselling and Psychotherapy.* London: Sage.

Locating yourself

Whatever methods you adopt as a qualitative researcher, they will involve you as a person in a way traditionally avoided in quantitative research. A quantitative approach does not acknowledge any reasons other than intellectual reasons for making decisions regarding research. In fact such an approach tries to remove all other possible factors such as political motives, personal motives, emotions, issues of identity and background, etc. It's as though research is a sterile zone where only intellect rules. A qualitative approach, on the other hand, attempts to understand the factors which create a context for the research by embracing them all. In fact as qualitative researchers we are behoven to try to identify, declare and acknowledge the possible effects of our motives, origins and identity. Since qualitative research is about humans, by humans and of humans, we would not seek to eliminate the human touch. We must mindfully include it in order to understand it better. As a starting point, you should reflect on why you want to do the particular piece of research, what you want to know from it, how and to whom you want to convey what you find and, perhaps most importantly, how, who and what you are may influence what you do and what you say – this is what we mean by locating yourself.

As a researcher using qualitative methods, your body is an instrument (and so is your mind). As with other instruments, the more finely it is tuned, the better it will perform. Much of the success of your research will depend on the amount, type and appropriateness of your preparation. As a qualitative researcher, you need to be more than a little self-aware so that your tendencies, attitudes, ways of seeing things, etc. are acknowledged and accounted for as factors contributing to the findings. Some things you can do to facilitate this are:

- examine your motives, personal, professional, financial. How will these colour your thinking?
- are you out to prove a point? What ideas are you trying to advance under the guise of research?
- what are your anxieties? Will you turn away from certain findings?
- make sure you have someone to turn to to check out your thinking on this research – get supervision
- keep a personal journal

Some of the questions you can usefully ask yourself in this process are:

Why am I doing this research?

Finding and declaring your reasons for research is the first step in calibrating yourself as the research instrument and locating yourself. For any of us, our reasons for doing research may vary from the positive and personal:

> 'Because I was involved in an armed robbery at my bank and I want to find out about support for post-traumatic stress disorder in my area.'
>
> 'I've always wanted to do research and this is a wonderful opportunity.'
>
> 'I'm fascinated by the whole area of spirituality and counselling and want to find out more.'

Note

Lots of researchers (whether they are doing quantitative or qualitative research) find a personal research journal useful. Keeping one helps organise and track the course of the research and also aids the 'creative' processes by which problems are solved, blocks overcome and ideas emerge. We think a personal research journal:

- helps you supervise yourself and work through the difficulties you encounter during your research
- facilitates self-reflection and self-analysis
- fosters the development of new ideas
- acts as a contemporaneous record of just what happens and how it happens

Activity

Make a list of all the things you think it may be useful, helpful and relevant to note in a personal research journal. It may be helpful to compare your list with that of one or more colleagues. We have listed some of our ideas in the margin of the next page.

Note

All this relates to 'formulating your research question' which we tell you about in Chapters 2.1 and 3.3.

To the distant, removed and reluctant:
> *'Because my boss told me to do it.'*
> *'I said I'd do it so I'll keep my word, even though I'm no
> longer interested.'*

Or the pragmatic:
> *'Because we have received funding to do this project.'*
> *'The future of the centre depends upon us being able to show
> that it's meeting a need.'*

Whatever the reason or reasons for embarking on your study, it will help you to get a sense of the context in which the research is taking place and the motives for the research. The reasons for doing the research will also point you in a certain direction in terms of how you will organise your work. For example, the reason: *'Because I was involved in an armed robbery at my bank and I want to find out about support for post-traumatic stress disorder in my area'* might point you in the direction of a case study approach (see p. 156, Chapter 2.7). Whereas: *'The future of the centre depends upon us being able to show that it's meeting a need'* might point you more in the direction of an evaluative study (see p. 130, Chapter 2.7).

You may have other motives for entering into research activity – political reasons such as interest in developing ideas and findings relating to sexism, racism, and other issues of oppression. It is really important to be up front about these and to declare your stance from the outset. For example, if your research is something to do with sexism in the workplace, isn't it important that the reader knows if you are a woman or man? Whether you work in or use the setting you are investigating? Perhaps your age is relevant too – do you remember the women's liberation movement of the 1980s? Or do you see yourself as living in a post-feminist world? What about your spiritual beliefs or religious views? Is your sexual orientation likely to shape your motivation and colour your findings? These things and so much more might be important and relevant – and because we can't always be sure of seeing the wood for the trees (or vice versa), it is important to think about and include things that may not immediately seem relevant.

Of course, your cultural background and life experience colours your research whether it is obviously value-driven or not. However, locating yourself with respect to your research doesn't call for absolute and total self-disclosure. Qualitative researchers are entitled to privacy just as much as any other human being. What you should do is honestly reflect on your own experience and motives and then make a judgement as to what is important and/or relevant and to somehow take this into account.

When you are pursuing a qualitative approach, this self-inquiry

Note
Our thoughts on what could be in a personal research journal include:
• an ongoing 'progress report' (a continual record of what was done, how it was done, what happened and so on)
• your cognitive and emotional processes as the research progresses
• descriptions of problems you encounter, speculations on how they might be solved (or the solutions you found)
• ideas you have along the way (however random they may seem at the time) and questions that occur to you as you do your research
• notes on what you read including summaries of anything you think you may want to reference when you write up (make sure you have the full details – it can be very frustrating to have to track down something you vaguely recall and know to be relevant right at the end)
• feedback from research supervisors and colleagues
• an outline of what your write-up/report may look like

at the beginning of your research work is not preparation for the research – it is the start of the research. Since qualitative research is of humans and by humans, your humanness becomes part of it. *Your research has already begun.*

What am I trying to find out?

Discovering and developing your research question is the next crucial stage in your research. There is no formula or approved procedure to follow that will guarantee a research question. What we can tell you is that it is much more likely that your research efforts will be sustainable if you have a genuine interest (and ideally a burning curiosity) in whatever it is you choose to do. There is something to be said for taking a good look at the world around you, your practice, your working or educational environment, your personal experience, and noticing what piques your interest. It may be that something is immediately obvious (indeed, perhaps you have come to this book with some notion as to what you would like to research) but whatever your situation, there are some useful guidelines for developing a research question. Useful research is more likely to arise from:

- personal involvement with fieldwork and activity, e.g. your practice. In other words, the best research is conducted by people who know something of what they are investigating from the inside
- the convergence of interests, for example, a person with a problem plus a person with an idea or method for solving it
- a feeling or intuition that the time and issue are 'right'. To a certain extent, it is OK to trust your instincts, your TACIT KNOWLEDGE
- good grounding in the theoretical issues. You must know about how what you are investigating is framed and understood – even if your motivation for the research is that you are unsure that the given theory is right or you have a hunch it may be incomplete
- projects which end up with tangible changes or benefits. Your research should result in some advantage (for example, a higher degree, service improvement, theoretical or practical advance)
- projects which are realistically achievable. There is no point in dreaming up a piece of research that you are just never going to get the resources or access to do. All research has costs and, to ensure success, these must be met

Disappointment is more likely to follow research based on expedience, a need to demonstrate or 'sell' a 'method', or motivation based solely on 'profit' (money, publication, fame). A healthy and effective way of proceeding can be developed by adopting a 'humble' approach:

TACIT KNOWLEDGE This is a term coined by Michael Polanyi (1967) who argued that the knowledgeable guesses, hunches and imaginings that inform, for example, the process of research, are motivated by what he describes as 'passions'. They might well be aimed at discovering 'truth', but they are not necessarily in a form that can be stated in propositional or formal terms. Polanyi (1967: 4) considered that we should start from the fact that *'we can know more than we can tell'*. He termed this pre-logical phase of knowing as 'tacit knowledge'. Tacit knowledge comprises a range of conceptual and sensory information and images that can be brought to bear in an attempt to make sense of something. Many bits of tacit knowledge can be brought together to help form a new model or theory.

Polanyi, M (1967) *The Tacit Dimension.* New York: Anchor Books.

- don't assume you know everything. Spend some time getting to know the background to the issue you are thinking of researching. This includes reading but perhaps it is also about talking to other practitioners or to service users. Do they experience things similarly or differently from you? Do they agree that the 'problem' you think you have identified exists?
- search around the area, not just in your narrow area of interest. For example, if you have identified an issue that relates to your field of practice, say occupational therapy, is the answer already known to one or more other professions allied to medicine? If so, can you apply this understanding in your investigation? What do theories other than the one(s) you espouse have to tell you about the issue?
- don't decide too early, be prepared to let ideas come and go; ask yourself 'Why am I holding on to this way of working or thinking?'
- get other people involved – ask for help, seek out others with experience in the area you are interested in. For a beginning researcher at least, serious consideration should be given to getting somebody to supervise the investigation. The job of a research supervisor is to provide help and guidance with respect to research methods, ways of processing data and expressing findings. A supervisor will also help you see when you are biting off more than you can chew – and conversely prod you when you aren't making all that you can of what you have done. They will also listen to your moans and groans and support you through the times when it all seems too much

How do I want to express myself through this work?

This question is about the extent to which your identity is consciously bound up with your research method. Do the decisions you make about research approach and methods have *congruence with various aspects of your person* at their heart? You may have gone some way to answering this question for yourself since you might have already decided that qualitative rather than quantitative approaches resonate more with your personality, or will allow you to express your *self* better through your research.

The answer to this question may also lead to a leaning towards, or wholehearted commitment to, a particular approach to research. There are very many approaches to qualitative research – more than we can tell you about in this book – and more are being developed all the time. For example, because qualitative research incorporates the values of the researcher, there are different approaches stemming from different value bases. There are feminist approaches to research, approaches that address issues of race and culture, approaches that resist the 'objectification' of the researched

Activity
By this time perhaps you are beginning to get some idea about what might interest you as a research project. If so, why not generate some preliminary ideas? You could try following our bullet point list in the text and answering the implied questions from your own perspective. For example:
- *What aspects of health and social care are you involved with?*
- *What do you see as a likely convergence of interest?*
- *What is your intuition telling you? Do you have a hunch about something?*
- *What are your theoretical strengths (or, if you identify weaknesses, how can you address them?)*
- *What will you get out of doing research?*
- *Is what you want to do possible within the existing constraints?*

Activity
- *Given what we have told you so far and what you already know, do you think that, as a researcher, you are more attracted by the idea of working with numbers or is it collecting stories that seems to appeal to you?*
- *Or perhaps you see no reason to place yourself in one camp or the other. If you are as yet unsure, you could try making a list of your personal pros and cons for each approach.*

PHENOMENOLOGICAL approaches to understanding and psychology are based on the study of immediate experience, where 'truth' or 'knowledge' comes from the perceptual field of the individual, rather than an external authority. Based on the work of the philosopher Edmund Husserl.

POSTMODERNISM is a reaction to the assumed certainty of scientific or objective efforts to explain reality. It is highly sceptical of explanations which claim to be universal.

and seek to incorporate them as co-researchers, research methods that are about changing systems, ones in which a spiritual element is built in and so on. There are approaches drawing on major disciplines – psychologists have come up with research methods, sociologists different ones, anthropologists yet others. Research can be PHENOMENOLOGICAL, POSTMODERN or humanistic to name but a few possibilities.

Even when it is agreed that what is important is, for example, 'narrative' and a decision is taken to interview research participants, there are then a number of ways of processing the interview transcripts to choose from. Content analysis (which we told you a bit about in Chapter 2.5) is one way, discourse analysis (concerned with the use of language) is another and narrative analysis *per se* (concerned with how the story is structured and its elements – plot, characters, etc.) is yet another – and there are more. Not only that, but each of these can be done from a variety of philosophical positions. When you add to this that every so often a researcher decides that there isn't a method to answer the question posed in such a way as to lead to the sort of answer required and so invents another approach, the choice of method can be baffling. However, there are broad classes of qualitative research methods and we will tell you about these (and some more specific ones) in Chapter 2.8. This should help you at least begin to choose an approach to research that is based in a philosophy more congruent with your experience, beliefs, values, cultural background or ethnic origins. For more help and guidance, take a look at the next few chapters.

Introduction

In the previous chapter we told you that in many ways qualitative research was about listening to, recording and processing stories. Sometimes, indeed often, this is about literally listening to another person but there are other ways too of collecting stories. Some stories exist in written form, perhaps as journals, diaries or other records of an experience – these can be used as the material of qualitative research either in their own right or to supplement information gathered in other ways. Sometimes it is the researcher who tells the story. This may be from observation of others as they act – the researcher being either an active participant in the action or a more passive witness to it – or it may be through a process of reflection.

Another way of coming up with a story may involve any two or more of listening, reading, observing, and reflecting – in some combination and proportion – for example, an in-depth single CASE STUDY may require all four. In some of the newer, more subjective approaches to research such as heuristic inquiry or autoethnography, it is the researcher's own stories that are collected. In this chapter we will tell you something about the various ways in which you can collect the stories that will become the foundation of your research.

We will also tell you a bit about some of the tools that will be helpful to you as you set out to collect your stories. Although we do this in relation to particular types of story – for example, you will find a bit about 'recording' in the section on interviews, and information about journal and diary keeping under the 'observing yourself' heading – one of the important things to remember about collecting stories is that the various methods don't always fall into neat boxes. It may very well be that keeping a journal is an important part of interviewing; so don't make the mistake of assuming because we tell you about something under one heading that it only applies to stories of that kind.

In many ways, flexibility and adaptability are keys to qualitative research and the various tools can be used in a variety of ways and for many different purposes. One of the things you are going to have to know before you set out to collect your stories is what it is you want to find out about – that is, you are going to have to have

Note
We told you a bit about journal keeping in the previous chapter.

CASE STUDY An intensive investigation of an individual, group, community or incident. For more about case study research see later in this chapter.

Note
Only a few years ago this would have meant audiotape and videotape, but with the advent of smaller and smaller digital recording devices (mobile phones, MP3 players, USB toggles, etc), we are reluctant to identify any technology, since it's sure to be superceded in short order.

a research question. We told you a bit about questions in Chapter 2.1 and much of what we said there applies to qualitative research as well as quantitative research. However, it won't hurt to remind you and there are some steps you can take to help you decide just what your question is and how to prepare to carry out your research.

How to formulate a research question

- list all aspects of particular interests or topics about which you are intrigued or about which you are curious – do you have a burning desire to *know* something? Do you have a hunch? Perhaps you are just vaguely wondering about something. Write down questions, thoughts, intuitions, even if they are vague and incomplete. Indeed, write down anything at all that seems relevant – you can always thin out things later
- take a good look at what you have written down and group things that seem similar such as related interests or topics into sub-themes
- now consider your sub-themes. You should set aside any which imply causal relationships and/or contain inherent assumptions
- look at all the remaining sub-themes and stay with them until one basic theme or question emerges as central, one that passionately awakens your interest, concern, and commitment
- formulate it in a way that specifies clearly and precisely what it is that you want to know

Once you know what it is you are seeking to find out, it may be that a particular way of collecting stories is immediately obvious to you. You may very well find that your question, how you would like to collect the stories, and your professional approach and underpinning ethics or philosophy point you towards a particular research method. It is really important that the method you use suits the stories you can collect and the question you are seeking to answer. However attractive a particular approach might be for you, don't use it unless it is going to take you to where you want to be – do you remember the screwdriver versus bread knife metaphor we used in Chapter 1.2, p. 10? To make the appropriate choice, you are going to have to know what options are available to you and that is what the rest of this chapter and Chapter 2.8 are about.

Evaluation studies

Before we start to tell you about how you can collect stories from other people, we thought we had best tell you something about a special set of circumstances in which you might need to construct a story of your own. Sometimes the focus of research is to 'evaluate'

Note

We return to formulating research questions in different contexts throughout the book and in Chapter 3.3, pp 263-4, where we come at it from a different angle.

Activity

When you are ready (and perhaps you want to read a bit more first or reflect on what you've learnt so far), work through the bullet point list opposite and see what you come up with. Remember, it commits you to nothing so far; it's just about the process of coming up with a question.

- *Are you getting anywhere near a viable research question?*

- *Don't forget that although here we are focusing on qualitative approaches this is an equally valid way of generating a quantitative research question.*

something, maybe a whole service, perhaps some aspect of service delivery or a particular way of working with patients or clients. The idea of evaluating something will be familiar to most of you. All of us have, at least intuitively, tried to evaluate the effectiveness of our practice at some time or another. Occasionally we may be asked to evaluate the effectiveness and/or the efficiency of a service. Behind the idea of evaluation is the notion of comparison and this can imply measurement. We could have told you something about evaluation when we were discussing quantitative approaches – and some evaluation studies are purely to do with measurement (for example, the whole idea of 'evidence-based' practice is actually about evaluation). However, here we mean evaluation in a much broader, richer sense and although effectiveness and efficiency became bywords for evaluation in the late 80s and early 90s, there are other themes that can be the subject of evaluation. Here are a few examples, the list is not exhaustive:

Effectiveness	Efficiency	Cost
Feasibility	Adequacy	Quality
Appropriateness	Usefulness/utility	Ethics
Legality	Validity	Reliability
Trustworthiness	Benefit	

These evaluative themes can be pursued at different times in the *life cycle* of a particular event. Looked at in this way, we can see a use for evaluation before, during and after an event or intervention.

- evaluation of the situation before something is started, e.g. feasibility studies
  Asking the questions, *'Is it worth doing?' or 'Will it work?'*
- evaluation of the changes in something as it happens, e.g. developmental analysis
  Asking the questions, *'How is it doing?' or 'How is it changing?'*
- evaluation of the process of something as it happens, e.g. process evaluation or monitoring
  Asking the question, *'What is happening?'*
- evaluation of the effect or impact of something, e.g. outcome analysis
  Asking the questions, *'Was it worth doing?' or 'Did it work?'*

Once you have decided what you are evaluating, for what purpose and at what time in the life cycle of an event, there are still some matters to resolve before you can start collecting data. Remember that an evaluation study is essentially comparative. In other words it is comparing whatever is being evaluated to a standard of some sort. It might be a norm of some description ('acceptable behaviour')

Note
The health and social care literature includes many case studies. If you'd like to see some for yourself you could try using Google Scholar to find publications with 'evaluation (insert the domain of choice)' in the title. Three we found are:

Ross, F, Rink, E & Furne, A (2000) Integration or pragmatic coalition? An evaluation of nursing teams in primary care. *Journal of Interprofessional Care* 14(3), 259-67.

Brännström, B, Tibblin, Å & Löwenborg, C (2000) Counselling groups for spouses of elderly demented patients: A qualitative study. *International Journal of Nursing Practice* 6(4), 183-91.

Merton, B, Payne, M & Smith, D (2004) An evaluation of the impact of youth work in England. *Research Report 606*. Department of Education and Skills.

or an absolute standard (set by legislation) or one you make up yourself. When planning your evaluation you might consider the following:

- do you need permission to get access to documents, areas, personnel?
- are you evaluating something against criteria or against some absolute idea or reference point?
- do you need and have you got a baseline measure?
- if you are using criteria, are you using someone else's criteria or are you generating your own?
- if you are generating your own criteria, what criteria are you using to evaluate against?
- who wants this work done – you, or is someone commissioning it?
- how will the findings be used – will you have the final say, or will someone else?
- if someone else is commissioning this work, how do they want it written up or presented?

When you have addressed all of the above issues to your satisfaction you will be at the stage of considering data collection. Any appropriate method can be used and there is much to be said for using a variety of methods. Documents, interviews, questionnaires, participant observation and other methods all have a valid contribution to make to an evaluation study. All these are described later in this chapter.

Finally you will have to have some sort of strategy when it comes to sampling. Much the same considerations apply to evaluation work as apply to case studies, see below. In fact your evaluation study may well be a case study with a particular purpose or aim, i.e. evaluation. In writing up your evaluation, you are in effect telling the story of whatever it is you have been evaluating.

Questionnaires

Although they are often used in quantitative research, questionnaires have a place in the tool kit of the qualitative researcher. Most of us are familiar with questionnaires of one sort or another. For example, you may have been stopped in the high street by a market researcher and asked to complete one or perhaps at the end of a training workshop or conference you have been handed a feedback sheet by the organisers and invited to tick boxes or answer questions. Then there are the 'tests' in the popular press that will tell you how good a lover you are, how fashionable you are or something similar. Perhaps it is this familiarity that leads many beginning researchers to think in terms of collecting the information they seek through using a questionnaire. However, there is a lot more to the questionnaire than simply compiling a list of questions. A well-designed and implemented questionnaire is a precise tool – a poor one can be a research disaster. So, we'll tell you a bit about them, how to design one and how to administer it.

Because a questionnaire is always an attempt to limit, direct and order the information coming from the respondent (the person answering the questions), they are most useful when you are after particular information of a particular kind. In this sense they are always leaning towards quantitative methodology. Questionnaires manage the data flow from the respondent by limiting and directing it according to the researcher's agenda. This makes the use of questionnaires almost a borderline qualitative/quantitative method, but one that those interested in developing qualitative methods will use with caution after much consideration. So, although genuine questionnaires *can* be structured to a greater or lesser degree, they are all structured and to some extent predetermined.

Essentially a questionnaire is a list of questions and instructions which the respondent is expected to fill in or complete themselves usually in the absence of the researcher.

We say 'usually' but sometimes (as in the approach to market research we talked about above) the researcher or an associate 'administers' the questionnaire by asking the questions and filling in the answers. Fairly obviously, this also happens when the questionnaire is administered by telephone. An advantage of doing it this way is that there is greater 'compliance' (more people you ask to complete the questionnaire will actually do it) than if you ask people to complete the questionnaire in their own time and return it to you. A disadvantage is that it is more labour-intensive and so limits the number of people you can ask to complete your questionnaire. However, for the purpose of this book, any method requiring a verbal response in the presence of the researcher we have decided to call an interview, including the use of the telephone, (although we have not dealt with the telephone separately).

In this section we will look briefly at the types of less tightly structured questionnaire that may be developed for use in qualitative studies. We will also look at other forms of self-completion activities which are much less structured than questionnaires. We will assume that the respondent has to complete the activity in writing.

The setting of the questionnaire

By this we mean the circumstances in which the respondent will be receiving and completing your questionnaire. This is something you should think carefully about because it affects the response rate you will get and maybe even how you design your questionnaire. There is a range of settings from formal to informal

Activity

As you might expect, there are hundreds of questionnaires available on the Internet. Some of these are simply fun, others are to be used with intent of the most serious kind. Find a short one online.

- *You could try filling this in for yourself.*
- *If you do, what do you think about your personal result?*
- *How do you rate this questionnaire in terms of how much it tells you and how accurate it is?*

If you would like to see a more detailed sample questionnaire you could try <http://patienteducation.stanford.edu/ research/diabquest.pdf> which is aimed at people with diabetes.

in which you might deliver your questionnaire to your respondents. For example:

- a room at your place of work or study, on their own, with an 'invigilator' to help with problems and misunderstandings
- as above in a group
- at home, delivered by prior arrangement by you. You staying to introduce the questionnaire and give some instructions
- at home by post, by prior arrangement
- at home by post, without prior arrangement
- as above but at the respondent's place of work

As we indicated, each setting will affect the level and quality of responses given by the respondents. You should consider the following factors:

- how many questionnaires are likely to be returned? (Postal questionnaires do not get a very high response rate – between 20 and 50%)
- what may distract the respondent during completion of the questionnaire?
- will it matter if there is an interrupted or non-continuous completion? What difference does it make if the respondent does not complete the questionnaire all in one go? Is this desirable or undesirable? (You may have this as a condition either way)
- what chance is there that your respondents will not complete your questionnaire according to the instructions?
- what is the possibility that someone other than the respondent will fill in the questionnaire?
- how many people's views are represented on the completed questionnaire? (The respondent might ask for other people's opinions before completing some questions)

Ensuring that the questionnaire is filled in according to your requirements is practically impossible when it is done anywhere other than in your presence. Even getting respondents together in groups for this purpose is very costly in terms of time and money. One of the main reasons for choosing a questionnaire is its cost effectiveness, so you may be limited to a postal questionnaire or something similar. If this is the case, you can maximise the response rate by following these common-sense guidelines:

- think about how your questionnaire looks. Make it attractive, easy to read and provide sufficient space for your respondents to enter their answers
- if you are going to send it to your respondents, consider how it will arrive. Send it to a named person and mark it 'personal'. Include a stamped addressed return envelope with your questionnaire. You may want to type addresses so that your

Note

There is at least a possibility that there are different quality ratings between respondents and non-respondents to a questionnaire. NON-RESPONSE BIAS can jeopardise the validity of questionnaire results. If you plan to use a questionnaire as a way of collecting data then reading the literature on dealing with questionnaire non-response bias is likely to be helpful.

NON-RESPONSE BIAS The bias occurring when analysis is limited to the available data (for example, completed questionnaires even though these may be a subset of those distributed). This is because those who do not respond may have different experiences and views from those who do.

Note

Remember that everything about your questionnaire should be congruent with your research aims and method. So if you are asking someone to keep a diary, you may wish to steer clear of devices that make it seem too formal or official.

efforts appear 'official' and – perhaps it would be as well to avoid, franked, brown envelopes that may be mistaken for junk mail and which would hit the wastepaper bin unopened. Think about the time you send out your questionnaire. It may be just as well to avoid the main summer holiday season (a lot of people go away in late July or August) and people can be very busy and distracted in the run-up to Christmas so December may not be a good time either. You might like to think through the implications of sending your questionnaire to your respondent's home address or to their place of work

- one of the big problems with using questionnaires as a way of collecting data is how to ensure that you get enough replies. Perhaps it is worth asking 'What is in it for my respondent?' Possible incentives include offering to let respondents know the result of your research (if it is about something they care about they may like to know) or sometimes a small gift may be appropriate. Another possibility is to include the names of everyone who sends in a properly completed questionnaire in a prize draw. Whatever incentive you offer, you should make it very clear at the outset – the information should be part of your opening statement about your questionnaire

- lastly, think about what you will do if you do not receive a reply. It is certainly worth sending a reminder saying that you would really value their participation in your research and that your research is important. If you still do not get a response, it is worth trying another reminder – but very probably more than three reminders is a waste of time

Developing a semi-structured questionnaire

Some researchers would not accept that there is any such thing as a semi-structured questionnaire. The point we are trying to make here, and indeed throughout this book, is don't be intimidated by the limited vision of others when it comes to qualitative methods. If you follow the planning and preparation process described in Chapter 3.3, you will develop a method with integrity.

Once you step outside the strict boundaries of quantitative, tightly structured questionnaires comprising weighted items that have been tested for reliability, validity, etc. (see Chapter 2.2, pp. 40-4), there are few 'rules' governing the structure of questionnaires. When using a questionnaire as part or all of your data-collecting strategy in qualitative research, always remember that you are compromising between being able to manage the data flow in order to quantify your results and collecting data that has the richness, spontaneity and natural quality you require. This is a difficult balance to strike.

When writing down questions and asking respondents to write their answers, you are limited to open and closed questions and the

> **IF YOU WANT TO KNOW MORE ABOUT**
> questionnaires

and how to use them, you could try looking at Robson (2002: 227-67) who includes some examples of self-completed questionnaires and how to design them, and McLeod (1999: 89-95) who has short sections on standardised PSYCHOMETRIC questionnaires, specifically designed questionnaires, personal questionnaires, open-ended questionnaires, the Delphi Technique and other types of questionnaire.

There are whole books devoted to the subject of the design of questionnaires and the analysis of data collected using them. These include Gillham (2000), Bradburn et al (2004) and Saris and Gallhofer (2007). As you might suspect, there are lots of Internet resources too. A helpful one is Alison Galloway's workbook at <http://www.tardis.ed.ac.uk/~kate/qmcweb/qcont.htm> retrieved 02/03/2010.

Robson, C (2002) *Real World Research: A resource for social scientists and practitioner researchers* (2nd edn). Oxford: Blackwell.

McLeod, J (1999) *Practitioner Research in Counselling.* London: Sage.

Gillham, B (2000) *Developing a Questionnaire.* London: Continuum.

Bradburn, NM, Sudman, S & Wansink, B (2004) *Asking Questions: The definitive guide to questionnaire design for market research, political polls and social and health questionnaires.* San Francisco, CA: Jossey Bass.

Saris, WE & Gallhofer, IN (2007) *Design, Evaluation and Analysis of Questionnaires for Survey Research.* Hoboken, NJ: Wiley.

PSYCHOMETRIC TEST Any standardised procedure for measuring aspects, qualities or attributes of mental functioning including, eg, sensitivity, memory, 'intelligence', aptitude or personality.

instructions which accompany them (see the section on asking questions in this chapter). The following suggestions may be useful:

- the instructions are the key to a successful questionnaire. Plan them carefully and state them clearly
- throughout your questionnaire, use simple, straightforward language and a large enough, simple, easy-to-read font
- pilot the questions individually and the questionnaire as a whole. That is, test your questions – find a willing volunteer or two to act as 'trial' respondents. Does your trial respondent understand the questions in the way you meant them? Are the answers you get in the form you want?
- use closed questions sparingly if you want to stick close to a qualitative style. All closed questions are 'forced choice' in that they give the respondent no flexible options

Here are some question types you might use:

Likert scale: a numerical scale from (for example) 1 to 5 offers your respondent the opportunity to rate an experience on a continuum. An example is in the margin.

Semantic differential scale: Asking respondents to decide between polar opposites in meaning. See margin.

Intensity measures: You ask 'How strongly do you feel about this?' and invite a response using either of the above types of scale.

Don't know: A mid point in a scale or a 'don't know' option allows respondents to not answer with dignity. Quantitative methods try to prevent this from happening but in a semi-structured questionnaire you may prefer to have this as an option in all cases.

The received wisdom of quantitative questionnaire design instructs us to avoid open questions like the plague. In qualitative work we do the opposite, since there is no need to tightly code the responses in numbers. You might, however, want to consider giving respondents a fixed space to write their answers to open questions.

Interviewing

As caring professionals, we are all familiar with interviews. At least to some extent, they are our stock in trade. In some sense or another, we interview our clients or patients in order to find out how they are, what they need and so on. Interviews in qualitative research have a different prime function; that is to collect information in the form of opinions, feelings and attitudes (otherwise called *responses*)

Likert scale

How likely is it that you will use this service in the next six months?

1	2	3	4	5
Highly improbable				Highly probable

Semantic differential

Put a cross on the scale to indicate what you think about your current therapist.

Strong • • • • • • • • • • • Weak
Kind • • • • • • • • • • • Cruel
Honest • • • • • • • • • • • Dishonest
Ethical • • • • • • • • • • • Unethical

Note

We go into more detail on the next page.

from the interviewee. If you are trying to get an understanding of the lived experience of another person, interviewing is probably a good way to do this. However, when you interview someone, you should remember that it isn't only the words spoken that are important. Part of the interviewee's story, part of the meaning given to experience, will be told non-verbally. Paralanguage (pauses, and grunts, etc.) and body language can both be important in aiding your interpretation.

Discovering things about the experiences of 'real' people in the 'real world' often hinges on somehow asking some group of individuals about their views, encounters, memories or whatever. Many researchers gather such information in one of two ways – that is, through the administration of a questionnaire or instrument or through interviewing (although there are other ways too). Perhaps if you want to know about human experience, the best way to find out is to ask the human beings who are having or who have had that experience. This means 'interviewing' and interviewing is a widely used method of collecting qualitative data. Put very simply, qualitative interviewing involves the researcher asking questions and listening and respondents giving answers. More technically, the way of knowing about the world assumed by qualitative interviewers tends to be more CONSTRUCTIVIST than POSITIVIST.

The purpose of most qualitative interviewing is to derive interpretations, not facts, from the stories told by the interviewee and the meanings they give to their experiences. In other words, when you want to know what sense a person makes of their experience and perhaps the conceptual or cultural framework in which it is embedded, qualitative interviewing is likely to be an appropriate vehicle.

The differences between qualitative research interviews and interviewing in quantitative research

The differences between interviewing in qualitative research and quantitative research are that the qualitative interviewer:

- recognises a wider range of responses as valid, for example, free-flowing speech, thoughts and feelings that appear to wander off the subject, anecdotes, etc.
- understands the importance of relationship variables such as rapport between the researcher and the respondent
- sees the respondent as a whole person (hence recognising the validity of all of their responses – see above)
- may be only interviewing one person if the research is a single case study
- may interview the respondent on more than one occasion, asking the same or different questions
- may ask the respondent to collaborate more actively in the

Note

As the title of Weiss (1994) *Learning from Strangers* implies, most commonly, interviews are conducted by researchers with people previously unknown to them. This requires a whole set of interpersonal skills and there are many references in the literature to what these may be. For example, Gubrium and Holstein (2002: 8) state 'Behind each bit of advice about how to interview effectively is the understanding that each and every stranger-respondent is someone worth listening to. The respondent is someone who can provide detailed descriptions of his or her thoughts, feelings, and activities, if the interviewer asks and listens carefully enough.' We return to interview skills later in this section.

Weiss, RS (1994) *Learning from Strangers: The art and method of qualitative interview studies.* New York: Free Press.

Gubrium, JF & Holstein, JA (2002) From the individual interview to the interview society. In JF Gubrium & JA Holstein (eds) *Handbook of Interview Research: Context and method* (pp 3-32). Thousand Oaks, CA: Sage.

Note

We told you a bit about a way of using interviews as a way of collecting quantitative data (survey interviewing) in Chapter 2.5.

CONSTRUCTIVIST Constructivism is a philosophy of learning founded on the premise that, by reflecting on our experiences, we construct our own understanding of the world we live in. Each of us generates our own 'rules' and 'mental models' which we use to make sense of our experiences. (From <www.funderstanding.com/content/constructivism> retrieved 11/11/2009)

POSITIVISM A doctrine asserting that sense perceptions are the only admissible basis of human knowledge and precise thought. In research, that the validity of knowledge can only be assured by experimental science.

Note

According to Warren (2002: 83) qualitative interviewing is based on conversation 'with the researchers asking questions and listening, and respondents answering'. This sounds similar to survey interviewing but Warren (ibid: 83) goes on to say that when you want to know what sense a person makes of their experience and perhaps the conceptual or cultural framework in which it is embedded, qualitative interviewing is likely to be an appropriate vehicle. Kvale (1996: 4) sees qualitative interviewing as journeying with the respondents and, on this journey, the interviewer is content to follow the lead and pace of the respondent.

Warren, CAB (2002) Qualitative interviewing. In JF Gubrium & JA Holstein (eds) *Handbook of Interview Research: Context and method* (pp 83-101). Thousand Oaks, CA: Sage.

Kvale, S (1996) *Interviews: An introduction to qualitative research interviewing.* Thousand Oaks, CA: Sage.

Note

It is Robson (2002) in his section on interviewing (pp 269-91) who defines an interview as a conversation with a purpose.

Robson, C (2002) *Real World Research: A resource for social scientists and practitioner researchers* (2nd edn). Oxford: Blackwell.

research by, for example, helping the researcher sort or categorise the responses

- will not be interested in counting or rating only a portion of responses as they are made but will be more interested in taking a more complete record of all responses
- may accept a wider range of possible interview techniques from asking predetermined questions right through to unstructured exploration through to helping the respondent reflect upon their experience

Conversation with a purpose

An interview is 'a conversation with a purpose'. As we said above, you probably conduct interviews of some kind with your clients or patients, for example, to discover how they are feeling or to take a case history. Broadly speaking, the same skills as you use in your practice will be required of you as an interview researcher. In the context of a research interview, this purpose is to gather data (a story) about the experience and/or views of the interviewee in such a way as to inform the research question of the interviewer. Accurate though this is, it is so vague as to be relatively uninformative and unhelpful. This is because, as simple as the process of sitting with someone and inviting them to respond to your questions while you listen to and record their answers sounds, it is actually a very complicated business and can be done in a multitude of ways and for many different purposes.

Most commonly interviews are conducted by researchers with people previously unknown to them. This requires a whole set of interpersonal skills – as we said above, it is likely that as a helping professional you already have these and use them in your day-to-day practice. However, there is no harm in pointing out what may be obvious. First and foremost, it is important to recognise and convey that everyone you interview is worth listening to. This shouldn't be difficult because, if you ask and listen carefully enough, the respondents can provide detailed descriptions of their thoughts, feelings, and activities, and your research depends on you getting this bit right. Careful listening is an essential skill of the research interviewer. Paying attention, responding to what you have heard and checking your perceptions will stand you in good stead as a research interviewer.

Although we tend to think of 'interviewing' as involving only verbal interactions and usually those in which the interviewer is a collector of information which is supplied by the interviewee, and this is probably the most likely form you will encounter or want to employ, it is worth thinking about other ways of collecting interview data. This might be particularly important if your interviewee finds expression through words difficult or has a limited vocabulary or if your form of practice is non-verbal and you would like to base your research in the same modality. For example, what about art as an expression of experience? Could someone talking you through a painting, a dance, a poem constitute an interview? And must all interviews in any one episode of data collection take the same form? Perhaps it is in line with helping practice that the research informant should be free to contribute to the data generation process in any way which makes sense to them and that it is the job of the researcher to seek to understand their expression.

Types of interviews

Interviews come in many different forms. You may already have come across the following types.

Structured interviews

When conducting a structured interview, the interviewer has specific questions and asks and records answers to only those and uses only standard prompts. This type of interviewing is more usually a quantitative research technique. For example, survey interviewing (see Chapter 2.5) is one way in which a structured interview technique is normally used.

Semi-structured interviews

In semi-structured interviews the interviewer has some specific points to cover but is interested in whatever else the interviewee might say and records everything and facilitates the interviewees telling of the story in a variety of ways. The researcher's main questions begin and guide the conversation and probes are used to clarify answers or request further examples. Also, there is sufficient flexibility for follow-up questions to find out more about what the interviewee meant by the answers given to the main questions. The advantages of semi-structured interviews include that they bridge the 'gap' between qualitative and quantitative methods and can add support to the findings in either approach. They are flexible yet allow the interviewer to control the flow of information. The disadvantages include that they are moderately time consuming at data collection (because the interview has an open-ended quality and it may be difficult to regulate the time) and data analysis (because the exploratory parts will generate lots of wordy unpredictable data).

There have been many attempts to define types of semi-structured interview in terms of the purpose for which they are conducted and the nature of the questions asked. Going into this is beyond the scope of this book. See box overleaf.

Note from research
It was Paul's (1997) experience of researching psychodrama (an action method of psychotherapy) that led him to think about action as a research method in its own right. Because a psychodrama is, in effect, a story, it seemed only natural to use it as a data-collection method. This led to speculation about expressive and creative methods as a whole being ways of telling stories. Also, because his informants chose a variety of ways to tell him their stories he had to find a way of taking adequate account of each story. The 'unification' of the views was expressed in the interpretative understanding.

Wilkins, P (1997) Psychodrama and research. *British Journal of Psychodrama and Sociodrama* 12 (1 & 2), 44-61.

Note
Peter Hawkins (1988) also wrote about the use of psychodrama in human inquiry.

Hawkins, P (1988) A phenomenological psychodrama workshop. In P Reason (ed) *Human Inquiry in Action: Developments in new paradigm research* (pp 60-78). London: Sage.

Note
For an expansion of these thoughts on questions in semi-structured interviewing see Rubin and Rubin (1995: 145-6) and Robson (2002: 270-2).

Rubin, HJ & Rubin, IS (1995) *Qualitative Interviewing: The art of hearing data.* Thousand Oaks, CA: Sage.

Robson, C (2002) *Real World Research: A resource for social scientists and practitioner researchers* (2nd edn). Oxford: Blackwell.

Types of semi-structured interview

As we said in the text, to give you a complete idea of all the subdivisions of the term 'semi-structured interview' that people have come up with is beyond the scope of this book. However, the scheme Frick (1998: 76-113) came up with demonstrates the complexity:

- *the focused interview* usually follows some stimulus (for example, the screening of a film) and an objective is to understand the interviewee's experience of and reaction to the stimulus
- *the semi-standardized interview* is a formal way of reconstructing the interviewee's subjective theory about the issue under study (for example, the use of trust in counselling)
- *the problem-centred interview* is a method for collecting biographical data with regard to a specific problem (for example, to understand a respondent's experience of a particular illness)
- *the expert interview* is a type of interview in which the interviewee has an area of 'expertise' and it is this and only this in which the interviewer is interested
- *the ethnographic* interview* is appropriate when the objective is to understand the subject's cultural milieu, way of living, etc. It demands a higher level of rapport between interviewer and interviewee than the previous kinds. * Ethnography is defined on pp. 17 & 164
- *the narrative interview* is mainly used in the context of biographical research. In other words, the interviewer requests an account of (some aspect of) the interviewee's life
- *the episodic interview* Frick (1998: 108) states 'the central element of this form of interview is the periodical invitation to present narratives of situations (e.g. 'If you look back, what was your first experience of television? Could you please recount the situation for me?')

Frick, U (1998) *An Introduction to Qualitative Research.* London: Sage.

Note

McLeod (2003: 74) notes that, with respect to interviewing, there are many situations in which 'the qualitative researcher may wish to make as few prior assumptions as possible regarding the topics to be covered'. For such occasions, he advocates the use of 'unstructured or open-ended interviews'. In such interviews, McLeod (p 80) states:

the researcher will invite the informant to discuss a broad topic or theme, with the emphasis being on recording the spontaneous, free-flowing meanings that the interviewee is able to articulate. The task of the researcher is to define or delineate the phenomenon to be studied and then to facilitate the exploration by the participant of what this phenomenon means to him or her.

McLeod, J (2003) *Doing Counselling Research* (2nd edn). London: Sage.

Unstructured interviews

In unstructured interviews the interviewer has only an initial question and then follows the interviewee's story wherever it leads, recording everything and responding in a facilitative way. At the more extreme end, unstructured interviews may be indistinguishable from conversations. The great advantage of unstructured interviewing is that it allows you to follow the story of the interviewee wherever it leads. Unstructured interviewing is congruent with the philosophy and practice of health and social care and respondents tend to feel respected, listened to and involved. This very flexible, 'naturalistic' form may lead to the discovery of things that you didn't even expect. Unstructured interviews can offer an unsurpassed richness of material. On the downside, the interviewee may never get round to answering the question as you thought it to be important and processing unstructured interviews is time consuming and requires the use of one or more interpretive techniques (see Chapter 2.8).

The practicalities of interviewing

We have told you something about the types and functions of interviews but just as for practitioners, there are some practicalities to be considered when conducting research interviews and these overlap with the professional skills of someone working in health and social care, but we will point out the similarities and differences.

Interviewing in the digital age

Although as yet there seems little written about it, email, and web-based services such as MSN Messenger and even chat rooms may provide alternatives to face-to-face interviewing. Such media are less restricting geographically (you could interview anyone with web access anywhere in the world) and, arguably, have the potential to offer greater confidentiality and allow participants and researcher a greater level of security. Email interviews are less personal than face-to-face or phone interviews and the spontaneity of the follow-up question is lost (and so, therefore, is some of the potential richness). However, they are convenient and fast, allow you to talk to people at great distances and, like face-to-face interviews, give you the benefit of adapting your questioning based on the responses you receive.

To give you some further pointers, Hamilton and Bowers (2006) offer some practical ideas on Internet recruitment and email interviewing, and Egan (2006) found that for traumatic brain injury survivors,

interviewing by email had the advantages of offering them increased time for reflection and composing their answers and that they appreciated the greater control over the email setting. She also found that using email got a greater depth of response than is normally found for this client group. Additionally, Opdenakker (2006) compared the advantages and disadvantages of face-to-face, telephone, MSN Messenger and email interviews.

Egan, J (2006) E-mail facilitated qualitative interviews with traumatic brain injury survivors: A new and accessible method. *Brain Injury 20*(12), 1283-94.

Hamilton, RJ & Bowers, BJ (2006) Internet recruitment and e-mail interviews in qualitative studies. *Qualitative Health Research 16*(6), 821-35.

Opdenakker, R (2006) Advantages and disadvantages of four interview techniques in qualitative research. *Forum: Qualitative Social Research 7*(4). Also available at: <www.qualitative-research. net.index.php/fqs/article/viewArticle/175/391>

Structure of an interview

The general structure of any interpersonal episode has a beginning, middle and end. You will be familiar with the structure of, for example, a typical assessment session and what you as a caring professional are trying to achieve as the session progresses. There are similarities between an assessment interview and a data-collection interview. In a data-collection interview these components have the following functions.

- *beginning* – introduce yourself to the respondent and build rapport (some people think of this as an opportunity to 'break the ice' or warm up). Set the boundaries appropriate to your interview, i.e. explain what the interview is about, how long it will take, whether you are offering confidentiality, how you will be recording the data (notes, audio, video)
- *middle* – this is the data-collection and recording stage. Depending upon the type of interview, semi-structured or unstructured, this will follow a different pattern. You might consider starting with demographic information such as the name, age, etc. of the respondent, followed by some relatively less intrusive, superficial, or 'safe' questions, building to more intimate, deep, or 'risky' questions as the interview progresses. Be careful – you may destroy the rapport you have established by clumsy, prematurely intimate or intrusive questioning early in the interview

Note from research
Paul supervised a student who was interested in the experience of using online dating agencies. It seemed natural to her to use the same facilities to recruit and interview her subjects. This worked very well and, since part of her interest was in the sometimes risky sexual behaviour of her respondents, meant she could keep herself safe while delving into some of the darker aspects of online dating.

Another research student was interested in the behaviour of people into BDSM (bondage, domination and sadomasochism) and how they used the Internet to chat to each other about their interests and arrange meetings. It seemed obvious to use the same medium to investigate their behaviour.

- *end* – an abrupt end can be quite a shock after a searching interview. You will want to thank your respondent and reiterate any arrangements for subsequent interviews, ownership of the data, publication, confidentiality, etc. This is both polite and gives you and your respondent the opportunity to 'wind down'. Counsellors are used to the 'door-knob' disclosures of clients where they get to the 'real' issues as they stand by the door on the way out. You may well find that your respondent does a similar thing whereby as you 'finish' the interview they start to tell you the most interesting and relevant material. Be prepared by having a strategy to capture this information – with the respondent's permission of course
- *follow-up/debriefing/support* – Depending on the nature of the topic or experience about which you are inquiring, it may be just as well to have in mind a number of resources which you can point your respondent towards if they seem in need of subsequent support. For example, if you are investigating the impact of bereavement on service use and interviewing bereaved people, it is possible that their grief will be reawakened. Have information about local support services for the bereaved to hand, perhaps in written form

Any interview should begin by the interviewer making some introductory comments (probably from a verbatim script telling something about the researcher, the purpose of the interview, confidentiality, what will happen to the interviewee's story) and end with some closing comments (thanking the interviewee, recapping the purpose, etc.).

The normal rules of research interviewing require some element of neutrality, objectivity and a degree of passivity in the interviewer. Also, deliberate attempts are taken to prevent interviewee 'cross-contamination', i.e. the interviewer does not disclose to one interviewee what has been said by another. This probably stems from a POSITIVISTIC notion that anything else risks contaminating the 'data'. Generally speaking, as a beginning researcher, if you want to be sure that what you are being told is the interviewee's idea, it is probably best to restrict what you say to asking your questions and making facilitative responses. However, there are other views and, briefly, we will tell you something about them so that you begin to get an idea of the huge possibilities and potentialities of interviewing.

Firstly, if you want to discover 'deep' information and knowledge – information concerning very personal matters, such as an individual's self, lived experience, values and decisions, occupational ideology, cultural knowledge, or perspective that is not normally accessible through surveys, informal interviewing or focus groups, a different approach may be in order. It is likely that a friendly, interested

POSITIVISTIC/POSITIVISM A doctrine asserting that sense perceptions are the only admissible basis of human knowledge and precise thought. In research, that the validity of knowledge can only be assured by experimental science.

Note

Don't forget that respondents of different types may require that you listen to them in different ways. For example, do you have to listen to women in a different way from how you would listen to men? That is an inference you could draw from Dana Jack (1999).

Jack, DC (1999) Ways of listening to women in qualitative research: Interview techniques and analysis. *Canadian Psychology* 40(2), 91-101.

Aspects of the qualitative research interview (after McLeod, 2003: 75)

• *life-world* The subject of qualitative interviewing is the life-world of the interviewee and his/her relation to it. The purpose is to describe and understand the central themes the person experiences and lives toward. The interview is theme-oriented, not person-oriented

• *meaning* The interview seeks to describe and understand the meaning of central themes in the life-world of the informant. The interviewer registers and interprets what is said as well as how it is said, and must be observant of and able to interpret vocalisation, facial expressions and other bodily gestures

• *qualitative and descriptive* The interview aims at obtaining nuanced descriptions of different aspects of the life-world

• *specificity* Descriptions of specific situations and action sequences are elicited, not general opinions

• *presuppositionless* Rather than coming with ready-made categories and schemes of interpretation, there is an openness to new and unexpected phenomena

• *focused* The interview is neither strictly structured with standardised questions, nor entirely 'non-directive', but is focused on certain themes

• *ambiguity* The statements of an interviewee may sometimes be ambiguous, reflecting objective contradictions in the world he or she lives in

• *change* During the interview, the informant may come to change his or her descriptions of and meanings about a theme. The process of being interviewed may produce new insight and awareness.

• *sensitivity* Different interviewers may produce different material on the same theme, depending on their sensitivity toward, and knowledge of, the topic

• *interpersonal situation* The interview is an interaction between two people

• *positive experience* A qualitative research interview may be a favourable experience for the informant. The interview is a conversation where two people talk about a theme of interest to both parties. A well carried through qualitative interview may be a rare and enriching experience for the interviewee

McLeod, J (2003) *Doing Counselling Research* (2nd edn). London: Sage.

interviewer who actively seeks to establish trust and rapport, rather than one who may appear detached or aloof, will encourage the interviewee to delve more deeply. Also, greater involvement of the interviewer's self than in most other kinds of interviewing is facilitative and self-disclosure on the part of the interviewee is a likely response to at least limited self-disclosure on the part of the interviewer. To do this safely and effectively, considerable self-knowledge on the part of the interviewer is a requirement.

Secondly, in some of the more subjective approaches to research which make use of interactions between the researcher and others, there is an assumption that a more relaxed 'conversation' in which the researcher not only self-discloses experiences but also offers interpretations of them will elicit deeper, more meaningful explorations on the part of the 'co-researcher'. Not only that but cross-contamination becomes cross-fertilisation in that when talking to Jane it is seen as actually helpful to say 'When I was talking to Bill, he said ... I wonder what you think about that?'

Interview schedule

1. 'Thank you for agreeing to take part in this survey. As I mentioned over the phone, I am conducting research into trainee counsellor's experiences in therapy. You also said that you would be happy to let me tape record the interview, does that still feel OK?'
   If yes – 'Fine, in that case I'll set the recorder up and switch it on now.' **Continue at 2**.
   If no – 'I appreciate your concerns. How do you feel about continuing with me taking notes?'
   If yes – 'OK, are there any other questions you have before we start?'
   If yes answer the questions and continue at 2.
   If no – 'I see. I realise that you have had more time to consider how you feel about this interview since we spoke on the phone. Since I need to record the information in certain ways, it wouldn't be sensible for me to continue with the interview, so thanks for your time so far.'
   Closing remarks.

2. 'The information you give is in confidence, your name will not be mentioned on the tape or in the notes and you will get a chance to look at this work before it is submitted for publication if you wish. Any extracts from the interview tape or notes will be worded so that you cannot be identified.'

3. 'Firstly then, are you in therapy at the moment?'

As can be seen in the example, the interview schedule is a mixture of aide-memoirs to help you if you dry up and instructions so that you know what to do next in order to get all the information you need. Use 'GOTO' instructions (sometimes called skips, e.g., 'if yes, skip to question 5') – 'If the answer to this question is yes, then GOTO question 5, if no, GOTO question 8.' And so on. Once the biographical and demographical information is collected at the beginning of the interview, you would proceed to collecting the main body of data:

7. 'How did you choose your therapist when you started the course?'
   Prompt 'Was the choice made for you by the course tutors?'
   Prompt 'Was the therapist recommended to you?'
   Prompt 'Is their orientation the same as that of the course?'

8. 'To what extent did you use the therapist to help deal with course issues?'
   Prompt 'Could you give me an example or two?'
   If worried 'Only go into as much detail as you feel comfortable with.'
   Allow to develop and finish with 'Is there any more you would like to tell me about that?'

Questions that might guide an in-depth exploration of human experience include:
- what does this person know about the experience?
- what qualities or dimensions of the experience stand out for the person? What examples are vivid and alive?
- what events, situations, and people are connected with the experience?
- what feelings and thoughts are generated by the experience?
- what bodily states or shifts in bodily presence occur in the experience?
- what time and space factors affect the person's awareness and meaning of the experience?

The setting of an interview

You will need only the briefest of reminders that interviews can take place in a variety of settings:
- in the respondent's home
- at the respondent's place of work
- a comfortable, private, quiet room, alone and face-to-face with the respondent, at the interviewer's premises
- as above but in a group
- on the street – on the hoof, permission sought and granted on the spot
- on the telephone – can be planned and arranged in advance or *ad hoc* with no appointment made (be ready for a refusal)

Each setting will require different planning and preparation. Things to consider include:
- distractions and interruptions
- confidentiality and privacy
- the amount of time the interview will take (don't expect your respondents to stand in the street for half an hour)
- the type and quality of the data you wish to collect
- how you are going to record the data

Other things you may want to know about qualitative interviews

In-depth interviewing

This may be a variant of the 'unstructured interviewing' but Johnson (2002: 103-19) sees it as being sufficiently different in form and function to be considered separately. He (p. 104) states,

> A researcher who uses in-depth interviewing commonly seeks 'deep' information and knowledge – usually deeper information and knowledge than is sought in surveys, informal interviewing,

Note

Whatever style of interview you are conducting, don't forget that how you behave may determine how much information you get and its nature. Your job is to get your informants to respond freely and openly. Robson (2002: 273) has four simple rules to help you do this:

1. *Listen more than you speak.* Except in a few approaches (for example, heuristic inquiry, see Chapter 2.8), a research interview is not an opportunity for the researcher to hold forth, giving expression to your own experiences and opinions.

2. *Put your questions in a straightforward, clear, non-threatening way.* A confused or defensive respondent is likely to clam up.

3. *Eliminate clues which lead interviewees to respond in a particular way.* In other words, check that the way you say things and/or how you respond doesn't amount to leading your interviewee, however subtly.

4. *Enjoy it (or at least look as though you do).* Don't give the message that you are bored or scared. Vary your voice and facial expression.

Robson, C (2002) *Real World Research: A resource for social scientists and practitioner researchers* (2nd edn). Oxford: Blackwell.

Johnson, JM (2002) In-depth interviewing. In JF Gubrium & JA Holstein (eds) *Handbook of Interview Research: Context and method* (pp 103-19). Thousand Oaks, CA: Sage.

or focus groups, for example. This information usually concerns very personal matters, such as an individual's self, lived experience, values and decisions, occupational ideology, cultural knowledge, or perspective.

Johnson (2002) goes on to state that in-depth interviews are seldom the sole source of data but are

> used in conjunction with data gathered through such avenues as the lived experience of the interviewer as a member or participant in what is being studied, naturalistic or direct observation, informal interviewing, documentary research, and team field research. In many cases, researchers use in-depth interviewing as a way to check out theories they have formulated through naturalistic observation, to verify independently (or TRIANGULATE) knowledge they have gained through participation as members of particular cultural settings, or to explore multiple meanings of or perspectives on some actions, events, or settings. (p. 104)

Johnson, JM (2002) In-depth interviewing. In JF Gubrium & JA Holstein (eds) *Handbook of Interview Research: Context and method* (pp 103-19). Thousand Oaks, CA: Sage.

TRIANGULATION is a way of assuring the validity of research findings through the use of a *variety* of research methods (usually more than two).

He goes on to consider what 'deep' information might be and ascribes four different meanings to that term in the context of this form of interviewing (pp. 106-7). In brief, these are:
- deep understandings are held by people who have the lived experience in which the researcher is interested. The interviewer seeks to gain the same level of understanding
- deep understandings transcend common-sense boundaries. An objective of in-depth interviewing is to discover what is normally hidden from view, what is not normally reflected on, or the 'irrational', emotional, TRANSPERSONAL or spiritual 'explanations' for phenomena
- deep understandings can show how our views of the world and values are actually constructed on the base of our experiences and interests
- deep understandings 'allow us to grasp and articulate the multiple views of, perspectives on, and meanings of some activity, event, place or cultural object'

TRANSPERSONAL Literally beyond (trans) the person, transcending the rational, physical and sensory to the mystical.

In summary, Johnson (p. 109) characterises in-depth interviews thus:
- in-depth interviews are conducted by a friendly and interested interviewer who actively seeks to establish trust and rapport
- in-depth interviewing calls for greater involvement of the interviewer's self than most other kinds of interviewing. Self-disclosure in the respondent is encouraged and supported by some reciprocity on the part of the interviewer
- in-depth interviewers must undertake considerable self-reflection

to get to know themselves and must make a self-conscious effort to observe themselves in interaction with others

The life story interview

Life story interviews are linked by Atkinson (2002: 121-40) to the classic functions of story telling. Myths and folktales bring us into accord with ourselves, others, the mysteries of life and with the universe around us. He argues that life stories serve the same classic functions. These four functions are (after Atkinson, 2002: 122):

1   stories, with their deeply human elements and motifs, can guide us stage by stage, through an entire life course. The stories we tell of our lives help us order and make sense of our experiences and assist us in forming our identities

2   stories can affirm, validate, and support our experiences socially and clarify our relationships with those around us. By underlining our similarities and differences, stories foster a sense of community

3   stories can serve a mystical-religious function by bringing us face-to-face with an ultimate mystery. Stories take us beyond the here and now of our everyday existence and allow us to enter the realm of the spirit, the domain of the sacred

4   stories can render a cosmology, an interpretative total image of the universe and help us understand how we fit into it

In defining a life story, Atkinson (2002: 125-6) offers the opinion that it is the story a person chooses to tell about the life he or she has lived and that it can take a factual form, a metaphorical form, a poetic form or any other creatively expressive form – whatever the teller prefers. He writes:

> In a life story interview, the interviewee is a story teller, the narrator of the story of his or her own life; the interviewer is a guide, or director, in this process. The two together are collaborators, composing and constructing a story the teller can be pleased with.

Atkinson goes on to consider the benefits of the life story interview. Of these benefits, he gives clear priority to those which are for the interviewee. These personal benefits include (pp. 126-8):

- in sharing our stories, we gain a clearer perspective on personal experiences and feelings, which in turn brings greater meaning to our lives
- through sharing our stories, we obtain greater self-knowledge, stronger self-image, and enhanced self-esteem
- in sharing our stories, we share cherished experiences and insights with others
- sharing our stories can bring us joy, satisfaction, and inner peace

Atkinson, R (2002) The life story interview. In JF Gubrium & JA Holstein (eds) *Handbook of Interview Research: Context and method* (pp 121-40). Thousand Oaks, CA: Sage.

- sharing our stories is a way of purging, or releasing, certain burdens and validating personal experience; this is in fact central to the recovery process
- sharing our stories helps create community, and may show us that we have more in common with others than we thought
- by sharing our stories, we can help other people see their lives more clearly or differently, and perhaps inspire them to change negative things in their lives
- when we share our stories, others will get to know and understand us better, in ways that they hadn't before
- in sharing our stories, we might gain a better sense of how we want our stories to end, or how we can give ourselves the 'good' endings we want. By understanding our past and present, we derive a clearer perspective on our goals for the future

Atkinson, R (2002) The life story interview. In JF Gubrium & JA Holstein (eds) *Handbook of Interview Research: Context and method* (pp 121-40). Thousand Oaks, CA: Sage.

Atkinson (2002: 128) states that telling a life story is not therapy 'but the act of telling the story can often help clarify things for the teller that he or she might not have understood before'. In considering the research uses of the life story interview, Atkinson (2002: 128-30) asserts it is 'inherently interdisciplinary'. The many uses to which it can be put include:

- understanding how the self evolves over time
- understanding how identity is constructed
- determining the range of possible roles and standards that exist within a human community
- defying an individual's place in the social order
- explaining an individual's understanding of social events, movements, political causes and so on
- determining the relation between language and social practice, the relation of self to other and the creation of social identity
- to get at shared cultural meanings and the dynamics of social change
- to discover value systems, beliefs and world-views
- to explore how life stories told currently fit with what is known of the universe or how people make sense of the world in which we live

Atkinson, R (2002) The life story interview. In JF Gubrium & JA Holstein (eds) *Handbook of Interview Research: Context and method* (pp 121-40). Thousand Oaks, CA: Sage.

Atkinson views the possibilities of the life story interview as limitless and says that the life story itself can be the focus of published research 'or segments could be used as data to illustrate any number of research needs' (p. 129).

Postmodern trends in interviewing

POSTMODERNISM is a reaction to the assumed certainty of scientific or objective efforts to explain reality. It is highly sceptical of explanations which claim to be universal.

This can be considered as a wholesale reconsideration of the supposed 'neutrality' of the traditional research interviewer – as such there is not one but many POSTMODERN influences on research interviewing. These are considered by Fontana (2002: 161-75) who (pp. 162-3) poses the sensibilities of the POSTMODERN interview as:

- the boundaries between, and respective roles, of interviewer and interviewee have become blurred as the traditional relationship between the two is no longer seen as natural
- new forms of communication in interviewing are being used, as interviewer and respondent(s) collaborate together in constructing their narratives
- interviewers have become more concerned about issues of representation, seriously engaging in questions such as, 'Whose story are we telling and for what purpose?'
- the authority of the researcher qua interviewer but also qua writer comes under scrutiny. Respondents are no longer seen as faceless numbers whose opinions we process completely on our own terms. Consequently, there is increasing concern with the respondent's own understanding as he or she frames and represents an 'opinion'
- traditional patriarchal relations in interviewing are being criticised, and ways to make formerly unarticulated voices audible are now centre stage
- the forms used to report findings have been hugely expanded. As boundaries separating disciplines collapse, modes of expression from literature, poetry and drama are being applied
- the topic of inquiry – interviewing – has expanded to encompass the cinematic and the televisual. Electronic media are increasingly accepted as a resource in interviews, with growing use of email, Internet chat rooms, and other electronic modes of communication

Fontana, A (2002) Postmodern trends in interviewing. In JF Gubrium & JA Holstein (eds) *Handbook of Interview Research: Context and method* (pp 161-75). Thousand Oaks, CA: Sage.

Fontana offers critiques of the detached interviewer (pp. 163-4), and (among other things) describes feminist influences on POSTMODERN ideas about research interviewing (pp. 167-9), and virtual interviewing (pp. 169-70).

Fontana, A (2002) Postmodern trends in interviewing. In JF Gubrium & JA Holstein (eds) *Handbook of Interview Research: Context and method* (pp 161-75). Thousand Oaks, CA: Sage.

Autoethnography

Autoethnography is a form of research in which the researcher is the subject – i.e. interviewer and interviewee are the same person – and where the aim is to connect the personal and the cultural. Autoethnography is usually written in the first person and may take a variety of creative/expressive forms. In autoethnographic texts, concrete action, dialogue, emotion, embodiment, spirituality and self-consciousness all have a place as 'relational and institutional stories affected by history, social structure, and culture, which themselves are dialectically revealed through action, feeling, thought and language'. Ellis and Bochner (2002: 739-43) name the many trends in or variants of autoethnography they recognise and consider the main types.

Ellis, C & Bochner, AP (2000) Autoethnography, personal narrative, reflexivity: Researcher as subject. In NK Denzin & YS Lincoln (eds) *Handbook of Qualitative Research* (2nd edn) (pp 733-68). Thousand Oaks, CA: Sage.

Moustakas, C (1990) *Heuristic Research: Design, methodology, and applications.* Newbury Park, CA: Sage.

Reason, P & Heron, J (1986) Research with people: The paradigm of co-operative experiential inquiry. *Person-Centered Review 1*(4), 456-76.

Wilkins, P (2000) Storytelling as research. In B Humphries (ed) *Research in Social Care and Social Welfare: Issues and debates for practice* (pp 144-53). London: Jessica Kingsley.

Collaborative interviewing

This is a term Paul coined to embrace the strategies employed in various collaborative approaches to research. These include co-operative inquiry (Reason & Heron, 1986), heuristic inquiry (Moustakas, 1990) – which shares with autoethnography 'self-talk' and the creative expression of findings – and 'storybuilding' (Wilkins, 2000: 147-8). Each of these involves the negotiation between a group of co-researchers who (among other things) talk to each other about their views, experiences and so on. Interviews most commonly take the form of conversations.

Conducting interviews

While, broadly speaking, any interview is a story-gathering conversation, different types of interview require different procedures, emphases and skills. We will give you some idea how to conduct semi-structured and unstructured interviews.

How to conduct a semi-structured interview

The semi-structured interview represents a compromise which many researchers find comfortable. The skill of getting the researcher's agenda into the interview without applying a rigid schedule should be within the repertoire of most helping practitioners.

The first task is to plan an interview schedule which could start something like the illustration on p. 144.

A schedule allows you to stray from the path of the questions when you feel it appropriate and yet it continues to remind you where you are up to, especially if each numbered item on it has a check-box next to it for you to tick when the question is asked. Because it encourages you to cover roughly the same ground with each respondent, this method holds the promise of a standardised procedure, without the straight-jacket feel of a completely structured interview. When the middle section of the interview is complete you should end the interview with some suitable closing remarks. You can include a sample of the wording of these in your schedule.

How to conduct an unstructured interview

It may be that exploratory, unstructured interviews are at the core of your practice and that you feel you instinctively know how they should be conducted. And, of course, to a certain extent you are right. However, a word of caution: in this context, remember that you are a researcher and not a practitioner. Your objectives will be different and so the skills you employ will have to be appropriately different. Your aim is to enable the respondent to explore their experience and tell their story. You will need to focus their reflective process on the important elements in the story, the meaning of the elements for them, the feelings and thoughts that these elements evoke and any consequences or outcomes. You may want to attend carefully to any sequences of events, etc. but if you are recording the interview on tape you will be freed from having to remember much of it apart from that which you need to facilitate further exploration. Don't forget that some forms of unstructured interviewing call for the active participation of the interviewer as an experiencing person. If you choose one of these, be prepared for the self-disclosure and self-discovery that is likely to be involved.

Whatever form they take, interviews are a very useful way of collecting stories. They can stand as the sole source or be used in conjunction with stories gathered in other ways (see below). Interviewing can be a way to check out hunches, ideas and theories you have formulated through, for example, observing or reflecting on your practice or that of your colleagues or in conjunction with other methods in order to TRIANGULATE your findings (see Chapter 2.6, p. 122). However, whether your interviews are structured, semi-structured or unstructured, your only source of information or one of several, you are going to need to know something about how to frame and ask interview questions.

TRIANGULATION is a way of assuring the validity of research findings through the use of a *variety* of research methods (usually more than two).

Recording an interview

When you decide to use one or more kinds of interview as a way of collecting your stories, you are going to need some way of making a record of what is said. Of course, you could do this by making contemporaneous notes but that would distract you from the actual process of the interview. Alternatively, you could write down what you remember immediately after the interview but this risks the loss of detail. Also, with either of these methods it is really difficult to get an accurate picture of all the 'paralanguage', that is, the things like pauses, grunts, tears, laughter, tone and hesitant or vehement responses. Sometimes these contain a wealth of information. Luckily, we have many other ways of recording interviews onto convenient digital media (audio and video) using very small devices including mobile phones. These have the virtue of offering a way of making a fairly comprehensive recording and, once set up and running, allow the interviewer to concentrate on the interpersonal process from which the story will arise. Of course they require the consent of the interviewee and access to the necessary equipment.

If you are studying at a college or university you may be able to borrow audio recorders and video cameras from the technical support section, but increasingly people have access to good quality digital equipment at home. Do not think that all equipment will be suitable – make sure you have appropriate equipment for the job, i.e. it has enough storage capacity and battery life to do the job you want it to do.

Once you have your hands on the audio or video equipment,

Note from life
My students used the recording rooms at my place of work to video-tape their practice interviews. Usually, everything appeared to go well but every so often when they came to review their tapes what was being said was drowned out by the sound of the tea trolley passing over a ridged hard surface outside or an aircraft approaching or leaving our local airport. They hadn't noticed these intrusions at the time. The sharper ones learned to keep focused on their informants and the interview process while keeping an ear open for intrusive, mechanical noises and, if it seemed necessary, pausing to allow the noise to pass.

Note

Reading this back, it sounds incredibly patronising. However, every researcher, regardless of their experience will have several tales of hours of work lost through equipment failure. Of course, what we really mean is that the work was lost due to human failure. The equipment was fine, but we forgot to charge the battery or plug the microphone in the correct socket.

you have to check that you know how to use it – if you don't know much about the machine you are going to use ask somebody who does know how to operate it. Failing that, read the instruction manual. Perhaps doing both is an even better idea. When you think you know how the thing works, practice. There really is no substitute for having a dry run or two before you set out to collect your data. Things to look out for include:

- do you know how to switch the machine off and on?
- does it have enough tape/memory for the length of interview you expect to conduct?
- what is the best distance from you and your interviewee to clearly record what is said and done without the device being obtrusive?
- is the power source adequate? If you are using batteries, make sure these are fully charged before you begin. If your audio-recorder or video camera requires mains power make sure that you can plug it in without the wires getting in the way
- when you play back the recording, can you hear or see what you need to?

You might like to think about the setting for your interview too. We have told you something about this already but it surprising what noises can loom large on a recording and obscure what is being said. For example, the tea trolley going past the window that you barely noticed at the time might very well drown out voices on the tape. Finding a soundproof room is beyond most of us but it really will help if you can find somewhere as far from disturbance as you can. Again, rehearsal is the key.

Once you have practised, have recruited your participants and found a suitable place to make your recordings, you are ready to start collecting stories. However, before each interview it is as well to run through the following check list:

- check that you can operate the equipment and that it is working properly before the beginning of each session
- make sure that the interviewee knows that they are being recorded
- make sure that the power source is adequate, batteries charged, and that you have enough memory or disk space
- ensure that you have the space for as long as you need and that you will not be interrupted

You are now ready to conduct your interview – for some guidance on how to do this, see above. When you have your recording, there are still some things left to do:

- an obvious point that regularly gets overlooked is to label the digital files of all recordings with the time, date and place as minimum. Back up the recordings and keep the backups safe –

both for your sake and to protect what might be confidential information
- as soon as possible after the recording is made and always before the next one is made, view or listen to the recording to check the quality. Attend to any technical problems that arise
- attach to each recording any special note – things to look out for or be aware of when watching or subsequently transcribing and processing the record
- make a separate recordings log – date, time, duration, place, name of participant observer(s), media and recording equipment used and any reminders for the next session regarding camera position, sound levels, etc.

When your recording is complete, you might like to think about what you noticed that the machine may not have picked up and how you can make a note of these. For example, automatic recording media cannot record your subjective thoughts and feelings. You will have to do this later. Make any such records as soon as possible after the session; your memory will only fade.

A word of advice, you should be judicious in your use of such recording methods. They generate a huge quantity of data which will take a very long time to transcribe and to code. Make sure you have the time and resources to analyse it in the way you want to. The flip side of this is that such records are very durable and can always be returned to at a later date. Indeed you may wish to do this anyway as a planned repetition of your research cycle.

As well as being more or less essential when collecting stories by interview, audio and video recording are frequently used in non-participant observation and can also be useful to augment participant observation (see below).

Last but by no means least, when you make audio or video recordings, you should think very carefully about to whom the information they contain belongs and what will happen to it at the end of the research project. Of course, there is an obligation to keep recordings safe in accordance with whatever the commitment to confidentiality you have given. Make sure you can do this in a way that will satisfy your interviewees. When you have finished with the recordings, dispose of them carefully. This means more than simply dumping them in the computer wastebin since you may forget to delete all files if your computer is sold on. Also consider giving a copy of the recording to the interviewee.

Some answers about questions

Unless you are opting for the extreme of an unstructured, reflective, respondent-centred interview with no questions at all, you will have to spend some time thinking about the sort of questions you want to use. Questions are common to both questionnaires and interviews, so we will review the options regarding questions before we look at how questions might be marshalled into some form of interrogation device. As caring professionals, you are probably familiar with the division of questions into two classes, closed and open questions. However, there is no harm in looking at them in relation to research.

Closed questions

These offer a fixed number of alternative answers to choose from giving the respondent limited freedom. Some closed questions ask for a response on a scale of some sort, perhaps of agreement or disagreement, preference or strength of feelings.

Advantages: Structured interrogation uses mostly (if not all) closed questions. They can be useful for getting basic demographic information – name, age, or whatever else may be necessary to identify and help categorise your respondents. If you are trying to approximate a qualitative method, you must use closed questions very sparingly.

Disadvantages: Closed questions are the stock-in-trade of quantitative researchers, since they lend themselves to having numbers applied to their well-ordered and (if you've set and asked them correctly) predictable responses. They require careful phrasing since it is easy to ask a question which does not give the full range of answers for a particular group of respondents (you will only get the answers you provide). This makes closed questions unpopular with qualitative researchers because they impose the researcher's agenda upon the respondent.

Open questions

Well known as a technique from the toolkit of, for example, many counselling approaches, the open question does not give an answer or range of possible answers. It structures the interrogation only to the point of introducing the researcher's preferred agenda topic but after that it does not direct the respondent to a set of permitted answers. The respondent can answer a well-compiled, open question in almost any way they choose – including giving a 'nonsense' answer or avoiding the question.

Advantages: Since fewer constraints are imposed on the respondent they are less likely to feel frustrated – a happy respondent is an honest and more accurate respondent. Open questions get richer responses. Answers are potentially more accurate and representative since the respondent can talk around the question and reveal any misunderstandings which may remain hidden in answers to closed questions.

Disadvantages: Open questions are more difficult to code in the

---

Closed questions

- Are you currently in therapy?

- How many times a week do you see your therapist?

- Do you find your therapist
  1 Very effective?
  2 Effective?
  3 Neither effective nor ineffective?
  4 Ineffective?
  5 Very ineffective?

Open questions

- Why did you decide to enter therapy?

- What do you look for when choosing a therapist?

- How would you describe the effectiveness of your current therapist?

traditional quantitative sense – you can't really apply numbers to the answers with ease. Open questions do not really lend themselves to questionnaires since respondents may get fatigued quite quickly. If respondents are writing their responses, it can be difficult to judge how much space to allow for an answer since people will assume they have to fill the space allowed and only that.

Other interrogation techniques

Questions aren't the only method of eliciting information in interviews. Caring professionals will know of a range of interview skills that all help the respondent to tell their story. In planning an interview we need to consider what methods other than questions we might need to use in order to oil the wheels of data collection:

Silence: Counsellors and all caring professionals know the value of silence in therapeutic and all helping interviews. Remember that the interviewer remaining silent is one way of getting the respondent to talk!

Continuation responses: Again, well known to caring professionals – the smiles, 'Uh-huh' and 'I see' type responses keep the respondent talking, so don't forget to use them.

Probes: Specific questions to get the respondent to elaborate on a particular point. These are particularly useful in semi-structured interviews and, in some styles of interviewing, may be restricted to a few agreed beforehand.

Prompts: A range or set of possible answers or set of reminders to let the respondent know of any options they might not have thought about. Again, these are useful in semi-structured interviews.

When it is done out of genuine interest and with a real intention to hear the answer, the simple question 'And what else?' can inspire further information even when the respondent thinks they have said all they have to say.

> **Probes and prompts**
>
> 'What do you look for when choosing a therapist?'
> **Probe**: *Ask for more about gender and ethnic origin.*
>
> What do you look for when choosing a therapist?'
> **Prompt**: *Show list of professional organisations if membership of a professional body is mentioned.*

Some principles of question asking

Wherever they are to be used, questions need to be carefully compiled, sensitively asked and their answers treated with respect. Here are some general rules which will help make your question asking effective and efficient.

Ask questions that can be understood – ask questions using language content and structure appropriate for your respondents. Try and put *your* question into the words your *respondents* would use. However, do this judiciously. What do you think would happen if you tried to interview teenage skateboarders using their street slang?

Ask questions that do not lead to an obvious answer – 'leading' questions either suggest an answer, or make an assumption or imply something about the respondent, e.g. 'Why do you like your physiotherapist?' is better asked as, 'Do you like your physiotherapist?' Similarly, 'What makes gestalt therapy superior to all other approaches?' should be rephrased as, 'What approach do you think is the best?' or, 'Do you think there are any advantages to gestalt therapy?'

Ask the simplest and shortest question possible – avoid jargon words unless they will be familiar to your respondents. People may only answer part of multi-part or long-winded questions or simply not understand the question because it is difficult to make sense of or see how it hangs together.

Ask only questions that **can** *be answered* – 'When was the last time you had a headache?' or, 'How many clients did you see in 1989?' will be difficult for respondents to answer accurately depending upon certain factors (e.g. whether they had a headache recently or whether they keep good records).

Ask only questions that **will** *be answered* – This includes the principle which says you should ask questions that will be answered truthfully. An untruthful answer is of little use since you will not be able to sort out the true responses from the untruthful ones. A refusal, although it will produce a 'hole' in your data, is often better. 'Do you enjoy oral sex?', or, 'Have you behaved unethically in the past year?' might get refused. Respondents also object to being forced by a structured question to give an answer that doesn't accurately represent their experience.

Ask as few questions as possible – your time is precious and you should respect your respondent's time too. You should collect only that data which you need for the purposes of your study.

Make sure the questions are relevant. This will make your project PARSIMONIOUS.

PARSIMONIOUS in general use means penny-pinching and miserly; in research terms it means efficient with no redundant elements.

Case studies

One of the ways in which social science researchers have sought to understand the experience of human beings is through examining case studies. At its simplest, a case study is an in-depth exploration and examination of the experience of one or more individuals who have had or who are having an encounter with the phenomenon of interest to the researcher. For example, one way of gaining a better understanding of depression would be to investigate the histories and views of people who are or who have been depressed. Case studies draw on a variety of sources including records and interviews (with clients, practitioners or both). The aim is to build up as complete a picture as possible of the experience or event the researcher is seeking to understand. The principle difference between case study research and other conventional approaches to inquiry is that in the former the focus is on reaching as full an understanding as possible of the individual case rather than seeking to comprehend something of a population. The intention behind a case study is for the researcher to present a holistic and meaningful interpretation of the characteristics of real-life events.

Case history and case study have played an important part in the development of health and social care. For example, in counselling and psychotherapy, Freud explained his theory and practice in relation to work with particular patients (for example, Little Hans and Ratman) and there is a famous exploration of work with 'Gloria' whose filmed encounters with Carl Rogers (founder of client-centred therapy), Fritz Perls (founder of gestalt therapy) and Albert Ellis (founder of rational-emotive behaviour therapy) are known to generations of counselling and psychotherapy students. However, these and similar examples are case illustrations rather than case study research for which there are more exacting standards.

Case studies provide a way of doing research involving the investigation of 'real-life' circumstances and offering a richness of detail inaccessible via a statistical study. As we indicated above, case studies rely on multiple sources of evidence and may be based on a mix of qualitative and quantitative data. The 'case' can be of almost any kind or nature: an individual of course, but also a group, an institution or a neighbourhood to name but a few.

As with any other form of qualitative inquiry, in case study research the objectives of the researcher must also be taken into account. When you conduct a case study, you are seeking to represent the case, not to represent the world. This, together with an awareness as to whether the study is intended to explain or explore a set of behaviours, circumstances, beliefs, etc. should be taken into account when considering the trustworthiness of conclusions and descriptions. The characteristics of an exemplary case study are that it must:

- *be significant* – that is the individual case or cases are unusual and of general interest and the underlying issues are of importance (theoretically, practically or in terms of policy)
- *be 'complete'* – Yin (2003: 162-3) acknowledges that this is difficult to describe operationally but he suggests that completeness can be characterised in at least three ways. Firstly, the boundaries of the case must be given explicit attention. This means that the study continues to an 'analytic periphery' such that any further information is of decreasing relevance to the study. Secondly, the complete case study report should demonstrate convincingly that an exhaustive effort has been

Note

For a synopsis of Freud's case studies of Little Hans and Ratman see <www.mag ma.ca/~mfonda/freud10.html> Also available in translation by James Strachey as Freud (1955).

Freud, S (1955) *The Standard Edition ... Two Case Studies (Vol 10).* London: Hogarth.

Note

Sections of the Gloria sessions (*Three Approaches to Psychotherapy*) are available on YouTube and <video.google.com>

IF YOU WANT TO KNOW MORE ABOUT the background to Gloria's interviews with the three psychotherapists and what happened to her later

you could take a look at her daughter's book (Burry, 2008).

Burry, P (2008) *Living with 'The Gloria Films'.* Ross-on-Wye: PCCS Books.

Note

Robert Stake (2000: 435) argues that case study is not a methodological choice but a choice of what is to be studied. This can be done in a variety of ways 'analytically or holistically, entirely by repeated measures or HERMENEUTICALLY, organically or culturally [or] by mixed methods'.

Stake, RE (2000) Case studies. In NK Denzin & YS Lincoln (eds) *Handbook of Qualitative Research* (2nd edn) (pp 435-54). Thousand Oaks, CA: Sage.

HERMENEUTICS The art and science of interpretation of meaning, traditionally of texts, but in social sciences more of human experience or social events.

Yin, RK (2003) *Case Study Research: Design and methods* (3rd edn). Thousand Oaks, CA: Sage.

made to collect all relevant evidence. Thirdly, the study should not be limited by, e.g. constraints of time and resources *unless* it is designed with those constraints in mind
* *consider alternative perspectives* – rival propositions, interpretations and evaluations to those of the researcher must be given appropriate consideration and be answered
* *display sufficient evidence* – an exemplary case study is one in which readers are presented with an effective presentation of the most relevant evidence so that they can form an independent view of the merits of the analysis
* *be composed in an engaging manner* – regardless of the medium used, the report of a case study must be accessible, well-written and engaging. The researcher should be enthusiastic about the study and want to communicate this and the findings from the study in a meaningful and enticing way

Case studies make a major contribution to our knowledge and understanding of human processes for a number of reasons:
* a well-researched case study that contradicts an existing theory, however previously well validated, can raise serious questions against the theory. Well-established ideas have been crucially undermined by good case study evidence
* case studies have been influential in the development of understanding, e.g. the work of Freud (treatment of hysteria), Piaget (stages of intellectual development in children), Osgood (multiple personalities) are based on seminal case studies
* our understanding of human processes would be very cold and dry without the detail and warmth contributed by the personal dimension of case studies. This is particularly true of our understanding of human distress, where case studies give a deeper insight into suffering: a good example is Virginia Axline's (1964) case study reported in *Dibs: In Search of Self*

More about case study research

McLeod (2003: 99) writes that case studies have 'the potential to contribute knowledge and understanding that is highly relevant to counselling practice' and it follows that this is true of other approaches to health and social care. Case studies provide a way of doing research involving the investigation of 'real-life' circumstances and offering a richness of detail inaccessible via a statistical study. Case studies rely on multiple sources of evidence and may be based on a mix of qualitative and quantitative data. Robson (1993: 5) gives the flavour of the term 'case study' (which he acknowledges is used variously) with the following definition: 'Case study is a strategy for doing research which involves an empirical investigation of a particular contemporary phenomenon

Note
Websites offering examples of case studies from the wider field of health and social care include:
<www.dh.gov.uk/en/Healthcare/Long termconditions/casestudies/index.htm> and
<www.careuk.com/content/case_studies> retrieved 03/02/2010.

Axline, VM (1964) *Dibs: In search of self.* Boston: Houghton Mifflin.

McLeod, J (2003) *Doing Counselling Research* (2nd edn). London: Sage.

Robson, C (1993) *Real World Research: A resource for social scientists and practitioner researchers.* Oxford: Blackwell.
[This idea does not appear in the same form in the second edition of the book.]

within its real life context using multiple sources of evidence.'

He uses this form of words because the 'contemporary phenomenon' (i.e. the 'case') can be of almost any kind or nature: an individual of course (for example, from the early development of client-centred therapy, Rogers', 1954: 259-348, study of Mrs. Oak) but also a group, an institution or a neighbourhood to name but a few. Robson (1993: 147) lists some types of case studies and cites examples. Yin (2003) offers an account of design and methods for case study research. He (p. 2) states that the value of the case study approach is that it 'allows investigators to retain the holistic and meaningful characteristics of real-life events'. Drawing on the work of other authors, Yin (pp. 33-4) describes four tests by which it is possible to judge the quality of empirical social research including case studies. These tests are of (after Yin, pp. 34-8):

- *construct validity* – to satisfy this test it is necessary to ensure that specific types of changes appropriate to the objectives of the research are studied and that it is demonstrated that the selected measures do reflect changes of these types. Case study tactics to ensure construct validity include (ibid.: 34):
  - using multiple sources of evidence
  - establishing a chain of evidence
  - having key informants review draft case study reports
- *internal validity* – this test is appropriate only to case studies where an objective is to establish a causal relationship, i.e. that one set of events or conditions leads directly to another set. Therefore it applies only to 'explanatory' research and not when the objective is to explore or describe. Tactics to establish internal validity include (ibid.: 34):
  - pattern matching
  - explanation building
  - addressing rival explanations
  - using logic models
- *external validity* – this test is to establish whether and/or to what extent the findings of a case study may be generalised. Tactics to establish external validity include (ibid.: 34):
  - using theory in single-case studies
  - using replication logic in multiple-case studies (ibid.: 47-51)
- *reliability* – this test is to demonstrate that the study can be repeated with the same results. Tactics to establish reliability include (ibid.: 34):
  - using case study protocol
  - developing a case study database

In evaluating case study research, the four tests described above may be helpful but, as with any qualitative research, the objectives of the researcher must also be taken into account. As Stake (2000:

Rogers, CR (1954) The case of Mrs Oak: A research analysis. In CR Rogers & RF Dymond (eds) *Psychotherapy and Personality Change* (pp 259-348). Chicago: University of Chicago Press.

Robson, C (1993) *Real World Research: A resource for social scientists and practitioner researchers.* Oxford: Blackwell.

[These examples are not in the 2nd edition of the book.]

Yin, RK (2003) *Case Study Research: Design and methods* (3rd edn). Thousand Oaks, CA: Sage.

Note
These terms are explained and expanded upon in Yin (pp 109-33).

Yin, RK (2003) *Case Study Research: Design and methods* (3rd edn). Thousand Oaks, CA: Sage.

Stake, RE (2000) Case studies. In NK Denzin & YS Lincoln (eds) *Handbook of Qualitative Research* (2nd edn) (pp 435-54). Thousand Oaks, CA: Sage.

Yin, RK (2003) *Case Study Research: Design and methods* (3rd edn). Thousand Oaks, CA: Sage.

McLeod, J (1994) *Doing Counselling Research.* London: Sage

Flyvberg, B (2006) Five misunderstandings about case-study research. *Qualitative Inquiry 12*(2), 219-45.

448) notes 'the purpose of the case report is not to represent the world, but to represent the case' and this, together with an awareness as to whether the study is intended to explain or explore a set of behaviours, circumstances, beliefs etc. should be taken into account when considering validity and reliability. Other criteria to bear in mind when evaluating a case study report are those given by Yin (2003: 161-5) as the characteristics of an exemplary case study.

It is important to note that there have been criticisms of the validity of knowledge produced by case study research (see McLeod, 1994). However, Flyvberg (2006: 219) presents an effective rebuttal of 'five common misunderstandings about case-study research'. In summary, these misunderstandings are (p. 219):

- *Theoretical knowledge is more valuable than practical knowledge.* However, Flyvberg (pp. 221-4) presents evidence and counter-argument leading to a revised proposition (p. 224):

  Productive theories and universals cannot be found in the study of human affairs. Concrete, context-dependent knowledge is, therefore, more valuable than the vain search for predictive theories and universals.

- *It is not possible to generalise from a single case study, therefore, the single case study cannot contribute to scientific development.* Flyvberg (pp. 224-8) demonstrates how this proposition may be refuted and (p. 228) offers the alternative:

  One can often generalize on the basis of a single case, and the case study may be central to scientific development via generalization as supplement or alternative to other methods. But formal generalization is overvalued as a source of scientific development, whereas 'the force of example' is underestimated.

- *Case studies are most useful for generating hypotheses, whereas other methods are more suitable for hypothesis testing and theory building.* Flyvberg (p. 229) points out that because of his correction to the second misunderstanding, this proposition falls. He revises this statement thus:

  The case study is useful for both generating and testing hypotheses but it is not limited to these research activities alone.

- *Case studies contain a bias towards verification.* Flyvberg (pp. 234-7) shows that case study research is no more likely to confirm the preconceived notions of the researcher than any other research method. Indeed he argues that case study research

Flyvberg, B (2006) Five misunderstandings about case-study research. *Qualitative Inquiry 12*(2), 219-45.

is less likely to verify preconceived ideas. He therefore revises this proposition accordingly:

> The case study contains no greater bias towards verification of the researcher's preconceived notions than other methods of inquiry. On the contrary, experience indicates that the case study contains greater bias towards falsification of preconceived notions than toward verification.

- *It is often difficult to summarise specific case studies.* While agreeing that it is indeed difficult and perhaps undesirable to summarise case studies, Flyvberg (pp. 237-41) establishes that the case study method can contribute to the cumulative development of knowledge. This leads him to revise the above proposition so:

> It is correct that summarizing case studies is often difficult, especially as concerns case process. It is less correct as regards outcomes. The problems in summarizing case studies, however, are due more often to the properties of the reality studied than to the case study as a research method. Often it is not desirable to summarize and generalize case studies. Good studies should be read as narratives in their entirety.

When reading accounts of case studies or planning and carrying out a case study, due attention should be given to the thoughts of Yin and Flyvberg.

The classic case studies of client-centred therapy include Rogers' (1954) analysis of his work with Mrs Oak, Shlien's (1961) account of client-centred therapy with a deeply disturbed hospitalised client and Axline's (1964) story of Dibs. Friere's (2005) case study of the experience of non-directivity in client-centred therapy is a recent example of case study research in person-centred therapy. McLeod and Balamoutsou (1996) have published a report based on the intensive study of a single case and Grafanaki and McLeod (1999, 2002) have published accounts of drawing on a multiple case study. These are written from the perspective of person-centred/experiential psychotherapy but other examples of psychotherapy case study research in the literature (e.g. Taylor & Loewenthal, 2001), although providing useful examples of how case study research may be used, are from different modalities. Drawing on previous work, Stiles (2009) discusses theory building from case study research.

Flyvberg, B (2006) Five misunderstandings about case-study research. *Qualitative Inquiry 12*(2), 219-45.

Rogers, CR (1954) The case of Mrs Oak: a research analysis. In CR Rogers & RF Dymond (eds) *Psychotherapy and Personality Change* (pp 259-348). Chicago: University of Chicago Press.

Shlien, JM (1961) A client-centered approach to schizophrenia: First approximation. In A Burton (ed) *Psychotherapy of the Psychoses* (pp 285-317). New York: Basic Books.

Axline, VM (1964) *Dibs: In search of self.* Boston: Houghton Mifflin.

Freire, ES (2005) The experience of non-directivity in client-centred therapy: A case study. In BE Levitt (ed) *Embracing Non-Directivity: Reassessing person-centred practice in the 21st century* (pp 113-38). Ross-on-Wye: PCCS Books.

McLeod, J & Balamoutsou, S (1999) Representing narrative process in therapy: Qualitative analysis of a single case study. *Counselling Psychology Quarterly 9*(1), 61-76.

Grafanaki, S & McLeod, J (1999) Narrative processes in the construction of helpful and hindering events in experiential psychotherapy. *Psychotherapy Research 9*(3), 289-303.

Grafanaki, S & McLeod, J (2002) Experiential congruence – Qualitative analysis of client and counsellor narrative accounts of significant events in time-limited person-centred therapy. *Counselling and Psychotherapy Research 2*(1), 20-32.

Taylor, M & Loewenthal, D (2001) Researching a client's experience of preconceptions of therapy – A discourse analysis. *Psychodynamic Counselling 7*(1), 63-82.

Stiles, WB (2009) Logical operations in theory building case studies. *Pragmatic Case Studies in Psychotherapy 5*(3), 9-22.

Organising a case study

You may organise a case study around:

- an individual
- a naturally occurring group of individuals – this could be, for example, a community, a family, or an organisation
- a specially constructed group of individuals such as a self-help group convened for the purposes of the study
- an event such as a disaster or crisis or a social occasion such as a wedding or funeral
- a relationship or set of relationships, for example, a particular practitioner–client relationship or the counsellor–supervisor relationships in a particular student counselling service
- roles – 'social worker' role or counsellor/teacher role conflicts

'What does a case study look like?' or 'How do you know if you're doing a case study?' are reasonable questions, since it could be argued that all qualitative work is case study work. A case study (simply) involves collecting information about an individual person or discrete, identifiable (small) group. The same general principles of research need to be followed when conducting a case study as are followed in other forms of research. For example, understanding and describing any theoretical background; locating the study in a context in the real world; finding a baseline; looking for, describing or measuring change; accounting for, explaining or interpreting the findings; referring back to theory.

Case studies can be approached in a more or less systematic and structured way. The following steps may be of use if you are unfamiliar with case studies or unsure how to proceed. We will assume that you have done all the necessary work on finding and developing your research question.

- identify the subject of your case study (individual, group, etc.)
- is there a theoretical background to the work you are planning?
- take a CASE HISTORY – this will help describe the real world context of the case and find a baseline (if necessary)
- when is the case study set in time? Case studies can be:
  - retrospective – describing events that have already happened and are being revisited, remembered or reviewed
  - present and ongoing – describing events happening now
  - forward-looking – setting up a situation to describe future events, e.g. setting up a case study to describe the early bonding experiences of your as-yet unborn child
- select a data collection method (see below) and collect the data

However, do not be mesmerised by the clinical case presentation style that may be familiar to you. This will only limit the opportunities for data collection, treatment and presentation. Although case studies

Note

If your group is very large, or the individuals do not have strong common strands, or you end up having to sample the people in some way, then the study might be more like a survey.

CASE HISTORY A detailed account of all the relevant information or material gathered about the development or condition of an individual, family, group, community or the like and arranged so as to serve as an organised record and to have analytic value. Used in, eg, social work, medicine, psychiatry and psychology.

are essentially simple descriptions of events, there are no real rules regarding how the material described should be collected or presented. Often case studies are presented in a chronological sequence, but this is not a requirement. If you feel a different form of presentation suits your collection method or data treatment better, then use it.

When conducting a case study, it really is open season as far as data collection methods are concerned. There is no 'not recommended' category of data collection in a case study, in fact the one suggestion we would make is to encourage you to use as wide a variety of methods as time, money, energy and other resources permit. The only warning note is to keep within realistic limits – don't collect a mountain of data that overwhelms you when it comes to data analysis – but at the same time be thorough.

Although having a *plan* regarding how you are going to collect the data in your study is necessary, sampling itself is not such a burning issue in the average case study as it is in a survey. This is usually either because of the small numbers involved or because you will be 'sampling' all of the actors' behaviour, thoughts and feelings. You will not be limiting your data collection to a small subset of information or from a small subset of people within the group. Some of the things to think about include:

- if you are doing a case study on an individual, you may have to sample their behaviour, thoughts or feelings in some way – it would be difficult to record their behaviour, etc. 24 hours a day. Interviewing may help, as will looking at any existing records (made by professionals, e.g. case notes, or the individual, e.g. diaries). Your observations of the individual may also be part of the material feeding into your interpretation and analysis
- if you are doing a case study on a group, family, community, or organisation, it may be difficult to record data from each individual, and again, it will prove impractical to record data 24 hours a day, 7 days a week. You could consider group interviews, perhaps even 'focus groups'. Not only are these efficient in terms of time but the 'cross-fertilisation' element can be productive. However, it is important to think about the dynamics of the group when thinking about such an approach. Will a group interview reveal or obscure?

As in other ways of collecting stories, the method you choose to record a portion of the data for only a portion of the time is your sampling method. Your sampling decisions are:

- from whom will you collect data?
- what data are you going to collect?
- when will you collect it?
- where will you collect it?

Note
Focus groups have been around as a qualitative research tool in some fields since at least the mid-1990s and are now an emerging tool in health and social care research. A useful resource to get a quick overview, advantages and disadvantages in the form of a PowerPoint presentation can be found at <http://hcc.cc.gatech.edu/documents/120_Fisk_focus%20group%20research%202004.pdf> retrieved 02/04/2010.

| IF YOU WANT TO KNOW MORE ABOUT |
| participant observation |

you could try:

DeWalt, KM & DeWalt, BR (2002) *Participant Observation: A guide for field workers.* Walnut Creek, CA: Altamira Press.

Emerson, RM, Fretz, RI & Shaw, LL (2001) Participant observation and field notes. In P Atkinson, A Coffey, S Delamont, J Lofland & L Lofland (eds) *Handbook of Ethnography* (pp 352-68). Thousand Oaks, CA: Sage.

Some reports of participant observation research are:

Latvala, E, Vuokila-Oikkonen, P & Janhonen, S (2000) Videotaped recording as a method of participant observation in psychiatric nursing research. *Journal of Advanced Nursing 31*(5), 1252-7.

Porter, S (1991) A participant observation study of power relations between nurses and doctors in a general hospital. *Journal of Advanced Nursing 16*(6), 728-35.

Power, R (1989) Participant observation and its place in the study of illicit drug use. *British Journal of Addiction 84*(1), 43-52.

These papers are also available online at <www3.interscience.wiley.com/journal>

ETHNOGRAPHY A branch of anthropology dealing with the methodical, scientific description of human societies and cultures, concerned with reaching an understanding of social and/or cultural phenomena through close field observation. No particular method is specified – what is important is that whatever the method of investigation it leads to describing people, their interactions and beliefs, through writing.

Participation

Since qualitative researchers are interested in the effects that the researcher has on the situation being studied and since they take the view that the best standpoint from which to develop an understanding is to see the world from the context within which the actors live, it stands to reason that participation is essential. Subjectivity is preferred to objectivity. Qualitative methodologists take the view that any observation interferes with the actions being observed anyway, so you might as well get right in the middle of it. This is broadly true of any approach to qualitative inquiry. However, 'participant observation' can itself be a way of collecting stories.

Participant observation

As you have probably deduced from its name, participant observation is an approach to research in which the researcher collects stories by directly observing the event or phenomenon that is the focus of inquiry. Of course, there is more to it than that. There are various levels of participation, from that of detached, passive watcher (perhaps even making use video, film or television) through active engagement in a new situation in order to learn about it from the inside, to total involvement as a natural participant. Participant observation is most normally part of an *ethnographic* approach to research and you may come across the term 'ETHNOGRAPHY' if you read more about participant observation.

The focus is on a 'community' but this can mean a group of almost any kind, for example, service users, people attending a day centre, a professional association and so on. The aim of ETHNOGRAPHY is to produce a descriptive account of a particular social system (for example, members of the Royal College of Nursing attending the annual conference) based on detailed observation of what people actually do. Ethnography is one of those approaches to inquiry that bridges quantitative and qualitative methods. Some ethnographic studies are wholly one or the other, some combine the two. Partly, this depends on, for example, the level of participation by the observer – so we will tell you a bit more about that.

How involved and active should you be?

In participant observation, at the one extreme is the systematic, structured observation where the observer is not connected with the action at all, sometimes separated from the action by glass (one-way mirror), or time and place (video recording). This can be a quantitative method because, firstly, it seeks to remove the observer and their effects from the action being observed. Secondly, the observer observes in a predetermined, highly structured and systematic way, using various numerical coding methods with which to capture the behaviour.

So, the observer is removed from the action in order to promote the objectivity and neutrality of the observations and the actions being observed are counted according to a scheme predetermined by the researcher. However, a qualitative approach to this form of participant observation is also possible. This would mean making 'field notes' (a record of what is actually going on as you are witnessing it) and treating these in a similar way to those made in other approaches to participant observation. However, we will look at this and the other qualitative types of observation in more detail.

IF YOU WANT TO KNOW MORE ABOUT
writing field notes

you could try:

Emerson, RM, Fretz, RI & Shaw, LL (1995) *Writing Ethnographic Fieldnotes.* Chicago: University of Chicago Press.

Qualitative non-participant observation

It is possible to observe and record the actions of others in an initially unquantified, descriptive form. This method involves unstructured observation where the observer describes what is observed rather than categorising or interpreting and counting actions. In all cases of qualitative observation, including those that follow, the term 'actions' can refer to any or all behaviour in whatever natural and complex form including language and interactions with others.

Advantages: Since the observer is removed from the action and hopes to interfere with it as little as possible, video and audio recording can be used. Data collection can be streamlined.

Disadvantages: The flip side of the advantages to streamlined data collection can leave you with quantitative data or data that has lost any human touch. The method also generates huge amounts of data such as voluminous transcripts of audio or video recordings or page upon page of the observer's frantic shorthand notes.

Observer-as-participant

This and the following two types of observation are distinguished by the degree to which the observer takes part in the action and the degree to which their role as observer is known by the other actors. The observer-as-participant is a person who is separate from the action in that they take no part in it but their role as researcher is known to the actors. It is a type of conscious journalistic approach to observation in which the observer reports on the action from the privileged position of researcher without having to get involved.

Advantages: Not as demanding as more involving or participatory styles of observation. Predetermined coding can be used, making the method lean more towards quantitative methods.

Disadvantages: It is debatable that anyone can reveal themselves to be an observer or researcher in the midst of the action without at some level becoming a part of the action and influencing it in some way. It is dangerous to assume that the observer has little or no effect. The effect of the observer will always be a central part of the action. This method makes it difficult to manage data collection.

Participant-as-observer

In this type of observation the observer might declare their role as observer at the start of the action being observed and then seek to establish relationships with other actors as if she or he were one of them. Alternatively, the observer role is seen as not the main reason for the participant's presence but as an adjunct to their already existing role, e.g. you may decide to observe relationships at your workplace. This is a difficult role to fill as it puts strain on the observer being in two roles. It also stands a great chance of disturbing or influencing the action as it develops.

Advantages: This method can be a convenient way to observe the action of which you are already a part. It holds the promise of not being too disruptive to any action that is already in progress.

Disadvantages: Can cause role tension and be subject to more observer effects than other forms of participant observation and necessitates careful preparation.

Full participant

Here the observer becomes an actor in the action without ever revealing their role as observer. The true purpose of their presence in the group is concealed from the other actors.

Advantages: This method suggests that it might get as close to 'real life' as possible by locating the observer incognito in the thick of the action. The aim is to be unobtrusive (indeed undiscovered) and therefore, so the argument goes, *unintrusive* as far as the recorded actions go.

Disadvantages: As with other methods requiring an element of deception, this raises ethical issues regarding informed consent of the participants. Also, following on from the advantages above, it is argued that even this method is not truly unobtrusive, since the presence of the observer is by definition an artefact. It could never be known what might have happened had the observer not been present. To extrapolate this idea, it might even be the case that researchers behave in a way that distorts the action through more active collusion with, or manipulation of, the actors to achieve a desired result. Such behaviour is clearly unethical.

Whatever the approach to participant observation, there are several key procedures to implement. The first task facing observers is to gain reasonable ethical access to the action being observed. This can be more involved than you might initially think. Participant observation hinges upon a number of factors including observer preparation and the quality of the relationship between the observer and the other actors. It can require many days, weeks or months for the observer to get to know the other actors and to varying extents become members of the groups they intend to observe. In some cases where the observer's role has been kept secret, this may have involved a period of induction into the group and the gaining of their trust.

As caring practitioners you will be familiar with the skills of relationship building. Entering a group as a participant observer is no more or less complicated than building relationships with the groups and individuals you meet in your professional role. The key qualities are genuineness (particularly *being yourself*), being non-judgemental (being judgemental is no more the role of the researcher than it is the role of any health and social care professional), and empathy (essential if your observations are to be worthwhile).

Secondly, the keeping of detailed records is the fundamental tool of the participant observer. These records should include exhaustive and meticulous notes on anything and everything that occurs whether seemingly extraordinary or commonplace and taken for granted. Keeping a personal log is a good idea and probably essential but don't forget other forms of record keeping like audio and video records (although you will have to take account of the effect that the intrusion of recording devices may have on whatsoever and whomsoever you are observing). Another strategy is, every so often, to step aside from the situation on which your study is focusing and in which you are immersed to review and reflect on what it is you have seen.

Here again, it is a good idea to make notes about your interpretations and understandings as you review your records. This too can become part of your data. Also, in a yet more deliberate way, continually monitor your observations, records and processing of records to see if you can find evidence of personal bias or prejudice – and remember to be aware of what you are leaving out as well as what you are including. You should also be aware that the 'observer effect' is a consequence of participant observation, i.e. how the actions of those being observed change as a result of being observed. It is never possible to be completely sure that the presence of an observer has no effect. However, there are some signs to look out for that the observer is successfully integrated into the group. These include:

- other actors show less and less interest in the observer, including making less contact which acknowledges the role of observer
- other actors say that the presence of the observer is having little or no effect. This can be checked with other participants, e.g. doctors may say that nothing has changed as a consequence of the observation, but patients may say that the doctors spend more time with each patient
- observations stabilise after an initial period

Some researchers believe that it is important to acknowledge the

Note
A 'research log' is a record of the process by which your research was undertaken, along with documentation of both positive and negative results. Essentially, it is the diary of your research process – what you did, when you did it, what happened, what was productive, what was less so. It should include all the sources you consult with a synopsis of the content and a full reference (you will be glad of this when you come to write up). You will also find it useful to make a note of the research terms on which you base literature and web searches. You can also use your log to record ideas you have along the way whether these be for things to do later, things to read about or further research. Either separately as a personal log or as part of your research log you may like to keep a note of your own emotional and cognitive processes.

inevitability of observer effects and incorporate them into the data collection. This can be done through deliberate collaboration and consultation with the participants. Self-observation is also crucial – see below.

Collecting and recording data

When you have decided how you will successfully install yourself as an observer you have to decide how you are going to collect your data and what methods you will use to record it. There are several recording methods to choose from, some helped by new technology, then the recorded material (raw data) needs to be treated or possibly refined in some way in order to reveal the meanings hidden in it. This is called *coding*. The accuracy and usefulness of coding depends to a large extent on how transparent or unbiased the coding instrument is and since the coding instrument in qualitative research is the researcher themselves, or their appointed helper, we will look at some ways of dealing with observational biases. Of course, in qualitative research this will occasionally mean not trying to eliminate bias but rather incorporating the effect and meaning of such biases into our study in a mindful way.

Sometimes recording observations and coding can be carried out simultaneously in the same operation. This is when the observation system is based on predetermined checklists or category systems where the observer ticks boxes at the time of observation. This is a more structured method leaning more than a little in the direction of quantitative methods. Whilst there is always an element of pre-planning in all research, we will not be dealing here with treatment and coding schemes which are heavily structured and predetermined. We will limit our attention to fairly lightweight coding at the time of observation as an aid to the observer.

We would find it almost impossible to collect any data if we were simply instructed to 'Observe and record the important bits of the following assessment session'. What are we expected to observe? How do we know what is important? We go into each observation period with some predetermined plan as to how we are going to look at the action in question and which bits we are going to record. There is a wide range of possibilities when it comes to recording and coding human actions, each of which we will have decided before we start. The following scale uses examples which only serve to illustrate the qualitative–quantitative, structured–unstructured continua on which observational studies can be placed. Each 'example' looks at *observation–recording–coding–data treatment*.

The scale has four positions on it to illustrate the degrees of structure possible relating to the points above:

1 *Observe as much as possible. Record everything, including your own thoughts, feelings and actions. Code nothing at the time of*

Note

The first phase of any observation study will be largely exploratory. After the exploratory phase the researcher will then determine what features the study will have:

• to what extent the observation will be structured and predetermined

• to what extent the observations will be coded on site

• how much the observer will record of their own behaviour

• what treatment of the data will take place once it is all collected in

Note

How and what you code varies with the research method you are using, the nature of your data and your research question. You will learn a bit more about this in Chapter 2.8.

observation. Sort and categorise later when all the data is in.

This is at the extreme qualitative end of the questionnaire spectrum. It requires a lot of time and patience both to build up relationships with other actors in order for the observations to stabilise and to make the actual observations. All data treatment is done after the event using qualitative methods since the recording of the observations is done in a 'freehand' style with no predetermined coding scheme.

2 *Observe as much as possible. Record a large sample of the action, record your own feelings, thought and actions. Use a loose general coding scheme to categorise the action at the time; consider your self-related data later. Further sort and categorise your observations when all the data is in.*

A largely qualitative approach with some features of quantitative methods to manage the amount of data coming in by sampling plus possibly coding the data in situ with a view to some small quantitative analysis for TRIANGULATION purposes. The person of the researcher is still very much at the heart of the data collection and analysis.

TRIANGULATION is a way of assuring the validity of research findings through the use of a *variety* of research methods (usually more than two).

3 *Observe a restricted portion of the action. Record only some of it, possibly keeping a separate diary of your thoughts and feelings e.g. whether you were tired and distracted. Use a structured coding scheme to categorise the data at the time of observation, possibly use your diary if it adds to the data significantly. Some limited further sorting and categorising to do when all the data is in.*

Leaning more towards quantitative than qualitative methodology, here the observer takes a more fringe position but is nevertheless involved in the study more than in quantitative non-participant observation. Coding is both predetermined to a large extent and geared towards numerical quantification of behaviour, but there is still room for the subjective impressions of the observer to add that qualitative edge in support of the findings.

4 *Observe a small, finite portion of the action. Record only that which falls into your coding scheme, ignore the rest. Use a tightly structured coding scheme to categorise data at the time of observation, don't record your own thoughts or feelings. There is no need for further data treatment when all the data is in other than statistical analysis.*

This is structured quantitative observation.

Recording your observations

Whatever form your observation takes, you are going to need to make some record of what you see and hear and what you think it may mean. Audio and tape recording may be useful and we told

ETHNOGRAPHY A branch of anthropology dealing with the methodical, scientific description of human societies and cultures, concerned with reaching an understanding of social and/or cultural phenomena through close field observation. No particular method is specified – what is important is that whatever the method of investigation it leads to describing people, their interactions and beliefs, through writing.

Note

We cover sampling (event and time sampling) from a quantitative perspective when considering structured observation on pp 111-12.

you a bit about these when we were discussing interviewing. However, the traditional method in participant observation and other ETHNOGRAPHICAL studies has been to make written field notes. Often these focus on 'behaviour' but in this context we mean something much broader than simply what is seen to be done. For example, field notes can include the interpretations and intuitions of both the observer and the observed.

There are many methods for recording behaviour. Firstly, you need to decide what sampling method you are going to use. That is to say, are you going to try to record all behaviour, or just a portion of it determined by, for example, time or location? Then you must decide which method of recording is most appropriate.

Sampling

Two decisions need to be made in sampling, firstly, what proportion of the action is to be recorded and secondly, what will determine the onset and offset of the recording.

- *time sampling* – when a time interval, predetermined according to some pattern (which may be random) is used to observe behaviour. For example, if a two-hour group supervision is being observed, it could be decided to record the whole session, or to record ten five-minute periods at random over the whole two-hour session
- *location sampling* – when only action occurring at a specific location is recorded, for example, nurses' behaviour whilst at the patients' bedsides
- *event sampling* – when you record all behaviour following or associated with a particular event, e.g. recording all counsellor or client responses after silences of ten seconds or more

Recording

However unstructured the observation method is, a careful and systematic recording of observations is essential. Some things to include are:

- description of the physical space, e.g. diagrams of layout
- other physical features and objects such as furniture
- the names of and relevant other information about the actors
- the actions of the actors
- specific events and occasions such as formal or informal meetings
- the timed sequence of events
- information about what the actors were trying to achieve in the way of aims
- feelings and emotions of actors

We might add to this list some dimensions concerning the observer in participant observation:

- how the observer is feeling before, during and after the observation session
- why the observer participated in the action
- any intuitions or interpretations occurring at the time of observation

Written records

Ideally, a record should be made on the spot, as it happens. You may need to develop a system of shorthand or abbreviations. When each observation session is finished, the abbreviated record should be augmented with detail and expanded accounts of the action. A well-documented record includes:

- *running descriptions* – specific descriptions of observed events without the observer's inferences or interpretations
- *recall of forgotten material* – bits and pieces of the action that you remember later
- *interpretive ideas* – the observer's interpretations, analysis, possible explanations and inferences. These can be focused on the research question or tangential to it
- *personal impressions and feelings* – the observer's subjective reactions either at the time or subsequent to the observation
- *reminders* – notes to attend to in the next session, perhaps to look out for a certain event, sequence or connection of events

You should add as much as is necessary so that you will be able to 'recreate' the action on subsequent reading of the record. Don't put this off – time will degrade your memory of events and after a few sessions you will start confusing one session with another, as well as the order in which events happened.

Collaboration

People participating in research programmes in the traditional paradigm are called *subjects*. This gives some idea of the role of the subject as being someone with little power, someone *subjected* to the experimental treatments, etc. Subjects are not asked for their views and historically have even been deceived as to the true purpose of the research. In qualitative approaches, we seek collaboration with our participants. They can be called actors, participants, people or whatever but never *subjects*. We will fully inform them of the purpose of the study, involve them in planning the work, ask about their thoughts and feelings during the research; we may even ask them to help in the data analysis. However, we can take it further than that.

So far, most of what we have told you about research is based on the idea that the researcher is somehow separate from what is

POSITIVISTIC/POSITIVISM A doctrine asserting that sense perceptions are the only admissible basis of human knowledge and precise thought. In research, that the validity of knowledge can only be assured by experimental science.

IF YOU WANT TO KNOW MORE ABOUT
action inquiry and action research

you could try:

Reason, P & Bradbury, H (eds) (2008)
The Sage Handbook of Action Research: Participative inquiry and practice.
London: Sage.

Some reports of action research are:

Kilgour, C & Fleming, V (2001) An action research inquiry into a health visitor parenting programme for parents of school children with behavioural problems. *Journal of Advanced Nursing* 32(3), 682-8.

Percy-Smith, B & Weil, S (2003) Practice-based research as development: Innovation and empowerment in youth intervention initiatives using collaborative action inquiry. In A Bennett, M Cieslik & S Miles (eds) *Researching Youth* (pp 66-84). Basingstoke: Palgrave Macmillan.

There is also the Sage journal *Action Research* available online.

being researched. This is in line with the traditional, POSITIVISTIC notion. In describing participant observation, we have begun to show that, in qualitative research, the idea of deliberate detachment is often spurious and attempts to achieve it may even limit the richness of the stories we can collect – but the idea of the researcher and the researched as separate remains. Not surprisingly, for some social scientists this separation has been seen as at odds with their philosophy and practice. They want research to be 'democratic' and to move away from forms of research *on* people to ways of researching *with* people. The essential principle is that people are self-determining, there is value in subjective experience and that power in the research community is shared. From this principle arises an array of *collaborative* approaches to research; that is, research *by* the people it concerns. In collaborative research, not only are there no 'subjects', but even the word 'participant' is inappropriate. We are now talking about 'co-researchers' who are all contributing to the focus and direction of the inquiry and commenting on the interpretations and findings resulting from it. There are many types of collaborative research but we will briefly tell you about three of the main ones: action inquiry/research, participatory action research and co-operative inquiry.

Action inquiry/action research

Action inquiry (or action research) is a form of research into practice often with a political or social dimension in that an aim is the facilitation of social change. It is concerned with the transformation of organisations and communities to bring about increased effectiveness and greater justice. It is really a way of balancing a problem-solving approach with the achievement of a deep understanding of the organisation or community that is the focus of the study. Action inquiry is:

- *practical* – it is based in real actions taken in real world situations
- *political* – it is intended to promote positive (even radical) social change
- *participative* – it is inclusive of the thoughts, impressions and intuitions of all those involved
- *collaborative* – its processes and results are co-owned by the whole research community
- *egalitarian* – the perspectives of all participants (including the lead researcher) are seen as of equal value
- *critical* – the programme of activity and research is carefully evaluated

You can probably already see why this may be an appropriate form of research in the context of health and social care. For example, a researcher (in the role of facilitator and monitor) could work with a user group to focus attention on the service they were receiving with an intention of increasing its effectiveness. Whatever the focus of an action inquiry, there are three essential practical elements involved and required. These are:

- an understanding and continual re-evaluation of the question 'What are we trying to accomplish (in the organisation as a whole and in any sub-units)?'
- the setting up of regular systems to test whether the organisation's strategies and operations in fact match its vision and to test its effect on the environment (including workforce, users, etc.)
- the facilitation and promotion of the capacity of the participants for exercising 'action inquiry' as a continuous learning from experience

Participatory action research

Just as with action inquiry, participatory action research (PAR) is fundamentally political in nature and it has been widely used with oppressed groups. A basic idea of PAR is that the researchers seek to establish a dialogue and rapport with the population with which they are working so that they can discover and address their practical, social and political needs. The two main aims of PAR are firstly, like action inquiry, to produce knowledge and action directly useful to the community and secondly, to raise awareness and empower people through constructive use of their own knowledge. This 'insider knowledge' then becomes a means of transforming their situation for their own benefit. Because PAR is an ideology rather than a method, there is no one way of doing it – by definition it arises from and is shaped by the community involved.

Many methods can be used in any one project and are as likely to include indigenous forms of expression arising from the culture itself (group meetings, song, dance, poetry, drama) as well as or even instead of more conventional investigatory techniques. In this way, a lot more is required of the researcher than technical research skills. Amongst other things, a PAR researcher has to have:

- a commitment to the empowerment of others
- a clarity of class, culture and gender analysis (and of anything else that may result in privilege, bias or disadvantage such as age and ability/disability)
- good communication skills
- an understanding of individual and group dynamics/behaviour
- an ability and willingness to self-disclose and share personal feelings and experiences

Co-operative inquiry

Like action inquiry and PAR, co-operative inquiry is concerned with the democratisation of the research process. However, while

---

IF YOU WANT TO KNOW MORE ABOUT
participatory action research
you could try:

Kemmis, S & McTaggart, R (2000) Participatory action research. In NK Denzin & YS Lincoln (eds) *Handbook of Qualitative Research* (2nd edn) (pp 567-605). Thousand Oaks, CA: Sage.

Reason, P (ed) (1994) *Participation in Human Inquiry.* London: Sage.

Note
Some research reports of participatory action research are:

Dickson, G & Green, KL (2001) Participatory action research: Lessons learned with aboriginal grandmothers. *Health Care for Women International 22*(5), 471-82.

Fine, M, Torre, ME, Boudin, K, Bowen, I, Clark, J, Hyton, D, et al (2003) Participatory action research: From within and beyond prison bars. In PM Camic, JE Rhodes & L Yardley (eds) *Qualitative Research in Psychology: Expanding perspectives in methodology and design* (pp 173-98). Washington, DC: American Psychological Association.

Ochocka, J, Janzen, J & Nelson, G (2002) Sharing power and knowledge: Professional and mental health consumer/survivor researchers working together in a participatory action research project. *Psychiatric Rehabilitation Journal 25*(4), 379-87.

Note

The original description of co-operative experiential inquiry is in:

Reason, P & Heron, J (1986) Research with people: The paradigm of co-operative experiential inquiry. *Person-Centered Review 1*(4), 456-76.

| IF YOU WANT TO KNOW MORE ABOUT |
| co-operative inquiry |

you could try:

Heron, J (1996) *Co-operative Inquiry: Research into the human condition.* London: Sage.

Wilkins, P (2000) Collaborative approaches to research. In B Humphries (ed) *Research in Social Care and Social Welfare: Issues and debates for practice* (pp 144-53). London: Jessica Kingsley.

Note

Some research reports of co-operative inquiry are:

Hostick, T & McClelland, F (2000) 'Partnership': A co-operative inquiry between community mental health nurses and their clients. 1. Research methodology, process and reflections. *Journal of Psychiatric and Mental Health Nursing 7*(4), 307-13.

Mitchell-Williams, Z, Wilkins, P, McClean, M, Nevin, W, Wastell, K & Wheat, R (2004) The importance of the personal element in collaborative research. *Educational Action Research 12*(3), 329-45.

West, WS (1996) Using human inquiry groups in counselling research. *British Journal of Guidance and Counselling 24,* 347-56.

all three involve participants in mutually deciding on the objectives of the research, it is most commonly only in the latter that the participants also decide on the operational methods to be used. Also, co-operative inquiry is holistic in that it makes use of and addresses feelings and spiritual dimensions of human experience as well as cognition and behaviour.

Co-operative inquiry can have similar aims to more traditional approaches to research – that is to increase the sum of 'knowledge' about a given topic, experience or area and to provide description and information. Equally, it can be aimed at transformation, exploring practice and effecting change. Sometimes the co-researchers develop and change in the course of the inquiry although this is not a direct aim. As it was originally proposed, co-operative inquiry depends on a rigorous cycling through four phases of action and reflection. These are:

- an initial phase in which the co-researchers decide upon the focus of their inquiry and come up with some basic propositions. They also decide what methods they will use in their investigation

- a second phase in which the co-researchers actively apply the agreed procedures using a special set of skills including, for example, being fully present with an openness to imagination and intuition. In this stage, the co-researchers make a deliberate effort to set aside their habitual, ingrained conceptual frameworks in order to generate new and alternative ways of seeing and interacting with the world. Depending on the nature of the inquiry, it may also be that all elements of practice must be critically appraised, re-evaluated and restructured

- in the third phase co-researchers are totally immersed in the activity and experience even to such an extent as to forget that they are involved in an inquiry. It is in this phase that the co-researchers are open to their experience and their environment in such a way as to see them in a new light

- the fourth phase is a return to reflection and the formulation of ideas and propositions. After sufficient time in phases 2 and 3, the co-researchers return to their original propositions and hypotheses and consider them in the light of experience. As a result of this critical appraisal, the original ideas are subject to modification, reformulation, rejection and so on. New propositions may be advanced and these become the focus for the next cycle

Because of a perceived ability of people (including researchers) to fool themselves and others, there is a need for a set of procedures to ensure the validity of co-operative inquiry. These are:

- *development of discriminating awareness* – the deliberate cultivation of a watchful and mindful state

- *recycling, convergence and divergence* – research cycling provides a set of corrective feedback loops. Convergent cycling allows for the checking of detail whereas divergent cycling introduces the creativity that comes from the deliberate adoption of many different viewpoints
- *authentic collaboration* – steps must be taken to ensure that the co-operative research endeavour is truly collaborative and not swayed by an individual or clique. This involves attention to group processes and group dynamics
- *falsification* – in order to counteract any consensus collusion, there is deliberate cultivation of the devil's advocate role. The devil's advocate is the group member who temporarily takes on the function of radical critic challenging the group's assumptions
- *management of unaware projections* – unacknowledged distress and psychological defences may seriously distort inquiry. This must be dealt with either by bringing it into awareness or by giving it creative expression. Attention to personal growth will probably be helpful
- *balance of action and reflection* – co-operative inquiry is a combination of action and reflection and these must be appropriately balanced. It is impossible to offer a definitive ratio because this varies with the nature and objectives of the inquiry
- *chaos* – a descent into chaos will often facilitate the emergence of a new creative order. It is important to be able to tolerate and welcome chaos

Although the above procedures were set out in the context of co-operative inquiry we have an additional reason for telling you about them. It seems to us that they are good guidelines for any approach to research, especially qualitative approaches that are deeply involving of the researcher as a person. Whenever you set out to collect and process stories it is probably just as well to keep them in mind – and perhaps even when you are measuring things.

Self-observation

As we have pointed out above, in many approaches to collecting stories the impact of the researcher on the research is an important consideration. Qualitative researchers are required to know about how they affect their participants, how their experience and background affect what they see or experience and how they record it, and not least how they process the stories they collect and present their knowledge to others. This requires self-knowledge and self-observation. However, not only is self-observation an important part of many approaches to qualitative research, there are some

Note
Some research techniques are rooted in self-observation. These include heuristic inquiry (Moustakas, 1990), autoethnography (Ellis & Bochner, 2000) and a variety of transpersonal research methods (Braud & Anderson, 1998).

Braud, W & Anderson, R (eds) (1998) *Transpersonal Research Methods for the Social Sciences: Honoring human experience.* Thousand Oaks, CA: Sage.

Ellis, C & Bochner, AP (2000) Autoethnography, personal narrative, reflexivity: Researcher as subject. In NK Denzin & YS Lincoln (eds) *Handbook of Qualitative Research* (2nd edn) (pp 733-68). Thousand Oaks, CA: Sage.

Moustakas, C (1990) *Heuristic Research: Design, methodology, and applications.* Newbury Park, CA: Sage.

forms of human inquiry which depend entirely on systematic self-observation and the critical evaluation of personal experience. If you like, the researcher is at once the storyteller and the story collector. For example, self-observation can be the backbone of a single case study covering a discrete event or sequence of events in your life. It can be at the heart of the investigation of a particular human experience such as loneliness or a way of understanding a particular professional or social milieu.

As well as many of the skills and techniques for collecting stories we have already told you about, when a researcher becomes the focus for the research a number of other things are required. First amongst these is an ability to honestly reflect on yourself and to tune into the intuitive and imaginative processes of your mind. We will tell you more about this when we discuss heuristic inquiry in the next chapter but remember that what we say in one place usually applies in others. The techniques of 'self-interrogation' used in heuristic inquiry have a valuable role in most other forms of collecting stories. However, there are some general techniques for recording self-observation that apply not only to qualitative methods focusing solely on the self of the researcher but are more generally applicable.

Techniques for recording self-observations
As part of almost any approach to collecting stories, what you notice about yourself in the process is important material to the research. Keeping some kind of record of your own thoughts and processes is useful and sometimes vital. Traditionally, this has been done in a variety of written forms and we will tell you a bit about some of these – but it is important to remember that each of these categories could just as well be in the form of audio or video recordings.

Memo writing: Involves writing memos to yourself, helping you develop your thoughts by writing them down as they occur. The ideas and thoughts don't have to be at any stage of completion, or even make 'sense'. One function of memo writing is to unburden your mind so that you are free to observe the action of others or free to have more ideas. A memo to yourself is also one way of trapping ideas, intuitions and interpretations before they are forgotten.

Diaries: Most readers will be familiar with the notion of keeping diaries. The distinction between diaries and journals is that diaries are usually thought to be more personal and reflective in nature. Diaries can tell the 'feeling story' behind the action, giving insight into your inner world of meanings which may be missing from more dry observations.

Journals and logs: Journals and field logs are a record of what happened to you and when. They are narrative and descriptive accounts of the period under study with dates, times and places as required. Some of these elements may be missing from the more haphazard and personal accounts in diaries.

Creative and expressive forms: Sometimes, for some people, the best and most meaningful way of recording a personal experience, particular one redolent with feeling, is in the form of a creative or expressive piece such as a poem, story or picture. Depending on the nature of your research and what use you intend to make of the record (not least how you will meaningfully interpret it for others), recording your impressions and self-observation in this way may be appropriate.

Other forms of story and how to collect them

So far we have concentrated on what many researchers see as the main forms in which stories exist or can be created or co-created. However, there are other forms of story that either exist out there independent of your research (for example, public records, novels and so on) or which you can cause to be created as part of your project (for example, the personal logs of your participants) so we'd like to finish this chapter by telling you a little about some of them. Our list isn't meant to be exhaustive – remember an important thing about qualitative research is that, although there are some well-established methods and it is sometimes safer to stick to them, it is mutable and adaptable. If you can justify it, almost any kind of story may be of value to a qualitative inquiry.

Diaries

You may ask your respondents to keep a diary focusing on a certain time period or sequence of events. You will need to take a careful approach to the planning of this method of collection. As with a questionnaire, the instructions are absolutely crucial and should be piloted before being used in the study proper. Some tips include:
- you might want to supply special forms on which the respondents are required to record the events and their thoughts and feelings. You will need to give as much attention to the layout and design of these forms as to any other type of semi-structured questionnaire
- this method is particularly useful where people's experiences of intermittent periods of illness are sought, for example, panic attacks. A log can be kept of when the attacks occur, an estimate of their duration and perceived severity. This basic information can then be supplemented by more detailed accounts of symptoms, thoughts and feelings accompanying the attacks

- you could ask your respondents to keep a tape diary spoken into a small tape recorder which may even be used to record key events in the respondent's life. (Recent television shows have used narrative-style diary accounts of peoples' lives in programmes such as *Video Diaries*)

Letters

Another even less structured data collection method is to write a letter to your selected respondents and ask them to write back detailing their experiences, opinions, thoughts and feelings. This is the least structured form of interrogation. You will nevertheless need to prepare for and plan the study. Working with letters as the source of stories can also be 'historical'. For example, you could review your correspondence with other members of your training group from ten years ago as a way of understanding the culture that developed, the intrapersonal and interpersonal processes occurring and so on. When you choose to work with letters, a major set of decisions hinges upon how you choose the sample of people to whom you will write. For example, you may start a letter-writing study by writing to a sample of members of the British Association for Counsellors and Psychotherapists about their experiences with clients' recovered memories. You could do this by systematically sampling the BACP list of members or you could invite potential correspondents to contact you by placing an advert in *Therapy Today*, the journal of the association. Whatever you do, remember to make sure that the people to whom you are writing (or have written) understand that they are taking part in a study and get their permission before you use any of their material.

Fiction and other creative forms

There is a wealth of distilled wisdom contained in the almost innumerable novels, plays, poems and stories written over the centuries. More recently, film and television have added to this. Admittedly, it is somewhat controversial but, when investigating any aspect of human experience, don't dismiss 'fiction' lightly. For example, if your study concerns something to do with the experience of ethnic minorities perhaps the poems of Benjamin Zephanniah or the stories of Alice Walker will greatly enrich your understanding.

Historical and contemporaneous accounts: Looking at what's left behind

Wherever human beings have been, we find evidence of their lives in a number of forms. We leave our mark by either adding to the environment or removing something from it. We leave behind us a trail, elements of which endure to different degrees. This trail can be followed to determine the effect that humans have had on history,

Note
Writing can be a method of inquiry in its own right.

IF YOU WANT TO KNOW MORE ABOUT
writing as a research method
you could try:

Clarkson, P (1998) Writing as research in counselling psychology and related disciplines. In P Clarkson (ed) *Counselling Psychology: Integrating theory, research and supervised practice* (pp 300-7). London: Routledge.

Janesick, VL (1999) A journal about journal writing as a qualitative research technique: History, issues, and reflections. *Qualitative Inquiry* 5(4), 505-24.

Richardson, L (1994) Writing: A method of inquiry. In NK Denzin & YS Lincoln (eds) *Handbook of Qualitative Research* (pp 516-29). Thousand Oaks, CA: Sage. [Note: this is not in the second edition of this book.]

the world and each other. A familiar example of this trail-following research is archaeology but although social science researchers might go 'digging' around in archives and litter bins, there are few similarities save painstakingly methodical procedures.

Looking at what's left behind in the wake of human living can provide data that supports other findings for the purposes of TRIANGULATION, or can offer a parallel narrative strand to illuminate other work, or occasionally can be a valid research method in its own right. The use of documents and quotations is well known in the social sciences; less so is the use of physical 'remainders'. Some recent social science research has made creative use of the various debris of human life, but any use of physical traces in caring practitioner research would need to be even more creative. However the material is used, it does not offer an easy route to cast-iron answers. The collection and collation methods involve painstaking and diligent searching, rigorous scrutiny and disciplined analysis. Do not underestimate the time and effort involved.

The human trail is divided into two broad categories – that which we have left in terms of additions to the world – products and the like, and the marks of destruction and removal of material from the world. These are called *accretion measures* and *erosion measures* respectively.

TRIANGULATION is a way of assuring the validity of research findings through the use of a *variety* of research methods (usually more than two).

Documents and records

By these, we mean official documents and records in both the public and private or personal domains. These include official records such as Hansard, the minutes of public meetings, company memos, letters, etc. These may be of limited interest to caring practitioners. We can, however imagine the history of the struggles to establish and keep a counselling service in a college being understood through content analysis of academic board papers. Local government provision for people with mental health problems could be elucidated by looking at council minutes.

Note from research
In her doctoral thesis at the University of Exeter, the counselling psychologist Barbara Douglas made extensive use of the correspondence between a woman patient, Louisa, held in a mental hospital in South West England in the early 20th century, and a variety of authorities, family members etc, in her efforts to understand the history of psychology, psychiatry and psychotherapy.

Published media

Published media include documents such as books, newspapers, magazines, advertisements, etc. The history of the practice of health and social care in the published media has been the subject of at least idle interest. There are a number of ways of working with stories (see Chapter 2.8) in the form of, for example, journal articles that could be used to understand gender bias, ethnocentricitry and other issues.

Broadcast media

Of increasing importance as documents of note are audio-visual records (television, radio, film, video, recorded speech and music, etc.). For example, a television documentary might be as or more relevant to your study as a paper in an academic journal. You might be interested in looking at the representation of nurses and nursing in the media: views of nursing in the popular press, how often the word 'nurse' is said on a television news programme and in what context, or images of nurses in film.

The Internet

Used judiciously, the worldwide web is a prodigious source of material. In a way, it can be considered as a combination of published and broadcast media but it is, of course, also much more than this. The potential of the Internet as a research resource has scarcely begun. Certainly, you will find stories of all kinds, many of which may inform your inquiry. However, it is sometimes hard to know the veracity of these stories, their source and so on.

Physical traces

By physical traces, we mean any physical addition to, or erosion of, the environment, including the infrastructure of human society as it impacts upon the natural world. This may seem of little relevance or use as far as health and social care is concerned, but at a stretch we could imagine being interested in the contents of the litter bins in speech therapists' offices or the patterns of carpet wear in and out of the various sections of a student services suite in a further education college.

Collecting stories over time: Chronologies

Another way of thinking about stories is as existing, growing and changing over time. Therefore it makes sense to collect them over time too – to make what you might think of as a chronological study. Chronological analysis is, as the name suggests, a time-dependent way of organising or categorising the data. Actually, we could just as well have included this section somewhere in our consideration of quantitative research because measurement over time is a very important aspect of some studies. But the thing about approaches to research is that they don't always fit into neat boxes. However, whether you are concerned with quantitative or qualitative approaches, there are two basic ways of using time in a research project, either longitudinal or cross-sectional:

- *longitudinal research* – is where data is collected from a single source over time, e.g. following a single person or group through a period of time (weeks, months, years), or a single record such as the minutes of a planning group for weeks, months, years. For example, the effect of a particular counselling method could be measured over time. A particular form of longitudinal study

Note
A quick trawl through Google Scholar or doing a literature research in some other way will demonstrate that a lot of papers to do with longitudinal research deal with problems of recruitment and retention. This is something to think about when you plan your study.

Note
We look at longitudinal and cross-sectional research from a quantitative perspective in Chapter 2.5, p 104.

used in qualitative work is a life history approach. These are 'autobiographical' accounts of the whole of a person's life (rather than 'key moments' or 'turning points') in narrative form. We put autobiographical in quotation marks because although what is being told is the participant's story it may very well be that it is told in response to prompts from the researcher who may also be the one who writes it down. This involves at least an element of influence and interpretation

- *cross-sectional research* – is where data is collected from many different COHORTS (to represent different ages in a process) at a single moment in time, e.g. looking at 5, 7 and 9 year olds at a particular school one September or taking the minutes from several planning groups that are currently at different stages in their life cycle

Arranging events in order of time also helps draw out some features in the data which might otherwise have been missed. There are some time-related data features which can be better demonstrated in a chronological sequence:

- *historical legacy* – where the weight of past events shapes present expectations
- *developmental effects* – changes over time
- *temporal association* – where two events happen so closely together that we can make a reasonable assumption that they may be causally related, e.g. although we've never seen the electricity in a wire, we assume that the flicking of the switch caused the light bulb to illuminate because they happen so closely together in time
- *temporal projection* – predicting future events by projecting current sequences of events into the future

When researchers, quantitative or qualitative are dealing with time, they are often looking for some kind of pattern to emerge over it. If it is possible to arrange data in a time sequence or series, these patterns sometimes emerge. If this approach is scaled up to use multiple data collections, any patterns in the data stand a greater chance of revealing themselves. It is always worth using as much data as possible when looking for possible patterns over time, since the cumulative effect of the layers of data is what reveals the patterns.

Advantages: Time is a natural feature, so arranging things in order of time will not distort events or oversimplify them to a great degree. Helps structure events in an understandable way.

Disadvantages: Can lead to spurious links, e.g. temporal associations might lead us to make causal links where there are none, i.e. build an idea on coincidences.

IF YOU WANT TO KNOW MORE ABOUT
longitudinal research
you could try:

Saldaña, J (2003) *Longitudinal Research: Analyzing change through time.* Walnut Creek, CA: Altamira Press.

If you want to see a few reports of longitudinal research together, in 2006 the *Journal of Pediatric Psychology* published a special issue Vol. 31, No. 10, 'Longitudinal Research in Pediatric Psychology'.

An example of a report of cross-sectional research is:

Hammersly, V, Hippisley-Cox, J, Wilson, A & Pringle, M (2002) A comparision of research general practices and their patients with other practices – A cross-sectional survey in Trent. *British Journal of General Practice 52*(479), 463-8.

COHORT A group of people sharing one or more common, defining characteristics, eg, an age cohort would be one of people all born in the same year.

Preparing for collecting stories

We have told you about lots of the possible ways to collect stories. There are others and you may come across them as you read about the research other people have done. However, when it comes to doing your own research, whatever way of collecting stories you choose you are first going to have to prepare yourself and your participants or co-researchers. Steps you can take include:

- developing a set of instructions that will inform potential participants or co-researchers of the nature of the research design, its purpose and process, and what is expected of them
- locating and acquiring the research participants. Developing a set of criteria for selection of participants, for example, age, sex, socio-economic and education factors; ability to articulate the experience; co-operation, interest, willingness to make the commitment; enthusiasm; and degree of involvement
- developing a contract which includes time commitments, place, confidentiality, informed consent, opportunities for feedback, permission to audio or video record and permission to use material in a thesis, dissertation and/or other publications, and verification of findings
- considering ways of creating an atmosphere or climate that will encourage trust, openness, and self-disclosure

Where to take the stories you collect

We don't think we have told you about all the possible stories out there and the ways to collect them – that probably wouldn't be possible – but we hope we have given you the general idea of where and how to look. However you collect your stories, you are going to need to do something with them in order to understand and distil them so that you can present your interpretation to others. For that you are going to need to look at the next chapter 'Working with Stories'.

Reflection and reflexivity

Important to health and social care practice are reflection, reflective practice and reflexivity. It might seem like stating the obvious that these are equally important to self-observation as a research practice – and indeed to the process of qualitative research as a whole. We are going to assume that you already know something about these elements or can find out more for yourself (see margin opposite) but a brief reminder will probably not go amiss.

Furthermore, what we have to say about reflecting on your research process should now be familiar to you, in that you will now understand that *all good researchers* (both qualitative and quantitative) think deeply about what they do, how they do it and why. However, what Donald Schön (1983) had to say about reflective practice applies as much to the research process as practice per se. The notions of reflection-in-action, and reflection-on-action were central to Schön's ideas about reflective practice. The former is sometimes described as 'thinking on your feet'. Reflecting-on-action on the other hand, involves looking to your experience, paying attention to your feelings and attending to your theories as you use them (and, in the case of research, as you develop them). The objective is to develop new understandings to inform your actions in the situation that is unfolding. The art is to allow yourself to experience surprise, puzzlement or even confusion in a situation you are encountering for the first time – to allow novel situations to suggest novel responses (while never forgetting the ethical and theoretical principles underpinning your research).

The process of reflection-in-action links directly to reflection-on-action. It is thinking about what has happened as you carried out your research. There are many ways of doing this. Perhaps it occurs as you 'debrief' with colleagues, as you write up your research log, transcribe an interview or talk things through with your supervisor. The purpose of reflecting-on-action is to explore why you did as you did, the process between you and your participants and within you and so on. In this way you will develop sets of questions and ideas about your ongoing research.

In simple terms, reflexivity involves the ability to stand back and assess aspects of your own behaviour, society, culture and other aspects of experience and upbringing in relation to such factors as their motivations, origins and meanings. Because we are all shaped and coloured by our environment, our thoughts, values and ideas are inevitably and inherently similarly shaped and coloured. In other words, as free and liberal as we may believe ourselves to be, we are all 'biased'. Moreover, we carry this bias into all aspects of our lives including our research. Reflexivity is a deliberate attempt to acknowledge and take account of our biases and to act with awareness of them. It is about delaying instinctive and unexamined reactions to what you are experiencing and analysing them before responding. If you are able to reflexively examine your situation and how you are reacting to it then you are able to engage in a pro-active analysis of your assumptions and how you relate to others, rather than just responding reactively. In this way, you can mitigate or ameliorate the effects of your assumptions on your interactions with others – including your research participants and the theories and practices on which your research is based.

Reflexivity is of two kinds. Personal reflexivity refers to how personal values, beliefs, experiences and interests influence research

Schön, D (1983) *The Reflective Practitioner: How professionals think in action.* London: Temple Smith.

Note
We hope it is clear that reflection-in-action happens while you are active, whereas reflection-on-action is looking back at what you did.

IF YOU WANT TO KNOW MORE ABOUT
reflexive research
you could read:

Etherington, K (2004) *Becoming a Reflexive Researcher: Using our selves in research.* London: Jessica Kingsley.

Hertz, R (ed) (1997) *Reflexivity and Voice.* Thousand Oaks, CA: Sage.

Schön, D (1983) *The Reflective Practitioner: How professionals think in action.* London: Temple Smith.

EPISTEMOLOGY Philosophy concerned with the nature of knowledge (what is it?), the source of knowledge (how do we know what we know?) and the scope of knowledge (what, if any, are the limits of knowledge?).

Etherington, K (2004) *Becoming a Reflexive Researcher: Using our selves in research*. London: Jessica Kingsley

Note

Carla Willig (2001: 10) gives a more complete description of the two types of reflexivity and their relevance to research. She writes:

> There are two types of reflexivity: personal reflexivity and EPISTEMOLOGICAL reflexivity.
>
> 'Personal reflexivity' involves reflecting upon the ways in which our own values, experiences, interests, beliefs, political commitments, wider aims in life and social identities have shaped the research. It also involves thinking about how the research may have affected and possibly changed us, as people and as researchers. 'Epistemological reflexivity' requires us to engage with questions such as: How has the research question defined and limited what can be 'found'? How has the design of the study and the method of analysis 'constructed' the data and the findings? How could the research question have been investigated differently? To what extent would this have given rise to a different understanding of the phenomenon under investigation? Thus, epistemological reflexivity encourages us to reflect upon the assumptions (about the world, about knowledge) that we have made in the course of the research, and it helps us to think about the implications of such assumptions for the research and its findings.

Willig, C (2001) *Introducing Qualitative Research in Psychology: Adventures in theory and method*. Buckingham: Open University Press.

while EPISTEMOLOGICAL reflexivity attempts to identify the foundations of knowledge and the implication of any findings.

Reflexivity is pro-active as its focus is on providing researchers with a tool that will simultaneously improve their communication and help make them aware of assumptions and priorities that shape their interactions with others. Reflexivity can be used to provide insight into 'biases' before reacting. Moreover, reflexivity is a dynamic process within and between the researcher, others involved in the research, the environment and the process – all inform decisions, actions and interpretations at all stages. Kim Etherington (2004) says this means you have to operate on several levels at the same time. In the context of health and social care research, reflexivity requires awareness of the researcher's contribution to the construction of meaning and an acceptance that 'objectivity', remaining outside and detached from what (or who) is being researched, is impossible.

working with stories

Introduction

In the last chapter we told you something about how you can collect stories – that is, the data for qualitative research. One of the tasks of qualitative research is to somehow reduce the stories you have collected in such a way as to refine, define and concisely express their meaning. You can think of this as finding a way to tell a new story that somehow encapsulates all the important features of all the stories you collected.

Now whereas in quantitative research 'meaning' can be found by statistical manipulation, the steps of which, once you have chosen your test, instrument or procedure, are more or less prescribed, the interpretation of qualitative data is not so rigidly dictated. Not only that, but even when using the same or similar methods of processing with the same tales, different researchers may see different things in a collection of stories. If that wasn't enough there are many, many ways of interpreting stories and what comes out of qualitative data depends upon the way in which it is processed and the experience, knowledge, interests and aims of the interpreter. It is, fair to say that the interpretation of qualitative data remains an art.

This is because whatever method of data transformation (that is analysis, synthesis or interpretation of your stories) you choose to use, you are in charge of making or discovering meaning in them and of making sense of your data. No one else can do that job since you are so intimately bound up with shaping your study and with understanding what you studied. In this sense, all qualitative data processing is idiosyncratic. This is why it is really important that you 'locate' yourself, that is, tell readers enough about you and your interests and expertise so that they can see the lens through which you are viewing your research (see Chapter 2.6) when writing or speaking about your investigation. It also explains the importance of self-observation (see the previous chapter) as part of any qualitative research. However, there are some general rules and principles when interpreting stories (by which we mean what other books may call 'treating qualitative data') and we will tell you something about them in this chapter. We will also tell you a bit about some of the particular ways in which stories can be collected and worked with – we can do this only to a limited extent because

Denzin, NK & Lincoln, YS (2000)
Handbook of Qualitative Research (2nd edn). Thousand Oaks, CA: Sage.

POSITIVISTIC/POSITIVISM A doctrine asserting that sense perceptions are the only admissible basis of human knowledge and precise thought. In research, that the validity of knowledge can only be assured by experimental science.

there are just so many methods used in qualitative research that to address them all would take us way over our word limit. Denzin and Lincoln (2000), in one of the best-known books about qualitative research, present 41 chapters covering 1100 pages and even that doesn't cover all the ways of doing qualitative research that we have heard of. Not only that, but new methods keep being invented.

So, we have chosen a few well-established approaches that are likely to be of use to health and social care practitioners to at least give you an idea of what is possible, but please remember that if what we tell you about doesn't seem to you as if it would quite do the job you want done, there is probably a method out there somewhere that will. Failing that, it is OK to combine elements of methods or, when you are more confident and experienced, even to come up with a new one. However, we do suggest that you only do these things in consultation with one or more people who have extensive knowledge of research.

One more thing before we move on to tell you some of the things you can do to make sense of the stories you have collected. In qualitative research, the boundaries between data collection (recording stories) and data treatment (interpreting stories) are not always as clear as they are when using POSITIVISTIC, quantitative methods. To at least some extent, qualitative researchers tend to begin the process of making meaning from the stories they are collecting in the actual process of collection. Also, some of the methods of working with stories we will tell you about later in this chapter imply one or more strategies for collecting the stories in the first place. So, there are some things in this chapter which could have been in the last one and vice versa. Please bear this in mind when planning your own research.

Qualitative data

Signs of successful, sound data treatment are, firstly, that it is planned, secondly, that it is congruent and in harmony with the aims of the research, the collection methods, and the data itself, and thirdly, that it combines more than one theme. So the data will be *described* and *elaborated,* or perhaps *reflected upon* before being *analysed.* However, when working with stories, analysis may not be the best way to go. It is true that some people find it difficult to imagine how to analyse data without quantifying it in some way. In fact the very word *data* brings numbers to mind.

There is a further problem which we have tried to address in the heading of this section. We have challenged the assumption that the only thing that can be done with data (or the only thing that researchers will be interested in) is to *analyse* it. This notion will confuse another group of readers. What else can you do with data other than analyse it? Read on to find out. But first a bit about 'data'.

Some useful questions about data
What is data?

This is not the first time we have asked this question, and tried to answer it in this book. On p. 14 in Chapter 1.2 we looked at this issue briefly in order to help us identify the sort of information we might be collecting in a qualitative study. The answer now is much the same as it was then – qualitative data is just about anything you can think of that lies within the realm of human experience, whether or not (with some emphasis on the 'or not') it can be put into numbers. In the language of this book, qualitative data is the stories you have collected.

What is our data?

Now this question is looking at what we have actually ended up with. It is important to consider this for a moment so that we can move towards deciding upon what method of treatment might be most appropriate. The answer to the question partly depends upon how it has been collected and recorded. For example, if you interviewed people then your data is the recordings you made of those interviews and/or the transcripts of them; if your study involved you in participant observation then your data is your field notes; whereas if you were part of a co-operative inquiry then your data is everything produced by the group in the course of the research (although you might want to focus most on the propositions generated in the inquiry).

What can be done with data?

This is one of those 'How long is a piece of string?' questions. You can use the stories you have collected in almost any way you can think of to distil meaning from them. However, there are some tried and tested principles when it comes to treating, transforming and interpreting stories. In processing stories, as qualitative researchers:

- we are interested in the natural patterns in the stories and consider these to be of more intrinsic value than any artificial enhancement or amplification
- we prefer to use treatments which involve humans as the instruments of treatment rather than mechanistic tests or numerical models. We seek to preserve the human quality in the data treatment by using treatments that are congruent and in harmony with both the data itself and ourselves as human instruments
- we understand that process and outcome are the same in qualitative data treatment

- in our search for patterns and qualities in our data rather than numbers and quantities, we will seek and develop novel and innovative treatment methods based on subjective and intuitive processes of synthesis in addition to more traditional processes of analysis

The major categories of methods of treating qualitative data

With these principles in mind, there are several major categories of data treatment available. These are:

Synthesis

Which is the putting together of information to arrive at new understanding. By adding information, or recombining it in novel ways, we synthesise some new patterns and meanings. This process is particularly good for understanding interactions between things. The study of human beings is more often than not the study of interactions, so some believe that synthesis, or making combinations and associations between information, is particularly useful in the study of human action. Synthesis is about looking for patterns and trying to grasp the 'wholeness' of things. A guiding principle is that a thing is greater than the sum of its parts.

Note
We explored the extent to which analysis and synthesis were fundamental characteristics of qualitative and quantitative inquiry processes on p 22, Chapter 2.1.

Analysis

More familiar to most of us is the process of taking something apart to understand it better or find meaning in it. This method is familiar to us when trying to diagnose why something mechanical or electrical isn't working, e.g. a washing machine or car.

Elaboration

This is the technique of extending, continuing, developing, embellishing or enhancing something until we find meaning in it. This is a little like completing a dot-to-dot picture or doing some painting by numbers. The basic pattern is there but we can only really make sense of it by further embellishment or elaboration. We may do this by adding extra material, possibly of our own.

Description

This is often seen as a first stage of data treatment in quantitative studies but can be the whole of data treatment in a number of circumstances. In qualitative research, describing data is seen as a highly skilled, illuminating and valid method of data treatment. Description is not simply writing about what has happened. There are many creative forms of description, many requiring careful preparation and discipline.

Reflection

At the unstructured end of data treatment is a reflective process where the researcher, though a 'tuned instrument', eschews any structured approach to data treatment. They still seek the same features in the data such as patterns, regularities and so forth, but do so through a process of deliberation and meditation that is at best semi-systematic.

Repetition

In order to understand it more completely, we may choose to repeat a type of data treatment to see what happens. Let's say we chose to categorise our data in a certain way at the beginning of our data treatment. Then, one month later we decide to do it all over again. We may find that the results of the second categorisation are the same as the first or different. Either way, we have learned something.

Repetition of research cycle

As we have mentioned before, repeating the data treatment is in itself a data treatment technique. Repeating the research cycle (not just the data treatment) is also a valuable method of elaborating the data further. It serves a number of purposes:

- as a check on the trustworthiness of the data. If the findings are the same the second time around, then the data is more likely to be stable and trustworthy
- as a method of elaborating the data further. It would be very suspicious if the data was exactly the same upon repetition of the research cycle. Nothing in the human domain remains absolutely constant, so we might repeat the research cycle to try to understand how things might have changed
- to detect changes in the researcher(s). Since human beings are the measuring instruments as well, we can check on what might be affecting them over time by repeating the measurements
- to check on first impressions. We may have had some 'gut reactions' the first time round, which, if they persist through the repetition, we might take more notice of
- to review and refine tentative hypotheses. The process of developing or possibly testing hypotheses is a continuous one in qualitative work, so the researcher goes through the research cycle again in order to gather more information which may help confirm (or otherwise) initial hypotheses

Advantages: Easy procedure to conduct, gives the findings a 'reliability and validity' check. Picks up changes in thoughts, feelings, and attitudes in participants and researcher. Allows modification of procedure after collaboration.

Disadvantages: Time consuming, questionable benefit in terms of findings since it can be difficult to know how to interpret any differences between findings on different cycles.

The importance of time and timing

The idea of repeating the same data treatment technique over and over serves to remind us of one very important fact in qualitative research: *Data treatment takes time*. More than this, it needs to take time in the same sense that a good wine needs time to mature; we might even see laying our data aside for a while (to let it 'mature') as another valid treatment method. Then there is the further issue of when the treatment of the data takes place. There is general agreement that data treatment can take place before, during and after collection. The timing of data treatment has a strong effect on the overall flavour of the research. The more predetermined the data treatment method is, the more quantitative in style the study becomes. Again, there are several available strategies:

- *predetermined data treatment* – this is the hallmark of structured, quantitative research. The data treatment is fixed before collection and therefore relatively inflexible. It is often fixed with a theory in mind or a hypothesis springing from a theory. Either way the effort is directed towards collecting evidence for a predetermined purpose, usually to support or refute an idea
- *data treatment during collection* – this can be researcher-directed or collaborative. It requires a more flexible schedule and almost inevitably leads to modified aims or avenues of exploration and inquiry from those originally planned
- *data treatment after collection* – can be determined by an original predetermined plan, collaboration with participants at the end of the data collection period, or the result of data treatment during the study

The last two data treatment occasions are more frequently (if not exclusively) associated with qualitative research. However, just because predetermined data treatment is presented here as a sign of quantitative methods, firstly, it doesn't have to be on every occasion and secondly, that does not mean that qualitative researchers shouldn't *plan* their data treatment as much as possible before doing it (usually this means before the collection stage). This plan will, of course, be flexible and open to modification as a result of data collection and treatment as the study progresses. As a general rule, in any research, qualitative or quantitative, it is as well to have a method of data treatment in mind before collecting your data. There is nothing more frustrating than realising that, if only you had collected your data in the right form, a particular way of treating data would give you answers of exactly the kind you are seeking.

Preparing your data for treatment

Before you can work with them, you have to get the stories you collected into a form in which this is possible. This may mean, for example, rewriting field notes so that they constitute a coherent narrative, collecting all the products of a co-operative inquiry group together or, if you have interviewed your participants, getting what was said into written form. Because we told you a lot about collecting stories by interviewing in Chapter 2.7 and because it is a very common way of conducting human inquiry, we will tell you some of the ways of working with interview data. A lot of what we say here is equally applicable to stories of other kinds such as the notes from participant observation, qualitative questionnaires, diaries, and notes from collaborative investigations, to name but a few. You can bear this in mind when planning your own research.

As we discussed in the previous chapter, interviews may be of a variety of types but they are most usually recorded either in audio or video formats. The recording then becomes the 'data' that will be processed in some way. This processing will, it is hoped, allow conclusions to be drawn and these will be presented as the 'findings' from the research. Until recently, it has been usual to process transcripts of the interview – and this is still the preferred technique of many. So, you need to know a bit about the practicalities of transcribing recordings.

Transcribing recordings

There is no way round it, transcribing recordings – that is, coming up with a written form of the spoken dialogue you recorded – is time-consuming and sometimes tedious. Even experienced transcribers can take 6–8 hours to accurately transcribe a one-hour interview (something else to think about when you set out to collect your stories). One way out of this is to pay an audio typist to do this for you. However, this is costly and, more importantly, if you do the job yourself you begin to immerse yourself in the data (because you have to listen intently to what is being said and how it is being said). The likelihood is that you will begin to sense the patterns and themes in the data even if at this stage this is a largely subconscious process. Unless you have a large number of interviews with which to work, it is probably best to do the job of transcription yourself. So, what is the best way to do that?

First, you have to decide what you want to include in your transcript. The simplest transcript comprises only the words actually spoken. However, in any interpersonal interaction a lot more is going on than just words and if you only write down those you may very well miss a lot of important detail. For example, as helping professionals, we know the importance of silence. Perhaps as you transcribe it is helpful to note when things go quiet – and for how

Note

Of course, rewriting your notes is in itself a form of data treatment. Of necessity, it involves an element of selection and interpretation: 'What did I mean when I wrote that?', perhaps elaboration 'Now I think about what was going on when I made this note, this comes to mind', perhaps exclusion 'This is rubbish – I'll leave it out' and so on.

Note

Here again, the process of data transformation (from audio or video record to written text) is inextricably linked to data processing. As you work with the 'raw' data (the contents of the recording) you begin to think about what it means, to sense the patterns it contains.

long. You can do this by literally timing pauses, but think about whether it is more useful to do this in a more subjective way. Perhaps whether the silence seems long or short rather than the actual time it lasts is what is important. Or maybe whether the silence is comfortable or uncomfortable is more relevant. Then there are all the noises other than words. You have to decide whether to include grunts, hesitations ('Errrr …', 'Ummm …'), laughter, chuckles, and so on. Perhaps on an audio recording you can hear yourself or your interviewee shuffling about. Might that have something to do with whatever is going on, if so are you going to note it? With a video recording, you will have a lot more information in the form of body language. You may decide to include this in your transcript noting, for example, open body posture, closed body posture, smiles, tearfulness and the like. As a general rule, it is probably better to note whatever you hear and observe than to limit yourself to particular kinds of interaction (you never know what is going to cast light on your sense of what the stories mean) but there is a balance to be struck. The more of the content and process of the interview you decide to include in your transcript the longer it will take you to complete it. Once you have decided what it is you are going to note it is time to get on with the task.

When you sit down to transcribe an audio or video recording make sure that:

- you will not be interrupted
- you have writing materials, or computer to hand
- you can easily reach the controls of the playback apparatus
- you can hear and (with a video) see well enough – some transcribers like to listen through headphones
- you have the file(s) you want to transcribe

When everything is in place there is nothing left but to get on with it. Each of us has our own preferences when it comes to transcribing a recording – it may take you a while to discover what the best way of working is for you. For example, some people like to listen/watch the recording a few times before beginning the task of transcription. This is good practice because it allows you to become familiar with the content and to begin the process of data transformation. Indeed, doing it this way is at the heart of some of the more subjective methods of inquiry. However, perhaps the easiest way is to listen to a short chunk of recording and then immediately write down or type in what you heard. You will find for yourself through trial and error how much dialogue you can remember before stopping the recording. This will depend partly on the quality of the recording, partly on the nature of what is being said or otherwise expressed and partly on you. Some playback machines can be connected to a foot-control to start and stop play. This may be useful

Note
Some digital recording devices and files let you put a marker at various points in the recording for quick return or reference. Make sure you get the equipment and software that will do what you want.

but almost certainly there will be times when you need to 'rewind' the recording and listen or watch something again just to be sure of what was going on so you will still need to be able to easily reach the controls of your machine. Once you know what it is you wish to note, everything is set up and you have discovered the best way of transcribing for you, it is just a case of carrying on with this until you reach the end of the recording. One of the good things about transcribing any kind of recording is that it doesn't have to be done all at the same time. You can get up, walk around, go for a coffee and the file will still be there, stopped at the place you left off. You don't even have to transcribe all of a recording on the same day – although you may get a better picture of what is going on if you do.

When you have finished working with a file, remember to clearly title your transcript and to store and back it up safely on some removable memory device. You might like to put it somewhere different from where you keep the recording equipment and computer. In this respect and in almost anything else connected with doing a piece of research, in general, a belt and braces approach is always a good idea. For example, can you imagine how it would feel to get towards the end of a research study and then lose your data? So, back everything up and store duplicates separately. Lastly, think about what you will do with the transcript when your inquiry is finished. Options include to destroy it (remember to do this safely too – shredding paper is a good option), to give it (with the file itself) to the interviewee who can then be assured that no record remains and dispose of it in any way they wish, or to keep it in case you can make use of it again. The last option requires that you take steps to protect the confidentiality of your participant by, for example, keeping it in a locked filing cabinet.

Working with what was said and done

Although it is common practice, transforming recorded data by making a transcript may result in the loss of information (subtle nuances of voice, the significance of silence, emotional content, etc. may all disappear) therefore some people think there is a case for working directly with the interview recordings. Whether you choose to work directly with recordings or transcripts, as an interview researcher you are faced with the issue of reducing field information into some other form so that conclusions may be drawn from it. This is equally true no matter how you collected your stories.

How this is done depends upon what is being sought, your philosophy as a researcher, the resources available (e.g. time, computing facilities), etc. This is a personal choice and it brings responsibility but also liberation. It is an essential task and it must be done in a trustworthy way but, on the other hand, providing you can justify it and explain clearly what you have done, you are free to interpret your stories in any way you want. However, like data of any other kind, stories should always be collected with a method of treatment or processing in mind, but just what might these methods be?

Broadly speaking, methods for processing interview data fall into one of four categories which deal with:

- *the characteristics of language* – how, in the sense of the words chosen and sentences structured, something was said (e.g. discourse analysis)
- *the discovery of regularities and patterns* – what things turn up regularly and/or commonly (e.g. thematic analysis)
- *the comprehension of meaning* – getting to the essence of human experience while accepting its subjective nature (e.g. grounded theory)
- *reflection* – for example, thinking deeply and critically about one's own thoughts, behaviour and experience (e.g. autoethnography)

You can think of this as a progression from more to less structured and formal. Most methods for treating qualitative data probably call on each of the categories. Another way to think about it is in terms of strategies that can be applied to understanding qualitative data. These are:

- *immersion* – we began to hint at this when we were telling you about transcribing recordings. What it means is reading or listening intently and attentively to your stories so that you assimilate as much of the meaning they contain as possible. Remember that sometimes meaning is explicit but often it is unspoken. You have to read between the lines and think about what might be being left unsaid (either because it is assumed that you will know, because the interviewee simply overlooks something, or because it is sensitive or difficult)
- *categorisation* – as you might expect, this is about coming up with groupings of things that have been said or done but which seem to be more or less the same thing. It involves systematically working through your data, assigning coding categories (we will tell you about coding a bit later), or identifying meaning within the story

PHENOMENOLOGICAL approaches to understanding and psychology are based on the study of immediate experience, where 'truth' or 'knowledge' comes from the perceptual field of the individual, rather than an external authority. Based on the work of the philosopher Edmund Husserl.

TRIANGULATION is a way of assuring the validity of research findings through the use of a *variety* of research methods (usually more than two).

- *PHENOMENOLOGICAL reduction* – when you have come up with some idea of the meanings contained in your stories, you have to think critically about them. Are they valid? Are there any other ways of looking at the data?
- *TRIANGULATION* – we told you a bit about the importance of triangulation in Chapter 2.6 when we were considering the importance of trustworthiness in qualitative research. Here it means something similar except that it is a way of ensuring that the categories in your different stories support each other. You

have to sort through your categories and decide which ones characterise the stories as a whole and which are less significant or are invalid or mistaken

- *interpretation* – the final stage of working with stories is to make sense of the categories and meanings you have found and to offer these in an accessible form. For example, you could construct a model or a META-STORY or use an established theory to explain your findings

META-STORY The story that tells everybody's story, the 'big story', or the story of stories.

Most approaches to processing qualitative data include these stages varying in the emphasis given to each stage and the degree of subjectivity with which they are approached.

Coding, description and categorisation as ways of treating qualitative data

As we have said more than once, you can do almost anything you want when you are making sense of qualitative data – providing you can make a reasonable argument for your actions. However, there are some tried and trusted techniques, one or more of which will usually get your stories into the form you want. These include coding, description and categorisation.

Coding

Codes are any device used to attach values to events in research. In quantitative research, this means using numbers in some way or other but in qualitative research we should not think of numbers as the first or only coding possibility. So what else can we use as codes and how do we go about the task of coding our data?

Coding is done to reduce data to manageable proportions. Traditionally, it is a way of allocating values via some sort of abbreviation or symbol, e.g. single words (as in TYPOLOGIES), letters of the alphabet (as in categories), or numbers (at this point the analysis becomes quantitative). One option is to use a predetermined coding scheme but this has the effect of imposing considerable structure on your data collection (because you decide beforehand what you are going to note), so we consider it to be leaning quite strongly towards a model mixed with quantitative methods. However, it may be useful for you to know something about how you might develop and/or use a predetermined code.

Predetermined coding schemes

The development of a coding scheme is difficult and time consuming. The following steps are involved, each one requiring some consideration and exploratory data collection (called piloting) to test it out before you go ahead and use it in your study proper:

TYPOLOGY Classification according to general type to aid the setting up and selecting of categories, so that you can process your data, eg, a typology of emotions could include happiness, sadness, joy, fear, etc.

Note
In fact a lot of this chapter is about coding, different methods of coding for different circumstances, some very general, some highly stylised. The purpose of this section is twofold, firstly, to give some idea of the types of activity that are traditionally used as coding practices, and secondly, to give ourselves permission to do whatever is appropriate and works for us regardless of what others have done in the past. Like all other areas of qualitative endeavour, there are no 'rules', save commitment to quality through a thoughtful, patient and rigorous application of common sense, plus our best attempt to preserve the humanness in our studies through practice that is congruent with our nature.

1 *How many observers are you going to use?*
If there is more that one you will have to train each observer to observe in a standard way using the coding scheme you have developed.

2 *Are the observations global or specific?*
When we create a coding scheme for global observations, we usually call this a rating scale. Specific observations are dealt with depending upon the number and type of categories of event being observed.

3 *How many types of event do you want to observe?*
If a small number of events are to be observed, it may be possible to construct a scheme which records some detail about each event in terms of subcategories. A large number of categories of event will limit your coding scheme to a checklist. You may have broad general categories each with a checklist, e.g. Non-verbal behaviours (plus checklist), Spatial behaviours (plus checklist), Extra-linguistic behaviours (plus checklist) and Linguistic behaviours (plus checklist).

4 *What use will your categories really be?*
Don't fall into the trap of trying to record everything just because you can see it. If absolutely necessary have a catch-all 'other' category to dump interesting bits into, rather than leave them out. Tie your coding to your hypothesis or research question as tightly as possible.

5 *How objective do you want it to be?*
It pays to be explicit about any inferences or interpretations you expect your observer(s) to make. Even if you are the sole observer, you need to be clear where on the subjectivity–objectivity scale you are. Using a predetermined coding scheme is more than a nod in the direction of objectivity and quantification, so try not to mix models.

6 *Make your categories mutually exclusive*
Do not have any overlapping categories. They should be independent, which means one category for each separate thing.

7 *Make life easy for your observer(s)*
Especially if you are the sole observer! If you are leaning towards quantitative analysis make the system user-friendly, e.g. tick-boxes where possible, simple abbreviations and explicitly defined categories which leave little or no room for error. If you are inclined towards a more qualitative approach be sure that you really want a predetermined coding scheme in the first place, then make your categories global with plenty of room for subjective opinion.

8   *Don't re-invent the wheel*
There are several good examples of coding schemes for human behaviour in the literature. You may decide to use one 'off the peg'.

Coding collected stories

Coding doesn't have to be predetermined – it can also be responsive or even collaborative. Coding done after all the data has been collected is more flexible and can be developed in response to the changing requirements of the study as the data is collected, or in response to collaboration between the researcher and participants. Collaboration is particularly valuable if *indigenous categories* are being used (see overleaf) since only the participants can usefully attach values to them in any coding scheme. Existing coding schemes (devised by others) can be used alongside coding schemes developed specially for the study in hand.

Since the purpose of coding is to *manage* data, the act of applying a code to data always reduces its complexity or changes it in some way. This is one of the basic arguments against quantitative methods, namely that applying numbers to human data is too restrictive, changes the nature of the data, is incongruent with 'human' data and oversimplifies complex processes. The trouble is, we find exactly the same problem in qualitative coding. All coding or data treatment methods become a trade-off between presenting very complex human data in an easily assimilated form and the unacceptable limitations, oversimplifications and distortions that are necessary to achieve this. Each coding or data treatment method will be assessed (where appropriate) for its degree of distortion/ oversimplification as it is presented.

The degree of elaboration in coding depends upon the data collection method. In its simplest form coding is the description of events in single words or prose, next comes the naming of categories and so on. At the other extreme it consists of developing elaborate schemes for allocating numbers to responses to questionnaire items or interview questions. There is no set method or procedure; successful coding is the product of common sense, thoughtful planning and, where possible, collaboration and careful piloting of the scheme. 'Coding' is an important part of thematic analysis and in our section addressing that we will give you some practical examples of how to code and identify themes.

Description

Along with categorisation (see overleaf), description is probably the most frequently used data treatment method. You may be wondering how *simply* describing something could be called data *treatment* when it doesn't appear to actually *treat* the data in any

Note
Some of the methods for processing interview data we look at later in this chapter, for example thematic analysis (pp 214-7 and grounded theory (see pp 212-4), are, or imply, particular coding schemes. Others are associated with other methods we describe later in this chapter.

way. As we hinted above, description *is* a coding method since the action (that is, behaviour, thoughts or feeling) has to be translated into words. This is coding of a sort, and most often the action is described by a third party (the researcher) who is not an actor. So, we have included description as a method of data treatment for the above and following reasons. Firstly, description isn't simple. There are different styles which can be adopted, some dependent upon the position of the researcher in relation to the action. For example:

- *narrative accounts* – telling the story based on a sequence of events, either as a participant oneself or from the viewpoint of other participants
- *journalistic accounts* – more external to the action, possibly as a non-participant observer, or partly participant observer

Secondly, description isn't transparent or neutral. It does interfere with, change or *treat* the data in some way. A descriptive account is filtered through the person doing the describing, so in that important sense there is a strong element of self-conscious data treatment. Once again, this indicates the importance of locating yourself when you are conducting qualitative research.

Description is usually used alongside other forms of data treatment. It is, however, a mistake to see it simply as a method of data presentation. In order to describe something we have to adopt a viewpoint from which to describe. This immediately changes or contextualises the description and should be recognised as a data treatment agent.

Advantages: The most flexible, least obtrusive data treatment method, offering the fewest opportunities for distortion or limitation of data. It is capable of acknowledging the full complexity of the data.

Disadvantages: May not limit the data enough for some purposes – is longwinded and doesn't 'manage' the data very well for simple presentation.

Categorisation
Categorising things is at the heart of qualitative methodology, so it would be surprising if it were not represented as a data treatment method. There is no magic in categorisation, simply the application of common sense and a systematic, well-prepared procedure. Two broad types of category emerge. There are *indigenous categories* which are those 'naturally occurring' categories used by the participants themselves in the situation under study. It is essential to the sensitive understanding of the action for the researcher to elicit these categories at some point during the research. Indigenous categories shape and determine the action and the participants' meanings in a number of ways. For example, a year group of students

may categorise themselves as 'goths', 'grunges', 'emos', 'stoners' or whatever. Then there are *researcher categories* which are those categories imposed on the action or data by the researcher according to some principle determined before, during or after the collection of the data. Such researcher categories may be determined by:

- a theoretical perspective
- the action or data as it comes in to influence the researcher
- a reflective process within the researcher
- a collaborative process involving the participants, but where the categories are still largely imported from a frame of reference external to the action

To go back to our example, from the perspective of the researcher, the same college year group might be divided into, for example:

- demographic categories such as age, gender, ethnic origin, socio-economic grouping, etc.
- friendship categories as a result of a sociographic analysis of their relationships
- categories based on experiences such as those who attend counselling sessions and those who do not

The type of categories used in any study will depend upon the particular data treatment method chosen. Categorisation as a basic technique is pandemic in qualitative research. It's usually just a question of *how* you're going to do it, not *whether* you're going to do it. In each of the methods below there is an expression of categorisation, often stylised to meet the needs of the data or theoretical perspective of the research.

Useful categories are ones that make life easy for the researcher. To some extent this should be under our control in the case of researcher categories. If we want to make things easy for ourselves we should aim for categories that are mutually *exclusive* and *exhaustive*, i.e. ensuring that there is no overlap between categories, or that one piece of data cannot fall into two categories and that no data is left uncategorised at the end. These features are impossible to guarantee in indigenous categories. In fact it may be an essential feature of an indigenous category system that it permits flexibility, overlapping and movement between categories.

Exclusivity and exhaustiveness are always to be aimed for when planning the category and coding system, and should be checked out for 'watertightness' during piloting of the category system.

Advantages: Indigenous categories offer the least interference, distortion and limitation of the data in a category system. They honour the participants' meanings in their experience. Aids simple presentation and helps understanding through sensitive simplification.

Disadvantages: Can get too complex. If researcher's categories are used they can get 'out of sync' with the participants' experience. Begins to simplify the experience of others to a point which easily becomes inaccurate or offensive.

Note

On p 277 we explain the difference between method and methodology. The difference is important to understanding this and the next section in this chapter.

EPISTEMOLOGY Philosophy concerned with the nature of knowledge (what is it?), the source of knowledge (how do we know what we know?) and the scope of knowledge (what, if any, are the limits of knowledge?).

ONTOLOGY The branch of METAPHYSICS concerned with the nature of being and, of special relevance to research, with particular theories about the nature of being and kinds of existence.

METAPHYSICS Philosophy concerned with abstract concepts such as the nature of existence or of truth and knowledge.

IF YOU WANT TO KNOW MORE ABOUT
narrative research

you could try:

Andrews, M, Squire, C & Tamboukou, M (eds) (2008) *Doing Narrative Research.* London: Sage.

Clandinin, DJ & Conelly, FM (2000) *Narrative Inquiry: Experience and story in qualitative research.* San Francisco, CA: Jossey Bass.

Elliot, J (2005) *Using Narrative in Social Research: Qualitative and quantitative approaches.* London: Sage.

Six major methodologies for working with stories

Way back in Chapter 1.1 we told you something of the importance and relevance of the way in which you view the world, the nature of people and how we know what we know influences how you are likely to conduct your research and interpret what you find. That is to say that EPISTEMOLOGY and ONTOLOGY underpin qualitative research methods. This leads to a huge array of possible ways of doing research. We cannot tell you about them all – especially as there seems to be no end to the development of new methods. However, there have been a number of attempts to classify or categorise qualitative research methods, grouping or clustering them into related methods (which is in itself an interesting reflection of many qualitative research practices). We have chosen one of these to tell you about because it is relatively straightforward and covers most ways of doing qualitative research of which we are aware. This classification sorts approaches to qualitative research into six categories as follows.

Narrative research

In the context of investigating human experience, a narrative is the story told or written about an event or experience or a series of events or experiences. An important characteristic of such a story is that it has a chronology 'first this happened, then that and we ended up here'. Such stories can be collected in any of the ways we discussed in the previous chapter. Interviews, biographical and autobiographical accounts, life histories and oral histories are all possible forms of narrative. Narrative research is a good way of collecting detailed stories of the experience of a small number of individuals. Collected stories are analysed or processed in any of a number of ways. For example, discourse analysis and narrative analysis as described below are ways used by narrative researchers, but thematic analysis (also below) might serve just as well. From the analysis, the researcher can re-cast the stories as a meta-story – a story that typifies them or one which 'tells the story of the stories'. Collaboration with the participants of a narrative study allows (amongst other things) a check on the meta-story. The researcher can take the re-cast story back to the participants asking 'Can you see yourself and your story in this account?' taking account of any feedback and addition to the plot and characters. This offers a validation of the original or subsequent analysis.

Phenomenological research

PHENOMENOLOGY has at its heart that 'reality' is subjective at least in as much as, for human beings, the world is interpreted. Our perceptions are filtered through the lens of our individual make-up and we decide the meaning of things in that light. If there is an objective reality, it is unknowable. As an approach to research, phenomenology leads in the direction of the determination of the meaning people give to their experience of a phenomenon (for example, a life event, an emotion such as anger) in an attempt to distil some universal essence. The basic questions of the phenomenological researcher are something like: 'What is your experience of this (phenomenon, action, feeling, life event, etc.)?' 'What circumstances/situations/settings have typically influenced or affected your experience?'

So, the phenomenological researcher collects stories about the phenomenon that is the focus of inquiry in much the same way as any other qualitative researcher and then seeks to develop a composite description epitomising what this encounter meant to all the participants. The objective is for this composite description to make clear 'what' (the perceived nature of the phenomenon) was experienced and 'how' the phenomenon or encounter was understood. To complicate things a bit, there are two different broad approaches to phenomenological research: HERMENEUTICS and 'transcendental' or psychological phenomenology. In the hermeneutic method, as well as the description of the phenomenon as experienced by the participants, the interpretations of the researcher are important, whereas the other approach is much less concerned (or not at all) with the researcher's interpretations. Indeed, transcendental/psychological phenomenological research requires the researcher to 'bracket off' (set aside) their own experiences to approach the phenomenon being investigated with fresh eyes. You can decide for yourself how easy or difficult this might be in practice. In phenomenological research, the processing of the raw data is about reducing it to significant statements that in some way exemplify the experience of the informants. These are then clustered into themes which are used to inform the writing of a description of the phenomenon as the participant experienced it. The individual descriptions then become the material from which a composite description is generated.

Grounded theory research

Although for some, grounded theory is a way of doing phenomenological research, it differs in that rather than simply to provide a description of a phenomenon an objective is to generate theory from the collected stories. That is, theories (general explanations) of processes, actions or interactions are 'grounded'

PHENOMENOLOGICAL approaches to understanding and psychology are based on the study of immediate experience, where 'truth' or 'knowledge' comes from the perceptual field of the individual, rather than an external authority. Based on the work of the philosopher Edmund Husserl.

> IF YOU WANT TO KNOW MORE ABOUT
> phenomenological research
> you could try:
>
> Cohen, MZ, Kahn, DL & Steeves, RH (2000) *Hermeneutic Phenomenological Research: A practical guide for nurses.* Thousand Oaks, CA: Sage.
>
> Moustakas, C (1994) *Phenomenological Research Methods.* Thousand Oaks, CA: Sage.
>
> Smith, JA, Flowers, P & Larkin, M (2009) *Interpretative Phenomenological Analysis: Theory, method and research.* London: Sage.

HERMENEUTICS The art and science of interpretation of meaning, traditionally of texts, but in social sciences more of human experience or social events.

> IF YOU WANT TO KNOW MORE ABOUT
> grounded theory
> you could read:
>
> Charmaz, K (2000) Grounded theory: Objectivist and constructivist methods. In NK Denzin & YS Lincoln (eds) *Handbook of Qualitative Research* (2nd edn) (pp 509-35). Thousand Oaks, CA: Sage.
>
> Corbin, J & Strauss, A (2008) *Basics of Qualitative Research: Techniques and procedures for developing grounded theory* (3rd edn). Thousand Oaks, CA: Sage.
>
> Glaser, BG & Strauss, AL (1967) *The Discovery of Grounded Theory: Strategies for qualitative research.* Chicago: Aldine.

in the stories of the people who have had the experience being investigated. We will tell you more about grounded theory in the next section 'Some story processing methods'.

Ethnographic research

Ethnography is an approach to research which is primarily of use when investigating a culture or cultural group, large or small. The purpose of an ethnographical study is to describe and interpret the values, behaviours, beliefs and ways and means of expression of a group of people sharing a culture. As you might imagine, it has been of great use to anthropologists studying particular societies but it can equally be of use to a caring professional wishing to know more about a particular group of clients or fellow practitioners. Ethnography is primarily an observational approach to research and one of the principle ways of doing it is as a participant observer. We told you something about participant observation in the previous chapter (see p. 164) so we won't repeat that here. As well as ethnographies of traditional form in which the researcher provides an account of what was heard or observed, there is an approach to ethnography, *critical ethnography*, which, something like action research, is concerned with political action and effecting social change through the emancipation of marginalised and disadvantaged groups. The focus of a critical ethnographer is likely to be on issues of power and inequality with the objective of empowering the participants.

IF YOU WANT TO KNOW MORE ABOUT
ethnographic research
you have a lot of choice but you could try:

Angrosino, M (2007) *Doing Ethnographic and Observational Research.* London: Sage.

Taylor, S (ed) (2002) *Ethnographic Research: A reader.* London Sage.

There is also a series of books '*The Ethnographer's Toolkit*' published by Altamira Press.

Case study research

This is something we told you about in the previous chapter (see p. 156) so what we will put here will mostly serve as a reminder. We included it in the last chapter because we see case studies as a way of collecting stories that can then be processed or treated in a variety of ways. However, another view is that case study is a methodology (i.e. a system of methods) in its own right. Basically, case study research involves the exploration of a particular issue or experience through the in-depth study of one or more 'cases' in a particular setting or context. As we wrote before, the basic idea is to take all the available information about the case or cases and to generalise from this.

IF YOU WANT TO KNOW MORE ABOUT
case study research
you could look at:

Gerring, J (2007) *Case Study Research: Principles and practices.* Cambridge: Cambridge University Press.

Simons, H (2009) *Case Study Research in Practice.* London: Sage.

Yin, RK (2009) *Case Study Research: Design and methods* (4th edn). Thousand Oaks, CA: Sage.

There is also the massive encyclopaedia intended to be the definitive compendium of case work research:

Mills, AJ, Durepos, G & Wiebe, E (eds) (2009) *Encyclopedia of Case Study Research.* Thousand Oaks, CA: Sage.

Intrapersonal/subjective research

Some more recent approaches to qualitative research are rooted in the assumption that while 'if you want to know about human experience, ask a human being' is a good guide, the human being each of us knows best is ourselves. This leads to a valuing of the in-depth exploration of personal beliefs, principles, thoughts and emotions as a way of understanding human experience. Most of the other five approaches can be used in this way – for example, one of the best-known forms of intrapersonal research is autoethnography in which the subject of the ethnographic study is the researcher. Heuristic inquiry, which we describe in the next section (see p. 217), is another such method and we will let that stand as an example of this group of approaches.

Some story processing methods

We will now list and explain a range of way of working with stories or, if you prefer, data treatment methods and techniques. What we have tried to do is to pick methods that are either somehow representative of particular philosophies or that we think are likely to be of particular interest and use to health and social care practitioners. Of course our list is incomplete and it is bound to be. There are more ways of doing qualitative research than we can count and, no doubt, there is some method lurking in the literature that will become the next 'big thing'. This is the exciting thing about qualitative methods – new approaches, new ways and new techniques are developing all the time. This should be encouraging to beginning researchers, since, as we have said already, in essence there is no reason why you should not develop a novel method that suits *your* data.

The list is an attempt to give you some reference points and starting points. Remember, if you want to use one or more of these methods in your own research you are going to have to read or ask more about it. Do bear in mind that qualitative research has a strong collaborative theme. By this we mean not only collaborating with your participants, but also with fellow researchers and supervisors. Seek out someone experienced to help with your data treatment, preferably someone who knows a little about the area on which your project focuses. We have already strongly suggested that you find a supervisor for your research. Now it is essential.

As we tell you about each approach, we will give you an indication of the ways in which that particular approach has been used in health and social care research. We aren't even going to try to be comprehensive in our coverage – our intention is just to raise some of the possibilities. You should remember that if, for example, we tell you that content analysis has been used to study whether it is the patient or the GP who initiates the prescription of psychotropic drugs, that doesn't mean you couldn't do it by using thematic analysis or some other approach.

Content analysis
Content analysis is the systematic analysis of the content of the document or text (the story) in question. All kinds of stories, from documents to video, can be subjected to content analysis. The main

IF YOU WANT TO KNOW MORE ABOUT
autoethnography
you could try:

Ellis, C (2004) *The Ethnographic I: A methodological novel about autoethnography.* Walnut Creek, CA: Altamira Press.

Ellis, C & Bochner, AP (2000) Autoethnography, personal narrative, reflexivity: Researcher as subject. In NK Denzin & YS Lincoln (eds) *Handbook of Qualitative Research* (2nd edn) (pp 733-68). Thousand Oaks, CA: Sage.

IF YOU WANT TO KNOW MORE ABOUT
content analysis

you could read:

Hsieh, H-F & Shannon, SE (2005)
Three approaches to qualitative content
analysis. *Qualitative Health Research*
15(9), 1277-88.

Krippendorf, K (2004) *Content Analysis:*
An introduction to its methodology (2nd
edn). Thousand Oaks, CA: Sage.

And, because content analysis is not
exclusively a qualitative technique:

Roberts, CW (ed) (1997) *Text Analysis*
for the Social Sciences: Methods for
drawing statistical inferences from texts and
transcripts. Mahwah, NJ: Lawrence
Erlbaum Associates.

areas of interest in health and social care concern mass media, i.e. newspapers, magazines, advertisements, photographs, television, radio, and films. However, the use of content analysis does not have to be limited to these 'mainstream' media. Minutes of meetings, letters, and speeches all have been subjected to content analysis to some limited degree. The approach has also been used on questionnaire and interview items and response content. Various 'specialist' versions of content analysis have been adapted and developed for use in different situations with different kinds of stories. We will consider one such specialist application in detail: discourse analysis.

Carrying out a content analysis is a straightforward procedure requiring time, patience and an orderly approach to categorisation. Assuming you have:

- developed your research question
- decided on your method
- found and assembled the stories you want to study

We suggest the following simple guidelines:

Sampling
As with almost every other method, one of the first tasks is to have a sampling strategy. In the case of content analysis, the purpose is to limit the flow of data to manageable proportions. Typically, the useful questions involve firstly, which factor will determine the sampling, e.g. time/date, person, event or place, and secondly, what type of sampling method will be used, e.g. random, stratified, opportunity, etc. Each type of medium will suggest appropriate sampling strategies. For example, television programmes may be best sampled randomly over time – a random sample of ten *Newsnight* programmes over a six-month period.

It may be necessary to have second or third stages in a sampling strategy, to continue with our example: we may then stratify the sample of *Newsnight* programmes so that all items are proportionally represented in our sample. Our final sampling stage will be to take segments of text from the programme (including or excluding visuals) for example, a two-minute segment, one minute into each item and every two minutes thereafter according to the length of the item.

Units of record
Now we have to decide what it is we are looking for and recording. Again, each type of media will suggest certain units of record. In a television programme we can choose from sentences, phrases and words spoken to camera, words in voice-over, moving images – live action, video footage, archive footage, still images, background music – all of this can be in the programme proper or the title sequence. We could record the number or type of whole items, programme segments,

length of time spent on each item and so on. There are many variations and decisions which are likely to be far from simple since each one will affect the nature of the material collected. (In case you haven't noticed, we're talking about a form of coding.)

If we were looking at newspapers we might use as our unit of record the number of times the word 'counselling' appeared, the size of the headline when counselling is the topic, the number of words in the article or whatever.

Context issues

Although content analysis is, fairly obviously, concerned with content, there is more than passing acknowledgement of the context in which the unit of record occurs. If we have chosen individual words as the unit of record, we know that the meaning of a word is entirely dependent upon the rest of the sentence, paragraph, page, article, book, etc. We would not draw the same conclusions from seeing the word 'counsellor' 20 times in a tabloid newspaper under different headlines:

> *Counsellors sold drugs to school children*
> *Counsellor saved my dog from drowning*
> *Counsellor awarded MBE for famine relief charity work*
> *Counsellors to help hostages recover from trauma*

Only one of these headlines has something to do with counselling. We would be further interested in whether the context had a positive, favourable, or negative, unfavourable, effect on the meaning of the word.

There are other contextual factors which must be taken into consideration, such as:

- what authority does the recorded material have:
  - who said or wrote or sponsored it: the Prime Minister or Paul Wilkins?
  - where was it published, broadcast, etc.: BBC News or *Therapy Today*?

Determine the categories

The task of constructing categories has been covered in the section on 'categorisation' on p. 198, where we outlined the general principles. The trouble with categorisation is that it is almost entirely situation and research-question specific. There is a huge range of possible categories that can be used in content analysis. Following on from the section on context, when constructing categories we must remember to consider not only the content but also:

- whether the meaning is favourable or unfavourable, positive or negative
- what overall goals the media might espouse

- what values are ascribed to or revealed by the media, its methods or the item(s) under study

As we have already said, categories in research, both qualitative and quantitative, should really be exclusive and exhaustive. Although these features are something to aim for in general, they can only really be checked out in practice by piloting the category system, see below.

Pilot the categories

In content analysis along with other methods in qualitative work, we would test the appropriateness, accuracy and trustworthiness of our data treatment method by collaborating with others.

Do the analysis proper

This means do whatever systematic acts of categorisation you have planned as part of your content analysis. There are devices which can be used as aids to the content analysis categorisation process. These can be either manual or computerised:

Frequency counts – counting the number of times a word or phrase, (or even a category) for example, occurs in a given text. These can be expressed in two basic ways:
- *key word counts* – the frequencies of key or target words, e.g.:

Counsellor	36
Counselling	76
Psychotherapist	12
Psychotherapy	16
Alcoholism	32
Drug abuse	53
Tranquilliser dependency	17

- *ranked frequencies of occurrence* – in order of most frequent to least frequent, regardless of relevance to the study in hand, e.g.:

Case	79
Debt	79
College	78
Counselling	76
Science	75

Such lists can be compared between documents or media or to 'absolute measures' such as official word counts which give the naturally occurring frequencies of words in various media. If category counts are being used, these will automatically be 'key categories' since it would be foolish to develop and include categories which have no meaning for your study!

Context lists – key word in context (KWIC) lists give the list of contexts in which the key or target words occur, e.g. the five words preceding and five words following the key word. These can be expressed as frequency counts as above, and the researcher chooses the extent of the context and any omissions. These will alert the researcher to any phrases which, once identified, can lead to further analysis.

Multiple criteria lists – listing those instances when a case (word, phrase or category event) meets more than one criterion at the same time. This can become complicated and time consuming and such multiple and combined category analyses are fast becoming the sole domain of computers.

*Advantages of **content analysis***: Has a 'natural' appeal in that it seems a common-sense form of analysis to most people. It is a flexible form of data treatment since the coding element can be made more or less structured and complex. Other advantages are the same as those of categorisation.

*Disadvantages of **content analysis***: Is an involved, disciplined procedure demanding of time and other resources. It has the same other disadvantages as categorisation.

What has content analysis been used to do?

In the general context of health care, television programmes have been subjected to content analysis to establish the safety behaviours of the characters portrayed in them and the implication this had for children's safety and injury (Potts et al., 1996). Fifty-two programmes were sampled and content analysis showed that, in the context of behaving safely, there was no perceivable effect of television on how the children behaved. Sleath et al. (1997), conducted a more specific study of 508 audiotapes of interactions between doctors in primary care and their patients, in which content analysis was used to find out if it was the patients or the doctors who initiated the prescription of psychotropic medicine. This study showed that about 47% of the time the request came from the patient. It also seemed that wealthier patients or ones who had known the doctor for a long time were more likely to ask for psychotropic drugs to be prescribed than poorer patients or those who had a relatively short relationship with the doctor.

Potts, R, Runyan, D, Zerger, A & Marchetti, K (1996) A content analysis of safety behaviors of television characters: Implications for children's safety and injury. *Journal of Pediatric Psychology 21*(4), 517-28.

Sleath, B, Svarstad, B & Roter, D (1997) Physician vs patient initiation of psychotropic prescribing in primary care settings: A content analysis of audiotapes. *Social Science and Medicine 44*(4), 541-48.

Discourse analysis

Although we have separated discourse analysis from the main body of content analysis, we see it as a specialist subdivision, dealing

IF YOU WANT TO KNOW MORE ABOUT
discourse analysis

there is a huge choice. However, you can try:

Jørgensen, M & Phillips, L (2002)
Discourse Analysis as Theory and Method.
London: Sage.

Phillips, N & Hardy, C (2000)
Discourse Analysis: Investigating processes of social construction. Thousand Oaks,
CA: Sage.

**Weatherall, M, Taylor, S & Yates, SJ
(eds) (2001)** *Discourse Theory and
Practice: A reader.* London: Sage.

with language (as opposed to images – photos, film etc. – music, symbols etc.). The term *discourse analysis* is not used consistently in qualitative research literature. Some use it to refer to all research which focuses on language and linguistics, others use it in connection with studies looking at language differences, and yet more people use the term to describe social psychology applications of a more general content analysis type. However, there is general agreement that discourse analysis is a way of understanding social interactions and that this is because the way we use language shapes the categories and constructs we use. Our sense of reality is socially and culturally constructed so language, meaning and 'reality' are inextricably linked.

All variations of discourse analysis have language (everyday talk) as the focus, which for many puts it at the centre of human studies, owing to the uniqueness and central role of human language in the structure of human relationships. Talk is not only about actions, events and situations, but also a potent and constitutive part of them. Another common feature of discourse analyses is the attention paid to the micro-components of language – individual words and phrases. These small units of discourse are analysed for meaning and then categorised and counted in the most structured examples.

Advantages: As for content analysis, but paying close attention to a uniquely human characteristic.

Disadvantages: As for content analysis, plus the concentration on small fragments can lose the contextual emphasis and therefore the meaning of the discourse.

What has discourse analysis been used to do?

In the context of health and social care, one of the very useful things you can do with discourse analysis is to use it to comprehend the meaning and usefulness of official guidelines. For example (Pattison, 2006), in the UK and in the context of nursing and the NHS, it has been used to reach conclusions about the impact of critical care documents on the provision of end-of-life care. Discourse analysis can also be used to understand what happens in interviews and other interpersonal interactions. For example (Reeves et al., 2004), it has been used to explore the evidence for the assessment of suicide risk being undertaken in the counselling process.

Pattison, N (2006) A critical discourse
analysis of provision of end-of-life care
in key UK critical care documents.
Nursing in Critical Care 11(4), 198-208.

**Reeves, A, Bowl, R, Wheeler, S &
Guthrie, E (2004)** The hardest words:
Exploring the dialogue of suicide in the
counselling process – a discourse
analysis. *Counselling and Psychotherapy
Research 4*(1), 67-71.

Working with narrative

The idea of working with narrative, that is, the stories people tell about themselves and their experience and how they tell them, runs across many approaches to qualitative research. Discourse analysis could be seen as one way of working with narrative and the feminist approaches we discuss later in this chapter can also involve looking at narrative. As you read more about research, you will probably come across the expression 'narrative analysis'. Narrative analysis is a way of understanding how people make and use stories to interpret the world, their lived experience of it and themselves in relation to it. In other words, we make sense of our experience and communicate it to others by telling stories. Not only that, but we tell stories that are rich in metaphor and these metaphors are often culturally defined. Public stories, accounts that are widespread in a particular community or culture, are a means by which people of that community or culture inform the construction of their personal identities and personal stories. Understanding not only the content of a story but at least something of how it was told can provide a great deal of information about the experience being related. It is also important to remember that for every story told, there is an audience, even if the story is self-talk or a daydream. Stories are shaped and told with the hearer in mind. In this way, all stories are co-constructed and to understand them something about the audience must be known. Getting to grips with all this is what narrative analysis is about.

It would be nice if 'narrative analysis' had only one meaning and we could neatly tell you what that is but, as we keep noting, in qualitative research things are rarely that simple. For example, it may be the structure and grammar of the story which is seen as important, or the focus might be on the cultural, historical and political context in which particular stories are (or can be) told, by whom and to whom, or it may be that what is sought is an understanding of the purpose of particular stories in people's lives. However, there are some shared characteristics we can tell you about. For example, whatever the exact approach, the stories people have to tell are not seen as 'factual' nor is 'truth' an issue. It is understood that narratives are subjective, rich in metaphor and personal meaning. They are social products produced in specific contexts and bounded by the social, historical, cultural and experiential milieu of the teller. As we have already said, narratives are a way people have of interpreting their worlds and representing themselves and their experience to others. You could even say that the stories we tell are a way of building up our identity – we know ourselves and are known to others through the stories we tell.

We called the last chapter 'Collecting Stories' – we could just as well have called it 'Listening to Narratives'. From this, you will immediately see that there is more than one form in which narrative can be collected. Interviews are often 'stories' but so are life histories, case studies and so on. All of these are likely to link to the past (what is being talked or written about happened 'then' rather than 'now') but it would be mistaken to think of the stories as objectively true or unbiased. What is being heard is an interpretation of a remembered event or experience. Arguably, memory involves

IF YOU WANT TO KNOW MORE ABOUT
narrative analysis

as well as the sources we gave you for narrative research on p 200, you could try:

Lieblich, A, Tuval-Moshiach, R & Zilber, T (1998) *Narrative Research: Reading, analysis and interpretation.* Thousand Oaks, CA: Sage.

Riessman, CR (2008) *Narrative Methods for the Human Sciences.* Thousand Oaks, CA: Sage.

reconstruction rather than accurate reporting; certainly it is always from the frame of reference of the teller and no two tellers see anything in the same way. What, then, are the characteristics of a narrative? Well, there is probably no single widely accepted definition. However, in *Poetics* Aristotle (yes, as usual the Greeks had a word for it) said that a narrative has a beginning, middle and an end. It seems that this is agreed as a necessary criterion even though it is insufficient for a total definition. Well aware that others may take different views, we offer you the following. Narratives are accounts:

- often containing at least an element of change over time – what you might even call transformation. That is, they have a temporal dimension. 'When I first went to music therapy I was really scared to make a noise until I found that it was OK just to sit in the corner and tap quietly on the drum'
- which contain some kind of action and which have characters. The characters and actions don't have to be 'real'. For example, we often tell stories about what might have been or what might come to be and also we sometimes populate our stories with imaginary characters. In the snippet above, there are at least two explicit actions – sitting and tapping the drum – and one character 'I', the storyteller although at least one more, the music therapist, can be inferred
- that have a plot line bringing together the other elements. Plots are not necessarily straightforward or linear. Most stories have subplots and digressions. The story of first coming to music therapy could very easily have a digression about the journey there (a difficult, cross-town bus trip). Digressions are not necessarily irrelevant, they will tell something about the narrator and maybe cast light on the apparent major theme in other ways.

    Perhaps the difficult journey as well as being a sub-story is also a further illustration of how difficult it felt to go to music therapy and so acts to emphasise the main story?
- which have a point and perhaps even a moral message. In a way, the story evidences and emphasises the point as well as explaining and clarifying it

Another way of looking at stories is as each comprising the same six elements. Including illustrations from our music therapy story, these are:

- the main character and where that character lives ('I', the music therapy client and the music therapy room)
- the mission or task that the character has to fulfil (participate in music therapy)
- the person or thing that will help the main character (we can infer that this may be the music therapist, but it could be other

group members, the storyteller's inner voice or someone else)
- the obstacle which stands in the way of the main character completing the mission or task (fear of making noise – perhaps being noticed, perhaps performance anxiety)
- how the character copes with the obstacle (finds a solution in the form of becoming less obtrusive)
- what happens next – does the story end or continue? ('when I first …' implies a continuing story)

One way of analysing a story is to look for each of these elements. They can also be used in the deliberate construction of a story. However, if you do collect stories by asking your participants to tell you about each of these elements be wary that your analysis doesn't just find what you fed in in the first place.

Analysing narrative
The analysis of narrative usually involves working with a transcript of the story as it was told as an interview, life history or similar. As we indicated above, how narrative is analysed will depend on the philosophy, question and EPISTEMOLOGICAL stance of the inquirer (that just means how they think knowledge comes about – see Chapter 1.1). A structural analysis of narrative will involve determining something like the six elements we told you about. More formerly these could be:

EPISTEMOLOGY Philosophy concerned with the nature of knowledge (what is it?), the source of knowledge (how do we know what we know?) and the scope of knowledge (what, if any, are the limits of knowledge?).

- the setting
- the initiating event
- the storyteller's internal response and reaction
- what the storyteller actually did about the situation
- what the consequences of the action where
- the reaction to events and the point of the story

Another way would be to look at the function the story has for the storyteller. From this perspective, the functions of stories include:
- a means of conveying meaning
- a way of solving problems, reducing tension and/or resolving dilemmas
- a way of sorting out the exceptional and the ordinary in such a way as to deal with and explain mismatches between them. We don't need to explain ordinary events to ourselves or others
- a means of re-casting extraordinary, chaotic or even traumatic experiences into explanatory, causal stories that help us make sense of them and which help us to feel safe

When taking a 'functional' view of narrative, the analysis involves looking at each of these (and probably other) aspects and working to understand how they fit the teller's experience.

A third category of narrative analysis involves determining the 'common-sense', cultural meanings of the collected stories. Another way of thinking about this is as the ways in which stories incorporate folk wisdom, social boundaries (how things are, how they should be and so on). This is narrative as contemporary myth where 'myths' contextualise, explain and teach about, for example, social mores. Finding themes like these in collected stories can tell you a lot about the social group to which the tellers belong.

What has narrative analysis been used to do?

The use of narrative analysis is widespread in researching health and social care. For example, it has been used to explore nurses' perceptions and experiences of psychological care giving and the ways these develop throughout nurse education programmes (Priest, 2000). It has also been used to understand how and why the parents of children with Down's syndrome make use of complementary therapies and, in Hok, et al. (2007) in Sweden, to understand how the combining of complementary therapies with more orthodox biomedical care is made sense of by patients who use both. In the field of counselling and psychotherapy, narrative analysis has been used by McLeod and Lynch (2000) to understand the relevance of both client and counsellor conceptions of the 'good life' in a successful example of client-centred therapy.

Grounded theory

Grounded theory was first described in the 1960s and it was one of the early attempts to come up with a systematic, rigorous way of doing qualitative research. Almost oppositely from POSITIVISTIC research, it is a 'data-driven' or 'hypothesis-generating' approach in that the intention in using it is to derive theory from the phenomenon being investigated. It is inductive, beginning with descriptive data (for example, interview transcripts but also 'texts' of other kinds) and subjecting the material to increasing levels of conceptualisation – that is, general principles are arrived at from a detailed examination of themes, content and context of the stories collected. To put it another way, in grounded theory research a first step is to unravel the elements of experience explicit and implicit in collected stories before reflecting on the way these elements link together. From this consideration, the researcher constructs a theory (or a series of theoretical propositions) which explains the nature and meaning of a particular experience for a particular group of people at a particular time and in a particular place. You will notice that grounded theory makes no claim to generate universal theory. Even if there is a hope and expectation that the theory generated from one grounded theory project may be applicable in similar circumstances, this cannot be assumed. Grounded theory approaches

Priest, HM (2000) The use of narrative in the study of caring: A critique. *Nursing Times Research* 5(4), 245-50.

Hok, J, Wachtler, C, Falkenberg, T & Tishelman, C (2007) Using narrative analysis to understand the combined use of complementary therapies and bio-medically oriented healthcare. *Social Science and Medicine* 65(8), 1642-53.

McLeod, J & Lynch, G (2000) 'This is our life': Strong evaluation in psychotherapy narrative. *European Journal of Psychotherapy, Counselling and Health* 3(3), 389-406.

POSITIVISTIC/POSITIVISM A doctrine asserting that sense perceptions are the only admissible basis of human knowledge and precise thought. In research, that the validity of knowledge can only be assured by experimental science.

> IF YOU WANT TO KNOW MORE ABOUT
> grounded theory analysis

as well as the resources we pointed you towards on p 201 you could try:

Charmaz, K (2006) *Constructing Grounded Theory: A practical guide through qualitative analysis.* London: Sage.

Rennie, DL (2002) Experiencing psychotherapy: Grounded theory studies. In DJ Cain (ed) *Humanistic Psychotherapies: Handbook of research and practice* (pp 117-44). Washington, DC: American Psychological Association.

include the following:

- the continual questioning of gaps in the data, checking for anything that seems to be missing or inconsistent or which can be only partly understood. There is also a need to understand just what it is that influences the environments and storytellers being studied
- an emphasis on open *processes* in conducting of research rather than fixed methods and procedures
- recognition of the importance of context and social structure
- the generation of theory and data from interviewing processes rather than from observing individual practices

In grounded theory research, data collecting, coding, and analysis occur simultaneously and in relation to each other rather than as separate components of a research design. It is an inductive process: theory must grow out of the data and be grounded in that data.

If you want to do a grounded theory study, because an objective of this approach is to reach an understanding of the 'lived experience' of the informants (storytellers), it is important that you do not 'review the literature' (that is, read about the particular circumstance, client group or whatever in any great detail) before carrying out your research. This is so that pre-existing ideas and theories do not influence the research and so prevent the possibility of making new discoveries.

Briefly, grounded theory analysis involves searching the text for meaning and coding that meaning. Codes are developed into categories (i.e. larger units of meaning/groups of related concepts). The next stage ('axial coding') is to search for linkages and connections between categories. Finally, core categories are identified which are used to generate a descriptive narrative. However, it would be a mistake to think of this as a linear process. Throughout a grounded theory analysis, it is necessary to continually check back to the original stories to make sure that the themes and story lines that are emerging accurately reflect the accounts you were given. Also, there is a process of recording questions the researcher has about theory, tentative hypotheses, etc. and re-examining the data in the light of these and subsequently refining them and so on. In a way, grounded theory analysis is about breaking the stories down into categories and then reassembling these to construct theories which are then checked to see if they explain the raw data in a reiterative, constantly refining process until a satisfactory end point is reached. It is a process that moves from description to interpretation and one which stops only when the researcher is satisfied that the human experience under consideration can be adequately accounted for by the proposed theoretical propositions.

Dent-Brown, K & Wang, M (2006) The mechanism of story-making: A grounded theory study of the 6-part story method. *The Arts in Psychotherapy 33*(4), 316-30.

Henretty, JR, Levitt, HM & Mathews, SS (2008) Clients' experiences of moments of sadness in psychotherapy: A grounded theory analysis. *Psychotherapy Research 18*(3), 243-55.

> IF YOU WANT TO KNOW MORE ABOUT
> thematic analysis

you could try:

Boyatzis, RE (1998) *Transforming Qualitative Information: Thematic analysis and code development.* Thousand Oaks, CA: Sage.

Ely, M (1991) *Doing Qualitative Research: Circles within circles.* London: Falmer Press.

What has grounded theory been used to do?

In a grounded theory study of the six-part story method often used in dramatherapy (Dent-Brown & Wang, 2006), it was found that, for a substantial majority, storytelling as therapy is very effective. Grounded theory has also been used extensively in the exploration of the client experience of psychotherapy, e.g. to explore moments of disengagement and of sadness in the psychotherapeutic process, see Henretty, Levitt & Mathews, 2008).

Thematic analysis

Thematic analysis is a process for encoding qualitative data. If you like, it is a way of 'seeing' what characterises the stories collectively. The idea is that until important moments are recognised and assigned to a category (coded as something) it is not possible to understand the data and thus to interpret it. Like grounded theory analysis, thematic analysis is a way of examining qualitative data for codes/ categories and then using these to generate themes. In this sense, themes are statements or units of meaning. The characteristics of thematic codes are that they have:

- a label (i.e. a name, usually one that indicates what is being coded)
- a definition of what the theme concerns (i.e. the characteristic or issue constituting the theme)
- a description of how to know when the theme occurs (i.e. indicators on how to 'flag' the theme)
- a description of any qualifications or exclusions to the identification of the theme
- examples, both positive and negative, to eliminate possible confusion when looking for a theme

A useful theme is either prevalent in the stories – occurring in all or most of them – or, although in a minority of stories it is significant because of its high emotional or factual impact. Unlike grounded theory, the objective is not to generate theory but to offer a rich description and/or interpretation of the phenomenon under investigation. An objective of thematic analysis is to 'tell the story' of the research participants; that is, to arrive at an understanding of the data through seeking out 'themes' which collectively convey the significant and typifying elements of the stories told. So, in performing a thematic analysis, the researcher is looking for 'meaning' rather than trying to prove or disprove a hypothesis. It is a technique suited to both exploration and explanation.

Rather than being a distinct and particular method, thematic analysis is an approach to working with stories that varies with respect to the degree of objectivity sought and the exact process by which it is done, according to who is describing and using it. The principal features of one of the more common ways of doing thematic analysis follow.

How to identify a theme

Firstly, the way themes are identified may involve either a theory-driven approach or be 'data-led'. In most cases, where the intent is to understand the lived experience of the participants, a data-led approach is likely to be most relevant and appropriate because it involves inductively constructing themes from the raw information.

The first step in identifying themes is to *reduce the raw information*. This involves the process of immersion in the stories (for example, by reading them, listening to or watching recordings or both together) until you are familiar with them. Out of this immersion comes an ability to paraphrase the stories and/or to recognise significant and salient points. As you do this, note anything that strikes you as interesting or significant. If you are working with a transcript, it is helpful to make this note in the margin in such a way as to directly link it to the point in the text that struck you. It may help to note things that:

- recur in at least two parts of any story but which reflect the same thread of meaning even though different words are used or that you recognise as being said in at least one other story
- are repeated – that is the same words, phrases or sentences are used in at least two parts of the story or in different stories
- are stated forcefully – that is, in a way that conveys some emotion or importance
- you intuitively recognise as important or meaningful

The next step is to note any potential themes arising – that is anything that seems to capture the essence of the text. What you are searching for is connecting threads and patterns in your data. List all the potential themes and look for connections and similarities between them. At this stage, your aim is to reduce the number of themes by combining them or eliminating them. Themes may be combined if they are substantially the same or are aspects of an overarching theme (in which case they may be considered as sub-themes). Themes which occur in only a small number of stories may be disregarded (because they do not help to explain or understand the stories as a whole) unless there is something particularly forceful or important about them. You may also elect to eliminate any emerging themes that do not relate to the research question, although this requires some caution. It is usual to end up with 3–5 key main themes.

You will find that your ideas as to what themes are in your data change as you analyse more stories. The aim of thematic analysis is to end up with themes that describe the essence of the collected stories.

When you have decided on your themes, you should re-read the stories noting each occurrence of each theme. It is helpful to have a colour-coding system for this and to underline or highlight each theme. Then read through the stories again noting anything that seems significant but that is not accounted for by your themes. Do you need a new theme or to modify an existing one?

When you are satisfied that the themes you have generated capture the essential nature of your stories and that they address your research question, you are in a position to name and explain your themes. For example, supposing that in reading through the transcripts of interviews about happiness you found repeated reference to the importance of being in relationship. You might decide that this constituted a theme which you could call 'Relating to Others'. This now needs an explanation, i.e. what was the informant talking about when you coded for this theme? For the sake of argument, let's say any reference to being in the company of others as a source of happiness was coded for this theme. This could be presented thus:

Theme: Relating to others
This theme reflected the importance informants attached to being in the company of other people as a source of their happiness. Sometimes this refers to relationships of deep and special affection (family, sexual partners, close friends) but also to looser alliances such as a night out at the pub with 'mates'. This theme was coded for when informants made any reference to friendship or affectionate relationships.

Having established this, you are in a position to state how many times and in how many transcripts your theme occurs. For example:

'Relating to Others' occurred 34 times in 9 out of 10 interviews

This semi-quantitative measure may indicate the significance of particular themes but it should be treated with caution. The next stage is to offer 'exemplars' of your theme. An exemplar is a typical example of the occurrence of the theme. Usually one or two will do. Exemplars should be presented as verbatim extracts from the collected stories. You indicate from which story you have taken the extract and the page and line numbers at which it can be found. For example an exemplar for 'relating to others' may be:

When I am with Jill my heart sings. It doesn't matter what we are doing, waiting for the bus, doing the housework, cuddling on the sofa – just being with her makes me happy.
(Interview 1, p. 5, lines 7-8)

You may decide that some themes can usefully be subdivided. Take the example of our 'relating to others' theme above. Perhaps relating to partners and family is categorised differently from relating to friends. That is, the two kinds of relationship are spoken of differently (in terms of content, emotional weight or forcefulness). In this case, although there is an overarching framework, it may be useful to tease the two apart. In this case each sub-theme will need defining and exemplars found for it.

A note of caution
Thematic analysis has its usefulness but we think that in the hands of a less experienced researcher the themes generated can simply reflect the questions asked or the information input by the interviewer in other ways. It is probably most useful for treating data from traditional unstructured interviews where the interviewer asks an initial question and then facilitates the responses of the interviewee without reference to his or her own experience, theory or the experience of others.

What has thematic analysis been used to do?
In a four-year study by Lambert (2007), first-time users of counselling were interviewed in order to ascertain their perceptions and how these changed over time. A thematic analysis-based interpretation revealed that before counselling, clients were uncertain as to what to expect, that there was positive change during the process, and post-counselling interviews confirmed further positive change and indicated some implications for practice in terms of assessment and the influence of cultural assumptions on theory and practice.

Lambert, P (2007) Client perspectives on counselling: Before, during and after. *Counselling and Psychotherapy Research* 7(2), 106-13.

In another study (Malik & Coulson, 2008), messages posted to a bulletin board used by men undergoing infertility treatment were analysed with the result that, contrary to received wisdom, men had similar fears about their infertility to those of women and of equal intensity.

Salmon and Rapport (2005), using audiotapes of meetings between staff of a Child and Adolescent Mental Health Service and other professionals such as social workers and educationalists, used thematic analysis to explore the problems of inter-agency working – in this study revealing that misunderstanding was rife and it seemed attributable to the different jargon ('discourses') of the different organisations.

Malik, S & Coulson, N (2008) The male experience of infertility: A thematic analysis of an online infertility support group bulletin board. *Journal of Reproductive and Infant Psychology* 26(1), 18-30.

Salmon, G & Rapport, F (2005) Multi-agency voices: A thematic analysis of multi-agency working practices within the setting of a Child and Adolescent Mental Health Service. *Journal of Interprofessional Care* 19(5), 429-33.

Heuristic inquiry
Heuristic inquiry is a way of discovering, learning and constructing knowledge through reflecting on experience. It is characterised by a highly personal, self-searching commitment to discovering inner truth. Indeed, it is so highly personal and subjective that some people wouldn't consider it to be research at all. Another view is that precisely because it *is* concerned with people's perceptions – the knowledge they create through doing, not from 'objective' reality

IF YOU WANT TO KNOW MORE ABOUT
heuristic inquiry

as well as the references we have given previously, you could try:

Moustakas, C (2001) Heuristic research: Design and methodology. In K Schnieder, JFT Bugental & JF Pierson (eds) *The Handbook of Humanistic Psychology: Leading edges in theory, research and practice* (pp 263-74). Thousand Oaks, CA: Sage.

West, WS (2001) Beyond grounded theory: The use of a heuristic approach to qualitative research. *Counselling and Psychotherapy Research 1*(2), 126-31.

– heuristic research has intrinsic validity. It is a demanding process because it not only requires continual questioning and checking to ensure the full analysis and development of your own experience and that of others, but also in the way it challenges patterns of thinking and creating and because it involves authentic self-dialogue, self-honesty and a deep commitment to understanding obvious and subtle elements of meaning inherent in human experience.

Deep immersion and personal reflection are two of the main characteristics of heuristic research. From the beginning and throughout an investigation, heuristic research involves self-searching, self-dialogue, and self-discovery; the research question and the methodology flow out of inner awareness, meaning and inspiration. In heuristic research, data is usually collected as informal, conversational interviews. Self-disclosure on the part of the researcher may be part of this conversation and it may spur the co-researcher to respond in greater, richer detail. Empathic listening is an essential quality of a heuristic researcher.

The characteristics of heuristic inquiry

Heuristic inquiry is a way of seeking out and expressing the depth and intricacy of human experience. How heuristic research questions are framed and inquired into reflects that. However, what is true for heuristic inquiry is broadly true for other approaches to qualitative research so we will go into it in some detail. The heuristic research question has definite characteristics:

1 it seeks to reveal more fully the essence or meaning of a phenomenon of human experience
2 it seeks to discover the qualitative aspects, rather than quantitative dimensions
3 it engages one's total self and evokes a personal and passionate involvement and active participation in the process
4 it does not seek to predict or to determine causal relationships
5 it is illuminated through careful descriptions, illustrations, metaphors, poetry, dialogue, and other creative renderings, rather than by measurements, ratings, or scores

Points 1–4 apply to most qualitative research as does most of point 5 – at least in spirit. However, in not all approaches would metaphor, poetry and other creative renderings be seen as legitimate.

Heuristic concepts and processes

Heuristic inquiry makes use of a number of concepts and processes. These are:

• *identifying with the focus of inquiry*: This is the process of 'getting inside the question', to understand something from another perspective, identifying with the focus of the investigation

- *self-dialogue*: Literally talking to your self – but with a purpose. Self-dialogue can take many forms. Sometimes it may be an internal debate – 'on the one hand, on the other hand', sometimes there may be a more deliberate evocation of a devil's advocate role or of a question-and-answer session. What is important is that self-dialogue involves a deep level of personal honesty and a willingness to confront personal experience as it is relevant to the question or problem which is the focus of the study
- *tacit knowing*: Tacit knowledge is the knowing we have about the wholeness of something from an understanding of the elements it comprises. Often, this contributes to a sense of knowing more than we think we can know. It is tacit knowing that gives rise to hunches and vague, formless insights that characterise heuristic discovery
- *intuition*: Intuition is the process by which we draw on knowledge we do not 'know' we have to reach conclusions without apparent intervening steps of logic and reason. It is through intuition (which, as a research tool, improves with practice) that people grasp patterns, see relationships and draw inferences – all of this is essential to good research
- *indwelling* is the process of turning attention inward with unwavering concentration to seek a deeper, more extended understanding of the nature or meaning of an aspect of human experience. The indwelling process is conscious and deliberate but not necessarily linear or logical. When indwelling, the researcher follows clues wherever they appear and expands their meanings and associations until a fundamental insight is achieved
- *focusing* involves the clearing of an inward mental space so that you can tap into the thoughts and feelings that will help you get to grips with a question. It promotes a relaxed and receptive state enabling you to clarify your perceptions and things you sense, however dimly. Focusing also allows you to tap into the essence of what matters, setting aside the inessential
- *the internal frame of reference*: 'Frame of reference' is a person-centred term – a person's frame of reference is the lens through which they see and experience the world. Inherent in heuristic research is the validity of the internal frame of reference of the person 'who has had, is having, or will have' the relevant experience

The phases of heuristic research
A heuristic inquiry progresses through six phases. These are:
- *initial engagement*: This is the process by which a question of intense interest to the researcher and one to which they have a passionate commitment is encouraged into consciousness and which awakens a real desire to 'know' resulting in a disciplined

commitment that will reveal its underlying meanings. Important to this phase are tacit knowing and intuition

- *immersion*: This is the process of becoming deeply involved with the issue or problem under investigation. It is about drawing it deeply into one's life so that it becomes entwined with all aspects of existence, waking and sleeping – even in dreaming. It is as the question is lived so the researcher grows in knowledge and understanding of it. Important processes are identifying with the focus of inquiry, self-dialogue, intuition and tacit knowing
- *incubation*: This is the process of withdrawing from the intense concentration of immersion, putting things on the back burner and allowing the internal processes of the mind, those below the threshold of awareness, to take over. Again, the intuitive process and tacit knowing are important but they are occurring below the threshold of awareness
- *illumination*: This is the process of the breakthrough into consciousness of new insights into the research question – it is the sudden switching on of a light, the 'Ah Ha!' experience. This occurs naturally when the researcher is open and receptive to tacit knowledge and intuition. There are many examples of illumination in the history of the development of human thought and human discovery – Archimedes' 'Eureka' experience is one of the best known, the story of Kekulé and the structure of benzene is another
- *explication*: To explicate is to make explicit. In this context, explication is the process of fully examining all that has emerged into consciousness as the result of other processes and to reach an understanding of what it may all mean. Focusing and indwelling are particularly relevant
- *creative synthesis*: The last stage of heuristic research is to pull together all the discovered components and core themes into a form which exemplifies the experience which has been examined and makes the findings of the researcher clear to others. This is the creative synthesis. Usually a creative synthesis takes the form of a narrative, probably using material taken from, for example, interviews but it could be in any creative form such as a lyric poem, a song, a narrative description, a story, a metaphoric tale, or an art work. What is important is that it encapsulates, expresses and explains the researcher's findings

What has heuristic research been used to do?

The primary focus of heuristic inquiry is always the researcher's own lived experience of a particular phenomenon. Thus it can be used to investigate almost any aspect of human existence. The classic (and first) use of the heuristic method by Moustakas (1961) was to explore the experience of loneliness. It has also been used by Atkins

Note

Archimedes noticed that when he got into his bath water was displaced. This gave him insight into the problem of how to measure the volume of irregular objects and he leapt out shouting 'Eureka!' (I have found it!). The organic chemist Friedrich Kekulé said that the solution to the problem of the structure of the benzene molecule (which has a ring of 6 carbon atoms at its core) came to him as the result of a daydream in which he saw a snake biting its own tail.

Moustakas, C (1961) *Loneliness.* Englewood Cliffs, NJ: Prentice-Hall.

and Loewenthal (2004) to address the question 'How do psychotherapists experience working with older clients?' allowing the principle researcher to question some of her assumptions about, for example, ageing.

Feminist approaches to research

As you will have gathered by now, people interested in the wider contexts of research have been inevitably drawn to ideas relating to perspectives other than the dominant quantitative perspective. Even within qualitative research and what have been called 'new paradigm' approaches there has been a tendency to challenge the old order and the established hegemony. One view that originated in the 1970s and is now well organised, takes a feminist approach to research. Notice the form of words. We are talking about an approach to research, not necessarily a prescriptive way of researching. Strictly speaking, feminist principles could colour and shade many different ways of doing research (for example, discourse analysis and participatory research can be feminist). We include feminist approaches to research here not only because of their importance in their own right but as an example of how approaches to research can legitimately draw on principles, ideas, ways of constructing knowledge and ideologies that challenge the orthodoxy rooted in white, male, heterosexual, middle-class thinking. Other examples include those to do with ethnicity, culture and sexual orientation. Taking any of these perspectives not only addresses issues of equality and inclusion, allowing 'non-dominant' voices to be heard, but also greatly enriches our knowledge of the human condition. We are all the better for that.

The field of feminist research grew from certain observations about the world of research as it existed in the 1960s and 70s and, some would argue, little has changed. Feminist research grew out of an awareness of the following dynamics of traditional research:

- *the absence of women in traditional research* – sadly unsurprising, traditional research in the social sciences has been and largely continues to be dominated by men
- *raised awareness of women's issues amongst women* – individually and collectively women have become more autonomous and have found a stronger voice. This has meant that women are more likely to stand up and make themselves heard
- *emergence of women's perspectives* – it is argued by some that women have a qualitatively different way of being. This different way of being leads to a different way of constructing and explaining the world, different values and different perspectives
- *increase in the perceived validity and value of women's experience* – more and more people are seeing the value of looking at the experience of others, including women. Women's experience is

Atkins, D & Loewenthal, D (2004) The lived experience of psychotherapists working with older clients: An heuristic study. *British Journal of Guidance and Counselling 32*(4), 493-509.

IF YOU WANT TO KNOW MORE ABOUT
feminist research

you could try:

Hesse-Biber, SN (ed) (2007) *Handbook of Feminist Research: Theory and praxis.* Thousand Oaks, CA: Sage.

Letherby, G (2003) *Feminist Research in Theory and Practice.* Buckingham: Open University Press.

Reinharz, S & Davidman, L (1992) *Feminist Methods in Social Research.* Oxford: Oxford University Press.

Ribbens, J & Edwards, R (eds) (1998) *Feminist Dilemmas in Qualitative Research: Public knowledge, private lives.* London: Sage.

Roberts, H (ed) (1981) *Doing Feminist Research.* London: Routledge & Kegan Paul.

of interest not only to other women but to anyone wishing to synthesise solutions through incorporating diverse experiences

One of the strong arguments in favour of creating a separate strand of feminist research is that the traditional research paradigm is sexist by its very nature; for example, it could be said that traditional research is biased in the following ways:

- it is androcentric, looking at the world from an exclusively male viewpoint, e.g. by assuming that a method piloted on males will be suitable for use with women, or making assumptions about patterns of availability, work, education, socialisation, etc. that do not acknowledge that things may be different for women
- it ignores gender, simply forgetting that gender might be an issue by, e.g. failing to report the gender of the protagonists, subjects or actors
- conversely, it may involve gender stereotyping making assumptions about what may or may not be appropriate for each gender, e.g. child rearing is necessarily 'women's work' or fire-fighting is necessarily a male activity
- it is prone to overgeneralisation as when a study generalises from a single sex sample to all the population (both sexes). For example, a study of abused women may draw conclusions about the behaviour and symptoms of all victims
- it can involve double standards; that is, the flip-side of over-generalisation such as when a study treats male and female participants differently for spurious or unacknowledged reasons

Feminist thinking leads to the desire for an approach to research characterised by:

- recognition of the interdependence of researcher and subject
- avoidance of the decontextualisation of the subject and researcher from their social or historical settings
- recognising and revealing the nature of your values within the research context
- accepting that facts do not exist independently of their producer's linguistic codes
- demystifying the role of the scientist and establishing an egalitarian relationship between science makers and science consumers

You will immediately notice that this accords with much of what we having been saying about qualitative research in general. Although some might argue about where the influences originated – feminism, sociology, humanism or general discontent with traditional research – it is clear that there is considerable harmony between the themes of the qualitative approach and the feminist approach. We say *the* feminist

Note

Feminist researchers have challenged power relationships including in the research process itself. This helps bring into focus a range of power issues as they relate to research as explored by Gitlin's (1994) edited book in which perspectives on power and method are explored from feminist, gay and lesbian and cultural perspectives.

Gitlin, AD (1994) *Power and Method: Political activism and educational research.* London: Routledge.

Note

Not all research informed by feminist perspectives is labelled 'feminist research'. This makes it harder to find when you are searching the literature. Other terms you could use include 'women's studies', eg, members of the Women's Studies Research Centre in Manchester have published papers on researching domestic violence and how this affects the lives of minoritised women (see, for example, Chantler, 2006).

Chantler, K (2006) Independence, dependency and interdependence: Struggles and resistances of minoritized women within and leaving violent relationships. *Feminist Review 82*(1), 27-49.

approach, but, as we indicated at the start of this section, of course there is no *single* feminist approach and there is much debate amongst those that own a feminist influence in their work.

As researchers interested in qualitative approaches we are behoven to listen to, and take account of, these views. One response might be to avoid the mistakes listed above in our own research. It is, however, not just a matter of developing an 'anti-sexist checklist' for your research project. It is necessary to develop and internalise an awareness of how our backgrounds and experiences bring certain ways of looking at the world, understanding our experience and working. We might then see how we are limited as researchers and how our work might be enriched by broadening our perspectives. Of course it is not possible to take one's perception beyond our experiences, for example, men cannot take a women's perspective.

Finally, it is worth recording that we two white, middle-class, able-bodied, heterosexual males are the least qualified to write with any authority on the subject of alternative perspectives. We happily acknowledge the valuable and positive contribution made by the feminist approaches to research, and would encourage all those interested to read more and become involved.

What has feminist research been used to do?

As you can imagine, there is a lot that has been done to investigate aspects of the existence and experience of women doing research guided by feminist principles. Of particular prominence have been issues of health and education. There have been studies focusing on women's health issues such as breast cancer and reproductive health, social issues affecting women (including domestic violence) and issues of sexual and gender identity. However, feminist approaches can be applied more generally, including to the experience of males: for example, research into exploring the relationships of boys (Way, 2001). There are also accounts of feminist research in some of the books to which we pointed you earlier in this section. Other examples of feminist research include:

- the effects of participating in the qualitative research process of women awaiting trial (Wincup, 2001)
- lesbian identity, e.g. research on lesbian mothers which demonstrates the greater importance of maternal rather than sexual identity (Lewin, 1993)
- disability and disability rights, e.g. addressing the 'invisibility' of disabled women including in the area of reproductive health and sport and even to feminists (Gill, 1997)

For some researchers, inquiry into issues related to the above topics may very well be best addressed by moving into paradigms more specifically related to the experience of the subjects of the research.

Note

Sue Wilkinson has written extensively about her feminist research and breast cancer. You could try doing a literature search (key words S Wilkinson, breast cancer, feminist research) or start with, eg:

Wilkinson, S (2000) Breast cancer: A feminist perspective. In JM Ussher (ed) *Women's Health: Contemporary international perspectives* (pp 230-7). Leicester: BPS Books.

Wilkinson, S (2000) Feminist research in health psychology: Breast cancer research. *Journal of Health Psychology* 5(3), 359-72.

Way, N (2001) Using feminist research methods to explore boys' relationships. In DL Tolman & M Brydon-Miller (eds) *From Subjects to Subjectivities: A handbook of interpretive and participatory methods* (pp 111-29). New York: New York University Press.

Wincup, E (2001) Feminist research with women awaiting trial: The effects on participants in the qualitative research process. In KR Gilbert (ed) *The Emotional Nature of Qualitative Research* (pp 17-35). Boca Raton, FL: CRC Press.

Lewin, E (1993) *Lesbian Mothers: Accounts of gender in American culture.* Ithaca, NY: Cornell University Press.

Gill, CJ (1997) The last sisters: Health issues of women with disabilities. In SB Ruzek, VL Olesen & AE Clarke (eds) *Women's Health: Complexities and differences* (pp 96-111). Columbus, OH: Ohio State University Press.

Kelly, GA (1955) *The Psychology of Personal Constructs.* New York: Norton.

PHENOMENOLOGICAL approaches to understanding and psychology are based on the study of immediate experience, where 'truth' or 'knowledge' comes from the perceptual field of the individual, rather than an external authority. Based on the work of the philosopher Edmund Husserl.

IF YOU WANT TO KNOW MORE ABOUT
repertory grid technique

the following are good starting places:

Bell, RC (2003) The repertory grid technique. In F Fransella (ed) *The International Handbook of Personal Construct Psychology* (pp 95-103). Chichester: Wiley.

Fransella, F, Bell, RC & Bannister, D (2004) *A Manual for the Repertory Grid Technique* (2nd edn). Chichester: Wiley.

Fromm, M (2004) *Introduction to the Repertory Grid Interview.* Münster: Waxmann.

Pollock, LC (2006) An introduction to the use of the repertory grid technique as a research method and clinical tool for psychiatric nurses. *Journal of Advanced Nursing 11*(4), 439-45.

Repertory grid techniques

According to a personality theory proposed by George Kelly, we make sense of the world and our experience of it by interpreting these in accordance with what he called *personal constructs.* He took the view that each of us is a 'scientist' seeking to understand the day-to-day events in which we are involved. We do this by evaluating our experiences and the phenomena we encounter according to a limited number of constructs that help us create our personal view. What lies behind people's actions is how we construct and interpret our personal worlds. We continually develop theories about the world and interpret our experiences in the light of these theories.

It was Kelly's view that the theories which people form are a set of bipolar ideas or *constructs* such as cruel–kind, aggressive–gentle. Kelly's most important point was that everyone has their own set of unique personal constructs. We each make up our own. This all makes personal construct theory an attempt to model and explain the PHENOMENOLOGICAL basis of individual personality. This means that if, as researchers, we can discover the personal constructs of our participants with respect to the phenomena in which we are interested, we can know something about their experience and how they make sense of the world. Repertory grids are a way of doing this.

Once a group of participants has been identified (say, clients of a particular counselling agency), as formulated for each participant, the basic repertory grid technique itself consists of the following stages:

- naming a set of 'elements' which depend upon the focus of the particular study, for example, if the research topic was *counselling,* or *interpersonal relationships* then the elements would be people who are significant in the life of the person being studied, maybe counsellors, friends and relatives
- taking these elements in groups of three, the person is asked to say in what way any two are different from the third. For example, my counsellor is different from my brother and mother because she is a more challenging person
- these elements are arranged in grid form to explore the emerging personal constructs

A computer will make analysis of the grids much easier if you are dealing with more than a couple of participants. In a large group, with many constructs a computer is practically essential if you are to extract the underlying constructs. The field of personal construct psychology and repertory grid techniques is filled with lively debate over such issues as whether it is best to stay with the idiosyncratic constructs generated by each individual, or whether to use ready-made constructs provided by the researcher. (You can, after all, only get out what you put in.)

What have repertory grids been used to do?

There are many examples of repertory grid techniques in the research literature. For example, it has been used to assess cognitive features underlying depressive states (Feixas et al., 2008) and clinical reasoning and decision-making in occupational therapy (Kuipers & Grice, 2009). In another study (Mitchell & Baher, 2000), repertory grids were used to establish how religious commitment is an influence on seeking help for psychological problems. The participants in this research were committed UK Christians and from working with them the researchers were able to propose a tentative model from which they deduced possible implications for members of minority groups of religiously committed people.

Interpersonal process recall

Developed by Norman Kagan in the 1960s, Interpersonal Process Recall (IPR) is a semi-structured method of eliciting storytelling from the actors in a dyad or group. It has the potential of revealing deep feelings and so does require careful consideration before being used. It also requires that the action in question (whatever your research involves, e.g. therapy, nursing care, etc.) has been recorded either as video or audio. The storytelling or *recall* is facilitated by a trained interviewer called an *inquirer*. The data elicited by the inquirer can itself be recorded on audio or video for subsequent analysis.

The technique involves the participants watching the action in question on video, or listening to an audio recording. They are asked to stop the recording whenever they remember anything about what was going on at the time. The inquirer helps them 'tell their story' by asking a series of semi-structured open questions and prompts such as:

- were there any feelings associated with what you said? What were the feelings?
- was this a familiar sensation? When has it happened before?
- what did you think the others were thinking at that moment?
- describe any images that flashed in front of your eyes when you did that

The 'rules' are simple:
- stay in the *there and then*
- stick to recalling your own (i.e. the recaller's own) stuff
- the recaller has control over the process and can decline to answer
- the recaller can start and stop the recording wherever they choose

The recall can be done individually or in pairs or groups (there are benefits to doing both group and individual recall). If recall is done in groups, interactions during the recall sessions, whilst very profitable in terms of yielding good data, must be managed carefully

Feixas, G, Erazo-Caideio, MI, Harter, SL & Bach, L (2008) Construction of self and others in unipolar depressive disorders: A study using repertory grid technique. *Cognitive Therapy and Research 32*(3), 386-400.

Kuipers, K & Grice, JW (2009) Clinical reasoning in neurology: Use of the repertory grid technique to investigate the reasoning of an experienced Occupational Therapist. *Australian Occupational Therapy Journal 56*(4), 275-84.

Mitchell, JR & Baher, MC (2000) Religious commitment and the construal of sources of help for emotional problems. *British Journal of Medical Psychology 73*(3) 289-301.

IF YOU WANT TO KNOW MORE ABOUT
interpersonal process recall

you could read:

Kagan, N (1984) Interpersonal process recall: Basic method and recent research. In R Larsen (ed) *Teaching Psychological Skills: Models for giving psychology away* (pp 229-44). Belmont, CA: Wadsworth.

Larsen, D, Flesaker, K & Stege, R (2008) Qualitative interviews using interpersonal process recall: Investigating internal experiences during professional–client conversations. *International Journal of Qualitative Methods 7*(1) online at:<http://ejournals.ualberta.ca/index.php/IJQM/article/viewArticle/1617> retrieved 22/03/2010.

or the process from the *there and then* will start up again in the *here and now*.

What has IPR been used to do?

IPR has been used to a limited extent as a research tool. However, it has been used by Rennie (2000) to investigate the client's conscious control of the psychotherapeutic process and also Cowie and Berdondini (2001) used it to enable children to explore (through action replays) their own feeling and those of others about incidents of bullying. It is our view that IPR is underused as a research tool in qualitative studies. It seems admirably suited to creative development as a method of reflection and learning. It may also have a place in understanding the interactions between practitioners and clients and for understanding assessment and psychotherapeutic processes.

Q-methodology/Q-sort

Q-methodology offers a systematic and rigorously quantitative means for examining human subjectivity in order to reveal the impressions and experiences of a phenomenon from the standpoint of the research participant. In other words, Q-methodology is a way of treating qualitative data quantitatively, so it is a bit of cheat to include it in this chapter. However, even though it is a 'hybrid' method it is about working with stories so we decided to include it.

It is as 'Q-sort' that aspects of this approach are most likely to be of use to practitioners of health and social care. Its attraction is that it allows the objective analysis of the points of view of the subjects of research. This is achieved by inviting respondents to rank a number of statements according to, for example, how much they agree or disagree with them. This ranking is normally using a *Lickert scale* (see p. 136) which is a way of quantifying the level of agreement/disagreement by, for example, ranging from 'strongly agree' (7) through 'neither agree nor disagree' (4) to 'strongly disagree' (1). Of course, there can be more or fewer elements than seven in the ranking. Most of us are familiar with this sort of scale from questionnaires in magazines or from being stopped by market researchers. Q-technique has certain resonances with the repertory grid technique described earlier and it is used most frequently with individuals to get some idea of changes in self-perception.

The statements (of which there can be any number) to be ranked or sorted are the *Q-sample*. One of the initial problems for a researcher intending to use Q-sort or Q-methodology as a whole is how to come up with a Q-sample. The statements to be sorted must make sense to the potential respondents and must relate to their experience but they must also fulfil the needs of the researcher. Perhaps too it is important that researchers work with the frames of

---

Rennie, DL (2000) Aspects of the client's conscious control of the psychotherapeutic process. *Journal of Psychotherapy Integration 10*(2), 151-67.

Cowie, H & Berdondini, L (2001) Children's reactions to cooperative group work: A strategy for enhancing peer relationships among bullies, victims and bystanders. *Learning and Instruction 11*(6), 517-30.

IF YOU WANT TO KNOW MORE ABOUT
Q-methodology
you could try:

Brown, SR (1996) Q-methodology and qualitative research. *Qualitative Health Research 6*(4), 56-7.

Corr, S (2001) An introduction to Q-methodology: A research technique. *The British Journal of Occupational Therapy 64*(6), 293-97.

McKeown, B & Thomas, T (1988) *Q-Methodology.* Newbury Park, CA: Sage.

Stephenson, W (1953) *The Study of Behavior: Q-technique and its methodology.* Chicago: University of Chicago Press.

Stephenson, W (1980) Newton's fifth rule and Q-methodology: Application to educational psychology. *American Psychologist 35,* 882-9.

Watts, S & Stenner, P (2005) Doing Q-methodology: Theory, method and interpretation. *Qualitative Research in Psychology 2,* 67-91.

reference of the respondents rather than impose their own perceptions. There is a variety of strategies for generating a Q-sample. These include:

- 'naturalistic' Q-samples where the items are drawn from interviews or written accounts about personal experience or from secondary sources such as the mass media. In other words, the items are drawn from what the participants are actually saying or from a source they are almost certain to have encountered and understood
- 'ready-made' Q-samples – that is, those derived from almost anything else other than the stories told by the participants. Ready-made Q-samples are more likely to conform with the researcher's agenda and/or previous findings
- 'quasi-naturalistic' Q-samples which, as the name suggests, can be considered as similar to naturalistic Q-samples but rather than coming from the stories told by participants they are derived from external sources, for example, other people in similar situations, accounts of similar experiences or the mass media
- 'hybrid' Q-samples which combine elements of naturalistic and ready-made varieties
- there is also the possibility of working collaboratively with respondents to generate the Q-sample

Q-sort may be conducted in a 'pen and paper' way similar to a magazine questionnaire – that is, by the respondent going through a list of statements and ringing the number on the Lickert scale most closely corresponding to their current view or experience or by, for example, arranging statements on cards along a spectrum – perhaps 'most like me' to 'least like me'. Once a Q-sort has been made it is possible to subject the resulting data to statistical analysis – principally by *factor analysis* which is a way of making sense of a large number of correlations between variables. What this means is that clusters of related items in the Q-sample can be discovered – that is the 'factors' generated summarise differences and similarities between Q-sorts. There are a number of computer-based packages to assist this analysis.

The Q-technique offers a way of exploring, for example, differences between practitioners or client groups, changes as a result of treatment ('before' versus 'after') or different interventions (brief, time-limited therapy versus 'open-ended' therapy, group therapy versus one-to-one therapy) and so much more.

What has Q-methodology been used to do?
Q-sort has been used extensively in investigations of 'personality', for example, to investigate the nature of abusive husbands (Porcelli et al., 2004). It has been used too to explore the influence of family

Porcelli, JH, Cogan, R & Hibbard, S (2004) Personality characteristics of partner violent men: A Q-sort approach. *Journal of Personality Disorders 18*(2), 151-62.

DeMulder, EK, Denham, S, Schmidt, M & Mitchell, J (2000) Q-sort assessment of attachment security during the pre-school years: Links from home to school. *Developmental Psychology 36*(2), 274-82.

Jones, S, Guy, A & Ormond, JA (2003) A Q-methodological study of hearing voices: A preliminary exploration of voice hearers' understanding of their experiences. *Psychology and Psychotherapy: Theory, Research and Practice 76*(2), 189-209.

life on children. For example, DeMulder et al. (2000) in a study of security attachment in pre-school children found that less family stress related to a more secure mother–child relationship whereas less securely attached children tended to be more angry and aggressive when they attended a crèche. This was more evident in boys than girls. Another example of the use of Q-methodology by Jones, Guy and Ormond (2003) was in the exploration of the understanding voice hearers have of their experience.

Introduction

When you read accounts of research, you will notice that they refer to the work of others. In theses and dissertations there will probably be a section headed 'literature review'. Indeed, it will probably be there even if under some other heading. In papers in academic and professional journals too there will be attempts to set the scene for the author's work by contextualising it in the light of what has already been published (that is 'the literature' – increasingly this includes not only print media but electronic forms). In conducting your research, whatever the scale of your proposed study, you too are going to have to search the literature and, in some form or another, write a literature review. Inevitably there will be some background reading to be done. There will be several functions that this reading will perform. These include:

- establishing the background against which your research will be set – including finding out what other researchers in the area discovered or what theorists proposed
- using this information to support the findings that you obtain or using the existing work as a starting point for your research with the intention of adding to the body of work, or arguing with the present state of thinking
- referring to the work of others may give ideas as to how your work should or should not be conducted, and regarding methods of data analysis, selection of people or situations to work with, etc.

Before you can read books, papers, dissertations (the literature) and the like you are going to have to know something about libraries and how to use them. So, for those of you who aren't familiar with academic publications, libraries and the Internet as a research tool, we'll define and explain a few terms and introduce you to the necessary practicalities.

Note
You might think that all research has to be novel and that your literature review is one way of establishing that the research you are proposing hasn't been done before. You would be wrong. A small amount of research is genuinely novel, but most is a variation on previous work and some is a deliberate copy of previously conducted research. This is done in an attempt to establish the validity of the findings and is called replication or TRIANGULATION. These terms are defined and covered in this book as follows:
- replication: Chapter 2.2, p 42.
- TRIANGULATION: Chapter 2.6, p 122 and Chapter 2.8, p 194.

What is 'the literature'?

In the sense in which you will come across the term 'the literature' in an academic or research context, it means all the information in the public domain. More specifically, it is the material published in

Note
Here we are referring to establishing the 'quality' of the information you are using, ie, how have the reliability and validity of the ideas and findings been evaluated? For a little more on this, see p 239 this chapter.

the form of books, conference proceedings, academic and professional journals, dissertations and theses and (as an increasingly important resource) on the Internet. The literature on which you can reliably draw for the purposes of research and writing should have at least an element of 'peer review'. With respect to journals (see below), peer review is the process by which a piece of writing is refereed (usually anonymously) by one or more experts in the subject matter addressed and/or the methods/methodology used. For books, we usually assume that this is part of the editorial process, but even then the ideas expressed in some books might be critiqued in reviews. Critical review in scientific publications is a part of the peer-evaluation process – see the side note.

What is published on the web is more problematic. Some journals exist in electronic form and so can be downloaded in return for payment or free as a perk of membership of a subscribing library. It should be possible to determine whether or not the material appearing in them has been peer reviewed. In other cases, the views expressed may be unsubstantiated or even downright biased. It is always advisable to treat such material with caution.

What is a journal?

Journals are periodicals devoted to publishing papers (articles) on current and contemporary scholarship and research in particular academic or professional domains. Most journals are published as two or more parts or issues constituting a 'volume'. Many journals publish one volume a year, usually of 2, 3 or 4 parts and at regular intervals. For example, the *British Journal of Guidance and Counselling* (BJGC) publishes one volume a year as four issues, one each in February, May, August and November. Journals may exist as hard copy, electronically or (as in the case of the BJGC) both. The 'Instructions for Authors' for a journal (usually found on the inside cover of a hard copy or on the relevant web page) will usually indicate if the papers published in it are peer reviewed. If you are a member of a professional organisation, it almost certainly publishes one or more professional journals. For example, to stay with the field of counselling and psychotherapy, members of the British Association for Counselling and Psychotherapy (BACP) receive both *Therapy Today* which keeps them abreast of professional and institutional issues and *Counselling and Psychotherapy Research* which, as the name suggests, contains papers giving accounts of research into the relevant domain.

Hard copies of journals relevant to the students, academics and professionals with access to them are kept in academic libraries (for example, those of universities, colleges, teaching hospitals and professional institutions). Good public libraries may also carry major journals. For some electronic journals, members of particular libraries have access as of right (because the institution pays for them). For information about these you should consult the online catalogue and/or the library staff.

Dissertations and theses

University and college libraries keep copies of the work their students submit to qualify for higher degrees by research (MA, MSc, PhD etc.), perhaps the dissertations of students who qualified for a Masters degree (or similar) by a taught route and sometimes at least the better of those submitted as part of a first degree. These are known as dissertations or theses. The difference between a dissertation and a thesis is not that precise and to some extent the words are interchangeable. However, 'dissertation' is the term most usually applied to work submitted for first and Masters degrees whereas 'thesis' tends to be reserved for work submitted for doctoral awards. Both dissertations and theses are usually available on the open shelves of academic libraries but they probably are for reference only. How they are shelved varies. Sometimes they are arranged chronologically by department or faculty. However they are shelved and wherever in the library they are, what these offer is yet another way of checking what is already known about the area you wish to research. Not only that, the literature reviews of the ones relevant to your own topic are likely to be helpful to you when you do your own literature search and the ones that use the same methodology and/or methods as you intend to use are probably useful even if they are about something completely different.

What is a literature review?

A literature review is a critical appraisal of the work published about a particular topic. In the course of your research, it is probable that you will be required to show evidence of having researched the literature currently available and use this to place your work in a context and demonstrate how it relates to that which already exists. Of course the depth and width of the literature review will largely be dependent on the nature of, or reason for your study and hopefully you will have been given guidelines as to what is expected of you.

In the context of your research, you could see your literature review as telling the story of what is known and/or what has been said about the area of interest to you. That it is a critical appraisal implies that more than a descriptive list of works is required. You should evaluate the work to which you refer, representing different arguments. There should also be a 'flow' to your literature review. Perhaps it will be 'historical', tracing the development of a line of thought through time; perhaps it will start with an overview, a broad discussion before focusing on one or more areas. Whatever the nature of your review, you should cite (and where appropriate quote

Note

Publications of professional bodies show an appropriate range of editorial and review processes often along similar lines:

• The Royal College of Nursing publishes *Nursing Standard* – a weekly current affairs in nursing magazine which carries a small research element, and *Evidence-Based Nursing* – a quarterly peer-reviewed journal. The RCN also publishes other specialist journals.

• The British Association for Counselling and Psychotherapy publishes *Therapy Today* ten times a year – more of a magazine than a journal – whereas *Counselling and Psychotherapy Research* is a quarterly peer-reviewed scientific journal.

Note

There is no point in reinventing the wheel. If an excellent literature review exists, use it *and adapt it* to your work (it will at least be out of date however recently it was completed, and no literature review can be comprehensive). We look at this point later in this chapter.

Note

We are not assuming that you are a student registered to do a Masters or Doctoral programme requiring research. One of the main aims of the book is to encourage practitioners (including independent practitioners) to collect data and evaluate their own practice. So, many readers will not have free access to the huge resources that students have available as a result of paying their course fee. Most (but not all) journals carrying good psychotherapy research will charge for access to their content (a charge per individual paper viewed) and these charges are not small. Independent practitioners must use their ingenuity.

Note

We realise that a lot of 'searching the literature' now happens online and we tell you about some strategies for this later. However, there is still a lot to be said for knowing how libraries work and, if what you want to know about is in a book rather than a journal, they are still often the best way of accessing material. Also, since beyond a certain point (usually the abstract) accessing journal content online involves payment (often tens of pounds per article), it is sometimes more cost-effective to search out online what may be relevant and/or interesting but then to go to a library holding the journal(s) to actually look at the full papers.

However, don't forget that academic libraries (and some public libraries) subscribe to journals and this usually means that online access to any journal they hold is available to members through the library website. That said, especially if you don't have easy access to a library, you might want to skip this section and go on to the next.

from) a range of works. These should certainly include contemporary journals. Further guidance about how to plan and write a literature review is available on the web (try Googling 'writing a literature review') and in books about writing up research.

OK, that was a bit sneaky. What we were trying to do was to get you started on using the available resources – both hard copy on the shelves of a library and the Internet – in other words to do a literature search about reviewing the literature. We'll tell you more about using these resources as we go along. You can of course buy books and subscribe to journals but there is really so much literature out there that to cover it all in this way is impossible. You are going to have to get at it in other ways.

Using a library

Although we both remember when libraries were places you went to borrow books and that was about it, we know that they are now much more than mere repositories of the written word. Not only do they now offer access to audio-visual material of various types (and some of that may be relevant to your research so don't forget to check it out) but they also have banks of computers. Some of these are likely to be devoted to allowing readers to search the online catalogue(s) while others are for accessing the Internet. However, in this section we are going to concentrate on hard copy (books and journals) and how to find the ones relevant to your research.

Finding books and journals

Libraries use systems to organise how they shelve their books and journals. Mostly, libraries in the UK use the same system to classify books – the Dewey Decimal System. In this, every subject area has a particular number. Firstly, books are allotted to one of ten numbered main classes. These are:

000 Generalities (including, for example, encyclopaedias, dictionaries and the like)
100 Philosophy and psychology
200 Religion
300 Social science
400 Language
500 Natural sciences and mathematics
600 Technology (applied science)
700 The Arts and recreation
800 Literature and rhetoric
900 Geography and history

Within each of these broad classes, specific subjects are given numbers of their own. This first division into a subclass is indicated by the second digit. For example, 360 is the number for books on social services (a subclass of social sciences).

Although this system is logical and it works well enough when subjects fall neatly into its particular system of logic there are a few idiosyncrasies. For example, books on counselling can turn up in the 150s (psychology), the 360s (social science) or the 370s (education). To some extent this seems to depend on the human being who coded the book in the first place. Also, quite why books on psychotherapy are classified in the 616s (diseases) baffles us – but because we know they are we can find them easily enough. Although the Dewey Decimal System is a bit difficult to grasp at first, once you have got the hang of it you can find books on a particular subject in any library because they always have the same code. However, this does not necessarily mean that particular titles by particular authors will be coded exactly the same by different libraries. Nevertheless, with this basic information you can wander along the shelves containing the books with the code numbers of your areas of interest and browse. Who knows what you might find?

Journals are also shelved systematically but usually separately from books – probably in a section of the library shelves specifically devoted to them. However, the system seems to vary from library to library. Some make use of the Dewey Decimal System; others shelve journals alphabetically by title. However the order is arrived at, once you locate a run of journals on the shelf it is likely to be arranged in date order. That is (if the library has every copy since the journal started), starting with Volume 1, Part 1 and ending at the most recent edition. Two things to watch out for are that libraries sometimes stop taking particular journals so their runs may be incomplete and journals sometimes change their names so you may have to look in more than one place. Also, current copies of journals (that is, the most recent ones) may very well be shelved separately in a sort of 'what's new' section of the library. When you are browsing current and recent copies of journals, you can quickly check their contents because these are usually printed on the back cover. However, most libraries bind older copies of journals in hard covers either by the year or the volume (in many cases these are the same) so you will have to look at the contents pages inside. Generally speaking, journals cannot be borrowed. However, libraries often have a photocopying facility and it is easy enough to copy papers in which you are particularly interested.

While we think that wandering around a library, picking books off the shelves, browsing current journals, etc. is a good way of becoming more familiar with the world of published material and of finding something that turns out to be relevant which you wouldn't have otherwise found, it can be a bit inefficient. Sometimes you

Note
A further refinement makes use of the third digit – thus the shelf number for books on social welfare is 362. It doesn't stop there. Subjects can be more precisely defined by digits after a decimal point (up to four or five is fairly common but the system allows for more). Child welfare is 362.7 – and so on. If there is more than one book with the same numerical code then three letters are added. These are usually the first three letters of the author's name. For example, *Becoming a Reflexive Researcher* by Kim Etherington is classified by Manchester Metropolitan University Library as 001.4ETH. 000 is 'generalities', 001 is 'knowledge', 001.4 is something to do with reflection, ETH is taken from the name of the author. A book is then shelved according to its number (for example, 362.079 before 362.18) and then alphabetically (362.079BAT before 362.079DEB). Most libraries then logically arrange their shelves such that the system starts with books at 000.00001AAA and ends at 999.99999ZZZ – but specialist libraries may be restricted as to which parts of the spectrum they stock. One other thing, although the Dewey Decimal System is used for both, loan stock (books you can borrow, taking them away to make use of) are shelved separately from reference books. The latter are for use only in the library itself.

will need to be more focused. There are ways to help you out. Libraries have catalogues. In the old days, catalogues existed as drawers of cards. These were superseded by microfiche (and in some libraries you might still have to use these to find older material) but now most catalogues are computerised. If you want to find a particular book and you know who wrote it, its title and perhaps even when it was published, you can enter this information into the catalogue and information as to its Dewey Decimal Number (thus, whereabouts in the library to find it) will pop up. You may also be told whether the book is currently available to borrow – which saves you a walk if it is already on loan. If somebody else has borrowed it, many libraries offer an online reservation system accessible from the catalogue so you can reserve the desired book at the click of a mouse. If you have less information, the catalogue may still be helpful. Most allow you to do a search on an author's name (which will bring up everything written by that person or people with a similar name that is held by the library) or a book title. Some even allow a keyword search which is particularly useful if you want to do the electronic equivalent of browsing the shelves. Needless to say, the more specific you can be the more efficient and useful a catalogue search is likely to be. Sometimes, given a very general term as a keyword, library catalogues just give up because there are too many titles to list. For example, the Manchester Metropolitan University online catalogue tells us that it holds 15,286 books it thinks relevant to our keyword search on 'research' but that this is too great a number to list. A keyword search on social care comes up with 1,307 works, also too many to list. However, when we combine the two ('social care research'), it came up with 149 works which it did list. If we had chosen, we could then have used the catalogue to find out a bit more about these books and eventually gone to the shelves to look at any that seemed particularly relevant or interesting. Many libraries also have a journals catalogue which can be used in much the same way.

One last piece of advice about searching for material in libraries is 'When in doubt ask a librarian'. Nobody knows as much about a library as the people who work there. Librarians can help you understand the shelving system, the catalogue and much, much more. They know the various ways there are to search their stock (more of that soon), they can tell you how to reserve a book, how to request a book from another library (every library has restrictions on the amount of stock it can carry but there is an 'inter-library loan' system – we'll come back to this) and so on. If you have access to a university or college library, the librarians may very well conduct introductory sessions on how to use the library and more specialist sessions on various aspects of library usage (for example, how to access online journals). There will probably also be a range of leaflets to help you use the library. Additionally, larger libraries may have specialist librarians who have a more detailed knowledge of particular aspects of their library. Their job is to help you when you require something that falls within their remit. Find out who these people are, what they can do and don't be afraid to ask. If you possibly can, make use of all these facilities and do this at an early stage in your research. You really should learn as much as you can about the libraries to which you have access as soon as you can.

What do you do if what you want isn't in the library?

As we said above, most libraries are restricted (by space and cost as well as subjects covered) as to what books they buy and keep and to which journals they subscribe. It might very well be that, as you do your literature search, you come across a reference to a book or paper that seems as if it is exactly what you are looking for but you can't find it in the catalogue of the library to which you have access. The first thing to do is to check with a librarian. You may have missed it somehow – perhaps it is not catalogued in quite the way you thought. Secondly, find out if what you want is available online. For example, if you are after an article published in a journal your library does not take, use a search engine to find out if there is a web page for the journal. If there is, it will almost certainly allow you access to at least the abstracts (see below) of recent papers. This may be enough to help you decide whether or not you want to see more. If you want the whole paper, you may be able to download it but it is likely that there will be a charge. If you can't get what you want online or don't want to pay what is asked, there is another system.

All the public and academic libraries in the UK (and lots of the others too) are linked by the inter-library loans scheme. Basically, this means that any member of a participating library can request a work not available at their own library and, as long as at least one library in the system does stock it, it will turn up sooner or later. Journal articles may come as photocopies (which you get to keep), books are sent on loan and must be returned before the loan period expires. Some libraries make a charge for this service but some do not. If your college or university library does charge, you could check out your local public library which may not.

Searching the literature

A lot of what we said about using libraries applies to either knowing exactly what you want or having just the vaguest clue. Doing a literature search involves going beyond material with which you

Note

There are several stages of doing research which challenge the researcher. Each stage presents its own challenge and the literature search is a challenge for most students and practitioners. Searching for literature is time consuming and frequently frustrating. And when you have located the literature you have to read it!

There are rewards as well. It's not possible to predict what exciting things you might discover as you broaden your knowledge, nor how new knowledge might benefit you and your clients regardless of whether you complete your research project.

are familiar but it requires something a bit more focused than browsing works on, for example, researching social care just to see what's there (although, to be fair, both these things have their uses). When you are searching the literature for material relevant to your research, you probably know a few things to get you started. Perhaps you can be specific enough with a keyword search to focus in tightly on your area of interest and this may be a helpful way of getting started. For example, 'alcohol counselling' will bring up books specific to working with people with alcohol problems and typing 'alcohol' in for a keyword search in a journals catalogue will draw your attention to journals dealing with alcohol use, other aspects of addiction and so on. Also, you probably know something about your area of interest already in the public domain. Perhaps your interest was sparked by something you read or heard, perhaps you know someone who has done some work in the area in which you are interested (an 'author' search on that person will lead you to any books they have published). If you are doing your research as part of a professional qualification or for a higher degree, then you will have a supervisor who should be able to point you in the direction of relevant literature. Once you have found even one relevant work, you can find others. The 'literature' is in effect a vast network and once you have found a way in you can, if you choose, follow its threads in many, many directions.

Searching the literature is time consuming and this may be an issue. Not only will you have to find your sources, but having identified possible sources you will also have to obtain them. You cannot reasonably expect yourself to follow every strand in this vast network. However, the better prepared you are for your literature search, the more effective and less time consuming it will be. As fascinating as a historical perspective might be or as absorbing as parallel work in an unrelated discipline is, don't pursue these to the neglect of the contemporary and current literature directly addressing your area of interest. One tip for those of you writing up your work for a dissertation or thesis is that when you know who your external examiner will be make sure you know about their relevant work.

The other time-related issue is knowing when to call a halt to your literature search – you don't just have to find the material, you also have to read it (and take notes). Be realistic, there will always be more you can do and when you eventually write up your research it is almost certain that someone will express surprise that you haven't made reference to a particular work. That's just how it is. Providing you have done enough reading to reinforce the background of and approach to your research and you can place your findings in the context of the literature, you will have done enough.

Tracing ideas backwards and following them forward

When you read any book or journal article you think may be relevant to your literature search, remember that its author has already performed the same task in writing what you are reading. As well as the author's original contribution, there will be reference to the work of others. Handily, these references will be listed alphabetically at the end of the paper or book (sometimes at the end of each chapter in the case of the latter). Now you have a key into the literature. You can look at the titles and/or the authors of the work referred to and make some decision as to which look as if they might be helpful to you in your research. Of course, you will then need to find a way of actually looking at what seems as if it might be relevant. One way of doing this is to go back to the library catalogue, find the book or journal on the shelf and read at least part of the work in question (sometimes the contents page of a book is enough to tell you if it is worth going further, sometimes you will have to check out a chapter or two). With journals, there is a handy short cut. Most papers in journals start with an abstract. An abstract is a compressed/SYNOPTIC version of the paper (of about 400–600 words). Usually, reading an abstract will be enough to know if the paper is likely to be relevant but don't be too hasty in dismissing things. Again, only a more thorough reading will confirm relevance.

Once you have found a book, chapter or paper in this way which is relevant to your research, you have access to yet another literature review and you can repeat the process. If you have the patience and it is relevant, you can in this way trace a line of thought back to its beginnings. Also, you will discover many branches and side turnings, some of which may be of great help.

Going backwards from a particular work is easy, perhaps time consuming and even tedious but easy. However, your entry point to the relevant literature, unless it is very recent, will not of itself give you access to an up-to-date picture of what is known about your topic because (rather obviously) it will only refer to works published before it was. It would be really useful to be able to find out who had subsequently published something relevant to your key book, chapter or paper. Luckily, other people think so too so for a long time there have been ways of checking to see who has cited any particular work. One way of doing this is to use a citation index which is an index between publications (almost always journals) showing which later documents cite (refer to) earlier ones. One likely to be of use to practitioners of health and social care is the Social Science Citation Index (available online and as a CD-ROM) which surveys 1,700 journals from 50 related disciplines in such a way as to help researchers make comprehensive searches and so discover where and by whom a paper in which they are interested has been cited. The obvious limitation is that anything

Note: Abstracts

The abstract of a research paper should tell the reader what the research question was, how the research was conducted, what was found and what was decided about what was found. Abstracts of papers dealing with something other than research per se will follow a similar format.

SYNOPTIC in the form of a synopsis or summary.

Note

The SSCI is not a free service. Students enrolled on Masters and Doctoral programmes will have access to it via their institution (most often by ATHENS, an online content management system which only allows access to registered users). Independent practitioners and private users will have to pay, and it's not easy even to do this.

Independent researchers do have access to free search services like Google Scholar (see pp 238–9), but these still don't match the combined power and flexibility available through an institution's online access facilities.

We explain a good free online source of systematic reviews, the Cochrane Library, on p 247 of this chapter.

published elsewhere than in one of the 1,700 journals will not be included in the index. However, when it works what you have once more is access to another bit of the massive web of the literature, this time going forwards and sideways.

Many libraries will have access to the various citation indices and the librarians will be able to help you use them and to point you in the direction of the one(s) most appropriate to your task. They will also know of other resources to help you track down subsequent citations of any work in which you are interested.

Doing online searches of the literature

For at least part of any literature search you do in preparing for or writing up your research you are likely to make use of online resources. We have begun to tell you something about this in previous sections of this chapter. For example, that you can often find at least the abstracts of papers published in journals via the web page for any particular journal and that the Social Science Citation Index is available online but there are other ways of finding out about what has been published in books and journals. We will tell you more about a couple of these as examples of what you can do. One thing you should know about is the free resource, Google Scholar.

This is an offshoot of the well-known Internet search engine which is specifically for searching the academic literature. Using the advanced search facility, you can specify that works contain either all the words you list, the exact phrase you give, at least one of the words you list or that specific words are excluded. These words can be anywhere in the paper or in the title. You can specify an author, a publication and/or a time period and make either a general search (that is of everything covered by the search engine) or restrict your search to a particular domain. When you have specified your criteria, Google Scholar comes up with works that fit. Usefully it also includes citations so you can come forward as well as go back.

Although sometimes you may find that you can get complete access, Google Scholar will usually only take you as far as the abstract for a paper or a summary of the content of a book. This may then mean that you have pay to see more online (but remember what we said about accessing online journal material for free via subscribing libraries) or seek out hard copy to get any further. However, Google Books and some book-selling websites have a 'look inside' facility which allows you to 'turn the page' and so access content. Sometimes, via a search engine you will be led to chapter published in an edited book which is available (in totality or part) as part of a 'look inside' facility on the bookseller's website. When you find such a chapter, it is not unusual to find that, at the very least, you can also take a look at the front cover, the title page, the page after (the one that lists date and place of publication, ISBN number and so on, all essential when you want to add it to your references) and the contents page(s). You may also find that you can look at other chapters published in the same book. Alternatively, you may be led straight to the front cover of a book in which you think you may be interested. If there is a 'look inside' flag or some other indication that you can access what the book contains you can usually get at least as far as the contents page(s) which may be enough to tell you whether or not seeking out ways of gaining greater access is worthwhile.

In these various ways, you will find routes into the vast amount of literature out there in the public domain. Having discovered it, all you now have to do is to make sense of it, learn from it and, when you are ready to write up your research, digest it, present it in a meaningful way both to give the background to your research and in exploring and explaining your findings. We will come back to that in the next chapter but first there are some more things it may help you to know about getting started.

Reading and evaluating the work of others

Whether you are doing research of your own or merely keeping abreast of developments in your field (which we think is a professional obligation) you are going to have to know what to read and how to make sense of it. Besides reports of research and papers or books advancing theory (what you might see referred to as 'conceptual' works, meaning they are about what somebody thinks rather than what they have demonstrated by research), you will need to become familiar with, for example, systematic reviews and meta-analyses, both of which are ways of summarising and/or interpreting bodies of research (see pp. 241-252, this chapter).

We have told you something about how to find information from the literature, but how do you make a judgement about the worth of what you find? In other words, while it is important to know that there is evidence of something, this is only going to be useful if you have at least an elementary understanding of the quality of that evidence. For example, you are going to have to know if the claims made for the presented evidence are valid.

You should never accept anything you read unthinkingly and uncritically. Publishing something does not make it 'true'. Presenting evidence for a claim or belief is a step towards establishing something as 'true', but evidence is a variable commodity and it may be variously interpreted. For example, an interaction that one therapist sees as evidence of transference is, for another, evidence of social learning, while yet another might see it as evidence of nothing at

Note

We think counsellors and psychotherapists would benefit from looking at Cooper (2008) for two reasons, firstly, it is a good contemporary evaluative review of counselling and psychotherapy literature, and secondly, it looks at many studies which readers can subject to their own scrutiny and sharpen their skills of evaluating research.

All readers (not only counsellors and psychotherapists) would find Gomm, Needham & Bullman an accessible and informative text for the same purpose.

Cooper, M (2008) *Essential Research Findings in Counselling and Psychotherapy.* London: Sage.

Gomm, R, Needham, G & Bullman, A (2000) *Evaluating Research in Health and Social Care.* London: Sage.

Note

... but even 'proof' has degrees – think about the requirement in criminal law for proof to be beyond reasonable doubt while in civil law the standard of proof is less rigorous.

Note

These are tests of the *validity* of the work and are similar to 'face validity' and 'construct' validity', see Chapter 2.2, pp 40-2.

Note

These are tests of the *consistency* of the work and are similar to 'reliability' in research methodology, see Chapter 2.2, pp 42-4. A further way of establishing the consistency of an idea or finding is to see if more than one person has published similar ideas or results.

all. Also, evidence does not necessarily constitute proof. The former is an indication of a possibility or likelihood that something is so, the latter is something much more definite. In some ways, it is up to you to decide how much evidence and of what quality you need before you regard something as proved. And don't forget that even what appears to be proved can later be disproved.

So, how do you decide if what you are reading is worth the paper on which it is written? Firstly, there is the issue of provenance. If you are reading a paper published in a reputable, peer-reviewed journal then it is safe to assume that there has been some check on the contents of the paper and that, if it is a report of a research study, there is agreement that the research has been carried out in a valid way and that the findings accord with the method of data collection and analysis. Similarly, books that come from reputable publishers have usually been subject to an editing process of some kind and so they can be relied upon to at least some extent. However, books are much more likely to contain 'opinion' and this has to be evaluated not only in terms of the internal argument but also in the light of your other knowledge. Papers appearing in publications other than refereed journals and books from less well-known publishing houses are not necessarily any less worthy, but a part of the monitoring process that has otherwise been done for you is down to you when you consult such works.

Whatever the provenance of the work you are reading, the first step in evaluating what you read is to assess whether it makes sense within itself. Does one thing follow from another? Is the reasoning logical? Secondly, comes the task of deciding if what the writer describes doing fits with your knowledge of how it should be done. We have told you a lot about both quantitative and qualitative approaches to research which will enable you to at least make a tentative judgement about this. For example, if there is reference to particular ways of collecting and processing data, does this conform to what you know about those methods? Are there omissions, exceptions, deviations or the like? If there are, are these explained? If so, does the explanation make sense and the difference seem legitimate? Are the findings clearly given and can you see how they follow from the data? Does the way the findings have been made sense of seem consistent and credible? Throughout, are there links to the literature and do these support what is written? The latter may involve you in actually checking for yourself. This is not so much because writers cheat by misquoting or wilfully misinterpreting the literature (although that may happen) but because your understanding of what Bloggs and Brown said may be different from that of the writer – this can cast a different light on everything else. Also, is the literature up to date? Does it omit particular papers, areas of study of which you are aware and so on. All of these things should raise questions in your mind. Before you can be totally satisfied with what you read, these questions need answers. Whatever you read, think about what may have been left out. For any omissions, seek reasons. Conversely, think too about what is included. Does it make sense? Does it follow on? Does it really belong?

At the end of this section we return to the possibly unsettling point we made above. That something has been published or stated authoritatively in any way does not necessarily mean it is true. Even the peer-reviewed literature is full of declarations as to why something could not possibly be so or is definitely so (often accompanied by convincing evidence) of which there are subsequent convincing rebuttals. Approach everything you read with openness to new ideas and different ways of thinking but also with a healthy scepticism.

Understanding strategies for summarising and evaluating large numbers of findings and aggregated data

Various ways of taking an overview of the findings of several studies have been developed over the years. In the crudest possible terms they are ways of determining 'average' findings or 'on balance' findings across several (sometimes dozens or even hundreds of) studies. It is not a new idea. Almost as soon as publication of scientific findings was established, scientists have, for various reasons, wanted to come to a general appreciation of big questions, from the topical 'does global warming exist?' to the more specifically relevant for some readers of this book, 'does psychotherapy work?'

For many years, the research community has tried to answer big questions like these by aggregating the results of many studies and summarising them. The first efforts to do this in psychotherapy proved how difficult it is to achieve trustworthy, widely accepted answers since the process required a number of adjustments to be made. Those involved in early quantitative research on, for example, the effectiveness of psychotherapy, did not conduct their studies with the idea in mind that one day their study would have its results aggregated and summarised alongside many others.

There are two phrases in common use associated with summary or aggregated results, *systematic review* and *meta-analysis*. We will go through the ideas behind contemporary strategies for such aggregations and summaries by looking at them in terms of the following principles:

- the hypotheses of the studies to be aggregated must be related
- the studies to be aggregated must be *primary* studies, i.e. they must be empirical studies which make direct measurements on

Note

It is probably OK to dip into this chapter at this point if you simply want to understand what a meta-analysis or systematic review is, but if you want to really understand how they work and arrive at conclusions, you will have to go back and start at the beginning of the book. These methods of summarising findings and aggregating results are sophisticated applications of research methods and assume you understand the basics of research thinking and methodology. We will not be defining terms that we have already covered in previous chapters.

Note

There is no real difference between *summarising* and *aggregating* results – the terms can be used interchangeably. We will be looking at types of summary/aggregate study and the methods of statistical analysis used later in this chapter.

the hypothesis in question, not summaries or reviews of other studies
- the aggregate/summary must try to be comprehensive. Whilst accepting that it cannot be, it must explain how it tried to be, including important issues such as the criteria by which studies were included and excluded from the summary
- summaries must make their methodologies, assumptions and judgements transparent
- the statistical procedures used to evaluate results across the studies must be appropriate and well-argued

When reading summary or aggregate studies, it will be helpful to look carefully at how the study has dealt with these principles. You will then be able to determine how confident you are about the conclusions of the study in question. Do not rely on others to do this for you, e.g. a peer-review process before publication. Although a study might be published, that is no guarantee that it is beyond criticism. Peer review does not make a study flawless and beyond criticism. Read carefully and do not be afraid to play devil's advocate.

Historical interlude

It is widely understood (see Lipsey & Wilson, 2001) that British psychologist Hans Eysenck's review of psychotherapy (Eysenck, 1952) kick-started systematic reviews in psychotherapy via the work of, for example, Smith & Glass (1977). In his review, Eysenck concluded that 'The figures fail to support the hypothesis that psychotherapy facilitates recovery from neurotic disorder' (p. 324). This work was one of the first systematic reviews of psychotherapy and is memorable for its contentious conclusions, exaggerated somewhat by Eysenck's larger-than-life reputation. Regardless of the resulting furore, Eysenck had to wrestle with some of the basic issues which confront anyone wanting to compare studies. In his review of 19 studies, 5 (in his terms) 'psychoanalytic' and 14 'eclectic' he realised that (a) he had to find a way of measuring improvement that could be used across all 19 studies, and (b) that to estimate how much patients had improved, he had to have a measure of how they were functioning at the start of the studies.

It is worth taking advantage of the York University 'Classics in the History of Psychology' online archive (see below) to read Eysenck's paper. It is a good preliminary to considering the whole area of review and meta-analysis.

Eysenck, HJ (1952) The effects of psychotherapy: An evaluation. *Journal of Consulting Psychology, 16*, 319-24. This (along with many other historic papers) can be downloaded from the excellent 'Classics in the History of Psychology' web resource at York University, Ontario, Canada. Retrieved 06.01.2010 from <http://psychclassics.yorku.ca/Eysenckpsychotherapy.htm>
Lipsey, MW & Wilson, DB (2001) *Practical Meta-Analysis*. Applied Social Research Methods Series (Vol. 49). Thousand Oaks, CA: Sage Publications.
Smith, ML & Glass, GV (1977) Meta-analysis of psychotherapy outcome studies. *American Psychologist 32*, 752-60.

The hypotheses must be related

The two general questions asked in the first paragraph of this section demonstrate the first 'principle' of looking at summaries or aggregates of studies, namely that you can only ask such a question about one hypothesis or a related and highly limited set of hypotheses. In the cases above ('does global warming exist?' and 'does psychotherapy work?'), this means we can obviously only include hypotheses and data concerning firstly, the evidence for and against the existence of global warming, and secondly, the efficacy of psychotherapy.

Even though the appeal and power of these questions lies in their promise to deal with the general, when trying to answer such overarching questions, it is crucial that we deal with issues of particular definition. We have been looking at how research processes and procedures refine our understanding of such definitions throughout this book. In the examples above, we need to have definitions of 'global warming', 'exist', 'psychotherapy' and 'work', and you should by now be familiar with such issues of definition, indeed you will be aware that the integrity and validity of research depends upon clear definition.

In the same way that the integrity of all research depends upon the precise wording of questions or definition of hypotheses, in a study summarising aggregated results, the more closely the studies are related in terms of their hypotheses, the better. A summary of studies will lose its usefulness if the hypotheses of the original studies are not closely related. This commonality can be from the closest relationship possible, i.e. when studies are essentially replications of an original study, through to a looser relationship based only on the conceptual bases of the studies. Understanding how closely the studies are related in a summary or aggregate study leads to considering the criteria on which work is included and excluded. We will look in a little more detail at this later in this chapter.

The studies summarised must be primary studies

This principle should be self-evident, but it's useful to remind ourselves that reviews are reviews of primary studies or original work, not reviews of reviews. Of course, there is such a thing as a review of reviews, and the title ought to declare this. We would expect reviews of reviews to be conceptual, rather than hard quantitative meta-analyses with related statistics.

Summaries must try to be comprehensive

This simply means that any summary or aggregate of studies will be judged on how many sets of results it is summarising. If there is a tightly defined hypothesis, the study should really aim to search the literature (remember literature searches?) to locate as many studies as possible to include in the summary. This is time consuming, but valuable work. Furthermore, there is an implicit acceptance that no study can be actually comprehensive. It is something that researchers doing reviews and meta-analyses *strive for* rather than can be confident in achieving. As each year passes two factors impinge upon this aspect of understanding aggregations and summaries of results:

- more studies are done
- search methods get better

The cumulative effect of these factors is that more recent reviews and meta-analyses tend to be larger and more comprehensive. More recent review studies can therefore also afford a tighter set of inclusion criteria, since there is a larger pool of original work to choose from. These factors all serve to make recent reviews much more robust in methodology and confident in the conclusions that can be drawn.

Note
This idea of rigour and transparency boils down to having a clear and declared protocol for the review and to follow it. The protocol is the sequence of tasks and methods followed in the review. It needs to be a clear and explicit list of the methods used to minimise bias and to ensure the results are reproducible.

A summary must make its methodology and judgements transparent

The fourth principle of summarising or aggregating findings is the principle of transparency. By this we mean that there is a reasonable expectation that, just as in other research, summaries of studies and aggregations of findings are essentially unbiased. Whilst it is assumed that this will have been an earnest aim of the researchers (the authors of the summary/aggregate, and also, of course, those conducting the original studies), a good summary or aggregation will demonstrate how it strove to be fair and unbiased and will reveal its methodology, warts and all. It will be transparent. Not only must it be transparent and unbiased, it must seek out inadequacies and possible sources of bias in the results of the studies which are being reviewed. This is all done in the spirit of acknowledging that no research is perfect, and that researchers never actively aim to deceive, but with hindsight the limitations of the original studies can be reviewed, evaluated and in some cases corrections applied in the form of more recent or specially dedicated statistical procedures.

Lipsey, MW & Wilson, DB (2001)
Practical Meta-Analysis. Applied Social Research Methods Series (Vol. 49). Thousand Oaks, CA: Sage Publications.

Note
The above book is a key text for students of quantitative analysis of psychotherapy research at Masters and Doctoral levels. If you need to get a handle on the details of meta-analysis this is a good place to start.

As we mentioned at the beginning of this section, we are going to describe two ways of looking at studies with a view to summarising or aggregating findings: *systematic reviews* and *meta-analyses*. The differences between these two ways of analysing aggregated results is subject to debate, but we will take as our basis the work of Lipsey and Wilson (2001) — one of the modern seminal texts still available and written in a very accessible style. Lipsey and Wilson make the traditional argument that the term 'systematic review' refers to the whole review process and should have an appropriate statistical comparison of the primary studies included (see also Wilson, 1999 – available as a free web download). If a review is entirely qualitative and/or conceptual, it would be more properly termed a 'narrative review'. A 'meta-analysis' refers to the statistical analysis applied to the review of quantitative primary studies.

Statistical procedures for use on aggregated results

The problem with aggregated results is how to make meaningful comparisons across studies with demonstrable differences. How can we get to the situation where we are confident we can compare like with like? Furthermore, the differences themselves will almost certainly not be simple. Studies not only will have different methodological structures, they will also have different sample sizes, sometimes from different populations of clients. Studies will then use different diagnostic criteria for including clients and use different outcome measures. The authors of a review then have to somehow determine whether there are any overall tendencies in the data worth staking their reputations on. A statistical solution is one way of standardising such judgements so that they are not merely a matter of whim.

Of course it is not quite that simple, since attention has been given to what statistical procedures are most appropriate for understanding what aggregates of results are capable of telling us, and there is still room for debate. In this book we have looked at both *statistical significance* and *effect size* (the latter to which we will return later in this chapter, p. 249), and the question you might be asking is 'which one is best for systematic reviews?'

The short answer is, when it comes to meta-analysis of outcome research, effect size is preferable. Some readers might be relieved to discover that we don't have the luxury of enough space to explain why, at a conceptual level, for a certain type of outcome study, using statistical significance has several disadvantages. Effect size has the further advantage that it is also inherently a way of making comparison of different types of quantitative data possible (there is a little more on this later in this chapter). Indeed, it is the advent and use of effect size that has made meta-analysis such a powerful and influential research review tool.

You might well come up against a number of other terms when reading meta-analyses. The field of psychotherapy research straddles social science and medical research conventions, so we find terms from both fields used, sometimes interchangeably.

Treatment effect can be understood fairly literally in caring professions research as meaning a measure of the effect of a deliberate intervention or 'treatment'. The treatment in question

Wilson, DB (1999) *Practical Meta Analysis.* PowerPoint presentation slides based on the work described in Lipsey & Wilson (2001) retrieved 04/01/2010 from <http://mason.gmu.edu/ ~dwilsonb/ downloads/ overview.ppt#256,1,Practical Meta-Analysis>

Note
We explain statistical significance in Chapter 2.5. We also have briefly touched on effect size on p 86 in Chapter 2.4.

Note
All of these terms refer to calculations which might be used to compare the results of studies aggregated and used as an *effect size*.

is usually a psychotherapeutic intervention or method, or different environment (as is sometimes the case in social care) and is usually being compared with a control or 'no treatment' group. Some texts use the term interchangeably with *effect size*, although, as we have seen, the latter is also used to describe the degree of effect between any two conditions in a study. The terms 'treatment effect' and 'effect size' can themselves refer to any of the following ways of analysing and comparing data ...

Odds ratio is the difference between the odds (chances or probability) of something happening in two groups, e.g. a group of men and a group of women, or in psychotherapy, a treatment group and a control group. Odds ratios are one of many ways of expressing what some people call 'risk' and so are related to ...

Risk ratio is the risk of something happening in one group set against the same thing happening in another group. Risk ratios are more frequently used in medical research where the researchers are, for example, trying to estimate the chances of a cancer developing in two different groups of patients (those who smoke versus those who do not smoke). In psychotherapy research it is likely to be used when looking at the risk of, for example, remission after treatment in two groups (treatment versus control).

Relative risk has a similar meaning to risk ratio, i.e. the relative risk of remission in two groups.

Standardised mean difference is the calculation used to compare the differences between means (of, say, the outcome measures of a treatment group versus a control group) between several studies when each study uses a different outcome measure. This is the essence of meta-analysis statistical comparison and is explained a little more below in the section on calculating effect sizes.

Rate ratio is simply the rate of a certain thing happening in group A set against the rate of it happening in group B. In medical and psychotherapy research it is often called the *improvement rate ratio* and as such is self-explanatory.

Rate difference or *improvement rate difference* is the difference between improvement rates rather than the ratio of improvement rates between two conditions. So it could show, for example, the improvements in social functioning between the control and treatment groups.

Systematic review

A systematic review is a method of summarising, analysing, and discussing the results of more than one (usually several) studies. The studies may have different methodologies and the results may have varying levels of concordance (indeed may be outright conflicting). The review will also come to conclusions regarding the types of methodology and trends in results. Readers might find

Note
A risk ratio of less than one means that the incidence of the event decreases (remission – eg, the chances of a participant's suicidal feelings returning – in the control group). When greater than one, the incidence increases (remission in the treatment group).

Note
The standardised mean difference is the difference in the means of the two groups divided by a standard deviation.

Note
Many, but not all, of these statistics use a confidence interval or level of probability to express how likely it is that such a ratio or difference could have occurred by chance. Some use arbitrary levels to express their strength, some of these levels have been the subject of peer scrutiny, some have not. Critical readers will have to understand the statistics in detail and make their own decision.

We look at confidence intervals and statistical significance in Chapter 2.5 in the margins on pp 93–5.

some texts using the terms systematic review and meta-analysis interchangeably. However, originally, systematic review referred to the *whole process* of aggregation, summary, statistical analysis, discussion and conclusion, and meta-analysis referred to the statistical analysis only.

The particular features of a *systematic* review are that:
• it is a *critical* review
• it is more than a *narrative review*, i.e. it brings a level of statistical analysis to the aggregated results
• it strives to be *objective* in its conclusions
• it strives to deliver *reproducible* conclusions through transparent methodology
• it is *systematic* in certain ways, i.e. it follows a clearly explained study protocol

The best-known example of the organisation of systematic reviews is the Cochrane Collaboration. It is an international organisation dedicated to collecting and disseminating current scientific evidence on the efficacy of medical treatments (including psychotherapy). It was founded in 1993 and named after epidemiologist Archie Cochrane. The website explains:

> The major product of the Collaboration is the Cochrane Database of Systematic Reviews which is published quarterly as part of *The Cochrane Library*.
>
> Those who prepare the reviews are mostly healthcare professionals who volunteer to work in one of the many Cochrane Review Groups, with editorial teams overseeing the preparation and maintenance of the reviews, as well as application of the rigorous quality standards for which Cochrane Reviews have become known.
> (Retrieved 14/01/2010 from <http://www.cochrane.org/docs/descrip.htm>)

The systematic reviews are thorough and rigorous, and the Cochrane Collaboration website explains the parameters of their reviews thus:

> • A structured format helps the reader to find his/her way around the review easily.
> • A detailed methods section allows the reader to assess whether the review was done in such a way as to justify its conclusions.
> • The quality of clinical studies to be incorporated into a review is carefully considered, using predefined criteria.
> • A thorough and systematic search strategy, which includes searches for unpublished and non-English records, aims to

Note
The Cochrane Collaboration, Cochrane Library and Cochrane Reviews are all available online. The main website address is <www.cochrane.org> and from there you can navigate to all the published material. The website explains:

> 'Cochrane Reviews investigate the effects of interventions for prevention, treatment and rehabilitation in a healthcare setting. They also assess the accuracy of a diagnostic test for a given condition in a specific patient group and setting.
>
> Each review addresses a clearly formulated question; for example: *Can antibiotics help in alleviating the symptoms of a sore throat?* The research is reviewed using stringent guidelines to establish whether or not there is conclusive evidence about a specific treatment. They are updated regularly, ensuring that treatment decisions can be based on the most up-to-date and reliable evidence.'
> (Retrieved 31/03/2010 <http://www.cochrane.org/cochrane-reviews>)

The library has a huge amount of information on evidence-based practice for a wide range of health and social care topics. The review groups are listed on <http://www.cochrane.org/cochrane-reviews>. If you intend to progress to more advanced research involving quantitative methods, we recommend you visit the Cochrane Collaboration to at least help with your literature review.

provide as complete a picture as possible to try to answer the question considered.

• If the data collected in a review are of sufficient quality and similar enough, they are summarised statistically in a meta-analysis, which generally provides a better overall estimate of a clinical effect than the results from individual studies. A meta-analysis also allows the author to explore the effect of specific characteristics of given studies (for example, study quality) on the reported results (for example, does exclusion of non-randomized studies change the overall result?). It also allows an exploration of the effects of an intervention on sub-groups of patients (for example, does the treatment have a different effect on smokers compared with non-smokers?).

• Reviews aim to be relatively easy to understand for non-experts (although a certain amount of technical detail is always necessary). To achieve this, Cochrane Review Groups like to work with 'consumers', for example patients, who also contribute by pointing out issues that are important for people receiving certain interventions. Additionally, the Cochrane Library contains glossaries to explain technical terms.

• Multinational editorial teams try to ensure that a review is applicable in different parts of the world.

• Reviews are updatable. Results from newly completed or identified clinical trials can be incorporated into the review after publication. Additionally, readers can send in comments and criticisms to any review, and reviews may be changed accordingly to improve their quality.

(Retrieved 14/01/2010 from <www.cochrane.org/cochrane-reviews/review-structure>)

Hunot, V, Churchill, R, Teixeira, V, Silva de Lima, M (2009) Psychological therapies for generalised anxiety disorder. *Cochrane Library, Issue 4*. Retrieved 14/01/2010 <http://mrw.interscience.wiley.com/cochrane/clsysrev/articles/CD001848/pdf_fs.html>

Note

An excellent general resource on meta-analysis is available for free download:

Valentine, JC & Cooper, H (2003) *Effect Size Substantive Interpretation Guidelines: Issues in the interpretation of effect sizes*. Washington, DC: What Works Clearinghouse. Retrieved 22/01/2010 from <http://ies.ed.gov/ncee/wwc/pdf/essig.pdf>

Readers can access Cochrane Reviews online without charge from the Cochrane Library website. The index of reviews by topic is at: <http://www.mrw.interscience.wiley.com/cochrane/cochrane_clsysrev_subjects_fs.html>.

The comprehensive nature, rigour and complexity of a Cochrane Review can be seen by looking at Hunot, Churchill, Teixeira and Silva de Lima (2009).

Meta-analysis

Meta analysis is a statistical protocol for analysing the aggregated results of more than one (usually several) studies. There are several statistical procedures that have been used for this analysis, and we have very briefly defined some of them earlier in this chapter. In this short section we are taking a closer look at effect size as a concept and a few of the statistical techniques used to express it.

However, we hope it's not too silly to point out that effect size is only useful when reviewing primary studies which are trying to show an effect (such as outcome research), and in recent years, psychotherapy research has become somewhat dominated by this type of primary study. It's worth reminding ourselves that there are many other reasons to do a systematic review and meta-analysis.

We are not going to give a comprehensive list of possible types of primary study amenable to systematic review, but, for example, other meta-analyses that do not look at *effects* might try to estimate the rate that something might happen in a particular sample, or the measurement of the strength of a phenomenon in one group at one time-point, or geographical location. For example, researchers might want to know 'What is the incidence of suicide in female students at UK universities?' or 'How many sessions did clients have in primary care counselling in 2009, compared with 1999?' Literature searches for either or both of these questions might generate sufficient primary studies to necessitate meta-analysis for a more powerful conclusion.

As we mentioned in Chapter 2.3, p. 66, the key to understanding effect size lies in unpacking the term, since it is intended to be used in outcome studies. Assuming that psychotherapists are looking for evidence that psychotherapy has a large effect upon the outcome for the client, in a meta-analysis of outcome studies we are looking for an effect and we want to know how large the effect is. In order to look across several studies and come to a meaningful conclusion we want to use a standarised measure that will make adjustments for the different measures used in each study. This is the rationale for effect size.

Why use effect size?
In a moment we'll look at the different types of effect size, but first the pros and cons:

- people with no research experience or previous understanding can quickly get to grips with the notion of effect size
- it evens out various complicating factors in the primary studies making comparison easier
- protocols *can* be agreed on how to interpret the degree of effect size (even though this has been somewhat problematical when the terms 'small', 'medium' and 'large' effect size have been used differently by different meta-analysers)
- if no agreement can be achieved on how big an effect size needs to be in order to be considered 'big enough', it is always possible to calculate, and use, confidence intervals (see pp. 92-4) as a benchmark for usefulness
- effect sizes are becoming *de rigeur* in research, for example, the *Publication Manual of the American Psychological Association* (5th edn) declares:

Note
You will find the terms associated with these other types of meta-analyses explained on pp 245–6.

American Psychological Association (2001) *Publication Manual of the American Psychological Association* (5th edn). Washington DC: American Psychological Association.

You, as an author, should familiarize yourself with the criteria and standards that editors and reviewers use to evaluate manuscripts ... Editors find in submitted papers the following kinds of *defects in the design and reporting of research*:

...

• failure to report effect sizes
(p. 5, emphasis added)

In the later section on adequate statistics, the APA *Publication Manual* advocates the use of effect size to help '... the reader to fully understand the importance of your findings' (p. 25).

• the use of significance testing (as we explored briefly in Chapter 2.5, pp. 92 & 110) has many more disadvantages when trying to compare outcome studies

Types of effect size

We are not going to give exhaustive coverage on this topic (for more information, see Valentine and Cooper, 2003), but will simply outline the main distinctions between effect sizes based on difference scores and those based on correlations. It is also imperative to understand that although we may have made effect size sound like a panacea to make results comparable, there is no such thing as the true effect size in any given situation. This area of research provides no silver bullets – you should be expecting that by now. So, condensing much continuing debate, in order for readers at the start of understanding outcome research, we offer a very simple explanation.

Effect size based on difference

These are called standardised mean effect sizes because they indicate the mean difference between two scores expressed as units of standard deviation (SD). *In principle* this is achieved as follows (bearing in mind that in practice, effect size must be calculated in a way that is appropriate for the data in the primary studies):

$$\text{effect size} = \frac{\text{the mean of group 1} - \text{the mean of group 2}}{\text{the pooled standard deviations of the two groups}}$$

In psychotherapy outcome research this equation would look like this:

$$\text{effect size} = \frac{\text{mean of the treatment group} - \text{mean of the control group}}{\text{the pooled standard deviations of the two groups}}$$

In crude terms, the comparative power of the effect size is given by dividing the difference between the groups by a standard measure of the variation, the standard deviation. So studies where there is even

---

Valentine, JC & Cooper, H (2003)
Effect Size Substantive Interpretation Guidelines: Issues in the interpretation of effect sizes. Washington, DC: What Works Clearinghouse. Retrieved 22/01/2010 from <http://ies.ed.gov/ncee/wwc/pdf/essig.pdf>

Note
For those of you who have an interest in outcome research for a higher degree or just want to know more, an excellent source of information about psychotherapy research, meta-analysis and the issues involved in outcome research, take a look at Robert Elliott's online blog (we've mentioned it before), and search for your topic: <http://pe-eft.blogspot.com>

Equation explanation
For explanation of 'mean' see p 54; for explanation of 'standard deviation' see pp 64-7.

Note
A pooled standard deviation is effectively the average standard deviation for the two groups.

quite a large difference will end up with a small effect size if the results are highly dispersed, i.e. have a large SD. Many texts use the 'pooled' SD in order to short-circuit debate on which standard deviation (the treatment group or the control group) should be used. Usually, the SD of the control group would be best, since it should be a representative group of the population who have not been affected by the treatment. However, often the control group is not large enough to avoid bias and in other cases it is not a true 'control' group. These factors can make an appreciable difference to the effect size, so any adverse influences are ameliorated by using the average.

In a classic book – though not one we would recommend to anyone without a very thorough understanding of statistics – Cohen (1988) offered the following guide to interpreting effect sizes based on standardised mean differences:

    0.8 = large
    0.5 = moderate
    0.2 = small

Effect size based on correlation
In Chapters 2.2 and 2.5 we introduced the idea of correlation as the expression of a relationship, an association, between two variables. We also made a note in the margin about it also being taken as an expression of the effect one variable might have on another. On p. 44, Chapter 2.2 we said:

> It is based on the idea that two things may be associated or co-related, for example:
> • my weight *increases* as I eat *more* food, or
> • the amount of petrol in my car's fuel tank *goes down* as I drive *more* miles

Clearly, in these everyday examples we can see the *implication* that one thing affects another. In caring profession research we might be interested to learn if the number of sessions of a particular treatment is associated with the degree of reduction of a set of problematical symptoms.

Studies investigating this would be correlational studies and any relationship could be expressed in one of three ways:
• as the number of treatment sessions increases, the symptoms decrease in intensity
• as the number of treatment sessions increases, the symptoms increase in intensity
• as the number of sessions increases, there is no change in the symptoms

When the results of correlation studies are aggregated, it is clear

Cohen, J (1988) *Statistical Power Analysis for the Behavioral Sciences* (2nd edn). Hillsdale, NJ: Erlbaum.

Note
Again, Robert Elliott has much more to say on this on his online blog. Search for 'effect size' <http://pe-eft.blogspot.com>

Note
We also were at pains to point out in Chapters 2.2 and 2.5 that correlation is generally accepted to be *only* a measure of association, not a measure of causation. So however logical it may seem, it is not possible to say that weight increases *because* more food is eaten purely on the basis of correlation. This is a problem when using correlation as the basis for effect size; it implies causality where there is none and causes confusion and misrepresentation as a result.

Note
Correlation coefficients are introduced and explained on p 107, Chapter 2.5. They can range from +1 (strong positive relationship: as one variable increases, the other variable increases) through 0 to -1 (strong negative correlation: as one variable increases, the other variable decreases).

Cohen, J (1988) *Statistical Power Analysis for the Behavioral Sciences* (2nd edn). Hillsdale, NJ: Erlbaum.

Note

These figures taken from Cohen (1988) – and those on the previous page – are only included to give readers a very rough idea of how terms like 'small', 'medium' and 'large' effects can be inferred from data. There are many detailed considerations which must be made when using these terms and figures, depending upon the particular nature of the methodology and statistics involved. Such considerations are beyond the scope of this book, but may have to be engaged with at doctoral and post-doctoral levels of research.

> IF YOU WANT TO KNOW MORE ABOUT
> understanding the trustworthiness
> of quantitative research

have a look at (with the most accessible first):

'Bad Science' The weekly column in the *Guardian* on Saturdays by Ben Goldacre, or his book:

Goldacre, B (2008) *Bad Science.* London: Fourth Estate.

Bausell, RB (2007) *Snake Oil Science: The truth about complementary and alternative medicine.* New York: Oxford University Press.

Mlodinow, L (2008) *The Drunkard's Walk: How randomness rules our lives.* London: Allen Lane/Penguin.

> IF YOU WANT TO KNOW MORE ABOUT
> understanding the trustworthiness
> of qualitative research

look at the references in the margin note on trustworthiness on p 121.

how correlation coefficients can be used as measures of how variable A (the number of treatment sessions) might affect variable B (the symptoms) and so constitute an effect size. A larger correlation coefficient means a stronger relationship between the variables, and so implies a larger effect size. Again, we find that although agreement on a protocol to determine what constitutes large, moderate and small effect sizes would be preferable, different writers have expressed different opinions on this. Cohen (1988) suggests:

$0.5 = \text{large}$

$0.3 = \text{moderate}$

$0.1 = \text{small}$

So is this paper really trustworthy?

You could be forgiven for thinking that although we have outlined strategies for engaging with the trustworthiness of research literature, we have failed to offer a sure-fire method of determining whether the paper or finding in question is really worth the paper it's written on. What we hope we have done is given you the tools to make the decision yourself based on evidence that you will find useful, rather than just passed the hot potato back to you. In doing this we are continuing to elaborate the philosophical problem at the heart of research – what is the truth?

Rather than sit on your own trying to work out where you stand it might help to be in dialogue with fellow researchers or others on a similar mission. Get together with other practitioner-researchers locally and debate the issues or take a look at some of the literature available.

A crucial aspect of organising, structuring and preparing for your research is to think through the ethical implications and ramifications of what you hope to do. In helping research, this will mean understanding and adhering to two strands of ethics, first, the ethics of scientific psychology research and second, the ethics of your professional helping practice. This is because as your research will probably involve directly working with people who are clients (as subjects, participants or co-researchers), it almost goes without saying that, as helping professionals, we must put their needs first.

It is more than likely that the professional body to which you belong, and perhaps even your place of work, will have codes of ethics that apply to both practice *and* research. In thinking about the design and implementation of your research, this should be your first port of call. It may even be that, if you are based in an institution as either a student or a worker, any research proposal you make will be scrutinised by an ethics committee. Such committees almost always have guidelines about how to make a submission. Here again, you should design your research to accord with these. Even if you don't have to submit your research proposal to a formally constituted body, it is a good idea to discuss it with a colleague, supervisor or manager to check its ethical implications. Needless to say, once you have come up with an ethical design that has been in some way reviewed, it is imperative that you conduct your research with integrity. Even though a proposal is a statement of intent (rather than a promise that you will follow the proposal to the letter), you should do your utmost to put the ethical elements of it into action.

As we have pointed out, you will not be short of resources to guide you – as an ethical researcher you are likely to have the guidance of your professional body, perhaps the institution in which you are based, the constructive criticism of friends and colleagues and your own common sense and professional integrity. However, we will give you a broad outline of the general principles of ethical social science research.

Competence

We may as well start with the obvious. Don't bite off more than you can chew. You must work within your own limits. If you are

Note

• The introduction to the British Association for Counselling and Psycho-therapy *Ethical Framework* says, 'This statement, Ethics for Counselling and Psychotherapy, … *is also applicable to counselling research* …' (emphasis added). Retrieved 3/12/2009 from <http://www.bacp.co.uk/ethical _framework/>

BACP do not publish an information sheet specifically addressing research ethics, though a short section appears in Information Sheet R4 *Using Measures and Thinking about Outcomes* by Tony Roth, with the subtitle 'Research ethics and research supervision'. In this paragraph, Roth directs readers to 'guidance on research ethics published by the British Association for Counselling and Psychotherapy, Bond, T (2004).' The publication in question is:

Bond, T (2004) *Ethical Guidelines for Researching Counselling and Psychotherapy*. Rugby: BACP (available for purchase from BACP).

• The United Kingdom Council for Psychotherapy does not appear to publish anything which specifically addresses the ethics of psychotherapy research, though it does have a 'Research Committee'.

• The British Psychological Society has lots of material pertaining to ethics and research. Our best advice is that you search the BPS site to see if they cover the topics you are interested in <www.bps.org.uk>

• The British Association of Social Workers has a section of its code of ethics (Section 4.4.4) in which it explains that social workers should abide by the code in all

…/ **continued in margin overleaf**

social-work related activities, specifically: The aims and process of social work research, including choice of methodology, and the use made of findings, will be congruent with the social work values of respect for human dignity and worth and commitment to social justice.

Several specific requirements follow. The code can be downloaded from several sites including <http://www.celtic knot.org.uk/links/baswcode.html> retrieved 2/12/2009.

• The Health Professions Council does not publish any standards specific to research since they are a multi-profession regulator and not all HPC professions would be involved in research. HPC expects all registrants involved in research to abide by the ethical standards set by their employer, education or training provider, or professional body.

• The Royal College of Nursing has a comprehensive online research resource including a clear policy on research governance and ethics. This can be found at: <http://www.rcn.org.uk/development/researchanddevelopment/policy/research_governanceethics> retrieved 02/02/2010.

• A search of HM Government website <www.direct.gov.uk> will provide links to department reports and advice on research ethics for several settings (e.g. children and families) and occupational groups (e.g. teachers).

unsure seek supervision. Seeking 'advice' is not enough since research is ongoing and has ongoing consequences. You will, therefore, need an ongoing relationship to plan your data collection and research. This is research supervision. If you are a student you should, at the very least, consult with your lecturer before proceeding. When conducting your study, do not claim to be more skilled or qualified than you really are. The general public are often very impressed by 'researchers'. Do not abuse this. If you are a student, say this from the outset.

Supervision

Although it has as much to do with good practice and increasing the likelihood that your research will be successful, supervision is also an ethical issue. If you are working towards a higher degree or professional qualification, you will be expected to have a designated supervisor for your research. Your research supervisor will be someone with more experience than you, have knowledge of a variety of approaches to research and may have a proven track record in published research. If you don't have automatic access to someone to supervise your research it is probably a good idea to find someone who can give you some guidance at least in the preparatory stages. It may be that your local university can offer support or that a senior colleague may be well placed to help. However you find one, the logical place to start working through the ethical implications of your research is under the guidance of a research supervisor. You will need a minimum of a couple of meetings, one to outline your ideas and have them vetted, and another to hear how you got on, look at your results to make sure you're treating them appropriately and check the sense behind your conclusions.

The avoidance of harm

It is axiomatic that any research you do should be designed in such a way as to avoid harm to the participants. You have a duty of care to them and to yourself. That has to be your starting point. Harm comes in a variety of forms. Of course there is physical harm but perhaps this is rarely an issue in practitioner research. In such a context, it is more likely that the potential for harm lies in two areas. Firstly, what you propose to do may cause emotional distress. For example, if your inquiry is into the effects of trauma there may be a risk that the pain of your participants is reawakened. Then it may be that the decision before you as an ethical researcher is whether to avoid such a risk altogether (which will circumscribe your inquiry) or to put some procedure or support in place for dealing with any upset and distress experienced by the participants. Secondly, harm may be caused by infringement of the participant's right to privacy. This means that you must develop a strategy for ensuring adequate and appropriate degrees of confidentiality and anonymity (see below). Last, but far from least, always put the welfare and safety of your participants first. Do not ask participants to do anything illegal. Do not put your participants at any risk at any time. Be prepared to abandon your study if it seems that harm is occurring or is likely to occur. In the prevention of harm, you should never:

- insult, offend or anger participants
- make participants believe they have harmed or upset someone else
- break the law or encourage others to do so
- contravene the Data Protection Act or any other relevant privacy legislation

Informed consent

Normally, research participants must be volunteers. Also, they must know exactly what they are volunteering for. It is unethical to deceive people by either commission or omission. If, after supervision, you conclude that the research cannot be carried out without some deception, ask yourself if the study is really worth it.

Researching ethically means that there is an obligation on you to tell your participants what you hope to discover from your research (your *research question*), how it will be done including what you will expect of them and what risks (if any) are involved (your *research method*) and to what use the outcome of or findings from your research will be put and what, if any, role they will have in the final product. It is also most important to tell them what will happen to the information they give you, who else will see it and how their confidentiality will be assured. You should also indicate the source of any funding you receive to carry out your research. You should emphasise sensitive aspects of the study, not cover them up. Research participants should be debriefed at the end of the research or at the very least at the end of their contribution to it, so that they know what the study was about and what was found (particularly as it relates to them). You should be prepared to answer all questions they may ask. Participants' own results should be made available to them. If this might cause distress you should not proceed. Seek supervision if the feedback at the end of a study is likely to cause distress. Also, be sensitive about the whole issue of involving participants in the later stages of your research. They may not care what you found so make an offer to tell them but don't force your enthusiasm on them.

It is a good idea to give your participants a copy of the ethical

Note
The last point also overlaps with the next section, in that informed consent also involves permission to be approached via personal data held on a database. For example, a member of the public may have their personal data stored on the database of an organisation, but this does not mean they can be approached by a researcher. A client's details may be stored by an agency but that does not mean that the client can be approached by a researcher from the agency without having given express permission.

guidelines governing your research. Also, in some approaches, for example, those involving participants as co-researchers, it may be possible and appropriate to incorporate their ideas and advice at various stages of the research project. Implicit in the notion of consent is the right of the participant to withdraw from the research at any stage. This should be made explicit. A good way to do all this is to come up with a 'research contract' setting out what the research is about, what will happen during its course, what you will provide for the participant and what are the rights of the participant. Each participant could then be offered a signed copy of this contract prior to the start of the research.

If you are carrying out a naturalistic observation of, for example, behaviour in public, you will not need the consent of those involved. You must, however, remember two things:

- many 'public' places are in fact private properties (for example, shopping precincts and airports) so ask permission first: including permission to conduct surveys. Think too about the security implications of your research: anyone walking around an airport with camera and clipboard risks being carted off by the police
- be discreet and respect the privacy of the people you are observing. You will not want to end up with a black eye

Another point to consider is that if your participants are not in a position to give their informed consent (possibly children, some people experiencing extreme emotional or mental distress or those with special needs), you should take special advice. In the case of children you will need the consent of the child's parent or guardian and a responsible person may need to be present or close by whilst you are conducting your study, e.g. a school teacher. In the midst of all of these 'responsible' adults, don't forget to ask the child themselves.

Confidentiality and anonymity

Social science research often involves asking questions about very personal and private experiences. Even when it doesn't there are good reasons for thinking about protecting subjects, participants and respondents from the curiosity of others. To do this, just like helping practitioners, social science researchers offer their research informants 'confidentiality' and often 'anonymity'. Rather than simply taking these as a given, it is useful to think through exactly what they mean and how, and to what degree, you can offer them in the course of your research. When you know, you can accurately inform your participants (see *informed consent* above). With respect to confidentiality, things to think about include who besides you as principal researcher will have access/limited access to the information provided by the participants. This could include, for

Note
You should also consider the advisability or necessity of Criminal Records Bureau checks for researchers working with children and vulnerable adults. It is the sign of a responsible researcher to not only ensure the safety of their participants but also to be able to create a safe research atmosphere by assuring participants, parents and carers that proper checks have been made. For more information go to: <http://www.crb.homeoffice.gov.uk>

example, your research collaborators, your research supervisor and the other participants. You should also think about under what circumstances, if any, you might breach a participant's confidentiality. This should be explicit in your research contract. Similarly, if you offer your research participants anonymity, exactly what will this mean and how will you ensure it? When reporting your research on Bill, it is probably not enough to simply call Bill 'Fred' if you then go on to offer a lot of biographical detail:

> *'Fred' is a 35-year-old, married secondary school teacher from North Manchester with two teenage sons. He presented for speech therapy following a head injury incurred in a road traffic accident in 2005.*

Now, it may be that more than one person fits this description – but probably not especially since, depending on the exact nature of the research, it may also be apparent where 'Fred' went for speech therapy and perhaps even who his speech therapist was. Anyone who knows Bill well enough will, when reading about Fred, be able to put two and two together. The easiest way to guarantee anonymity is to leave out identifiers of all kinds but, in making sense of your findings, it may be important to convey at least a limited amount of information about, for example, the age, sex, occupation, cultural heritage, class, geographical location and/or educational background of the participants. How to do this while protecting them is something you must think through beforehand.

The first thing to do is to ensure that anything you do state about your participants is actually relevant to the study. A lot of demographic information that gets collected is useless in the particular context. Does it matter to the research if your participant is married, divorced or single? If not, why collect information about marital status?

Secondly, think about how you can offer crucial information in such a way as to be at a maximum distance from any particular participant. One way to do this may be to write 'fictionalised', composite accounts. For example, if it emerges from your research that the experience of Maisie, Dianne and Pat who are in their fifties is fundamentally different from that of Kylie, Leanne and Tracey who are in their twenties, you could take the pertinent details from each set and write about a 'typical' fifty-something ('Kate') and a typical twenty-something ('Gemma'). In this way, the anonymity of Maisie, Dianne, Pat, Kylie, Leanne and Tracey is protected but the important features of your findings are conveyed. Of course, this isn't always possible and it may be essential to understanding your findings that more information is conveyed. In such cases your only option is to obtain the informed consent of your participant to the relevant degree of disclosure.

The promotion of benefit

It is vital that research does not cause harm either to the participants or researchers, or in a wider context. However a further ethical consideration concerns its benefit to the people who are participating in it and perhaps to the client community at large. If we are being scrupulously honest, research is often a selfish act. It is our burning question, our higher degree, our publication that it is about, but there is also an ethical obligation to think about the personal and *social* consequences of the research. Essentially, perhaps ideally, ethical practitioner research should enhance, for example, service provision, the client experience and/or the skills of the practitioner. So, when designing a research project with ethics in mind not only should you consider the matter of harm, but you should deliberately address the issue of benefit. Put bluntly, should any research involving clients, not aiming to yield information which will benefit clients, be done? Are clients there to be simply the objects of our curiosity?

Independence and transparency

Wherever possible, research should be conducted in such a way as to be independent and unprejudiced by vested interests. This is far from as easy as it may sound. For example, if your research is funded by an outside body it may be that this inevitably shapes the investigation and how and where findings are reported. Similarly, you as a researcher are a being with views and opinions. However careful you are, these will colour how you do your research and how you interpret what you find. This is not a bad thing. However, there is an ethical obligation on practitioner-researchers to be transparent about the things which are likely to influence their research. The easiest way to do this is, for example, to declare sources of funding and under the auspices of which (if any) organisation the research is being conducted and for you to 'locate' yourself. That is to offer enough relevant information about yourself in the context of the research you are conducting/have conducted to allow others to understand the views and opinions you bring to it so that they may understand something of the lens through which you are likely to view your research.

Honesty and integrity

Perhaps it goes without saying but part of researching ethically is to act honestly and with integrity at all times. In the context of research and scholarship, this includes avoidance of the following:
- *illegally copying tests and materials* – if you want to use an existing test, unless it is freely available in the public domain,

Note
You might have thought that the only point of ethical scrutiny is to eliminate research that is too risky. Here we are suggesting that psychotherapy ethics might also eliminate research that is too trivial. Psychotherapy ethics demand that involvement with clients is for the active benefit of clients, not the benefit of the therapist or researcher.

you must get permission and you may have to pay a fee. Similarly, unless your sponsoring institution allows it because it has a licensing agreement with the publisher, if you photocopy materials for use in your research you are liable to pay for them

- *making up data* – we shouldn't have to say this – and probably we don't have to. However, it has happened. It is unlikely that most researchers will be tempted to make up data completely but there can be a temptation to tweak data and findings to confirm an existing view. Resist the temptation. Remember that the facts are friendly and act accordingly
- *copying other people's work* and/or claiming that someone else's wording is your own. This is one of the most heinous of academic crimes – plagiarism. If you are quoting or citing somebody else's work or making use of it in any way, always give full credit to the originator

Power issues and dual roles

Something to bear in mind when designing and implementing a research project is the issue of power. Just as there is a power imbalance in the professional/client relationship so there is (or at least can be) in the researcher/participant relationship. This is especially true when the researchers seek to engage their own clients or clients of the agency or institution for which they work as participants. Research participants from marginalised groups (for example, ethnic minorities, the lesbian, gay, bisexual and transgender (LGBT) community, poorer people, young people and older people) in particular may all experience themselves as lacking power whereas they are likely to experience the researcher as having structural power – that is, power conferred by the 'expert' role, relative position in society and the (perceived or assumed) relative difference in their experience of power and powerlessness (see Proctor, 2002 for an analysis of the dynamics of power in therapy). This may very well influence what they are prepared to tell the researcher. For example, one possibility (especially for the researcher in a dual role), is that the researcher is only told what the informant thinks they want to hear. Another possibility is that a researcher who is perceived by participants as 'different' may well not be told the complete story. For example, LGBT participants may not include a straight researcher in tales of all their experiences; women may be reluctant to communicate fully with a male researcher and so on.

Marshall and Batten (2004) cite evidence that issues of power may be less problematic for a community when researchers join the community rather than enter as experts or interlopers and that creating a partnership with research participants may reduce the

Proctor, G (2002) *The Dynamics of Power in Counselling and Psychotherapy: Ethics, politics and practice.* Ross-on-Wye: PCCS Books.

Marshall, A & Batten, S (2004) Researching groups across cultures: Issues of ethics and power. *Forum: Qualitative Social Research* 5(3). Available online <www.qualitative-research.net/index.php/fqs/article/view/572> retrieved 05/04/10.

risk of unethical or unintentionally insensitive behaviour. They also state that participatory research is more likely to be effective both in terms of ethical conduct and accurate research results.

Although in this section we may seem to have concentrated on issues of power in qualitative research, the power of the researcher is at least as much an issue in quantitative approaches – particularly as the collaborative and participatory options are less available to the quantitative researcher.

Getting through an ethics approval process

Kirshen Rundle

This is an account of my personal experience in getting ethics approval for my research. The research was not designed to be an outcome study – rather the study aimed to collect the lived experience of clients in the counselling process by interviewing people at the end of their counselling. The participants were to be clients of mine from my work as a counsellor at a counselling agency, at an NHS mental health trust and in a low-security psychiatric unit.

At first all the admin seemed an irritating hindrance. But one of my supervisors was right when he told me 'Research is like decorating; you get a better result if you prepare properly first.' Once the research proposal got done I thought the ethics procedure would be easy. After all, I am a qualified and experienced counsellor so I know all about working ethically and protecting vulnerable people don't I?

It is also worth mentioning that I had three supervisors who all had experience of supervising others through this procedure. They all helped me enormously; talking with me, giving me written feedback on drafts and generally encouraging me.

When I first saw the forms, though, I immediately felt overwhelmed and a bit resentful of the effort that would be required to complete them. The university procedure didn't seem so bad but, when I looked at the NHS Integrated Research Application System (IRAS), I felt I couldn't even begin to get to grips with what they wanted. It's an online system which selects the questions you need to answer according to your project outline and enables you to complete things once for both research ethics and trust governance approval. It is complex, detailed and has over 80 questions – the completed submission was 31 pages of text with 22 enclosures. But *please don't worry*; that first glance at the procedure was the low point!

I tried to complete the IRAS pack alongside the university application. This was my first real understanding of what I had been taught in research methods lectures – that operating as a researcher is different from operating as a counsellor. My previous research had been a reflexive study of my experience of setting up a counselling service and working as a counsellor in a prison. Although I had to get consent from my clients for their stories to be used, data was in the form of *my* recollections of our work together. So I did not really operate as a researcher with them except insofar as I was constantly reflecting on the experience in order to write about it later – much the same as the constant reflection therapists and helping practitioners do anyway, particularly when we take things to supervision. This research was going to be different. I would be taking on dual roles, interviewing my own clients about their experiences of their counselling.

As a therapist I try to operate always from within the client's frame of reference, trying to ensure I stay aware of whether I am tempted to ask a question only because I want to know the answer rather than because I want clarification or feel it may help the client in their process. As a researcher I would have an agenda, would need to ask questions that I wanted the answer to. The research interviews were going to be recorded and transcribed. I was also going to be recording therapy sessions so that, as a control, they could be confirmed as being person-centred therapy by independent assessors. The issues of dual roles and power associated with these things were, I assumed, going to be central.

The other main concern was likely to be the protection of confidentiality. I have been used to managing the confidential storage of information in my work as a counsellor – keeping names and contact details separate from session notes and so on. So it was relatively straightforward for me to consider all the implications of 'how' to store research data. But there were still some issues related to 'where' that I had to think about, depending on whether participants were recruited as patients of the NHS mental health trust or not.

I think that was when I first started to enjoy working through the IRAS application. The questions are so detailed and specific that I could not copy information I had produced before. I had to think from scratch which made me consider how this project was *actually* going to operate day to day.

I sent off my application to the university ethics committee and it was approved quite quickly without the need for a meeting which encouraged me. I also applied for a date for my application to be considered by the local NHS Research Ethics Committee (REC). Once my application had been allocated to one of their meetings I had to start getting all the information and documentation together as well as signatures from my Director of Studies, and a couple of other people in senior management at the university. I also had to get letters drafted by the university confirming indemnity insurance and that I was registered as a student there. I thought this would all be quick and easy but, in the end, it took ages to organise and involved much traipsing backwards and forwards between offices on different campuses. Luckily, people were very helpful even though, in my ignorance, I had left things until the last minute.

Just after I submitted the application I was invited to present my research to a panel of clinicians and service users at a research day organised by the mental health trust I work at. For an hour we discussed my study. Many people contributed valid views about the ethics of research, what information was useful to potential participants and what was needed to protect people. I realised I had not made

enough effort to contact local service user groups, assuming that would happen once the project started.

On the day of the Research Ethics Committee meeting I was terrified. I had been told horror stories of committees that were aggressive and pernickety; I knew that person-centred therapy is not widely used in mental health services; I knew that my critical position to the medicalisation of distress might appear too radical, unprofessional or threatening. As it happened the meeting was a pleasure.

The ten members of the committee plus the REC Co-ordinator/Minuting Secretary and a senior manager from the research ethics service appeared genuinely interested in enabling research in the Trust. There were a few questions about my dual roles and the potential power imbalance, but I was able to answer these in such a way as to properly discuss the person-centred attitude to power in the therapeutic relationship. We talked of service user involvement in research and I mentioned the amendments I had made to my documentation in the light of feedback from users.

One of the committee members had been at the research day organised by the NHS trust I attended and it was agreed I could submit amendments as part of this application. It was over very quickly, I left feeling hopeful and was delighted when the provisional approval letter arrived less than a week later. All I had to do was change a couple of sentences on the participant documents and I was good to go! I was thrilled and felt immediately more confident about the whole study. Almost as if I had been accepted into some research 'fraternity'. It was a great experience and it helped my overall research process hugely.

So what is there to learn from my experience?

Get help from people who know
Access people from the population from which you will be recruiting your participants and seek their feedback on your study design and the documentation – e.g. the consent form and information for participants. I wish I had done it earlier. The input I received was invaluable.

Just answer the questions
Don't think you can copy and paste from what you have already produced in your research protocol. It is quicker and easier to approach each question afresh. That way you will make your answers specific

and relevant. It will move you forward in your planning and help to refine your design, alerting you to things you might not have thought of.

Check, check and check again

Go through all the sections and all the documentation attached to each section to make sure you provide the information required and in the right format. It helped me to put headers on everything using the IRAS terminology, to number pages and to present it neatly. That sounds so basic and I did it to help myself check things. But it was surprisingly well received by the REC Co-ordinator and the committee members. It seemed to get them on my side from the start. When the REC Co-ordinator acknowledged formally receipt of the application she commented on the 'beautiful, organised presentation' and thanked me. The Chair of the committee thanked me at the meeting and then mentioned it yet again in the formal letter which summarised the meeting and gave me ethical approval!

You may be passionate about your research project but the members of the ethics committee may not be even vaguely interested in it. I knew my justification for the research needed to be well argued but I know now that anything else that makes it easier for the committee to plough through the (*many!*) pages of your application will be appreciated.

Be prepared

Imagine the sort of questions which might be asked and make sure especially that you can answer challenges about areas that are likely to be contentious or possible limitations of the study. New research is, by definition, different from the status quo and so may be challenging to some people. I was aware that my critical stance on the medical model of mental distress might appear threatening to some members of the committee who had worked within the mental health field. I said I was aware of the issues raised and explained how I was going to minimise potential problems. The horror stories I had heard beforehand helped me here I suppose and, in the end, it was fine – all studies have limitations after all.

Enjoy it!

It is a laborious process but I gained a lot from it. It really enhanced my study design and enabled me to put myself fully in researcher rather than therapist mode. I also felt a great sense of achievement when I submitted everything; the meeting going so well was the icing on the cake; getting the approval was a wonderful cherry on top! The preparation had taken so long and at last I was going to start *doing* my research. A bit scary, but very exciting too.

Introduction

We could have called this chapter 'Preparing to conduct a research project'. Whether you think about it as preparing for research or actually getting started, there are a number of things you will need to do before you begin to collect your data (whatever form that takes). If you have decided to do some research, it's important to not get carried away with your enthusiasm to get going. Careful planning and preparation, dull though they might seem, are essential. This chapter covers the topics you will have to think about, plan and prepare for.

Formulating your research question

At the risk of stating the obvious, the starting point for any research is to decide just what it is you are interested in. You may, for example, have a hunch about something that you want to put to the test, have a curiosity about a process, have an idea about how to improve the efficiency of your service, be asked to determine the need for your service or have a desire to involve colleagues and/or clients in service development. From this will come something you can pose as a question, for example, 'What do social work clients value most about the service provided by Midshires Social Service Department?' or 'What aspect of my counselling practice do my clients find most useful?' These are 'research questions' and from them flow the whole process of research. Just how they are formulated and presented is therefore the fundamental starting block to any research project. It is essential to develop a research question that you're interested in or care about in order to focus your research. Remember that whether you are seeking to explain or to explore something, somewhere at the back of what you want to do there is a question. To develop a strong research question from your ideas, you should ask yourself these things:

- Do I know the field and its literature well?
- What are the important research questions in my field?
- What areas need further exploration?
- Could my study fill a gap? Lead to greater understanding? Develop new thinking?

Note
We took this list from:
<www.theresearchassistant.com> retrieved 02/12/2009.

- Has a great deal of research already been conducted in this topic area?
- Has this study been done before? If so, what can I learn from previous research and is there room for improvement?
- Is the timing right for this question to be answered? Is it a hot topic, or is it becoming obsolete?
- Would funding sources be interested?
- If you are proposing a service program: Is the target community interested?
- Most importantly, if you are wanting to get your research published: Will my study have a significant impact on the field?

Note

See the section on costing your research later in this chapter.

Note

These points have varying importance if you are interested in practitioner research for its own sake. For example, if you are interested in examining your own practice in a systematic way, qualitatively or to collect practice-based quantitative evidence, you may not be so interested in getting your work published, and funding might not be on your horizon either.

We are offering these points as a generic list of issues which researchers might have to engage in. It's worth working through them all, if only to eliminate those that are not relevant to your project.

One of the things to think about as you begin to engage with the idea of research is what has been called the 'So what?' test. We encourage you to think about what is likely to happen as a result of your potential research. What will be the benefit of answering your research question? Who will gain from it? What difference is it going to make? If you are seeking funding (direct, in the form of hard cash or indirect, in the form of, for example, time off your normal work schedule) then being able to make a definite statement of the potential benefits of your research is essential.

Another thing to remember about formulating your research question is to keep to what is practicable. The constraints on you are likely to include the available time and money, so pitch your question with these in mind, and there is also the question of scale. Generally speaking, you should aim to keep your research focus reasonably narrow rather than making it broad based, local rather than global. For example, it is almost impossible to answer a question like 'What causes alcohol misuse?' whereas 'What can the clients of Midshires Alcohol Treatment Centre tell me about their experiences?' may be an answerable research question.

Once you have a potential research question, it is just as well to take a critical look at it to make sure that it is a practical possibility. Some questions to ask include:

- Am I interested enough in this question to have the energy and enthusiasm to pursue the answer to it?
- Is answering the question a practical possibility?
- What type of information will I need to answer this question? Is it likely that I will be able to get it? Are there people who can help (informants/participants)? Will I have access to the resources I will need?

Later sections of this chapter will help you decide the answers to these questions. However, if the answer to one or more is 'no' then you are probably better off exploring whether there is another, more practical question to which you *could* get an answer.

Recruiting participants and gaining access

Once you have decided on your research question and done some reading around your area of interest, you will also have reached some conclusions about how you are going to collect and process your data. You will probably want to get straight on with things. What should you do next? Well, the next big step with any human inquiry is finding the human beings to participate in it. Most of us are more optimistic about this than turns out to be justified. However, there are things that you can do to improve your chances of recruiting enough people who will be able to help you answer your question.

Firstly, it is always imperative to remember that, as important as your research is to you, it doesn't necessarily matter to your potential informants/participants. It is always worth asking yourself the question 'What's in it for them?' If there is something likely to be of direct benefit to your participants (for example, perhaps you think an improvement to a service may result from your efforts) then find a way of making this clear. If you are depending entirely on the good will of people to give up their time and to make an effort on your behalf without apparent reward, then be upfront about this too. In either case (and all the intermediate ones too), not least because you need the informed consent of all involved (see Chapter 3.2 'Researching Ethically'), you are going to need to have a good, clear explanation of who you are, what you want to do and why you are asking that particular individual.

Who? What? Why?

Although the most obvious issue is that of the consent of the actual people who will be involved in the study, there are others who must also be considered. For example:

- the management of the institution where the research is to occur (perhaps involving an approach to an ethics committee)
- the staff working in the area in which you will be conducting your research
- other service users, particularly if your research will impose on them in any way at all

Note
We look at ethics and ethics committee applications in Chapter 3.2.

This may be particularly important if you are conducting your research at a location where you would normally be viewed as a friend, colleague, therapist or employee and where on occasions you will be occupying a different role – that of the researcher.

At various stages in the preparation for your research you will be required to provide either a verbal or written statement concerning it. One way to approach the question of what information should be provided is to put yourself in the position of those who you are approaching – institutions or potential co-researcher/participants.

What would *you* want to know before granting your permission to be included in a research study? The chances are that you would require a mixture of information and reassurance – what is being done, why is it being done, what is expected of me, and what safeguards do I have? Since qualitative research is congruent, open, respectful, involving and collaborative – honesty is not so much the *best* policy as the *only* one recommended for use in qualitative work, even if it were not required by ethical guidelines. Any hint of deception would distort your relationship with the participants in your study and therefore distort your findings. We take the view that this is equally true of quantitative research.

In approaching people for both permission to conduct your research and when seeking participants, it will help you to have a 'cover story'. That is, an open and honest statement of:

My name is Sarah Jones. I am a nurse working in the community with people who experience mental and emotional distress. I am employed by Midshires NHS Trust and currently studying for an MSc at Midshires University. This research project is part of my studies. I can be contacted at <s.jones@midu.ac.uk> or 0155 777 2142.

• *Who you are*
This should include at least a brief statement of your relevant background, your institutional and professional credibility and how you may be contacted.

I am investigating the experience of people who use community-based mental health services in Midshires. I want to do this by interviewing service users so they can tell me about what happens to them, what they think about the service and so on. I am going to ask people who use the service if they will give up an hour of their time to talk to me about their experience. I would like to record our conversation.

As well as gaining me my Masters degree, I hope that this research will lead to some real and effective improvements in the service in which I am employed.

• *What you are doing*
It may be that a statement of your research question will suffice but you might like to expand on it or state it in terms most likely to be easily understood by your target audience.

• *Why you are doing it*
Perhaps you are just satisfying your curiosity, perhaps you are furthering your career, perhaps you hoping to effect change of some kind.

My findings will be presented as part of my dissertation which will be put in the library at Midshires University. I will also be making them available to my work colleagues as well as the managers and users of the Midshires Community Mental Health Service in the form of a short report. If you wish, I will send you a copy of this report.

• *What will be done with the findings*
For example, who will see the result of your research? Will your findings be published? If so where? It is good practice to ask the participants what they would like to see happen with the findings. In particular, ask them if they would like to know what you find and, if they do, make sure that they get at least a summary statement (and that they know they will).

I have chosen to look at the Midshires Community Health Service because I work for that organisation and I want to know what service users think we do well and what they think we could do better. I am asking people who have been service users for at least a year if they will help me with my study.

• *How the location and subjects were chosen*
It is important to get across to potential participants why you have chosen to approach them.

• *What are the possible benefits and risks to participants*

These will vary with the context of the study but, after you have come up with your own list, you could and should ask the participants if there is anything they would like to add.

• *The promise of confidentiality and anonymity to participants (and organisation if appropriate)*

There is normally an expectation that what you are told by participants will be 'confidential' and that they will be guaranteed anonymity but it is worth thinking through exactly what, in the context of your research, this means and then being very clear about it. For example, if your research method involves the inclusion of verbatim quotes in the findings, what implications does that have for confidentiality? Similarly, if you are writing about and at least in part for a closed community then how are you going to offer anonymity? It is certainly going to take more than a simple name change. Don't make promises you can't keep and do make sure that the limitations of what you are offering are apparent to your participants and that they willingly and fully consent to these with understanding.

• *How often and for how long subjects will be required to participate*

Make a realistic estimate here – don't make their involvement sound less that it really is going to be.

• *Requests to record information – and a statement of what methods of recording are intended*

If you haven't done this already when discussing some other aspect of the process, make sure that your participant knows exactly what you will record, how you will make your record and where and how securely the record will be kept. Make sure you have the right permissions – see 'Gaining access' later in this chapter.

I hope that what you tell me will enable me to make some real, positive suggestions as to how the Midshires service might be improved and that this will make things better for you. I guess there is a chance that, as you tell me your story, old fears and troubles will be re-awakened. I will arrange for support and counselling to be available to anybody who thinks they need it. Is there anything else about being involved in this study that worries you?

What you tell me when we talk will be recorded but only I will hear the tapes. I will make a transcript of our conversation. When the study is complete I will destroy the tapes and transcripts or, if you prefer, you can have yours and do what you like with it. I will use short quotes from the interviews in my dissertation but you will not be named and I will make sure that you cannot be identified from what I write. I will not tell your key worker or anybody else in the service what you said.

In the first place, I would like to talk to you in a private setting for about an hour. Later, I would very much like to tell you about what I find out and to know your opinion about it. We can either do this by meeting again (probably 30 minutes would be long enough) or I can send you something in writing and phone you to talk about it when you have had a chance to think about it. If you like, we could even do this by email.

In our interview, I would really like to know what it is you think about the service you receive. I will not be judging you nor will I tell anyone else what you said. There are no right or wrong answers to my questions but the more open and honest we can be with each other the more I can learn and the better the results will be for us all.

Thank you for taking the time to read this introduction to me and my research. I hope that you are willing and able to take part – if so or if there is anything else you would like to know please contact me by email <s.jones@midu.ac.uk>, phone (0155 777 2142) or you can write to me (Sarah Jones, Community Mental Health Team, Midshires NHS Trust, 77 Park Way, Midtown, MT1 3QQ). If you want to help with my research, please contact me before the end of June.

Note

Some issues here include:

• to be aware of the effect of your materials, eg, do they create demand characteristics? (Chapter 2.5, p 96)

• the effect you have as a person, ie, your demeanour, how you are dressed, etc. In quantitative work these are called experimenter effects (Chapter 2.5, p 96) and we look at some qualitative dimensions of this on pp 123-4.

• the structural power of the researcher-as-expert (Chapter 3.2, p 259).

• *Clarification that the intention of the researcher is that of understanding rather than judgement*

All this requires is a similar attitude to that you would take to your client in, for example, an assessment meeting or ongoing therapy. What you are interested in is what the participant has to say.

• *Concluding comments, etc.*

Here, you are thanking the prospective participant for their time thus far, reiterating the invitation and explaining how you may be contacted and, if there is one, the time frame in which this should be done. A little tip about time and timing, you should always give people enough time to reflect on what you are asking but not so much that they delay responding and then forget altogether. Four to six weeks is probably about right. But don't forget to follow up anyone you don't hear from.

Depending on who you are addressing, you will have to modify or expand these points. We have used communicating with prospective participants as a model because whoever you have to approach for approval and permission will probably want to know how you are going to do this. However, other agencies and individuals likely to be concerned with, or have an interest in, your research may want to know more about certain aspects of it and you. Use your common sense in deciding what to include for whom – but do check if the agency or institution you are approaching has expressed protocols or requirements of prospective researchers and make sure you conform to them.

You will of course be faced with the dilemma of exactly how precisely you describe the intentions of your research. Obviously there should be no deliberate intention to mislead anyone regarding the purpose of your study, but there will also be the need to consider the degree to which prior knowledge may influence the behaviour of the participants. As yet another rule of thumb, the best policy may be to give an initial general statement of intent, which may become progressively more specific as the study develops, particularly as piloting of the study may cause a shift in focus. It should go without saying that a copy of any document describing you and/or your research should be included in your research proposal (see below).

Gaining access

Having decided where you intend to carry out your research, and who with, you may now be faced with the problem of gaining access. The degree to which this may be a difficulty will depend to some extent on your relationship with the institution within which you intend to carry out your research; this may be a reason for conducting your research at the place where you work. Your cover story may also prove to be of considerable importance in gaining the access you require, as it will set out the important elements of your research for consideration by whatever authorities will make the decision. It is likely that any public institution (and many others) will have ethical and perhaps even legal requirements you will have to look at and comply with. For example, if you wish to work with children or older, vulnerable people you may need to have had a CRB check. Certainly, as part of your research proposal, you will have to show that you have given thought to the ethical issues raised by your research and that you have satisfactorily addressed them. You may even have to have your proposal considered and approved by one or more ethics committee before you can gain access.

Note
Criminal Records Bureau checks can take some time – remember to allow enough time for this, especially if you have changed address recently.

Note
We look at ethics and ethics committee applications in Chapter 3.2 and give a real-life account on pp 260-2.

Locating gatekeepers

If you are going to be conducting research within an institution of which you are not already a member, one problem may be identifying the channels through which access may be gained. There are likely to be individuals or groups who are of particular use. Even if you are familiar with people within the institution, you should still make sure you go through the appropriate people, groups and channels. You could think of these groups as gatekeepers. You will find life much easier if you work with and through them. It is also worth remembering that the wheels of institutions may grind but slowly and that the process of gaining access may add considerably to the time required to conduct your study.

Note from research
As an example of a worst case scenario (other than being refused access) Pete remembers waiting eight months for a quorate meeting of the committee that could grant the permission he sought. And this was in an institution in which he worked and thought he had some influence! Delays like this can at least sap your enthusiasm or mean that you pass critical deadlines for accessing client groups, funding, etc.

The location of your research

Much of what we have already said about locating yourself and your research and gaining access is at least partly predicated on the assumption that you are likely to be investigating some aspect of your own practice, workplace or client group. This is because, for most practitioners, an interest in research develops out of our practice – we get curious about something we are involved with in the course of our professional activities. Research becomes an addition to, but different from, our professional role. This means that, often, the proposed site of your research will be related to your current field of operation, i.e. you will be playing the role of practitioner-researcher. It is worth looking in more detail at the advantages and disadvantages of this choice.

Advantages: The majority of the advantages of conducting research within a known location are fairly obvious. The routes for obtaining access are more likely to be well known and are likely to take less time to negotiate:

- rapport between the researcher, participants and other interested parties (for example, managers and colleagues) is likely to be well established
- the existing social network will also provide great opportunities for support and advice
- conducting research within the work location, even if it has not been requested by the organisation, may have personal and professional benefits

Disadvantages: It may be argued that researching in a familiar environment will aid the research process by providing insights and ideas, both for the actual data collection and with respect to the most appropriate methods of investigation. However, others may consider that the experience of researching in the work setting will cause problems because their existing relationships and resulting expectations may be difficult, if not impossible, to work around. Additionally, there is the problem of switching roles from practitioner to researcher – not only for you as a researcher but also for your work colleagues and clients.

The researcher/practitioner role

There are always ethical and political considerations attached to doing research. However, being a practitioner researcher, especially if you are researching some aspect of your own practice or work setting, brings a special set of its own. For example, on occasions when the researcher will be acting as observer, there is the question of how explicit this transition should be.

It may also be the case that, in the course of the research, information or practices that are undesirable or unethical may come to light – the reporting of these may have severe consequences, whilst the non-reporting may have equally severe, but different consequences. In brief, the researcher-practitioner may become compromised as a result of the dual role. Finally there is the difficulty of maintaining confidentiality when compiling the final report of the research.

If a decision is made to choose a location external to the normal working environment, the situations are more or less reversed. The advantages of the first situation become disadvantages, whilst the disadvantages of the practitioner-researcher situation become

Note

Should the researcher wear a green hat whenever they are acting as observer and a different coloured one at all other times? Well, probably not, but it might be important to be obvious and apparent about your role at all times. Even the researcher needs reminding from time to time.

Note

As helping practitioners we are already sensitive to the likelihood of problems arising from dual roles, and here is another. Holding two roles at the same time can be problematic. Furthermore, making the transition between being a practitioner and being a researcher is also challenging, eg, when it comes to ethics. Kirshen Rundle writes of her experiences in this regard on pp 260-2.

advantages when the researcher has only one role. The initial stages of the research may take longer, but the objectivity and ethical considerations are less likely to be problematic.

These issues of duality of role impinge upon choice of location and on the selection of people to work with, and both of these issues should be explicitly addressed within the research proposal.

Choosing your participants

Researchers have to find people who can give them the information they need in order to answer their research question. Often, who can be of help is clear but even so two basic problems remain. Firstly, how do you choose your participants from the (possibly many) people who can tell you what you want to know? Secondly, how do you persuade them to take part? These are problems for both the qualitative researcher where some aspect of human inquiry is likely to lie at the heart of the matter and for quantitative researchers, since active, informed participation is necessary for all contemporary ethical research. For the sake of simplicity and because what we say about it will be equally applicable to, or easily adapted for, quantitative research we are going to concentrate on discussing qualitative research in this section.

Deciding on who to ask

In quantitative research, where 'generalisation' may be an objective, establishing a representative sample of a population is of major concern. This isn't normally an issue for qualitative researchers. However, even for qualitative research, sampling still remains the best way of limiting your field of study from all of humankind down to the people or person with whom you want to work. This may be achieved through random selection, selecting a stratified sample that matches the characteristics of the population, or using a convenience/opportunity sample. A lot of qualitative research relies on the latter approach – that is, we tend to ask people who we suspect know what we are after and to whom we can reasonably easily gain access to help us with our research. It is important to remember that however you choose the people you want to work with, your rationale must be clearly explained and the criteria for selection made explicit – including reasons why certain people may be excluded from your study. For example, it may be that everybody attending a particular service could be considered for inclusion. Often this will be a far greater pool of potential informants than you need so you have to find a way of limiting those you ask to participate. There are lots of ways you could do this. For example, you could select a number of individuals at random from the service users as a whole and ask them to participate in the study (always

Note
We look at sampling and generalisation in Chapter 2.4.

Note

The requirements of sampling for a pilot study are just as stringent in qualitative research as they are in quantitative. This is simply because since a pilot study is a test of your procedure from which you can foresee problems and avoid pitfalls; you are more likely to do this if the pilot sample resembles the actual sample as closely as possible.

Note

These points also echo the principles of conducting ethical research, see Chapter 3.2. They all in some way address the issue of transparency and integrity in research.

This also intersects with the issue of structural power of the researcher which we look at briefly on p 259. We hope it does not need emphasising to health and social care practitioners who would normally be aware of the power implicit in their roles as helpers. The same concerns apply to the role of researcher.

invite at least a few more than you think you need, some will say no, some will fall by the wayside and it is a lot easier to deal with an excess of data than to have to go out and find more). Alternatively, you could ask for volunteers (using news sheets, notice boards, messages to clients via your colleagues and so on) or for recommendations from third parties (managers, colleagues, service users). Don't forget that, if you are going to do a pilot study (which is desirable if at all possible), then as far as is possible, the people taking part in the pilot should resemble the final selection of people for the study proper.

Giving potential participants a reason

As researchers, we depend on the goodwill of the researched and those who control routes to them. Here, we are particularly concerned with the former. Sometimes, we are so excited by our proposed research that we unconsciously assume that everybody else will be too, but why should they be? After all, there is profit in the research for us (a higher degree or professional qualification, a publication, promotion, the itch of curiosity well and truly scratched) but what about the participants? It is always worth asking the question 'What's in it for my participants?' To some extent, we can depend upon the altruistic nature of people. A lot of us like to help – just as long as we are not too disadvantaged by our efforts and as long as we feel appreciated. However, offering your participants reasons and encouragement to join your endeavours is always a good idea. Precisely what this might be will vary with who they are but there are some things that are worth considering:

- be very clear about your aims and objectives and explain why these are important. Be upfront about what you hope to gain from the research
- if there is a possible advantage in, for example, the form of improved service, make this clear both in your cover story and in any direct approach
- be nice to your participants, that is, be grateful but not obsequious or smarmy, keep them as informed as they want to be and be appropriately thankful to them
- build and maintain rapport with your participants. It is essential to be interested in what the participants are doing. Be polite, look happy, be grateful. Occasionally research may put us in contact with disturbed, disturbing or abusive people. It is the researcher's job to try to understand the world of the participant or respondent – not to judge or run away too soon
- involve your participants in aspects of your research other than merely as providers of raw data. Perhaps invite them to comment on your interim findings (their comments then become material for a further refinement) and on your ultimate discussion. Unless

they have specifically declined the offer, make sure that they get a copy (or at least a digest) of whatever you write up about your research. Acknowledge their efforts in your writing

Although the above will often be enough to get you the number and quality of responses you want, there are other tactics you can consider. For example, what about offering a small reward? This could be in the form of a gift for everybody you interview (a small bunch of flowers, some chocolates) or perhaps entry into a draw with the winner taking a somewhat bigger prize. If your practice usually involves clients or patients incurring a charge, you could offer a 'free' service conditional on helping with the research by, for example, being interviewed or writing about their experience. If you adopt this strategy you might consider over-recruiting. We have known a researcher to meet with his participants in the pub to review and comment on preliminary findings – he bought everybody a drink. Really, what we are saying is that people like to be valued and to be involved and you should make sure that they are.

> **Note from research**
> When he was researching the process of a psychodrama group Paul did this and although everybody took the free offer in its entirety, only about 60% kept their side of the bargain and one or two only sketchily.

> **Note**
> Remember that participants' anonymity and confidentiality need to be protected in most social sciences research. Would the example of meeting participants in the pub get your ethical approval?

Costing your research

Doing research costs money. Whether you are conducting your research on behalf of an organisation, as a student on a course or as an individual practitioner-researcher, there will be costs involved and these should be considered, particularly if you are to shoulder the burden yourself. You may also wish to look for ways to lighten the load in the form of sponsorship or support. Getting some realistic idea of what your costs will be before you start is essential if you are going to apply for funding and a good idea in any case. But just what do you need to consider?

Perhaps the first and most obvious cost (but one novice researchers in particular tend to overlook) is that incurred to cover the time of the researcher(s). Mostly, we get away without considering this one to any great extent because it is taken for granted as part of our employment or our studies. However, if as a practitioner you are researching rather than practising (or doing associated admin tasks) then either something else doesn't get done or someone else has to do it. This is costly and you need to address this at least to the extent of engaging with and getting the consent of your managers and colleagues. If you are applying for funding (in terms of money or time) then you must come up with a realistic estimate of how much time you will need, over what period and how much this is going to cost. You could calculate this as an hourly rate but if you do you should be aware that how much your time actually costs is more than simply what you are paid (institutions and businesses have what they call 'oncosts' for their employees including, for

Note
Ask your employer what your oncosts would be. Reckon for the true cost of replacing you to be anything between 1.25 and 2.00 times your actual salary.

Note
People are increasingly doing research using 'free' electronic media, such as emails. While this might well avoid the costs of photocopying and postage, do remember that a proper interactive questionnaire that *is secure* (participant information must be confidential), will take more than basic computer skills and more time than just bashing off a few emails.

Note
Estimating how much time your research will take (and cost and the other parameters covered in this short section) are all best worked out with another person to help you. If you have a research supervisor, they are the obvious choice. Otherwise a colleague who knows your work and research plans will be a good choice. Two heads are definitely better than one.

example, pension contributions and holiday pay – your actual cost to your employer is your salary plus oncosts). If you are in private practice it is equally important to know how much it will cost you to do your research and how you can cover this cost.

The second consideration is that of expenses you will incur and those of your participants that you agree to cover. Probably the chief of these will be transport but do think it through to determine whether there are others. Next, we come to materials. This includes library fees, photocopying costs (if your college or place of work does not have a licensing agreement this may very well include a fee payable to the originator of the material you copy), postage (think about all the SAEs you may send out if you use a questionnaire), phone calls (consider using email where possible – it might be cheaper and some people prefer it) and any clerical support you decide to use, as well as any equipment you decide to use (borrow what you can for free, hire what you can't, buy as a last resort or if you have further use for it). If you are going to produce a dissertation or thesis you will also have to cover the cost of typing, printing and binding. For every project there will be costs we haven't listed here – and the likelihood is that there will always be ones you didn't think of at the outset, so you had best add on a bit for 'contingencies'.

Timing your research

Your research will take time – and in our experience almost always more of it than you at first thought. Organising your research requires that you make a realistic assessment of how long it will take in total and how long each constituent stage will take. You can then come up with a timetable.

We can regard the research process as containing three major phases – planning, implementation and reporting. Each of these will require time, though to some extent each may run concurrently with another. Inevitably, you will be working to a deadline, and while this may prove to be flexible, this simply means that the time available for other activities also becomes restricted.

In the planning stage, the literature search is likely to take up the bulk of the time required. Remember that you must also read and extract information from the sources you identify. Although the temptation is always there to wait for one more source, it is important to set a deadline and stick as closely as possible to it. Try to be as ruthless as possible – this can be a self-development challenge to many of us pathological perfectionists.

When planning the research, remember that not only is your time involved but also that of others. Besides giving reasonable consideration to others when placing demands on their time, make sure that you are aware of any restraints on their availability. It may appear obvious to readers, but be aware of seasonal variations in the activities of organisations; for example, do not plan to conduct a survey of college staff during the summer.

Wherever possible, negotiate some sort of time allowance with employers that is also recognised by colleagues. This will make it easier to arrange visits or interviews within working hours; any other arrangement may make it difficult to gain access to people.

Be sure to draw up a research timetable. Whatever your timetable looks like, make sure that a degree of flexibility is built in; you cannot legislate for the illness of others, transport difficulties, machinery breakdown, incompatibility of computer equipment, etc. It is also worth considering drawing up deadlines after which alternative methods or approaches will be considered rather than sticking to an approach that is obviously becoming unfruitful.

It is also true that your research is unlikely to be as important to others as it is to you and that their full co-operation and immediate attention cannot be guaranteed at all times. Expect the unexpected, the unforeseen disaster and the inevitable frustration, and you will only be mildly surprised when it proves to be even worse than that!

Your research proposal

Once you have a research question, for most research, particularly if it is going to be done under the auspices of an institution or you hope to attract funding or support of some other kind, you are going to have to write a formal research proposal. A research proposal is a statement of who you are, what your question is, why it is relevant and important, how you intend to carry out your research, with whom, what the resources implications are and so on. Even if your research is totally independent it is good discipline to go through the process of thinking through your research in the way necessary to write a research proposal. To do this effectively you are going to have to think about everything we have so far told you about in this chapter – and other things as well.

Your sponsoring institution, if you have one, will almost certainly have rules which determine exactly what will have to go in your research proposal and how long it must or can be. Likewise, if you are applying for funding the grant-awarding body you are approaching will probably have a preferred format for research proposals it will consider. Your starting point is always to find out how whomsoever you are writing for wants a research proposal to look. You then write yours accordingly. However, whatever the required form, your proposal is likely to include more or less the same type of information and to draw on all the things we have already told you about in this chapter.

Note
Kirshen Rundle writes about how important presentation and adhering to the required format and style of the proposal is on p 261. Although she is writing specifically about ethics committee requirements, the general point is equally important.

IF YOU WANT TO KNOW MORE ABOUT
writing a research proposal

a web search will bring up several university websites (from the UK and the US – some require a student ID, others are free-access) with good advice and guidance, or take a look at:

Bell, J (2005) *Doing Your Research Project: A guide for first-time researchers in education, health and social science* (4th edn). Maidenhead: Open University Press.

Punch, K (2006) *Developing Effective Research Proposals* (2nd edn). London: Sage.

It may be the case that you look on the writing of a research proposal as an inconvenience prior to conducting the study, but a well-constructed proposal offers many opportunities:

- firstly, it gives a focus to the planning stages of a project. The proposal will require details of all elements of the proposed work. In turn, this will aid the development of a well-structured piece of research. A frequently used analogy of the research proposal is that of a blueprint. From consideration of the plans, any defects can be identified and corrected before the project commences. Additionally, it will allow consultation with others and viewing from different perspectives, once again offering the opportunity for alterations to be made before they become too costly and time consuming
- the proposal may also act as an indicator of the competence of the researcher, and its acceptance may therefore be beneficial in terms of the confidence of the researcher – often an issue with first-time researchers
- you should also remember that eventually there must be a written report of the research. Much of the preparatory work will be of benefit in producing the final report

Whatever the purpose of your proposal (academic or professional) and whatever the subject of your proposal, two requirements should predominate, those of *clarity* and *organisation*. The purpose of your proposal is to inform others of what is intended and will therefore require clear statements of aims and methods. As the research is unlikely to have arisen in a vacuum, the proposal will also have to place the research in some sort of theoretical or situational context (or both). The person who reads the proposal may not have the same level of knowledge about the topic area that you will have developed through the various stages of the construction of your proposal. They will be seeking *clarity of explanation* rather than a megalith of jargonistic, pedagogic obfuscation (see what we mean?) of the main issues masquerading as a demonstration of your academic rigour and prowess. So, your research proposal is to be clear and both succinct and comprehensive!

Whatever structure is used for your proposal, and how much resemblance it has to the proposal format suggested here, the need for organisation is paramount. It should be clear to whoever reads the proposal exactly where particular types of information will be located within the document. The sections should be identified in a clear and consistent manner:

Proposed research: Your research proposal needs a title. This is the headline, the thing that is going to invite the reader to continue.

It may be that your research question itself will serve but you may want to reframe or rephrase it for this purpose.

Aims: What are you hoping to achieve as a result of your research? Come up with two or three major aims that encapsulate what it is about and state them briefly but clearly. A bullet-point list is a good idea.

Background: This section should establish a context for and background to the research. You need a brief statement indicating from where the idea for this research comes. This may include a historical overview (what is already known, the starting point for your work), something about why what you propose to do is topical (perhaps it relates to new legislation or a change in policy or direction) and how it relates to your work situation or practice. You should define your terms and provide a background by making links to existing theories and reference to previous research. If you feel it is appropriate, you may wish to include a personal statement (that is 'locate yourself') as to why you have chosen the particular topic or area. This should include why it is relevant to you and what makes you a suitable person to carry out this research. If the research is concerned with a particular organisation, a description of the organisation, identification of its aims and objectives, plus some historical detail will be appropriate.

Literature review: You should contextualise your research by writing a short review of the relevant literature. What is already known? Who has raised questions similar to yours? Who has indicated the importance of what you are setting out to find? And so on. Your task here is to provide a summary of key points and key texts rather than an in-depth critique (although that will be the task when you write up what you find). Sometimes, the literature review can be incorporated into the 'Background' section.

Note
To do this, it may help you to look at what we have written about references and referencing in Chapter 3.4.

Rationale: As an optional extra, when you have discussed the background to your research and reviewed the relevant literature, you can make a short, clear statement of your rationale for the research.

Methodology: Firstly, METHODOLOGY and method are not synonyms. Method is the precise way something is done (the recipe if you like which is why some people prefer the term 'procedures') but a methodology is a system of methods, arguably it is about the philosophy of an approach to doing something rather than a way of doing something. So your methodology has to do with the thinking behind your approach to research rather than the way you actually do it although, of course, the latter flows from the former. So here

METHODOLOGY A coherent collection of theories and practices relating to a field of inquiry; the underlying principles and rules of organisation of a process of inquiry.

you are writing about the overall approach you will take to your research and why. You may also like to explain why this leads you to particular ways of data collection and data processing and name your research method. You could consider explaining why possible alternatives were not chosen.

Procedures and materials: In this section you will concentrate on the practicalities of the research, how it will be conducted, where, with whom and why. You should ensure that sufficient detail is provided of all aspects of the way in which you propose to do this. Unless it is clear what is intended, and sufficient detail is provided so as to determine the suitability of the chosen method, the proposal is unlikely to be successful. However, the proposed method should be realistic in terms of time, resources and the experience of the researcher. It is probably best to write to the following subheadings:

- *participants*: This section should provide a description of the people chosen for the study – how they will be chosen and why. You should also provide a description and justification of the location(s) at which the study will be conducted
- *materials*: What are you going to need to collect your data? This section should begin by listing and/or describing all materials to be used in the study. Where appropriate (e.g. if the study involves use of a published questionnaire) the choice of materials should be explained/justified. If any 'home-grown' materials are to be used, these should be described, with reference made to their development – including the piloting of the material. This is particularly important in the case of questionnaires/structured interviews
- *data collection*: This is your opportunity to explain the nature of your data and how you will collect it. If this is to happen in stages, make this clear especially if later stages are contingent on what happens in the earlier ones
- *data analysis/interpretation*: Here, explain what you will do with your data once you have collected it. Will you be processing your data as the research proceeds or will it all be processed when data collection is complete?
- *ethical issues*: You should provide a review of ethical considerations involved or raised by your study. Where appropriate you should offer an explanation of how ethical issues impact upon the proposal and at what points your decisions may have been influenced by ethical considerations
- *pilot study*: It is a good idea to indicate here how and when you will carry out your pilot study and how it will relate to each of the above sections
- *timetable*: Indicate how long you expect your research to take and what will happen when

- *resource considerations*: You should also include some appropriate references to financial or other resource considerations
associated with your proposed research. Be realistic about this
especially if you are applying for funding. There will be a cost
for the services of anybody else involved and for the hire of
equipment. Don't forget that there is also a cost to your time,
you will have transport costs and you may have to pay the
transport costs of others. Allow a realistic amount for all this.
Remember too that, say, even your literature search can take
many hours and cost many pounds. For example, we told you
that some libraries charge for the inter-library loan service.
Accurate costing is particularly important if your proposal is to
be read by someone who controls funding

As we said at the start of this section, you may well have a specified
format and a specified number of words for your proposal (as well
as a deadline). Of course, these should be adhered to. How long
each section will be will vary according to the individual piece of
research, so the length of other sections may have to be altered to
accommodate this. However, skimping on the amount of information
offered, or padding out with unnecessary information are not options
that should be considered.

Note
Yes, you have to negotiate a course between the devil and the deep blue sea. Your supervisor will help and give you invaluable feedback on your efforts.

A final point to be remembered is that what you are producing
is a proposal – not tablets of stone. As the project unfolds, one or
more aspects may change, through interest, development or
necessity, so a flexible approach is required. If one aspect of the
proposal changes, for example, the method or sample of subjects –
this may have an effect on other aspects, such as the objectives.
Flexibility should not be presented as a lack of consistency between
aspects of the proposal – a feature which will not enhance the
likelihood of acceptance.

Your pilot study

Let's move on a bit. You have submitted your proposal, it's been
vetted by the ethics committee, you have funding in place and/or
have been released from your other duties. It is time to start. So,
where do you begin? Well, the best thing to do is to check that
everything is in working order. What you need to do is pilot your
method.

A pilot study should be a vital part of your research planning.
The main purpose of your pilot study will not be to collect data or
information, but to test or clarify as many aspects of your proposed
research as possible. For example, it is obvious that if you are
proposing to use a questionnaire or interview, a significant aspect
of the pilot study will be to identify any problems with the

questionnaire or interview schedule. However, through this process other problems may emerge that can be dealt with before the study proper. As the pilot study should be as close as possible to the actual study you intend to conduct, the people used in your pilot study should be as similar to the people used in the final study as possible – so the pilot will also help you identify any problems with obtaining persons to work with. It should also be made clear to subjects that they are in fact taking part in the piloting of a piece of research rather than the final piece of research itself, though all the other ethical considerations relating to treatment of subjects should obviously still apply.

Practical considerations of the pilot: Perhaps the first question you may ask about your pilot study is how many people should be involved. As the pilot is to be used to fine-tune your final study, the main consideration should be that enough people are used to give a real representation of the intended final study and to explore all the problems that are likely to arise – without overdoing it! Every study is different and what you will need to pilot for yours, only you can know. However, there are a few things we can suggest to give you the flavour:

- if you are conducting a questionnaire or interview, besides checking that the questions are clear and precise or even necessary, it will also help determine whether the instructions and information given to participants/respondents are clear and sufficient and also to check the time required for conducting or administering the questions. Again, whilst using people that represent your final targets will help answer some of the above questions – such as the timing and clarity – it will be essential to consult colleagues and supervisors to check on such aspects as appropriateness of questions, and whether there are any important omissions
- if observational methods are to be used, the pilot will help investigate elements such as: how participants respond to being observed; how well the recording technique operates; are the categories of behaviour being considered comprehensive or realistic?
- piloting will also help fine-tune yourself – are you presenting yourself as you would wish. Are there any difficulties in establishing rapport with subjects?

Finally, conducting the pilot study may also throw up questions that you had not previously considered, and may in fact add or subtract elements to or from the research that had originally been proposed.

Introduction

You have collected and processed your data and thought about your findings and what they mean. This *could* be enough but it might be argued that the research process isn't complete until what you have done and what you have found is in the public domain or at least available to peers in some other way. So an almost inevitable consequence of research is that you are going to have to present your work to others. If you are studying for a higher degree or professional qualification you will be expected to write a thesis or dissertation. This counts as putting things in the public domain, although you may also want to think about writing one or more papers for publication in academic journals based in your research.

Similarly, if you are conducting research for your institution, company or service there may be a preferred way of presenting it internally (for example, as a report, via an in-house journal or as a PowerPoint presentation to colleagues and/or clients). Otherwise there are two major forums for the presentation of research: as a paper in an academic journal (or membership-based magazine) or a conference presentation. Of course there is nothing to stop you presenting your work in two or more of these ways – in fact we would encourage you to do that. The more widely disseminated practitioner research becomes the more we will all benefit.

Presenting your work

However you choose to present your work, the first rule is to find out what is expected and to conform to that expectation. If you are writing a thesis or dissertation your university or college will have a preferred format for it. This will include word count, how it is to be bound and so on. Similarly, any journal to which you think you might submit your work will have 'instructions for authors'. You should locate these and make sure your paper is in the form the journal expects. Editors can at the least get very annoyed, and in some cases reject the paper, if it doesn't. The same applies when you decide to present at a conference. For example, there will be clear guidelines as to what is expected in terms of an abstract and the length of time you will have in which to present so make sure that your presentation fits. Timing a

Note from research
As co-editor of a leading academic journal, Paul found it the best policy for all to return to the authors papers that clearly did not conform to the house style.

Note

Beginning researchers, including students on diploma and degree-level courses may find a poster a good way of presenting their work to others. Posters as a method of presentation are not restricted to presenting emerging research or early results at conferences.

If you are not familiar with the notion of poster presentations, we do mean literally a poster – a large A2 or A1 piece of paper summarising your research using various illustrative devices (just filling the whole sheet with text would make for an extremely boring display and people would simply move on to the next one without reading yours). A good resource for planning a poster presentation can be found at <http://lorien.ncl.ac.uk/ming/dept/tips/present/posters.htm> retrieved 03/04/2010.

Note

This looks like a long list and you only have a limited time, but many of the items can be covered with brief, well-chosen words. It can be a daunting prospect, so if you have no idea at all what a presentation might be like, try to get to a research conference locally or nationally which has short presentations of modest research projects, eg:

• The British Association for Counselling and Psychotherapy Research Conference is held annually: see <www.bacp.co.uk/research>

• The Royal College of Nursing Research Society organises annual International Nursing Research Conferences: <www.rcn.org.uk/development/researchanddevelopment/rs>

• The British Association for Social Work organises specialist events, many with a research element. Look on their events page: <www.basw.co.uk/pubevents>

presentation isn't easy. It is a good idea to have a core of things you must get in, some things that you would like to get in but could cut out if time goes more quickly that you thought. It is also a good idea to have some extra things to include if everything goes more quickly than you had imagined. If it isn't catered for separately, make sure you allow enough time for questions.

Increasingly, conferences not only allow the formal presentation of papers as part of the proceedings but also the submission of posters summarising research. There may be a formal slot in which posters are presented but the general idea is that delegates can look at them as and when they fancy. Designing a good poster is an art and we won't go into it here except to say that the conference organisers will have rules about posters and their presentation. If you want to use this format, find out what the rules are and get your poster right.

By now you are probably thinking, yes, OK, I get that bit about not upsetting the university, editors and conference organisers by ignoring the rules but what do I actually include when I present my work? In some ways this is one of those 'how long is a piece of string?' questions. However, whatever the format and regardless of how traditional or unconventional your research and the way you choose to present it is, the basics to include are:

• *what is this about?* This may include a statement of your research question and/or your aims but it may be that these have been refined and redefined in the course of your research. Also, you may only be reporting on part of what you did

• *what was my thinking about this research?* Something about the background to your study (including the literature) and why you chose the approach you used

• *what did I do?* Your method, the materials and procedures you used and the participants who took part. Also how you processed your data

• *what did I find?* What was the result of processing your data (that is the manipulating of numbers or working with stories)?

• *what sense do I make of what I found?* This is about how you interpret your findings. Again, here you should make links to the literature and illustrate your points by reference to the data and/or the findings

• *where would I go from here?* Consider what was good about what you did, what was less good (what didn't lead you where you hoped and what would you now do differently?) and what questions are raised as a result of your research and how you think they could be answered

Another suggestion we have to make is that before you write, you should read. If you are writing a thesis or dissertation, go to the library shelves and find a few that relate to what you have done and/or the way you have done it. Notice how they have been written and take that as a starting point. Similarly, if you are thinking about submitting a paper to a particular journal take a look at recent editions of it to see the acceptable form. As we mentioned in the margin on the previous page, the same applies to conferences – notice how others present and what the posters look like. We are not inviting you to slavishly copy the way others have done things but to use their work to get an idea of the conventions – and their innovations – and to inspire you to do even better.

We have deliberately chosen not to go into the detail of how to structure a thesis or paper. We have two main reasons for that. Firstly, to do a thorough job requires more space than we have and it is quite easy to find out more elsewhere. Secondly, we want to encourage you to write or present in a way that suits you and what you have done. However, whatever form your presentation takes, it is essential that you know something about how to indicate who has informed your work. This is usually done by 'referencing' in a conventional way.

References and referencing

In Chapter 3.1 we told you about how to find things in the literature. Now you need to know a bit about how to incorporate what you find into your writing. The most important thing to realise is that when you use the ideas of others you must always acknowledge your source. This is the art of referencing which is an essential skill of an academic writer.

What is a reference?

Simply put, making a reference is a way of pointing to the relevant work of another. When you cite or quote something in your writing, you are making a reference. Conventionally, all books, papers, etc. you cite or quote in your writing are listed in an organised way at the end of your thesis, dissertation or paper in a section headed 'References'. Another convention less common in social science research is to give references as footnotes.

A reference is a way of indicating to the reader not only where you got an idea from but where to find out more about it. Not only does this avoid a charge of plagiarism but, more importantly, it allows others to check your interpretation and understanding for themselves. A reference is also a way of honouring precedent, helps you to explain who has a view similar to, or different from, your own and indicates the range of ideas there are about a particular topic. Referencing is done systematically most commonly by using the Harvard scheme, American Psychological Association (APA) scheme or some variation

IF YOU WANT TO KNOW MORE ABOUT
writing or presenting a paper

there is lots of guidance available on the Internet, and some printed sources we found are:

Markham, R, Markham PT & Woddell, ML (2001) *10 Steps in Writing the Research Paper* (6th edn). Happauge, NY: Barron's.

Porter, S (2007) Writing and publishing a research paper in a peer-reviewed journal. *The Journal of Applied Research in the Community College 14*(2), 115-23.

Thody, A (2006) *Writing and Presenting Research*. London: Sage.

Note

'References' are not the same as a 'bibliography' – the former is a list of authors and works from which you have extracted ideas and words to use in the presentation of your own ideas; the latter is a descriptive list of books and papers which are relevant to the general area – you may have read them but you have not necessarily cited or quoted them.

Note

The APA scheme is very detailed and continually developing. It is published as a manual and cut-down versions can be found in various places online. The paper version (running to over 400 pages) is:

The American Psychological Association (2009) *Publication Manual of the American Psychological Association* (6th edn). Washington, DC: American Psychological Association.

Note

Each journal has its own preferred scheme, so when submitting a paper, make sure you find out what is required and make sure your referencing conforms to the 'house style'.

Rogers, CR (1959) A theory of therapy, personality and interpersonal relationships, as developed in the client-centered framework. In S Koch (ed) *Psychology: A study of science, Vol. 3: Formulations of the person and the social context* (pp 184–256). New York: McGraw-Hill.

Mearns, D & Thorne, B (1998) *Person-Centred Therapy in Action*. London: Sage.

of them (you must be consistent and use only one scheme, not change conventions partway through). Basically any work you cite or quote should be indicated in a conventional way in your text at the point at which you make the citation or quotation and then, also in a conventional way, be given in full in the last section of your writing which will be headed 'References'.

Citing and quoting

When you indicate the source of an idea but use your own words, you are 'citing'; when you use the exact words of another, you are 'quoting'. In both instances, the convention is to write the surname of the author followed (in parentheses) by the year of publication of the work and the page or pages in which the ideas you are discussing or presenting appear. For example:

Rogers (1959: 249) indicates that when the individual perceives such unconditional positive regard, conditions of worth are weakened and unconditional positive self-regard is strengthened.

is a *citation* because it represents Rogers thought without using his actual words.

Alternatively:

Mearns and Thorne (1988: 59) define unconditional positive regard thus:

Unconditional positive regard is the label given to the fundamental attitude of the person-centred counsellor towards her client. The counsellor who holds this attitude deeply values the humanity of her client and is not deflected in that valuing by any particular client behaviours. The attitude manifests itself in the counsellor's consistent acceptance of an enduring warmth towards her client.

is a quotation because it uses the actual words of Mearns and Thorne. Notice that in both cases the reader is pointed towards the exact location of the relevant words – that is, a page number (or, where appropriate, a range of pages) is given. This has long been the convention when quoting but it is increasingly common for citations too as you will observe from your reading of recent books and current journals. Sometimes the separator between date and page number is a comma (1999, 7) rather than a colon (1999: 7) and sometimes the numeral indicating the page is preceded by 'p.' (1999, p. 7).

There is likely to be a preferred option for whomsoever you are writing; you have a choice but however you do it, it is good practice verging on the essential to indicate to which page or pages of a particular work you are referring. This is because unless you point the reader to exactly what it is that is relevant to your argument they cannot pursue your point for themselves. For example, if you think that something Rogers wrote in *On Becoming a Person* is pertinent to your research and you indicated this by writing 'As Rogers (1961) said …' how is the reader supposed to know on which of the 400 or so pages this thought was conveyed? The reader must be able to check the exact context of the quote to appreciate its full meaning. Quoting out of context is not good academic practice.

Something else to notice in the above example is that, when there are two authors, both names are cited (and in the order in which they appear in the original). When there are three or more authors, it becomes tedious to write (and to read) a handful of names over and over again, so it is normal to cite just the first in the main body of the text and to use the Latin abbreviation 'et al.' (meaning 'and other people') to indicate that there are others, and *all* the names should appear in the actual reference section.

If you quote or cite authors sharing a surname, then it is usual to use their initials in the main body of the text. For example, using the person's initials in the citation – e.g. C. R. Rogers (1961: 65) and N. Rogers (1985: 7) – distinguishes between Carl Rogers and his daughter Natalie who is a practitioner, academic and author in her own right. Also, if you cite or quote more than one work of a particular author with the same year of publication, it is usual to use the letters of the alphabet as 'suffixes' to distinguish these. So, for example, if you refer to three works published by Anne Smith in 1999, the first to which you refer becomes Smith (1999a), the second Smith (1999b) and the third Smith (1999c). If, in the body of your text, you quote any one of these for a second or subsequent time, you use the same letter as before. In your reference section, these works are presented in the order in which you refer to them, i.e. a before b before c.

Another common convention is demonstrated above. When a large section of text is being quoted, it is now usual to separate the quotation from the main text and to use a smaller point size. The rule (this does vary between publications) seems to be 40/50 words or more, separate and/or indent the quote, less than 40/50 words, run the quote on in the text but indicate that it is a quotation by using quotation marks. For example, Bozarth (1998: 82) unambiguously declares 'unconditional positive regard is the curative factor in client-centered therapy'.

Don't relax just yet though, there are different conventions

Rogers, CR (1961) *On Becoming a Person.* Boston: Houghton Mifflin.

An illustration of the differences between APA and Harvard style in two straightforward references

APA

Rennie, D. L. (2000). Aspects of the client's conscious control of the psychotherapeutic process. *Journal of Psychotherapy Integration, 10*(2), 151–167.

Wilkinson, S. (2000). Breast cancer: A feminist perspective. In J. M. Ussher (Ed.), *Women's health: Contemporary international perspectives* (pp. 230–237). Leicester: BPS Books.

Harvard

Rennie, D. L., 2000. Aspects of the client's conscious control of the psychotherapeutic process. *Journal of Psychotherapy Integration,* 10(2), pp. 151–67.

Wilkinson, S., 2000. Breast cancer: a feminist perspective. In J. M. Ussher, ed. *Women's health: Contemporary international perspectives.* Leicester: BPS Books, pp. 230–7.

See if you can spot the differences!

You will also find that the Harvard style has been liberally interpreted by different universities. Although claiming to prefer Harvard style, various university websites show a range of differences.

Bozarth, J (1998) *Person-Centered Therapy: A revolutionary paradigm.* Ross-on-Wye: PCCS Books.

Note
The variations of rules regarding speech and quotation marks are too numerous even to list. You will need to pay attention to details if you want your work to have a trouble-free passage.

Cooper, M (2008) *Essential Research Findings in Counselling and Psychotherapy.* London: Sage.

regarding speech and quotations within a quotation. These conventions concern whether you should use single ' ' or double " " quotation marks, and how you should indicate a quotation within a quotation. The APA requirement is as follows:

> Cooper (2008, p. 47) helpfully explains "This is known within the counselling and psychotherapy fields as the 'research allegiance effect.'"

Some other things of which you should be aware when you are quoting are that you should preserve the spellings of the original (did you notice our use of the American spelling 'centered' above in the Bozarth quote?) and, normally, also any emphasis in the original text – by this we mean that any word which is stressed (conventionally by the use of *italic* script when using Roman and vice versa) in the original is also stressed in the quotation. You would indicate this as follows:

McLeod, J (2007) *Counselling Skill.* Maidenhead: Open University Press.

> McLeod (2007, p. 77) points out that "Sensitivity to the person's 'helping belief system' lies at the heart of competence in working effectively with *difference*". (original emphasis)

Bozarth, J (1998) *Person-Centered Therapy: A revolutionary paradigm.* Ross-on-Wye: PCCS Books.

Note
Here we show how to do it in APA style. Remember that other styles will be different, perhaps using the phrase 'my emphasis' or 'emphasis added' either in the text or at the end of the quote in brackets. APA style incorporates the expectation that anything you quote, you will quote scrupulously, and therefore the use of a term such as 'original emphasis' is not used.

Sometimes, if you want to make a point, you may choose to stress a word in your quotation which was not stressed in the original. This is OK but you must indicate that you have done so, for example:

> Bozarth (1998, p. 83) unambiguously declares "unconditional positive regard is *the* [italics added] curative factor in client-centered therapy".

How to present a reference
Conventionally, although different kinds of works are not presented differently in the main body of the text – i.e., the format 'author (year: page)' – is used regardless of whether the work is a book, a journal, an edited volume or a website, they are distinguished in the reference section at the end of the work, again in a conventional manner. The normal conventions are as follows (but do check the requirements of the journal, publisher or institution you hope will publish your work):

Reference to a book written in its entirety by the person (or persons) who you are citing or quoting always take the form:
Author (surname, initials)/Year of publication/ Title (usually written in italics)/Place of publication: Publisher.
For example:

> Robson, C. (1993) *Real World Research: A Resource for Social Scientists and Practitioner Researchers.* Oxford: Blackwell.

Journals are referred to thus:

Author (surname, initials)/Year of Publication/Title of the article or paper/Title of the Journal (in italics)/volume number (also in italics, or bold)/part number (in parentheses)/page numbers.

For example:

> Ablon, J. S., & Jones, E. E. (1998). How expert clinicians' prototypes of an ideal treatment correlate with outcome in psychodynamic and cognitive-behavioural therapy. *Psychotherapy Research 8*(1): 71-83.

When quoting from a work which appears in an edited book, the form is:

Author (surname and initials)/Year of Publication/Title of the paper or chapter/Editors (usually with initials followed by surname, followed by (ed.))/Title of the book, (in italics)/Place of Publication: Publisher.

For example:

> Jones, A. (2000). Exploring young people's experience of immigration controls: The search for an appropriate methodology. In B. Humphries (Ed.), *Research in social care and social welfare: Issues for debates and practice* (pp. 102–118). London: Jessica Kingsley.

For websites, there is no established convention but here we illustrate the American Psychological Association (APA) preferred protocol:
Author/Year of Publication/Title of paper/Web Address in Full.

For example:

> Forester-Miller, H., & Davis, T. (1996). *American Counseling Association: A practitioner's guide to ethical decision making.* Retrieved March 2, 2009, from http://www.counseling.org/ counselors/practitionersguide.aspx

With minor variations, these are the forms which you are most likely to encounter in the literature and which you should use yourself.

Getting published

As we said above, although we aren't going to tell you how to write your thesis or exactly what to put in a paper aimed at an academic or professional journal, we thought you might like to know a little more about your options. Firstly, although a peer-reviewed paper in a prestigious academic journal is seen by some as the gold standard – the ultimate vehicle in which to present research – there are other options. For example, if it is your first attempt to get your thoughts and findings into print and you are a little daunted by the thought, why not write a letter to the editor of a relevant professional journal? This is a way of telling others a little about what you know, to begin making your mark and you may get some useful feedback. Once

Note

To give you an example of the variations, we show the same reference first in the style used by the British Association for Counselling and Psychotherapy in *Therapy Today* in 2009:

> Dalal, F. In White K Unmasking race, culture and attachment in the psychoanalytic space. UK Karnac Books Ltd; 2005.

and second in the style required by the American Psychological Association (APA):

> Dalal, F. (2005). Racism: Processes of detachment, dehumanization and hatred. In K. White (Ed.), *Unmasking race, culture and attachment in the psychoanalytic space* (pp. 10–35). London: Karnac Books.

Note that there are differences in punctuation, and the inclusion of titles of chapters, pages and author's initials.

Note

As we have explained, each publication has its own style and requirements including citations and referencing style. Many follow an accepted style, eg, Social Work Today publishes its writer's guidelines on: <http://www.socialworktoday.com/ writers_guidelines.shtml> in which it states that it requires writers to follow the APA referencing style.

again, if this seems a sensible possibility to you, we recommend that you look at the letters pages of the journal(s) you think may be interested in what you have to say with a view not only to checking that the editor is likely to agree with you about the relevance of your letter but to get some ideas of the preferred style. If you have more to say but are not yet prepared for the rigours of submission to a major journal then writing a shorter piece for a professional journal may be the way to go. For most helping professions there are specific 'profession-focused' publications and many professional associations have a house journal of some kind. These may welcome accounts of practitioner research which are, say, summaries of findings or methods or which deal with the experience of research but which are not research papers in the full sense.

However, if you are really excited about your research and what you have found it is likely that you are going to want to publish a full account. This does lead in the direction of a peer-reviewed journal or a high-level conference (which may also include a peer-review process). So, we thought we would tell you a bit about the peer- review process.

Note
Some publications (the 'magazine' type rather than the academic journals) may have a limit on the number of references and/or footnotes you can include. Be prepared to review your writing to prune some references, but find out from the publication what their preferences are first.

Taken from the authors' guidelines for the art & science section of *Nursing Standard*

References in the reference list
Each journal reference should include:
- The author's surname and initial(s) (in bold): print the surname and initial of all authors for references with six or less authors. For seven or more authors, print the first three and add *et al* (in bold italics).
- The year of publication in brackets.
- The title of the article in full.
- The name of the journal in full.
- The volume, issue number and first and last page numbers.
- Use alphabetical order for references. If there are two or more references to the same author, use chronological order.

Each book reference should include (in the order listed):
- The author's surname and initial(s) in bold. Please indicate if the people cited are authors or editors.
- The year of publication in brackets.
- The title of the book in italic.
- The edition (if applicable).
- The publisher.
- The city of publication, and state if in US.
- If you are citing a chapter within a book, supply the author's name, title of the chapter and page
  Use alphabetical order for references. If there are two or more references to the same author, use chronological order.

Retrieved 01/04/2010 <http://nursingstandard.rcnpublishing.co.uk/shared/media/pdfs/authorguide.pdf>

Submitting your work for peer review

In what we told you about journals in Chapter 3.1 we referred to the process of peer review. The process for written papers and peer-reviewed conference presentations is essentially similar so we'll concentrate on the former. To recap, when you submit a paper to an academic journal or indeed many professional journals, the editor will take a look at it to see if it falls within the domain covered by the journal. If it does and it seems to be competently written in line with the journal's instructions for authors and it appears to be of sufficient standard, the likelihood is that it will be sent out for peer review.

What this means is that your paper is sent to 'referees' (usually two or three) who are briefed to comment on what you have said in their capacity as experts in the field. Your personal details will be blanked out or removed so that the referees can judge on the merits of the paper and not be swayed by your professional status (either positively – if you are a 'famous' professor – or negatively – if you are an unknown student). The referees send their reports to the editor usually making a recommendation as to whether or not the paper should be published.

Although the referees may also make a confidential report to the editor, their comments and feedback are conveyed to the author(s) of the paper along with the editor's decision with reference to publication. In our experience (as editors, referees and authors) it is very rare for a paper to be accepted without amendment as it is first written. So, if your paper comes back from the referees with all sorts of suggestions and comments don't take it to heart. It happens to even the most experienced of researcher writers. The best way to look at submitting a paper to a peer-reviewed journal is as a process of soliciting feedback as to how you can make your work sharper, more focused and more complete. In practice, even if the editor says 'sorry, this paper is not for us' you will often find some sort of guidance as to how you may improve your paper and even recommendations as to where you may submit it. At the very least you should expect an explanation as to why your paper has been rejected, although if you submit a paper on the evaluation of a speech therapy service in Midshires to *The Astrophysics Journal* you may get a somewhat dusty answer. But, given what we told you about making sure you address your work to a journal you know to be relevant, in the form that is required, you wouldn't be that silly would you?

On the next page we give an example of a review response letter.

Note
In actual fact many journals ask the referees to make a selection from a list indicating how close to being a suitable publication for the relevant journal the paper in question is. The list would be something like:
- Accept ☐
- Accept subject to minor revision ☐
- Request major revision ☐
- Reject and resubmit ☐
- Reject ☐

Note
In practice, getting your paper ready for publication may be a reiterative process involving two or more cycles through the peer-review process. So, don't get disheartened, take the advice offered by the editor and the referees and you are likely to get there in the end. And if you don't, don't give up – try another journal. It may even be that some sort of cascade system occurs to you – Most Prestigious International Academic Journal, Next Most Prestigious International Academic Journal, National Academic Journal, Professional Journal, Niche Journal for my particular form or place of practice. Don't give up until and unless you have been through the entire gamut.

Example of a review response letter

Dear [Author's name]

I have now received reviews on your paper from three very prominent colleagues. As you will see in the attached comments, they all had very positive and similar reactions: that your manuscript was coherent, well written, and somewhat polemical, and that you could give your argument a broader impact by mentioning some other literature and acknowledging and addressing some additional, perhaps contrary views. I agreed that with some further work, your manuscript might recognise a wider audience and speak more forcefully to others who don't share your assumptions. The reviewers have suggested some specific ways that this might be accomplished. I ask that you consider their comments carefully and respond in a revised version.

Your manuscript was near the upper limit for the length of articles in [Journal]. As you revise, please ensure that any elaborations or additions are balanced by condensation elsewhere. In the same vein, I ask that, as you review your manuscript, you look for ways to make the prose more succinct and crisp. Although the writing is good, I think it could be made more punchy by some selective word pruning.

Please send me the revised version by [date] (preferably sooner), with a covering letter that describes how you have responded to the reviewers' comments.

Thank you for your work on this. I look forward to seeing your revision.

Example of review evaluation of submitted paper

Evaluation (use Poor = 1; Marginal = 2; Adequate = 3; Good = 4; Excellent = 5)

Significance of topic	5
Contribution to knowledge	3
Coverage of literature	4
Clarity of presentation	4
Validity of conclusions	4
Likely reader interest	3

Recommendation (choose one) …

1. Accept in present form
2. Accept conditionally: Needs minor revision *(circled)*
3. Revise and resubmit: This version is not acceptable, but a revised version could be
4. Reject: Definitely not publishable
5. Inappropriate for [Journal]

practice-based research
in the real world

doing
practice-
based research

3.5

An evaluation of person-centred counselling in routine clinical practice in primary care: A five-year study

Isabel Gibbard

The rationale for the evaluation

The NHS is driven by government policy and the end of the nineties saw the start of a series of government initiatives to improve the quality of patient care within the NHS. They have had an enormous effect on counselling in primary care. One of these initiatives was the requirement for evidence-based practice, which was meant to ensure that only effective treatments are given to patients. The National Institute for Health and Clinical Excellence (NICE) was established to assess the evidence and produce clinical practice guidelines. Another initiative was the requirement for clinical governance, whereby a service undertakes routine monitoring and evaluation in order to demonstrate a continuous improvement in the quality of patient care.

The primary care counselling service I manage offers short-term person-centred counselling (a maximum of twelve sessions). The original rationale of the evaluation was to fulfil the requirement for clinical governance by monitoring the counselling service and relaying information to managers and commissioners on an annual basis. As time went on, the rationale changed in response to two main developments. The first was the publication of the NICE Guidelines for anxiety and depression (NICE, 2004a, 2004b). There is a considerable amount of evidence for the effectiveness of CBT and the NICE guidelines recommend CBT as the treatment of choice for all primary mental health conditions. There is a lack of the kind of evidence NICE requires for primary care counselling in general and person-centred counselling in particular.

The second development influencing the change in rationale was the introduction of Primary Care Mental Health Workers (PCMHWs). They work in GP surgeries, offer guided self-help

NICE (2004a) *Clinical Guidelines for the Management of Anxiety in Adults in Primary, Secondary and Community Care.* <www.nice.org.uk/CG22>

NICE (2004b) *Clinical Guidelines for the Management of Depression in Primary and Secondary Care.* <www.nice.org.uk/CG23> both retrieved 5/02/2009.

Barkham, M & Mellor-Clark, J (2003) Bridging evidence-based practice and practice-based evidence: Developing a rigorous and relevant knowledge for psychological therapies. *Clinical Psychology and Psychotherapy 10*, 319-27.

Bower, P & King, M (2000) Randomised controlled trials and the evaluation of psychological therapy. In N Rowland & S Goss (eds) *Evidence-Based Counselling and Psychological Therapies* (pp 70-110). London: Routledge.

Clark, DM, Fairburn, CG, & Wessely, S (2008) Psychological treatment outcomes in routine NHS services: A commentary on Stiles et al. (2007). *Psychological Medicine Volume 38*(5), 629-34.

Mellor-Clark, J, Connell, J, & Barkham, M (2001) Counselling outcomes in primary health care: A CORE system data profile. *European Journal of Psychotherapy, Counselling and Health 4*, 65-86.

Evans, C, Connell, J, Barkham, M, Marshall, C & Mellor-Clark, J (2003) Practice-based evidence: Benchmarking NHS primary care counselling services at national and local levels. *Clinical Psychology and Psychotherapy 10*, 374-88.

based on CBT principles and carry caseloads of 50 to 60 patients with mild to moderate anxiety and depression. They therefore occupy a position within primary care which was traditionally occupied by counsellors, but they are more cost effective and fulfil the NICE Guidelines. I was concerned that the counselling service would find itself in competition for funding with the PCMHWs and so it became vitally important to demonstrate the effectiveness of the person-centred counselling we offered.

In this study I employed a practice-based evidence research model (Barkham & Mellor-Clark, 2003). This is a naturalistic or observational study where the effectiveness of a therapy is measured in routine clinical practice. All clients attending a service are measured before and after they receive counselling and any change is attributed to the therapy. A study like this has high external validity as it demonstrates how the therapy works in 'real life' situations but there is a corresponding reduction in internal validity due to a number of methodological difficulties. There are an unknown number of confounding variables other than the therapy which could affect the outcome, such as events in the client's life outside therapy. In addition, without a control group with which to compare the outcome of therapy, there is no way of knowing whether the same outcome would have been achieved without an intervention (see Bower & King, 2000; Clark et al., 2008).

Measures used

Traditionally the outcome of therapy has been measured by self-report questionnaires, completed by the client, which concentrate on the severity of problems or symptoms. A reduction in symptoms at the end of therapy is reflected in an improved score on the outcome measure. Some measures are specific to a particular condition such as anxiety or depression while others measure general distress. Often researchers have developed measures in response to their own theoretical preference or the intervention under test. This has resulted in thousands of different outcome measures with new ones being developed all the time.

I decided to use the CORE system because it measured overall distress and was not specific to a particular condition, and because of its widespread use in primary care (Mellor-Clark et al., 2001; Evans et al., 2003). The CORE system consists of three forms. The Therapy Assessment Form is completed by the therapist after the first counselling session. It records demographic information such as age, gender, medication, presenting problems, risk assessment, waiting time and assessment outcome. The *End of Therapy Form* is completed by the counsellor after discharge. This records information about the therapy including the number of sessions, and type of ending. When collated these forms provide information profiling the whole service.

The CORE-outcome measure is a self-report questionnaire consisting of 34 items covering four domains of subjective well-being, problems, functioning and risk. There is a mixture of intrapersonal and interpersonal experiences, positive and negative items and high and low intensity items. Each item is scored and the average for all the items is calculated and expressed as a number on a scale of 1–4, where the higher the score, the greater the level of severity. The reliability and validity of the measure have been extensively tested and parameters for reliable and clinically significant change have been calculated together with cut-off points between clinical and non-clinical populations. The overall effectiveness of the service is calculated in terms of the percentage of individuals who demonstrate clinical and reliable improvement (Barkham et al., 2001; Evans et al., 2002). This information was collated on an annual basis and relayed to the service commissioners.

In addition to the CORE forms, exit questionnaires were administered. The exit questionnaire consists of a number of open questions where clients may write about their experiences of counselling with an opportunity for the client to sign the form enabling negative comments to be addressed. Clients are asked to rate how helpful they have found the therapy and how much better they feel. This information was used quantitatively as an additional measure to compare with and to complement the CORE data. The exit questionnaires also provided valuable qualitative feedback about the client's experience of counselling and this was given to counsellors for their personal reflective practice then collated for the service as a whole and given to the commissioners along with the CORE data.

Barkham, M, Margison, F, Leach, C, Lucock, M, Mellor-Clark, J, Evans, C et al. (2001) Service profiling and outcomes benchmarking using the CORE-OM: Toward practice-based evidence in the psychological therapies. *Journal of Consulting and Clinical Psychology 69*, 184-96.

Evans, C, Connell, J, Barkham, M, Margison, F, McGrath, G, Mellor-Clark, J et al. (2002) Towards a standardised brief outcome measure: Psychometric properties and utility of the CORE-OM. *British Journal of Psychiatry 180*, 51-60.

Method

Counsellors employed at the onset of the study were given a three-hour training session in the use of the CORE system, and a user manual containing information and guidelines for completing the forms. Initially, we held regular meetings for discussion, support and encouragement and to ensure that we were all using and completing the forms in the same way. Counsellors who joined the service during the period of the evaluation were provided with training and regular mentoring regarding its use.

All clients were sent information about counselling when they were first referred. This included information about CORE, and stressed that if they did not want to complete the forms, this would not interfere with their therapy. Clients were asked to complete the pre-therapy form during their first counselling session and those who reached a planned ending were asked to complete the post-therapy form at the last counselling session. The exact timing of administration, in or around the session, or its use as a therapeutic tool within the session was left up to the individual counsellor. If the client was unable to complete the pre-therapy form during the first session it was given to them to complete and to be brought to the second session. If the client was unable to complete the post-therapy form during the final session it was sent to them with a pre-paid envelope to return by post. For a period during the study clients who reached an unplanned ending were sent a form in the post, but we discontinued this due to the low return rate.

Complete sets of forms were submitted when the client was discharged and the information entered onto CORE-PC. This is a computer software package that collates and analyses the data. As the information obtained from a system like CORE is entirely dependent on the quality of the data which is put in, I monitored that quality on an ongoing basis. Incomplete forms were either returned to the counsellor for completion or missing information was added from administrative and client records.

Collecting the data

From a person-centred standpoint, there were several concerns about using the CORE system. Many person-centred counsellors are uncomfortable with therapy outcome as a concept, regarding therapy as a unique encounter between two individuals which defies measurement. There were concerns that the administration of an outcome measure would be detrimental to the counselling process because it would affect the balance of power in the relationship and introduce an agenda external to the client. There were reservations about using a measure concentrating on symptom reduction as this conflicts with the person-centred aim of empowering the client to take control of their own therapy, and to decide for themselves what should be the outcome of their therapy. It acknowledges an external value system, which again conflicts with the person-centred aim of facilitating the client's discovery of his own internal value system. Understandably, counsellors were concerned that they would be expected to reach a positive outcome and that the data would be used to measure their individual effectiveness. However, on the whole, their fears went unrealised and most counsellors came to value using CORE. It was evident that an outcome measure such as CORE cannot capture the complex, subtle and personal nuances of therapeutic personality change. However, it can provide insights into a client's process and give an indication of what has occurred during therapy, and it is associated with changes in a person's thoughts, feelings and behaviour which it is possible to measure.

Some counsellors used the CORE form as part of the therapy. It was very useful to indicate the level of risk, which might need further assessment. Sometimes completing the form would prompt clients into beginning an exploration of their problems, or enable them to identify or focus on important issues. Some counsellors used the form as a prompt when the CORE scores did not 'fit' with what the client was saying. Often it was used during the last counselling session when the counsellor and client together compared the post-therapy with the pre-therapy answers. Counsellors found that their clients valued this process as it provided evidence in 'black and white' of how they had changed and facilitated joint reflection on the counselling process. Counsellors also used the CORE outcomes as part of their personal reflective practice. If a client did not score as an improvement some found it useful to ask themselves why and to look in more detail at what had gone on in the counselling process.

McLeod (2001) writes about the methodological difficulties associated with the use of outcome measures. When administered at the beginning of therapy they give an expectation that the individual will have emotional and psychological problems and most people realise that an improvement is expected at the end of therapy. This may well influence how the client responds. The use of outcome measures requires that the client is honest in completing them and this is not always the case. Some clients respond in the way they think they 'should' or think will be acceptable. Some clients minimise their difficulties, possibly because they do not want to appear 'weak', while others do the opposite, possibly to justify why they have come for counselling. This raises the question whether the change being measured is real or whether it is a change in the way the client has completed the form. A client may feel less anxious and depressed at the end of therapy, but also be more self-aware and self-accepting. He may therefore be more honest with himself and his score may not change or even deteriorate. On the other hand an individual who scores an improvement may respond in order to please the therapist, to appear a 'good' client, or they may have learned to operate a kind of benign self-deception. Sometimes counsellors were concerned that a successful episode of therapy was not reflected in an improvement in the CORE scores. Such an underestimation of improvement would inevitably be counterbalanced by an overestimation of improvement, where the positive change in scores was due to life events outside therapy or to wide fluctuations in mood from week to week. I found it was important not to make judgements based on individual or small numbers of cases, and that to be meaningful conclusions had to be based on numbers greater than 100.

McLeod, J (2001) An administratively created reality: Some problems with the use of self-report questionnaire measures of adjustment in counselling/psychotherapy outcome research. *Counselling and Psychotherapy Research 1*, 215-26.

Analysis of the data

I collected data over a five-year period, from April 2002 to March 2007. After 12 months I had pre- and post-therapy scores for 129 individuals and 83 exit questionnaires. The outcome scores showed that nearly 70% of those who completed post-therapy outcome measures demonstrated reliable improvement in their scores and 75% of the exit questionnaires reported that the client felt better or very much better after counselling. I wrote my annual report, included some favourable comments from the exit questionnaires and went to meet the commissioners. They were sceptical of the results and asked if the clients might have improved without counselling. In other words they highlighted one of the methodological limitations of a naturalistic study such as this where there is no control. Clients waited several months for counselling, and because of this I was able to address this by asking clients to complete a CORE form when they were first referred. The change in scores after the waiting time would, I thought, give me a control against which to compare the change in scores after therapy.

After five years I had pre- and post-outcome data for 697 clients and the additional measure at referral for 382 individuals. I also had 469 exit questionnaires. The results continued to show that there was a marked difference between the average score for the whole service at the beginning and end of therapy, and that nearly 70% of those who completed both pre- and post-therapy outcome measures showed a reliable improvement. There was some improvement during the waiting time, but this was much smaller than the improvement after therapy. Traditionally, in the NHS, counselling has only been considered suitable for clients who present with mild to moderate symptoms associated with the common mental health problems. By comparing clients with mild to moderate symptoms with those with moderate to severe symptoms I found that a greater percentage of clients with moderate to severe symptoms showed reliable improvement than clients with mild to moderate symptoms.

Publishing a paper

I realised I was in a unique position to demonstrate the effectiveness of person-centred counselling to a wider audience. However, I did not have the confidence to publish the evaluation by myself so I enrolled on an MA at University of Manchester. My tutor, Terry Hanley, was supportive in terms of writing and structuring the work, checking the analysis of the data, helping me decide on the most relevant journal to send it to, and he became my co-author.

At this time I attended the BAPCA (British Association for the Person-Centred Approach) conference to present some of the data in a workshop. Only 7 people attended, which was disappointing, but one of them was Professor Robert Elliott who introduced me to the concept of 'Effect Size'. Effect size is a way of expressing the difference between two groups and is calculated by using a formula which incorporates the means and standard deviations of the two groups. Where the two groups are actually the same group before and after an intervention, such as counselling, then the effect size demonstrates the impact that the intervention has had on the group. The larger the effect size, the larger the impact of the intervention. Using the formula sent to me by Robert, I was able to calculate the pre-post therapy and pre-post waiting time effect sizes. This showed that the counselling had a large effect on the sample, and while there was some improvement during the waiting time the effect size was considerably smaller. By comparing the effect sizes of the different severity bands I found that counselling had the greatest impact on clients with moderate to severe symptoms and that these clients showed very little improvement during the waiting time. This challenges the traditional view which is that counselling is not suitable for such individuals.

With regard to the need for ethical approval within the NHS an evaluation such as this is a 'grey area' and opinions differ between individuals and organisations, and change over time. There is the view that ethical approval cannot be given in retrospect and as this study involves audit of existing data rather than research involving the collection of new data it does not require a submission to the local Research Ethics Committee. Alternatively there is the view that, although the data is already in existence and is in the public domain within the organisation, the data is also being used to generate new knowledge that requires ethical approval and permission is required for it to be made public. I therefore went through the procedure of applying for an ethical review, but it was not necessary and I only required the permission of my line manager for the data to be used and made public.

I wrote a paper describing the evaluation and demonstrating the effectiveness of person-centred counselling using the reliable change calculated by CORE-PC, and effect sizes calculated by the formula given to me by Robert Elliott. Terry, my tutor recalculated the effect sizes using a different method and the results were the same. We decided to send the paper to *Counselling and Psychotherapy Research*. This is a peer-reviewed journal where papers which have been submitted are sent to two anonymous reviewers for their comments. When the reviews were returned one was very favourable but the second was quite critical. The second reviewer pointed out that we could not use the term 'control' for the measurement during the waiting time, as this was not contemporaneous with the therapy, but we should call it 'quasi control' or 'comparator group'. She or he provided a list of points which were unclear, or unnecessary, or which should be included in the paper to improve it. S/he also questioned the way we had calculated the effect size. This concerned

Note

We look at calculating effect size in Chapter 2.4, p 86 and Chapter 3.1, pp 249-51.

us so Terry checked what we had done with the statisticians in the university. He discovered that there are various ways of calculating the effect of an intervention on a group and the method employed will depend on a number of factors, but that the method we had used was suitable for measuring the effect of a therapy. I incorporated as many of the suggested changes as I could and these did make it a much better paper when it was finally published (Gibbard & Hanley, 2008).

I cannot emphasise enough how beneficial this evaluation has been. It has convinced both managers and commissioners that person-centred counselling is effective and as services are commissioned locally it has resulted in an increase in funding. Locally it has resulted in the establishment of the person-centred approach as a valued alternative to CBT and the person-centred counselling service is now established as a specialist service within primary mental health.

Future plans

Since completing the study I have taken over the management of the CBT service in addition to the counselling service. Decisions are made on a daily basis about an individual's suitability for either CBT or person-centred counselling, but no one is quite sure on what basis this decision is made. The two approaches are very different and yet both are similarly effective and beneficial. There are several possible reasons for this equivalence. Bohart and Tallman (1999) believe the explanation lies with the client's capacity for self-healing and his ability to use whatever is provided by the therapist. Another possibility is that the characteristics of the client influence outcome so that different kinds of people find different therapies helpful. Some research has been conducted into the helpful aspects of a range of different approaches (Timulak, 2007; Nilsson et al., 2007). Some helpful factors are specific to a particular approach while others are common to all approaches.

Little is known about how these helpful factors are linked to the process of change. Outcome studies have been the main method of investigating client change as a result of therapy, but they do not help our understanding of the process of change within the client. In other words, we know what works, but we don't know how. My future plans are therefore to conduct a qualitative study comparing the process of change in the two different therapies. The aim is to help our understanding of the ways in which the different therapies may complement each other within an integrated service and to help develop a sound theoretical basis for the integration of different therapies within such a service.

Gibbard, IM & Hanley, T (2008) A five-year evaluation of the effectiveness of person-centred counselling in routine practice in primary care. *Counselling and Psychotherapy Research* 8(4), 215-22.

Bohart, AC & Tallman, K (1999) *How Clients Make Therapy Work: The process of active self-healing.* Washington, DC: APA Publications.

Timulak, L (2007) Identifying core categories of client-identified impact of helpful events in psychotherapy: A qualitative meta-analysis. *Psychotherapy Research* 17(3), 305-14.

Nilsson, T, Svensson, M, Sandell, R & Clinton, D (2007) Patients' experience of change in cognitive behavioural therapy and psychodynamic therapy: A qualitative comparative study. *Psychotherapy Research* 17(5), 553-66.

• ● •

C	linical	
O	utcomes in	**Frequently Asked**
R	outine	**Questions**
E	valuation	

The following is the 'Frequently asked Questions' leaflet produced by CORE, reproduced by kind permission of CORE Information Management Services.

What is CORE?

CORE is an acronym for Clinical Outcomes in Routine Evaluation. It was launched in 1998 as the result of a three year collaboration between researchers and practitioners seeking to design an evaluation system to resource the growth of practice-based evidence that could help inform the development of client care in and across psychological therapy services.[1,2,3,4]

As a paper-based evaluation system, CORE is free to use and comprises three A4 inter-dependent tools:

- The *CORE Outcome Measure* is a client self-report questionnaire designed to be administered before and after therapy. The client is asked to respond to 34 questions (such as 'I have felt OK about myself' or 'I have felt criticised by other people') about how they have been feeling over the last week on a 5-point scale from 'not at all' to 'most or all of the time'. The responses are designed to be summed by the practitioner to produce a mean score to indicate the level of current psychological global distress (from 'healthy' to 'severe').[1] Following the last session, the questionnaire is repeated, and the comparison of the pre and post-therapy scores offers a measure of 'outcome'. That is, whether or not the client's level of distress has changed, and by how much.[5,6,7]
- The *Therapy Assessment Form* is completed by the practitioner and helps profile the client, their presenting problems/concerns, and their pathway into therapy
- The *End of Therapy Form* is also completed by the practitioner and helps profile the pathway through and out of therapy, alongside a range of subjective outcome assessments

Why use CORE?

In the last few years an increasing proportion of psychological therapy services (and a range of individual therapists) have begun to use CORE to create a large, active learning community. We believe the reasons behind such growth are that:

- Many practitioners have looked for a good quality, free outcome

1. Barkham, M, Evans, C, Margison, F, McGrath, G, Mellor-Clark, J, Milne, D & Connell, J (1998) The rationale for developing and implementing core batteries in service settings and psychotherapy outcome research. *Journal of Mental Health 7*, 35-47.

2. Mellor-Clark, J, Barkham, M, Connell, J & Evans, C (1999) Practice-based evidence and need for a standardised evaluation system: Informing the design of the CORE System. *European Journal of Psychotherapy, Counselling and Health 2*, 357-74.

3. Mellor-Clark, J & Barkham, M (2006) The CORE system: Quality evaluation to develop practice-based evidence base, enhanced service delivery and best practice management. In C Feltham & I Horton (eds), *The Handbook of Counselling and Psychotherapy* (2nd edn). London: Sage.

4. Barkham, M, Mellor-Clark, J, Connell, J, & Cahill, J (2006) A core approach to practice-based evidence: A brief history of the origins and applications of the CORE-OM and CORE System. *Counselling and Psychotherapy Research 6*(1), 3-15.

5. Evans, C, Mellor-Clark, J, Margison, F, Barkham, M, McGrath, G, Connell, J & Audin, K (2000) Clinical Outcomes in Routine Evaluation: The CORE-OM. *Journal of Mental Health 9*, 247-55.

6. Evans, C, Connell, J, Barkham, M, Margison, F, Mellor-Clark, J, McGrath, G & Audin, K (2002) Towards a standardised brief outcome measure: Psychometric properties and utility of the CORE-OM. *British Journal of Psychiatry 180*, 51-60.

7. Barkham, M, Margison, F, Leach, C, Lucock, M, Mellor-Clark, J, Evans, C, Benson, L, Connell, J, Audin, K & McGrath, G (2001) Service profiling and outcomes benchmarking using the CORE-OM: Towards practice-based evidence in the psychological therapies. *Journal of Consulting and Clinical Psychology 69*, 184-96.

2. Mellor-Clark, J, Barkham, M, Connell, J & Evans, C (1999) Practice-based evidence and need for a standardised evaluation system: Informing the design of the CORE System. *European Journal of Psychotherapy, Counselling and Health 2*, 357-74.

3. Mellor-Clark, J & Barkham, M (2006) The CORE system: Quality evaluation to develop practice-based evidence base, enhanced service delivery and best practice management. In C Feltham & I Horton (eds) *The Handbook of Counselling and Psychotherapy* (2nd edn) (pp 207-24). London: Sage.

4. Barkham, M, Mellor-Clark, J, Connell, J, & Cahill, J (2006) A core approach to practice-based evidence: A brief history of the origins and applications of the CORE-OM and CORE System. *Counselling and Psychotherapy Research, 6*(1), 3-15.

6. Evans, C, Connell, J, Barkham, M, Margison, F, Mellor-Clark, J, McGrath, G & Audin, K (2002) Towards a standardised brief outcome measure: Psychometric properties and utility of the CORE-OM. *British Journal of Psychiatry 180*, 51-60.

8. Mellor-Clark, J, Curtis Jenkins, A, Evans, R, Mothersole, G, & McInnes, B (2006) Resourcing a CORE Network to develop a National Research Database to help enhance psychological therapy and counselling service provision. *Counselling and Psychotherapy Research 6*(1), 16-22.

measure that could be used for routine evaluation since the mid 1990s as an alternative to fee-based measures, and/or client satisfaction tools[2]

- Since the late 1990s the number of NHS psychological therapy and counselling practitioners needing an accessible outcome measure has increased substantially with the introduction of quality standards culminating in Department of Health (2004) guidelines recommending the introduction of routine outcome measurement with all clients

- The actual responses to the CORE questions provided by the client (for example, answering 'often' to the question 'I have felt terribly alone and isolated') provides the therapist with clinically useful information for starting the session, and therefore supports and resources their own clinical assessment

- Six of the OM questions provide client risk profiles – a very important measure where the therapist suspects or needs to explore any risk of self-harm, suicide, or risk to others

- The therapist can examine the extent to which the client's CORE OM score profiles in a 'clinical population' by comparing their score at referral with national 'clinical cut-off' scores. The clinical cut-off has been established by asking a large sample of people in the UK population to complete the questionnaire and comparing their scores statistically with those for large samples of clients in therapy [4,6]

- By using the full CORE System within a service (or by a group of therapists sharing some common professional interest) it becomes possible to explore how outcomes (recovery and improvement rates) vary by client factors (e.g. age, ethnicity, gender, medication, problem presentation, etc.) and/ or therapy factors (e.g. therapy type, duration, intensity, etc.).[3,4] Services are increasingly using this information to help develop referral and treatment guidelines designed to improve clinical outcomes

- The CORE System captures information to help explore recognised service quality indicators such as waiting times, premature client termination of therapy, and attendance rates, etc. to help contribute to the development of client management guidelines [3]

- Individual therapists or services can compare their own CORE data profile with national 'benchmarks' for services seeing similar clients across such measures as outcomes, waiting times, client severity, therapy endings etc.[8]

How is CORE used in practice?

The way that CORE is used in practice divides into two camps – independent users and supported CORE Network users.

Independent users typically introduce CORE into their service through the use of the CORE Outcome Measure rather than the full CORE System. It's understood that this appears an attractive start to service evaluation as it has minimum impact on practitioners' time, whilst providing an opportunity to collect data that profile therapy outcomes. In practice this typically means that either a service administrator or practitioner invites each client to complete a CORE Outcome Measure when they attend their first session, and again when they attend their last. On average this takes the client little more than 5 minutes on each occasion and provides a clinical profile of the symptoms, quality of life, and subjective well-being of the client, as well as an assessment of the clients' risk to self and/or others. The merits of this first-step approach is that it's simple and therefore generally achievable. The yield provides an objective risk assessment, offers opportunity to reflect with the client on their responses to each of the individual[3,4] questions both before and after therapy, and once appropriately scored – provides a way to reflect on the proportions of clients whose outcomes fall into improved, recovered, unchanged and deteriorated categories. This latter reflective and empirical profiling activity is generally referred to as 'outcomes monitoring'.[3]

Unfortunately, talking to independent users it appears common that the results of outcomes monitoring can often be something of a frustration. Firstly, this is because practitioners have differing levels of comfort and (hence) success in introducing routine outcome measurement to their clients, Secondly, on average less than half of those completing a CORE Outcome Measure at the beginning of therapy complete a measure at the end of therapy,[10] and thirdly, the proportion of people who cannot be shown to have demonstrably benefited from therapy can be higher than expected and raise questions that require more detailed evaluation. The combined impact of these three findings can mean that as few as one-in five clients can demonstrably be shown to have benefited from therapy, and for those who become aware of such profiles, many join the CORE Network community for support in learning how to assess and develop their service quality. Consequently, network users can either be services who start out as independent users, or services who perhaps assess the benefits of support and network membership as beneficial and choose to be trained in how to get the most out of CORE from the outset.

CORE Network members are encouraged to use a common methodology that combines: (a) preparatory training; (b) specialised data analysis software; and (c) service benchmarking designed to help secure the maximum yield for continuing professional development.[8,9] The characteristics of each of these elements helps define how CORE was designed to be used – and the current adopted

3. Mellor-Clark, J & Barkham, M (2006) The CORE system: quality evaluation to develop practice-based evidence base, enhanced service delivery and best practice management. In C Feltham & I Horton (eds), *The Handbook of Counselling and Psychotherapy* (2nd edn) (pp 207-24). London: Sage .

4. Barkham, M, Mellor-Clark, J, Connell, J, & Cahill, J (2006) A core approach to practice-based evidence: A brief history of the origins and applications of the CORE-OM and CORE System. *Counselling and Psychotherapy Research,* 6(1), 3-15.

8. Mellor-Clark, J, Curtis Jenkins, A, Evans, R, Mothersole, G, & McInnes, B (2006) Resourcing a CORE Network to develop a National Research Database to help enhance psychological therapy and counselling service provision. *Counselling and Psychotherapy Research,* 6(1), 16-22.

9. Evans, R, Mellor-Clark, J, Barkham, M, & Mothersole, G (2006) Developing the resources and management support for routine evaluation in counselling and psychological therapy provision: Reflections on a decade of CORE development. *European Journal of Psychotherapy and Counselling* 8(2), 141-61.

10. Bewick, BM, Trusler, K, Mullin, T, Grant, S, Mothersole, G (2006) Routine outcome measurement completion rates of the CORE-OM in primary care psychological therapies and counselling. *Counselling and Psychotherapy Research,* 6(1), 50-9.

methodology for an estimated 3,000+ practitioners working across more than 200 services.

CORE introductory training is now in its tenth year. The principal content continues to evolve in light of both evaluative feedback, and national policy guidelines creating opportunities for professional development. Currently, the focus of training attempts to prepare and guard practitioners against some of the challenges we know have been experienced by the small minority of services who have failed in their attempts to introduce the CORE System by contrasting them with factors linked with success. These include:

- understanding future opportunities for evidence-based high quality services
- clearing practical, philosophical and ethical obstacles to evaluation
- creating a shared vision and service coalition focused on developing client care
- learning how to use the CORE Outcome Measure for both assessment and client feedback
- developing an appreciation of real clients' pathways through our services and how they can be improved

Whilst training has evolved to help compensate for the lack of research methods teaching and appreciation in counselling and psychotherapy training, data analysis support has also had to be developed to help service users and practitioners manage and understand their CORE data.

CORE-PC is now in its fifth year of provision.[8] Developed in response to services' requests for a closer relationship and understanding of CORE System data, the software has been designed as a tool to help resource service quality assessment and development. Based on a pluralistic research paradigm, CORE helps quantify clients that fall into specific categories (e.g. age bands, ethnicity, gender, employment, medication, problem presentation, therapy ending, etc.), and then offers tools to help identify and explore individual sub-sets of clients who fall into specific categories outside service quality targets (e.g. long waiting times, early termination of therapy, clinical deterioration, and poor attendance, motivation, alliance and/or psychological mindedness).

CORE benchmarking is now in its third year of provision and is evolving to help offer a sense of relativity to service performance assessment. In brief, when services have learned how to implement CORE and are collecting good quality data in CORE-PC, the next learning stage is to understand the strengths and weaknesses of the service. This is resourced by the collection of annual anonymised data donations from the CORE Network published as guides to key service performance indicators. In 2005 we developed a CORE

8. Mellor-Clark, J, Curtis Jenkins, A, Evans, R, Mothersole, G, & McInnes, B (2006) Resourcing a CORE Network to develop a National Research Database to help enhance psychological therapy and counselling service provision. *Counselling and Psychotherapy Research,* 6(1), 16-22.

National Research Database for NHS primary care counselling and psychological therapy services for almost 35,000 clients, seen across 34 services and published a selection of benchmarks in the March 2006 edition of BACP's *Counselling and Psychotherapy Research*. These included:

- waiting times between referral and first contact sessions
- CORE Outcome Measure completion rates
- first contact sessions outcomes
- incidences where clients and practitioners have differing views of risk
- client-initiated termination of therapy
- recovery and improvement rates

Over the next 12 months further benchmarking guides are planned for NHS secondary and tertiary services as well as workplace, voluntary sector, and student counselling services.

Who resources CORE?

Operationally, CORE is a self-financing, action research partnership between four groups learning how to maximise the practice impact and research yield of CORE tools and resultant CORE System data. The *CORE System Trustees* are a small group of voluntary senior advisors who act as copyright guardians to the measurement tools to protect against infringement. *CORE Information Management Systems Ltd* support a CORE Network by providing CORE-PC software system to grow a CORE National Research Database [NRD] to resource benchmarking for service quality development.[8,9] *The Psychological Therapies Research Centre* at the University of Leeds analyse CORE data to both develop and refine the tools, and maximise the academic yield through peer-reviewed publications. Finally, the *CORE Benchmarking Network* is made-up of volunteer service managers that are interested in exploring the experiential impact of CORE on service delivery to help identify and develop best practice, and represent data donors in planning the strategic use of CORE data to help inform national policy and practice development.

What alternatives are there to CORE?

There are a wide range of alternative tools and methods for routine evaluation. Psychometric questionnaires divide into fee-based and fee-free measures. In the UK popular fee-based measures[2] include the Beck Depression Inventory [BDI], General Health Questionnaire [GHQ], and Hospital Anxiety and Depression Scale [HAD]. More recently developed fee-free measures tend to focus on specific

8. Mellor-Clark, J, Curtis Jenkins, A, Evans, R, Mothersole, G, & McInnes, B (2006) Resourcing a CORE Network to develop a National Research Database to help enhance psychological therapy and counselling service provision. *Counselling and Psychotherapy Research*, 6(1), 16-22.

9. Evans, R, Mellor-Clark, J, Barkham, M, & Mothersole, G (2006) Developing the resources and management support for routine evaluation in counselling and psychological therapy service provision: Reflections on a decade of CORE development. *European Journal of Psychotherapy and Counselling* 8(2), 141-61.

2. Mellor-Clark, J, Barkham, M, Connell, J & Evans, C (1999) Practice-based evidence and need for a standardised evaluation system: Informing the design of the CORE System. *European Journal of Psychotherapy, Counselling and Health*, 2, 357-74.

symptoms such as depression and include the Depression, Anxiety and Stress Scales [DASS-21] and the Patient Health Questionnaire 9 [PHQ9]. Client satisfaction questionnaires remain an option, but returns are usually constrained by poor representativeness relative to the total number of clients seen. Finally there are the 'in-house' approaches such as those developed by employment assistance services [EAPs], and whilst these have their strengths in fitting the values and objectives of their users' organisations, they have their limitations for benchmarking relative service performance.

Key support resources

The support website for the CORE System can be found at <http://www.coreims.co.uk>. As well as providing a thorough introduction to the background and development of CORE, the site also provides free access to the measures and manual, and descriptions of the support services that include CORE implementation training, CORE data management training, and CORE-PC. The March 2006 edition of *Counselling and Psychotherapy Research* [Vol. 6 No. 1] distributed freely to members of BACP is a special edition on CORE that provides a comprehensive introduction to the history, use and utility of the system for benchmarking and service quality development.

This leaflet is available from CORE IMS, in a trial pack together with multiple copies of sample tools and manuals for £10.00 available from: <http://www.coreims.co.uk/site_downloads/core_trial_pack_order_form.pdf>

Anyone interested in using CORE materials is advised to visit the CORE website <www.coreims.co.uk> or call 01788 546019.

if you are bitten by the research bug …

If you have read the majority of this book – or indeed if you have only cherry-picked the bits that interest you most – you may by now be thinking that you would like to do some research of your own. You can see that by engaging in research not only will you develop personally and professionally, so advancing your career, but also you will make a step (however small) that advances your profession as a whole, improves things for your clients and fellow service providers and/or results in a more efficient and effective service. If so, you are probably wondering how you can get started. In this chapter we will give you a few clues as to how you may become an active researcher.

Research as part of a qualification

It is likely that as either part of your professional training at Masters level or above (and increasingly at diploma or degree level) you will be required to undertake a piece of independent research. This may also be true if you seek to develop as a practitioner by undertaking further study. Such research will be contained and relatively short. You will be offered guidance, support and supervision by the institution providing the qualification for which you are studying. You will probably have some input about a variety of research methods and how to use them. Therefore, we don't think there is much we have to tell you about this except to say that you will find various sections of this book helpful in getting started. In particular we draw your attention to the sections on:

- different approaches to research (Are you instinctively drawn towards the use of numbers or do the stories people have to tell engage you more?)
- developing a research question (What do you want to know? How can you find out?)
- encountering the literature (What is already known?)
- writing up your research (What have I found and how can I let others know?)

Higher degrees by research

One of the possibilities open to you as a health and social care professional wishing to undertake research is to register for a higher degree by research – that is a qualification awarded solely on the basis of a thesis or dissertation which is an account of a piece of independent research. The precise award will vary with the length and depth of study with (for example and traditionally) the period of full-time study for an MA or MSc by research being perhaps 1 year, an MPhil, 18 months and a PhD, 3 years. There are part-time equivalents for these timings (the rule-of-thumb is twice the full-time length) and in practice most people take a bit longer than the minimum specified time – but do beware, most institutions also have maximum times in which the study must be completed. The length of dissertation or thesis also varies with the nature of the award, although the exact requirement varies between subjects and institutions; in social science the length of a dissertation or thesis is about:

- Masters by Research (e.g. MA, Msc)   30,000 words
- MPhil   40,000 words
- PhD   80,000 words

IF YOU WANT TO KNOW MORE ABOUT
higher degrees by research
you could take a look at:

Brewer, R & Lawler, G (2007) *Your PhD Thesis: How to plan, draft, revise and edit your thesis.* Abergele: Studymates Books.

Kar, J (2009) *How to Survive Your PhD: The insider's guide to avoiding mistakes, choosing the right programme, working with professors and just how a person writes a 200 page paper.* Chicago, IL: Sourcebooks.

Finn, J (2005) *Getting a PhD: An action plan to help you manage your research, your supervisor and project.* London: Routledge.

Murray, R (2002) *How to Write a Thesis.* Buckingham: Open University Press.

We guess that the most likely route for a health and social care practitioner to proceed towards a higher degree by research is to register for a part-time course of study and to base the research in some aspect of their own practice.

For a practitioner, there are many benefits of this way of doing research. These include:

- it results in a qualification – as well as personal satisfaction, this may lead to professional advancement and/or better career prospects
- the research will be supervised by one or more experienced researchers (who may also be practitioners in their own right). Support and guidance will be on hand
- there will be access to libraries and online resources – this will ensure that 'the literature' in all its many forms is easily available
- there is likely to be training in research methods and access to research SEMINARS
- it confers membership of an active research community including peers with whom to share feedback, doubts, fears and enthusiasms (this can be very important because doing a long piece of research may, at times, be experienced as lonely and dispiriting)

SEMINAR Any meeting for an exchange of ideas; a course offered for a small group of advanced students; a class held for advanced studies in which students meet regularly to discuss original research.

If you think proceeding to a higher degree by research is right for you, then, once you have a broad idea about what you might do (your research question, something you really want to know – although it doesn't have to be all that refined at this stage) and that you are likely to have access to suitable resources (this is about subjects/co-researchers, permission and so on) then it is time to look for a suitable supervisor working for an appropriate institution of higher education. It will be helpful if your potential supervisor has some acquaintance with at least the broad area of your chosen topic but perhaps a familiarity with the process and methodology of research would be even more useful. People able to supervise research can be found in university departments offering programmes in many aspects of health and social care (for example, schools of nursing, psychology departments, counselling and psychotherapy units, social work departments, departments offering programmes in one or more professions allied to medicine). One way of finding someone suitable is to look at the part of the university prospectus or online resource that lists the research interests and publications of its academic staff. This will often provide enough information about the interests and research inclinations of individuals to tell you if they are worth approaching with your proposal or not. The research literature too may provide a guide to suitable sources of supervision. A critical reading will indicate who and/or what institutions are working in similar or sympathetic areas to the research you propose to carry out.

Doing independent research

Of course, not all research is undertaken by academics and you don't have to be part of an institution of higher education to do valuable research. If, for whatever reason, you want to answer a question about your form of practice, the people who use or provide your service, or you want to check out an idea or hunch you have then you can come up with a research project that takes you where you want to go – and one aim of this book is to help you do that. Don't be deterred. As we told you at the beginning of this book, there are ways in which research is an ordinary activity and, as a practitioner, in a way, you carry out a research process every time you reflect on your practice or try out something you have learned. To be a researcher, you don't have to be a student; you don't have to think in terms of a 30,000-plus-word dissertation as being the product of your efforts. A short paper of, say, 4,000 – 6,000 words, a presentation at a conference or even an in-house document are all perfectly respectable research outputs. And if your research is aimed more at change or transformation than the production of information then you may not even need these. However, you will still profit from following the steps of the research process as we have outlined them.

Note
We strongly suggest that you first check out a local university or equivalent – or at least somewhere you can get to easily and with minimal expense. Although there may be reasons for choosing a particular supervisor far away from your home (for example, they have particular expertise in the methods that attract you or your type of practice), this can lead to all sorts of inconveniences. However, in the days of electronic communication, these can be minimised.

Note from research
Don't be too literal about departments in which you expect to find a suitable supervisor. It may very well be that the most appropriate person for you is not in the department offering programmes in your particular aspect of health and social care but in another. So, if your closest universities don't deal with your exact area of practice and expertise don't dismiss them out of hand. For example, Paul wanted to proceed to PhD in the particular area of person-centred psychotherapy. It was far more convenient for him to work locally than to register with any of the institutions housing academics with particular expertise in that orientation but the university he favoured didn't even have a counselling department. He didn't despair but checked out the psychology department where he easily found suitable supervisors.

A reminder about steps in the research process

1. Find something that inspires you or about which you are curious

2. Formulate a research question

3. Search the literature. Is the answer to your question already known? What is known that may help you answer your question? Who knows it and how did they find out? How might you answer your question?

4. What ethical issues are raised by your question and the way you propose to answer it? How can you resolve these issues?

5. In the light of the above, conduct your research, collect and process your data. This will involve at least one cycle through 'observation, reflection, experimentation' or the like and probably more.

6. Consider what you have discovered as the result of the process so far. Is it satisfactory? What new questions has your research raised? Do you need to answer them at this stage? At all?

7. Present your findings and what you think they mean in such a way as to make them accessible to others (for example, as a thesis, as a paper or article for a journal or online, by presenting at a conference or a meeting, running a workshop or in audio-visual form

---

Note

In 'Introductions' p v, we explain the online resources associated with this book as follows:

readers will find much of the margin information, including references and live web links on the PCCS Books website <www.pccs-books.co.uk>. Click on 'VIP section' on the left of the home page, then 'click here to access the protected area'. Type in the password 'FSIPR01'.

The advantage of using the resource is that the weblinks are live and you can cut and paste references into search engines or your own documents.

If you decide to do your research independently and you are a novice researcher then it is probably just as well to keep things simple. Start off with something you can do with the resources and time you know you have. Although you will be without the sustained and automatic supervision available to students, you might like to think about talking through what you propose to do with someone who does have a proven track record of research. Perhaps a senior colleague or a former tutor who you know well enough to approach for advice. You could even consider engaging someone as a research 'consultant' paying for their time in the way that you might for any other form of professional advice. Above all, use this book and other resources you may discover to steer you through the process of doing your research. We have told you everything you need to know and/or pointed you in the direction to find out more. Also, one of the possibilities open to you as an independent researcher not normally available to someone who has to produce a dissertation or thesis is that you don't have to work alone. It is perfectly possible and allowable for a group of colleagues to work together to carry out and present a piece of research. Indeed, if you look at published accounts of research you will find that there are often two or more authors.

Our final words to you are '*Go on – give it a go!*' As a health or social care practitioner, you have the ability to contribute positively to the growing pool of knowledge about your particular form of practice and to health and social care in particular. You can improve life for yourself, your colleagues, your service users. You can demonstrate your value and the value of what you do to the people whose hands are on the purse strings. When you think about it, you'd be silly not to, wouldn't you?

drawing graphs and charts

Introduction

This appendix is intended to give a little confidence to those readers who have never had to represent numbers in a graphical form before. It is simply a matter of data presentation. No calculations have to be done, and you don't really have to know much about how to draw a graph either. All you need to know is what is logically possible and most appropriate with the data you have. We explained the logical possibilities of presenting different types of data in Chapter 2.3. Here we show you an easy way to make your findings look understandable and attractive. The only cautionary note we would sound is to remind you that data presentation is about clarity and understandability, not colour and drama. It is easy to get carried away with special effects – the message is in the numbers, not the Day-Glo colours available for the pie chart.

We have chosen Microsoft PowerPoint as the vehicle for data presentation since we think it's the easiest to use for the non-mathematician and it comes bundled with computers, although of course you could use any equivalent presentation software. Other types of software also have graph-drawing capabilities, for example, you may have a good understanding of Excel or another spreadsheet – if you feel competent, you should use it, especially since you might already have entered your data for storage or to do some calculations. The tutorial is written so that you progress from example to example – starting with the scattergram might be confusing.

Using PowerPoint to draw graphs, histograms and charts

Getting started

We are starting at the very beginning for those of you who have never used PowerPoint before and then we move on for those who have never used PowerPoint to create a graph or chart.

- Open a new PowerPoint presentation (your screen will look like Diagram 1, right

- On the toolbar, hover your cursor over the graphics until you find one which looks like a bar chart and shows 'insert chart'. Click on it

- The first slide will change so that it looks like Diagram 2, right. It is a standard panel which you will have to change

- This is the starting point for all graphs and charts. The lower panel (with 'Presentation - Datasheet' in the titlebar) can be moved independently around the screen. That is where you enter your data – it's very clearly laid out

You are now ready to draw any chart, histogram, graph or scattergram

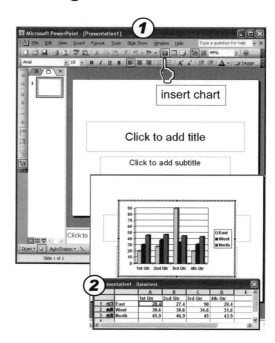

Using PowerPoint to draw a pie chart

• Starting with the standard chart on your screen (where we left off on the previous page), hover over the icons on your toolbar (you might notice that this has changed slightly now that you have inserted a chart) until one shows 'chart type'

• Click on the little black downward pointing arrow to see the types of chart available. Hover over them in turn and you should find that row 5, column 1 is the pie chart (Diagram 1). Click on it

• The first slide will now change so that it looks like Diagram 2, right. It is the pie chart panel which you will have to change. The lower panel is where you enter your data

• Enter your data. We will use the example from page 50, Table 2.3.8 showing the number of clients attending the college counselling service by faculty in 1992:

> • Starting with column A top row (the unnumbered row which reads '1st Qtr'), click on the cell and type 'engineering' then enter all the faculties in turn in the cells along the top row

> • In the first column of the second row (the row numbered '1' which reads '20.4') enter the data for engineering ('14' – see page 50) and continue to enter the data for the other faculties in this second row – the appropriate figure below each faculty

> • Now delete the cells left over from the standard chart which you don't want – the cells containing 'east', 'west' and 'north', plus the ones containing the numbers in rows numbered '2' and '3'. Your screen should now look like Diagram 3

• Tidy up and finish your presentation by adding a title and deleting unwanted frames:

> • First click anywhere on the white area of the slide and it will put itself in the first slide position (number 4, on the right)

> • Next click on and delete the unnecessary grey outline box (for text on the slide) at number 5 on the right

> • Finally click on the title box, move it up away from your chart, enter your text, choose an appropriate font and point size using the toolbar and your slide will look something like the bottom diagram, on the right

Now that you've done it once, play around a little by altering the size and position of your chart, and the colour, size and font of your title. Get it just the way you want it.

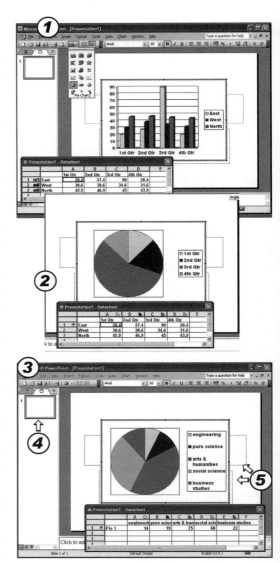

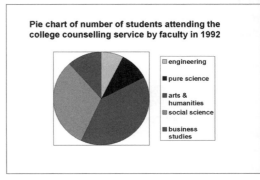

Pie chart of number of students attending the college counselling service by faculty in 1992

Using PowerPoint to draw a histogram or graph

• Starting with the standard chart on your screen (where we left off on page 309), hover over the icons on your toolbar (you might notice that this has changed slightly now that you have inserted a chart) until one shows 'chart type'

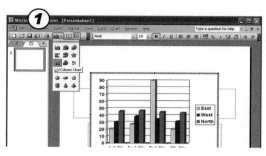

• Click on the little black downward pointing arrow to see the types of chart available. Hover over them in turn and choose the column chart (Diagram 1). Click on it

• The first slide will now change to the column chart panel which you will have to change. The lower panel is where you enter your data

• Enter your data. We will use the example from p. 48, Table 2.3.3 showing the number of clients returning to drugs after treatment has finished:

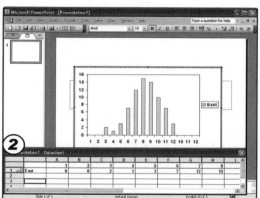

  • Starting with column A top row (the unnumbered row which reads '1st Qtr'), click on the cell and type '1' then enter all the months (2–12) in turn in the cells along the top row

  • In the first column of the second row (the row numbered '1' which reads '20.4') enter the data for month 1('0' – see p. 49) and continue to enter the data for the other months in this second row – the appropriate figure below each month

  • Now delete the cells left over from the standard chart which you don't want – the cells containing 'east', 'west' and 'north', plus the ones containing the numbers in rows numbered '2' and '3'. Your screen should now look like Diagram 2

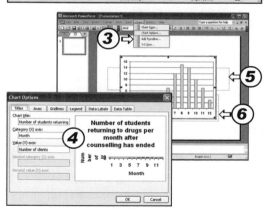

• Tidy up and finish your presentation by adding a title, naming the axes and deleting unwanted frames:

  • First click on 'chart' and then 'chart options' on the toolbar (number 3, right). A new panel will appear where you should enter the title of the chart and the names of the axes (number 4, on the right)

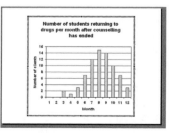

  • Next click on and delete the unnecessary grey outline boxes at numbers 5 & 6 on the right. Click 'OK' and your screen should look like the bottom diagram, right.

  • Finally click anywhere on the white area of the slide and it will put itself in the first slide position and you are ready to copy and paste the chart into a word processor file

Now that you've drawn a bar chart, you can play around a little by altering the size, colour and position of your chart on the slide. You are also ready to change the type of chart you choose using the same data, for example immediately overleaf we use this data (which we drew as a histogram on this page) to plot a graph …

Using PowerPoint to draw a histogram or graph

• To draw a different type of graph, simply click on 'chart type' and choose, say, the line chart. Using the same data we entered overleaf you get the graph opposite

• Experiment by choosing different styles of graph. If you have more than one data set to show on a single set of axes (e.g. the data at the bottom of p. 50 showing the students' improvements in skills over the academic year) simply add these in separate rows. You will soon get the hang of using the data sheet to enter and illustrate your results. Have fun!

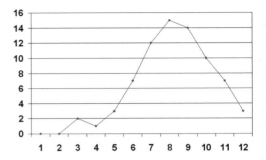

Using PowerPoint to plot a scattergram

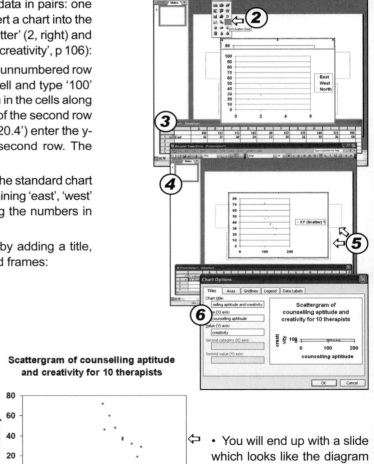

• Enter your data. Since we are plotting a scattergram, you will know that we have two sets of data in pairs: one for the x-axis and one for the y-axis. Insert a chart into the slide (Diagram 1, right), choose 'XY Scatter' (2, right) and put in the data ('counselling aptitude and creativity', p 106):

   • Starting with column A top row (the unnumbered row which reads '1st Qtr'), click on the cell and type '100' then enter all the x-axis values in turn in the cells along the top row. Then in the first column of the second row (the row numbered '1' which reads '20.4') enter the y-axis data and continue along the second row. The screen will now look like Diagram 4

   • Now delete the cells left over from the standard chart which you don't want – the cells containing 'east', 'west' and 'north', plus the ones containing the numbers in rows numbered '2' and '3'

• Tidy up and finish your presentation by adding a title, naming the axes and deleting unwanted frames:

   • First click on and delete the unnecessary grey outline boxes at number 5 on the right. Then click on 'chart' and then 'chart options' on the toolbar (number 3, right). A new panel will appear where you should enter the title of the chart and the names of the axes (number 6, on the right)

   • Finally click anywhere on the white area of the slide and it will put itself in the first slide position and you are ready to copy and paste the chart into a word processor file

Scattergram of counselling aptitude and creativity for 10 therapists

• You will end up with a slide which looks like the diagram on the left. Can you tell from this whether it is a positive or negative correlation?

index

This is Survivor Research

Edited by *Angela Sweeney, Peter Beresford, Alison Faulkner, Mary Nettle & Diana Rose*

2009   ISBN 978 1 906254 14 8   202 pages

£20.00 Discounts and free p+p from
www.pccs-books.co.uk

There has been a major development in health and social science research: it is now being carried out by people who had previously only been seen as its subjects. At the forefront are people with experience as mental health service users/survivors who have taken a lead in pioneering a new approach to research which is now commanding increasing attention and respect.

This is Survivor Research for the first time details this important new approach to research. Written and edited by leaders in the field, it:
- explores the theory and practice of survivor research,
- provides practical examples of survivor research, and
- offers guidance for people wishing to carry out such research themselves.

This is a ground-breaking book for policy makers, researchers, educators, students, service users and practitioners in the mental health field and beyond.

Praise for This is Survivor Research

'This is Survivor Research' is an important and timely publication. Clearly written, comprehensive, interesting, useful, this is a book anyone concerned with survivor research should have readily to hand.
Peter Campbell, mental health system survivor

The authors of this pioneering book spell out the ways in which research in mental health can [deliver benefits] in every respect by the direct participation of service users. Underlying this recently achieved consensus is a basic challenge to the traditional way that biomedical research has been undertaken. These arguments for service user-/consumer-/survivor-led or participatory research are powerfully argued, strongly justified, and persuasively marshalled in this very important addition to the literature.
Graham Thornicroft, Professor of Community Psychiatry and Head of the Health Service Research Department, Institute of Psychiatry, King's College London

This book marks the coming of age of user- and survivor-led research. It maps out the why, what and how of an important strand of research whose influence is growing in strength. It needs to be read by researchers, policy makers and the wider mental health community to increase understanding of the impact and integrity of user- and survivor-led research.
Paul Farmer, Chief Executive, MIND

This book helps us understand exactly how far survivor-led research has taken us and how much further there is to go. It is essential reading for all interested in mental health research, whether it is survivor led, survivor informed or not. No one can question the substance or relevance of survivor-led research after reading this book.
Andrew McCulloch, Chief Executive of the Mental Health Foundation